Introducing Social Po

Pearson Education

We work with leading authors to develop the
strongest educational materials in social policy,
bringing cutting-edge thinking and best learning
practise to a global market.

Under a range of well-known imprints, including
Prentice Hall, we craft high quality print and
electronic publications which help readers to
understand and apply their content,
whether studying or at work.

To find out more about the complete range of our
publishing please visit us on the World Wide web at:
www.pearsoneduc.com

Introducing Social Policy

CLIFF ALCOCK

SARAH PAYNE

MICHAEL SULLIVAN

Prentice
Hall

An imprint of **Pearson Education**

Harlow, England · London · New York · Reading, Massachusetts · San Francisco · Toronto · Don Mills, Ontario · Sydney
Tokyo · Singapore · Hong Kong · Seoul · Taipei · Cape Town · Madrid · Mexico City · Amsterdam · Munich · Paris · Milan

Pearson Education Limited

Edinburgh Gate
Harlow
Essex CM20 2JE
England

and Associated Companies around the world

Visit us on the World Wide Web at:
www.pearsoneduc.com

———————————

First published 2000

© Pearson Education Limited 2000

ISBN 0 132 72212 7

British Library Cataloguing-in-Publication Data
A CIP catalogue record for this book can be obtained from the British Library.

10 9 8 7 6 5 4 3 2 1
04 03 02 01 00

Typeset by 60 in 10/13pt Palatino
Produced by Pearson Education Asia Pte Ltd.
Printed in Singapore

Contents

Preface

Social policy as an academic field of study has grown tremendously over recent years. Social policy, or welfare, in its widest sense represents probably the largest area of government ativity. Social policy as an academic subject however, claims a very mixed parentage and can trace its roots via sociology, politics, economics, history and most directly social administration.

This book is intended as an introduction to social policy for undergraduate students in British Universities, but also for the range of students, perhaps studying social policy for the first time in a range of other types of course including BTEC, NVQ or even A level. Additionally, students who are studying social policy as a subsidiary part of their degree, health studies, nursing or social welfare/social work, will find this book valuable.

This book aims to provide students with a comprehensive introduction to social policy in Britain and is divided into four parts: the first part provides a brief historial outline of the development of the welfare state in Britain during the nineteenth and twentieth centuries. Secondly, we examine the contemporary context within which social policy is practised in the late twentieth century. Thirdly, we examine the range of theoretical or ideological explanations for the development of welfare and the normative prescriptions they offer and finally we take what we term a more traditional approach to social policy and outline and examine the main policy areas.

Although students may wish to 'start at the very beginning, a very fine place to start' and work through to the end of the volume, the book will also allow students to 'dip into' particular parts or chapters as their interests, or studies dictate. At the end of each chapter are a list of references together with suggested further readings by which students may be able to explore in greater depth and detail some of the ideas discussed in the chapter. At the end of the book is a glossary of terms explaining some of the abbreviations and phrases that are common currency within social policy.

We hope you enjoy it.

Authors and Contributors

Cliff Alcock is a Senior Lecturer in Social Policy in the School of Health and Social Sciences, Coventry University.

Sarah Payne is a Lecturer in Social Policy in the School for Policy Studies at the University of Bristol.

Michael Sullivan is Professor of Social Policy at the University of Wales, Swansea.

Judith Carlson is a Senior Lecturer in the Department of Social Sciences at the University of Hertfordshire.

Mike McBeth is a Lecturer in Health Policy in the Department of Social Policy and Social Work at the University of Birmingham.

Tony Colombo is a Lecturer in Sociology in the Department of Sociology at the University of Warwick.

Acknowledgements

We are grateful to the following for permission to reproduce copyright material:

Figure 5.3 from Christopher Ham, *Policy in Britain*, 3rd Edition, © 1992 reproduced by permission of Macmillan Press Ltd. This figure is included in 1999 edition.

Whilst every effort has been made to trace the owners of copyright material, in a few cases this has proved impossible and we take this opportunity to offer our apologies to any copyright holders whose rights we may have unwittingly infringed.

1 Introduction: What is social policy?

Social policy as an academic field of study is one of those curious items, rather like an elephant, which we recognise when we see it but which is notoriously difficult to describe. It is, at one and the same time, the theoretical pursuit of norms about how we think society 'ought' to behave, but also the practical application and implementation of those policies that we consider to be 'social'. We could, of course, argue that all areas of policy inherently have implications for the well-being of society. Consider, for instance, the debate in the years since the falling of the Berlin Wall and the realisation of the so-called 'peace dividend' which has employment implications both for the armed forces and those industries involved in their supply. Yet we do not automatically consider either defence or armed forces policy to be within the remit of 'social policy'. What, then, is social policy?

Exhibit 1.1

> Social policy is the study of the social services and the welfare state. The field of study has grown over time, and it stretches rather more widely than at might first appear, but the social services are where the subject began, and they are still at the core of what the subject is about. The social services are mainly understood to include social security, housing, health, social work and education – the 'Big Five' – along with others which are like social services, including employment, prisons, legal services or drains (Spicker, 1995).
>
> The term social policy is not only used to refer to an academic discipline and its study, however, it is also used to refer to social action in the real world. Social policy is the term used to describe actions aimed at promoting well being; it is also the term used to denote the academic study of such actions (Alcock, 1997).

The two quotations in exhibit 1.1 provide us with fairly standard definitions of the term social policy and both suggest that, as an area of study, it is concerned with the welfare or well-being of society and its members. Furthermore, as an area of study, social policy is closely concerned with the activities of the 'welfare state', that is the range of government policies and social services used to enhance the welfare of citizens within a country. Some writers (Spicker, 1995 and Hill, 1996a) suggest that social policy is intimately concerned with the activities of the 'Big Five' which make up the classic welfare state. This classic welfare state (though the Big Five may not be universally agreed) will normally comprise policies of income maintenance and social security, health policy and services, the personal social services, education and training policy, and employment policy and housing policy. Some writers might consider that policies concerned with employment rightly belong to the field of economics and economic policy rather than social policy, similarly policies of criminal justice enjoy a transience between social policy and legal studies. Such an apparent confusion, however, does provide us with an insight into the difficulties in defining social policy. We can suggest that all government policy has a social element but that is not to suggest that all government policy is social policy. We may also note here, the multi-disciplinary nature of social policy; it is an academic subject which draws upon the academic techniques and skills of many other disciplines – sociology, economics, politics and policy making and history. This itself remains an unresolved debate amongst social policy academics between those who regard social policy as a 'field of study' which draws heavily upon other academic disciplines and those who regard social policy as an academic discipline in its own right drawing together those other academic elements (see the chapters by Alcock and Erskine in Alcock, Erskine and May, 1998).

Exhibit 1.2

> ... although it is on the one hand, an academic discipline – to be studied and developed in its own right – it is also an inter-disciplinary field – drawing on and developing links with other cognate disciplines at every stage and overlapping at times with these in terms of both empirical foci and methods of analysis ... the boundaries between social policy and other social science disciplines are porous and shifting ... (P. Alcock, 1997).
>
> While social policy cannot claim to be a science, it draws its legitimacy as a subject on its ability to draw upon the methods of a number of social sciences and apply these in a rigorous and disciplined way to understand the field in which we are interested. ... social policy involves understanding a range of philosophical and political perspectives (Erskine, 1997).

THE SCOPE OF SOCIAL POLICY

Although debates such as those indicated above may prove interesting to those academics employed within social policy departments, they do not necessarily hold the same interest for students of social policy. Instead, students of social policy may be (rightly) more concerned with the study of social phenomena, such as poverty, inequality and social justice, and policies that attempt to address such phenomena. Implicitly and following such a definition, the student of social policy is concerned to discover whether such policies may be said to be effective – that is whether the policies achieve the aims they set out to pursue and crucially

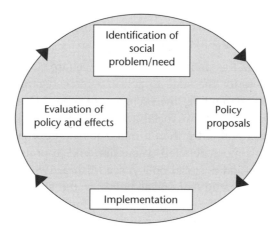

Fig. 1.1 The policy cycle

whether social welfare can be said to have been improved as a result of the introduction of one or other policy. Here we can borrow, from policy studies, the notion of a cyclical policy process.

Though this might be described as a simplistic model of policy making it does, nonetheless, provide us with a useful frame of references for thinking about social policy (for a detailed exposition of policy making and its study, see Hill, 1997). Social policy, then, is not simply the study of society and its problems, but is intimately concerned with how to address and ameliorate social problems and with the analysis of the success or failure of policies designed to improve welfare and well-being. Implicitly too, the study of social policy is concerned with the creation and appropriateness of structures and institutions designed to implement social policies.

Here we have introduced the term 'welfare' to our notion of social policy and often the terms social policy and welfare, or welfare state, will be used interchangeably in texts about the subject (Ginsburg, 1992). This interchangeability has been and can continue to be the source of confusion as we may be tempted to regard the activities of the welfare state as coterminous with social policy. Indeed for many years, under the guise of social administration, the distinction between welfare and the welfare state was not clear, and may still today be blurred. Yet social administration determined the content and direction of social policy and framed its debate for much of the post-war period.

The discipline of social policy is relatively new, ... [T]he first department of social policy opened at the London School of Economics in 1950 headed by Richard Titmuss. This department ... [was] primarily concerned with the training of welfare professionals during a period of expansion in the welfare state ... The scope of the discipline in these early years was therefore strongly influenced by the institutional structures of the welfare state. Academic concern thus focused on the role of the state as the primary provider of welfare. (Ackers and Abbott, 1996)

Social policy was, by this definition, what the welfare state did and no longer was it simply possible for the state to act; it became regarded as the 'natural' provider of welfare apparently at the exclusion of others. During the decades of the 1960s and 1970s this view of social administration as social policy became somewhat discredited and since then a more holistic approach to social policy has developed. (For a more detailed discussion and appraisal of the transition from social administration to social policy, see Mishra, 1981.)

Broadly speaking the study of social policy is the study of the role of the state in relation to the welfare of its citizens. This leads immediately to two questions. First, since the welfare of citizens is affected by their own actions and by the actions of others, including those of collective organisations of different kinds, what is it about the role of the state in relation to welfare that is different? Secondly, what are the kinds of actions that have an impact on welfare? (Hill, 1996b.)

THE STRUCTURE OF THE BOOK

This volume is intended to be an introduction for students having their first experience of social policy whether as undergraduates of social policy, or taking relevant A-levels, BTEC courses or access students. It is written on the assumption that students have little or no prior knowledge or experience of social policy but may have encountered social policy in other contexts. The text aims to provide an up-to-date yet accessible overview of the development of and the context for the provision of social welfare in contemporary Britain. Chapters are included that discuss the historical, ideological and political context within which social policy has developed and discuss the changing contemporary context within which social policy is developing today.

The book is divided into four substantive parts. Part I explores the historical development of social policy through the nineteenth and twentieth centuries with one chapter devoted to the development of welfare services following the introduction of the Poor Law Amendment Act of 1832 and a second chapter charting the changes from the Liberal welfare reforms through to the widespread adoption of the welfare principles laid down in the Beveridge Report in 1942. The distinction between the two centuries is somewhat arbitrary but the chapters seek to explore the ideas and principles laid down during those years that we might say still guide the implementation and delivery of social policy in late twentieth-century Britain.

Part II examines the policy and political context within which social policy is made and begins by examining the changes to the political environment that the welfare state has experienced in the last two decades. The first chapter of this part considers the so-called 'crisis of welfare states' that heralded the end of the Beveridgean consensus in British politics generally but in social welfare in particular. The other chapters of this part consider, first, the policy-making process, that is how policies come into being and are implemented, and, secondly, the financial environment of social policy making. That is, how we prioritise and allocate resources to welfare services and the mechanisms by which resources are collected and distributed.

Part III considers the ways in which different ideologies are used in explaining social policy and how such theoretical concepts are necessary for an understanding of social policy. The first chapter assesses why theory is regarded as a useful tool for analysing welfare policies and whether we can apply certain basic principles, such as need, to the allocation of welfare resources and as a foundation for social policy. The second and third chapters in this part go on to explore particular social theories and how each seeks to explain welfare and the welfare state. First, we explore the so-called traditional theories of welfare, such as classical liberal theory, Marxist theories and Fabian analysis, and how each understands the development of social policies and the welfare state. Secondly, we turn to more 'contemporary' theories which both criticise the traditional theories and present social policy in the context of modern-day political and social environments.

The final part looks at the 'policy areas' that form the backbone of the British welfare state and have traditionally been considered the very essence of social policy thinking and analysis. Therefore we have chapters considering developments in social security: education and training, health, housing, personal social services and employment. Each of these chapters presents a brief historical overview of developments since the publication of the Beveridge Report and outlines the development of our modern 'social services'. We also include in this part, however, chapters examining less-traditional areas, including the development of 'family' policy and the role of the criminal justice system in social policy which, although not regarded as social policy, have a considerable impact on social welfare. Although we do not go so far as to consider the so-called 'new' social policy (see Cahill, 1994) neither do we dismiss such considerations as invalid. Finally we consider the impact on British social policy of the international policy environment encountered principally in the development of a social policy agenda within the European Union but also in a wider international context.

The structure of the book is intended to provide the reader with a flexible and accessible introduction to social policy making in modern Britain. It is hoped that readers and students of social policy will be able to approach the text in a linear fashion but also to be selective and take a more random approach to their study of social policy.

REFERENCES

Ackers, L. and Abbott, P. (1996) *Social Policy for Nurses and the Caring Professions*, Buckingham: Open University Press.

Alcock, P. (1997) 'The Discipline of Social Policy', in Alcock, P., Erskine, A. and May, M. (eds), *The Student's Companion to Social Policy*, London: Blackwell.

Alcock, P., Erskine, A. and May, M. (1998) *The Student's Companion to Social Policy*, Oxford: Blackwell.

Cahill, M. (1994) *The New Social Policy*, Oxford: Blackwell.

Erskine, A. (1997) 'The Approaches and Methods of Social Policy', in Alcock, P., Erskine, A. and May, M. (eds), *The Student's Companion to Social Policy*, London: Blackwell.

Ginsburg, N. (1992) *Divisions of Welfare: A critical introduction to comparative social policy*, London: Sage.

Hill, M. (1996a) *Understanding Social Policy*, 5th edition, Hemel Hempstead: Harvester Wheatsheaf.

Hill, M. (1996b) *Social Policy: A comparative analysis*, Hemel Hempstead: Harvester Wheatsheaf.

Hill, M. (1997) *The Policy Process in the Modern State*, Hemel Hempstead: Harvester Wheatsheaf.

Mishra, R. (1981) *Society and Social Policy*, London: Macmillan.

Spicker, P. (1995) *Social Policy: Themes and approaches*, Hemel Hempstead: Harvester Wheatsheaf.

Part I

THE HISTORICAL CONTEXT

Introduction to Part I

This part examines the historical context within which social policy in Britain has developed over the nineteenth and twentieth centuries and seeks to establish the background behind much of contemporary social policies and welfare structures. An historical perspective helps us to better understand the present climate of social policy and may lead us to speculate about the future. We also may be able to trace the development of particular social policies over a considerable period of time and to understand what is often the apparently cyclical nature of policy developments.

Any historical approach to policy development inevitably involves an amount of arbitrariness, especially in deciding where to begin. Since this volume is intended to explore contemporary social policy issues and debates these two historical chapters are brief and seek merely to explore context and environment. Inevitably then they may omit or deal only briefly with aspects that some readers may feel deserve more detailed consideration. Since our focus is to introduce social policy in the British 'welfare state' in the late twentieth century we have chosen to begin in the year 1834.

Chapter 2 introduces the reader to a range of developments in welfare policy that were pioneered in the nineteenth century. The year 1834 is a landmark year since it marks the point at which government announced its own permanent presence on the welfare stage. The introduction of a New Poor Law, founded upon scientific principles, marked a fundamental turning point in social policy and heralded interventions in many other aspects of society. The chapter goes on to discuss legislative developments in public health, employment regulation and education, each of which experienced reform to a greater or lesser degree, though in each case developments were tentative and sporadic.

Chapter 3 discusses developments in the early decades of the twentieth century, beginning with the Liberal governments in power before the First World War. These governments, armed with new ideas and new thinking in social policy, established the roots of what was to become, after the Beveridge Report in 1942 and the legislative programme of the post-war Labour government, the welfare state. Successive governments adopted, usually in the face of deep-seated opposition, wider and more pervasive powers in the regulation of our social life. These governments also laid down welfare principles, such as insurance, that remain with us today.

The distinction between the developments of the nineteenth century and those of the twentieth is another arbitrary choice since, as many writers will indicate, many of the ideas adopted by the Liberal governments were the result of a process of debate that began in the late nineteenth century. Similarly the philosophical and ideological foundations of the Beveridge era have roots going back some decades. There are many other texts available that examine these and other developments of this era and to which readers are directed within both chapters and the annotated readings.

2 Welfare before the welfare state

OBJECTIVES

- To provide a broad historical overview of the development of British social policy.
- To explore the development of the principles of welfare and the foundations of contemporary social policy.
- To describe the development of welfare services, including public health, income maintenance, education and employment regulation.

INTRODUCTION

It is often tempting when examining the modern welfare state to trace its beginnings to its contemporary, post-1945, founders. But taking William Beveridge and his ground-breaking report of 1942 runs the risk that we omit to consider some of the principles that have characterised the development of British social policy and the welfare state before Beveridge. Similarly it may be tempting to take a lengthy historical detour in order to provide the fullest possible background to the contemporary picture and contemporary developments. We may for instance wish to elaborate the feudal and religious foundations of welfare, which stressed both the religious duty of caring for those less fortunate and the duty of the feudal lord to protect those within one's own domain.

We can also suggest, with some degree of accuracy, that many of the founding principles, for instance the distinction between the deserving and undeserving poor drawn in the Elizabethan Poor Law of 1598, remains with us today or that the parable of the good Samaritan is still apposite. Similarly we might argue that the residency qualification, embodied in the Elizabethan Poor Law, which parishes used to limit the burden on their own funds by driving the 'travelling poor' from their boundaries, may be found in the modern day treatment of both travellers and the single homeless. However, although such an approach may prove interesting for both reader and writer, it remains a detour from the contemporary scene that we wish to examine. And, of course, there are numerous historical accounts already available to which we might usefully refer the reader (Fraser, 1976; Marshall, 1985; Slack, 1995).

We have chosen instead to begin our historical overview with the year 1834 and the Poor Law Amendment Act, which, although not the first instance of the involvement of the state in the welfare of its citizens, represents a fundamental turning point. For it is with this Act that the state's role is consolidated in an attempt to redefine the Poor Law on the basis of universal laws and principles; it is here then that we can discern the foundations of the modern 'welfare state'. It is also from this point that the state begins to adopt ever-greater responsibilities in the everyday lives of its citizens and gradually, over the next century or so, increases the number of activities for which it assumes responsibility or control. And, although we do not wish to characterise the expansion of state activity as linear or necessarily progressive, and about which there has been much debate, 1834 nonetheless represents a significant turning point in the history of social policy.

We turn from the Poor Law Amendment Act to examine other areas of increased state involvement in the regulation of the social sphere. For example in the regulation of working hours and conditions, in the attempts to improve the sanitary conditions in our major towns and cities of the nineteenth century and in the beginnings of the development of state education. We also briefly examine popular reaction to an increasing state role in the provision of social policy and welfare services as compared to the range of provision already made by individuals and groups. Finally in this chapter we discuss what we have called the 'winds of welfare change', by which we mean the period towards the end of the nineteenth century during which to continue a 'hands-off' approach with the minimum of state provision no longer seemed adequate or sufficient. We refer here to the ideological roots of what was to become a 'new liberalism' in which the state in Britain was to re-evaluate its own social role and was to conclude, along with other modern industrial nations, that a far greater level of intervention was right and proper. In Britain this provoked constitutional crisis which was itself to help redefine not only the course of social policy for the twentieth century but also the role and function of government and the balance of power within the British constitution.

POOR LAW REFORM

The 1834 Act was founded on the many concerns and worries in the minds of officials and reformers. First, was the often random nature and application of the existing Poor Law, which was administered by local parishes. The often cited, we may say famous, systems of parish relief, such as that of the parish of Speen in Berkshire, were by no means universal and there remained great diversity in the availability and generosity of parish relief. Secondly, was the fear that the Poor Law of the previous two and a half centuries was no longer able to meet the demands of nineteenth-century Britain. The dual processes of industrialisation and urban development were attracting new populations to towns in search of work. In times of unemployment, existing residency qualifications, embodied in the various Acts of Settlement, would disqualify individuals from turning to the parish for help; indeed we may argue that the parish boundaries themselves had become outdated and meaningless.

Finally, and possibly uppermost in the minds of reformers, was the issue of rising costs. Parish relief was felt to be an expensive luxury which, instead of simply relieving the poor, was encouraging them to remain idle and burden the parish and its ratepayers. A burden that fell disproportionately, they felt, on the aristocratic rich and new groups of wealth-creating capitalists. We might further suggest that the existence of parish relief itself was a cause of poverty, since employers were able to maintain wages at low levels in the knowledge that the parish would 'top-up' the wages of their labourers. This was most keenly felt in rural areas as employers felt able to artificially reduce local levels of pay in the knowledge that the parish would supplement a labourer's income. Those same employers, this time as ratepayers, also pressed for a reduction in the burden of their parish rates and thereby a reduction in payments of relief. Such factors were themselves cited in the Swing riots of 1830 which witnessed in Hampshire the breaking of agricultural machinery and the destruction of local workhouses in some parishes (Hobsbawm and Rudé, 1969, pp. 119–20).

THE 1834 AMENDMENT ACT

The combination therefore of the rising costs and inconsistent application and outdatedness of the existing system of the Poor Law together paved the way for its review and subsequent amendment. The intention behind the review was to found the New Poor Law on more rational and 'scientific' principles. The establishment of a centralised administrative system, laying down the rules to be implemented at a local level, was a keystone in the new system. Similarly the random distinction between 'deserving' and 'undeserving' poor would be more systematically, and bureaucratically, defined leading in time to the establishment of notions of 'rights to welfare'.

Exhibit 2.1

Poor Law Report 1832

The first and most essential of all conditions; a principle which we find universally admitted, even by those whose practice is at variance with it, is that his situation on the whole shall not be made really or apparently so eligible as the situation of the independent labourer of the lowest class. Throughout the evidence it is shown that in proportion as the condition of any pauper class is elevated above the condition of independent labourers, the condition of the independent class is depressed; their industry is impaired, their employment becomes unsteady, and its remuneration in wages is diminished. Such persons, therefore, are under the strongest inducements to quit the less eligible class of labourers and enter the more eligible class of paupers.

The 1834 Act removed the responsibility of the Poor Law from the parish and instead created a locally elected Board of Guardians who were to administer relief in 'unions' (groups of parishes) which were supervised at a central level by the Poor Law Board. (The Local Government Board replaced this in 1871.) Central supervision, which was advisory rather than directive in nature, was intended to ensure that the principles of the Poor Law were applied uniformly. These principles were, first, the ending of most 'outdoor relief' and the application of the workhouse test. Each Poor Law union was to establish a workhouse, the intention of which was to discourage all but the destitute from turning to the Poor Law for relief. Secondly, was the notion of 'less eligibility' which dictated that levels of relief would not be so generous as to discourage the poor from finding work. The system of relief founded by the 1834 Act then was one which, in theory, offered relief to those individuals whose poverty was not their own fault and whose behaviour was respectable (Fraser, 1976; Thane, 1996).

Individuals, who could satisfy the local board of their need, that group of individuals referred to as the deserving poor, might still receive outdoor relief but otherwise would have to rely on the provisions of the workhouse. The work-house system put the poor to work in return for assistance and discouraged the (re)production of further mouths to feed. The notion that no one should receive something, in this case assistance, without a corresponding duty to work, is one we find resonant in some of the notions of 'workfare' and the 'New Deal' debated in contemporary political circles.

In theory then, the able labouring poor would be provided for by the work-house whilst other groups, the elderly, widows, sick and physically or mentally unfit, would continue to receive outdoor relief. In practice the workhouse came to dominate Poor Law provision in the later years of the nineteenth century as the deterrent principles of the Act were enforced most vigorously. The poor often instead refused to submit to the indignities of the Poor Law and the ultimate indignity of a pauper funeral. This might suggest that the poor of the nineteenth century had only the prospect of destitution and the Poor Law as some kind of safety net, cast so narrowly as to miss the bulk of the poor (Fraser, 1976).

The above brief account of the Poor Law may leave one with the impression that the Act concerned itself primarily with the income maintenance of the poor and destitute. However, there was too the much wider consideration of the health and moral welfare of the poor. Local Boards of Guardians also sanctioned the creation of other forms of institutional welfare by way of infirmaries providing medical care and secure hospitals providing for the incarceration of the mentally ill. Such 'indoor relief' we might usefully suggest remained within the twentieth-century welfare system, in the provision for both the elderly and mentally ill, until perhaps the practical development of ideas about community care.

The Poor Law was not, however, the sole form of provision available to the poor: savings, insurance schemes, Friendly Societies and trades unions all offered the working class ways of providing for themselves and their families in bad times. Unemployment, sickness, old age and death could all be covered by the variety of schemes operating, often by the working people themselves and outside the realm of Poor Law Guardians, especially as the century progressed (Johnson, 1985). Alongside the various forms of self-help that the Poor Law was keen to encourage, there also developed wide-ranging elements of charitable poor relief. Attempts to co-ordinate charitable relief under the auspices of the Charity Organisation Society (COS) and to deliver charitable relief according to 'universal and consistent principles' so that help was distributed systematically and to those 'deemed capable of becoming self-supporting' (Thane, 1996) proved largely unsuccessful. However, the 'casework' approach pioneered by the COS involving attempts to deal with the problems facing an individual or family has persisted in much charitable and, in the personal social services, state provision today.

This brief foray into the world of the Victorian Poor Law, whilst not attempting to be a wholesale review of nineteenth-century attitudes towards the poor, does illustrate that many of the principles upon which state intervention in individual lives was predicated remain with us today. Distinctions between the deserving and undeserving, the discouragement of dependence and the targeting of help to the most needy are all the stuff of the welfare reform debate initiated by successive governments in the 1980s and 1990s. However, though crucial in the development of a welfare state, the Poor Law was by no means the only factor in the evolution of British social policy. The state also began to develop its responsibilities in public health, employment regulation and education, and it is these other areas of state intervention to which we now turn.

PUBLIC HEALTH

If the need for change in the operation of the Poor Law can be attributed to the rapid growth of an industrial, urban population then the pressure for action over public health was doubly felt as a result of rural migration. The population of Britain doubled in the first half of the nineteenth century, with a fourfold or even eightfold increase in the populations of some urban areas (Fraser, 1984). Such accelerated growth heralded the development of towns and cities in which housing was closely built, so as to be near places of work, and lacked amenities which we now take for granted, such as a clean water supply, and sewerage and refuse disposal.

The development of public health as a legitimate concern of government and indeed the development of systems of both a clean water supply and sewerage disposal are often credited to one man, Edwin Chadwick. Chadwick had been crucially involved in the collection of evidence for and the preparation of the Poor Law review which itself formed the basis of the 1834 Poor Law Amendment Act. It was in this capacity that Chadwick and his colleagues first began to perceive the link between sanitary conditions and the spread of illness and disease and in its turn the contribution of disease (and death) to the prevalence of poverty and, of course, the costs of the Poor Law.

The acceptance by government for public health responsibilities was, however, faltering. Death rates, it was generally agreed, particularly in towns and cities, were rising and the increasing incidence of epidemic diseases such as cholera alarmed the middle classes. They were, even in the 1840s, diseases that were preventable. Chadwick, in preparing his report on sanitary conditions, was able to use the newly founded central machinery of the Poor Law to collect his evidence. Poor Law Assistant Commissioners, Boards of Guardians and Poor Law medical officers were all used to give testimony to the health and sanitary conditions endured by the 'labouring classes' (Fraser, 1984). His report, published in 1842, was not, however, widely and readily accepted and it was not until 1848 that legislation, in the form of the Public Health Act, saw the light of day. Political infighting and unwillingness to raise additional revenues – the costs involved in creating a water supply and sewage disposal systems would be considerable – resulted only in inaction. Also the whole debate was itself overshadowed by the debate surrounding the proper role for the state in regulating its people, again an issue frequently revisited since.

Provision for clean water and sewage disposal were initially a discretionary responsibility of municipal authorities who found themselves facing a host of vested interests in the form of the building industry, landlords, water companies and ratepayers. The Public Health Act made provision for setting up local boards of health and the appointment of Medical Officers of Health (MOH), although this was only permissory unless death rates were unusually high. Although some earlier legislation had provided, for example, for the creation of a municipally controlled water supply in Leeds and an MOH in Liverpool, the development of the state's role in public or environmental health was initially patchy. An overseeing role was ascribed to the General Board of Health, also established under the Act, although so ineffective was the legislation that the Board was eventually abolished in 1858 with Chadwick himself dismissed from the Board in 1854.

Only with the Sanitation Act of 1866 did municipal local government derive compulsory powers to act in the interests of public health or for the prevention of 'nuisances'. Other Acts had been passed in the intervening years, but the significance of the 1866 Act was its universality. It was not until a decade later under the 1875 Public Health Act, introduced following the report of the Royal Sanitary Commission in 1871, that the situation was further clarified and responsibility for public health and sanitation laid with the newly developing local authorities. Further change came in an Act of 1890 (the Housing of the Working Classes Act), which allowed local government to impose minimum standards in the construction of housing and to develop municipal (council) housing.

Other developments in the provision of public standards of health derived from improvements in medical technology and knowledge. The increasingly widespread use of immunisation against disease together with increasing knowledge about disinfection made hospitals themselves safer places to be treated. Later still the provision of public hospital services was distanced from the Poor Law. The provision of hospitals also gradually became a responsibility of local authorities, as it was they who from 1929 assumed control of Poor Law infirmaries.

Many of the public health provisions discussed here, like the Poor Law itself, have been retained as principles by which the modern welfare state continues to operate. Much responsibility for public health today remains with local authorities, and for reforms pioneered by Chadwick and others responsibility lies with Environmental Health Officers as well as with the National Health Service. And, although the priorities of public health may have developed such that the provision of clean water, sewerage systems and refuse disposal are taken for granted, new areas of responsibility, for example in food hygiene standards or noise pollution control, have been incorporated. Once again we are able to see how the contemporary welfare state owes a debt to an age long forgotten.

EMPLOYMENT REGULATION

Looking back to the nineteenth century it often appears that the pioneering spirit of laissez-faire capitalism, the industrial revolution and the creation of an empire were foremost in the minds of the government of the day. Yet within that century of revolution we can discern the seeds of latter-day social policy developments, tempered though they were by considerations of the moral virtue of the working classes and a strongly held principle that the state should only become involved when absolutely necessary. That meant a clear understanding that the free market had failed to provide and that any intervention should not itself be the cause of harm – sentiments clearly resonant of many debates today.

Employment regulation was, however, possibly one of the most sacrosanct areas of welfare and like the Poor Law and sanitation change was slow to come. Government involvement in the control of employment and conditions in the work place at a time when supply and demand determined the price and conditions of labour was, to say the least, a tentative venture. Many employers and politicians of the time continued to believe in the value of free trade, and thereby regular employment, as the most effective way of providing for the welfare of the working classes. At a time when trades unions, though legal, were effectively emasculated by the law, legislation to regulate hours and safety in the work place was patchy and slow to develop. Many employers were able to do little more than comply with the minimum standards in the full knowledge that enforcement was lax and punishment light.

Exhibit 2.2

Commission of Enquiry into Factories 1833

In recommending legislative restrictions of the labour of children, as not being free agents, and not being able to protect themselves, we have been careful not to lose sight of the practical limits...

The restrictions we venture to propose ... are, that children under nine years of age shall not be employed in mills or factories ... that until the ... fourteenth year the hours of labour during any one day shall not in any case exceed eight ... until the fourteenth year children shall not in any case be allowed to work at night; that is to say between the hours of ten at night and five in the morning.

Since the whole of our recommendations have for their object the care and benefit of children, we have been desirous of devising means for securing the occupation of a portion of the time abridged from their hours of labour to their own advantage. We think the best mode of accomplishing this object will be the occupation, supports of three (or four) hours of every day in education.

Reformers initially focused their attentions on the employment of children in factories. Child labour itself was of course nothing new and children would be put to work in agricultural regions or cottage industries as soon as they were able. But the conditions in which children worked and lived in industrialising Britain proved an offence to the humanitarian sentiments of a country that came to regard itself as the most civilised in the world. The conditions endured by children, the long hours and the physical hazards they faced when operating machinery, were likened to slavery, since children in contrast to adults often had little choice over their labour. They could not trade their labour in the free market as laissez-faire economics predicted and gradually, though by no means easily, the case for government regulation was accepted. Employers constantly stressed the damage to their industry if child labour were banned and often sought to place the blame at the doors of parents who insisted that their children work as soon as they were able. Similarly they stressed the likely increase in poverty amongst the labouring classes, and therefore the increased Poor Law burden, if children were prevented from working.

Some employers, enlightened reformers such as Robert Owen, sought to show that they could continue to profit whilst maintaining a watchful eye on the welfare of their employees, but they were often the exception in the early industrial revolution. So it was that children, often as young as four, came to work in coal mines and factories across the country, often simply because their stature allowed them to work in places adults could not reach. Indeed in many districts workhouses and Boards of Guardians would 'apprentice' children to colliers or factory owners and so reduce the burden on their local rates (for a description of children's working conditions in the coal industry see Pollard, 1984).

Restrictions on the hours that either children or women were able to work, or the industries in which they were able to work, were also beset with problems. An overall reduction in the income available to a family placed that family under greater pressure and strain and might lead them to the doors of the workhouse. Such proposals also raised in the minds of Victorians the prospect of social unrest as children, out of gainful employment and in families under increased social pressure, might turn to crime. Images such as this were reinforced in the popular conscience by stories such as those of Fagin and the Artful Dodger in Dickens' *Oliver Twist*. But reformers too were concerned with the moral and educational welfare of children, and accounts of long hours, beatings, sexual promiscuity, drunken and indolent parents and the physical injuries suffered by many children meant that the intervention of the state could be put off no longer.

As we might expect, however, the introduction of legislation to regulate the conditions and hours worked by children, and later by women and men too, was slow and hard fought. Credit for the ending of child labour is often given to Lord Shaftesbury and his parliamentary campaigning but, as Fraser notes, his work was the climax to that started by others before the passage of the 1844 Factory Act (Fraser, 1984). Indeed the previous decade and a half had heralded vigorous efforts in the pursuit of a legally enforceable ten-hour day. Incremental legislative change throughout the middle decades of the nineteenth century gradually introduced protection first for children, for instance prohibiting their employment in textile mills at ages younger than nine years and limiting their daily hours of work to eight, rising to 12 hours at age 13. Legislation also introduced the factory inspectors who had powers to enforce rules governing the employment of children.

The legislation, however, remained weak and difficult to enforce – only one mines inspector was appointed by the 1842 Mines Act – and this itself indicated the difficulty of and opposition to something as fundamental as control of the 'free market'. Indeed the ten-hour day was not achieved until the 1874 Factory Act by which time pressure from workers themselves was growing which is indicated by the growth of the 'new unionism' (the TUC had formed in 1868) and gradual reforms in the franchise giving more working men the right to vote.

EDUCATION

Education and its provision during the nineteenth century remained very much a minority undertaking. Formal and structured education remained, as it had done for previous centuries, largely a privilege for the aristocracy and the emerging middle classes who could afford the costs of private tuition, fee-paying grammar schools and eventually perhaps Oxford or Cambridge. But, for the mass of the population, education, where it existed at all, remained basic, often little more than basic literacy and numeracy. There was, of course, much between these two extremes, for example church-run schools, industrial schools, dame schools or those provided by charitable funds; for the mass of the population, however, education was both scarce and patchy.

Indeed there remained for much of the century deep-seated opposition to mass educational provision, with those arguing variously that anything more than a basic education would upset the given social order. Similarly, the state had no business in deciding the education of individuals and that compulsion in education would pauperise the labouring classes whose children would no longer be able to work and learn their trade. Much of the opposition had its roots in the religious divisions of the time and successive governments had to tread very carefully between the various churches and their dogmas. These factors in their turn guaranteed that formal state involvement in the provision of learning was delayed until the final quarter of the nineteenth century. So difficult did it prove for governments to agree on the nature and extent of its role in education that early interventions were confined to the regulation of teacher training which was felt could help overcome often bitter conflict over the teaching of religion (Fraser, 1976; Henriques, 1979).

There existed some state support for schooling in that provided for children under the care of the workhouse. However, Poor Law education was not considered to be of very high status, offering low pay and low status to teachers. Efforts towards education for pauper children continued to attract voluntary and charitable effort, notably in the form of the Ragged Schools from the 1840s, but government support for such schools was rejected. Other provision came in the form of the Factory School that proved attractive to some owners as a method of disciplining and improving the standards of their workforce. But herein lies the roots of a conflict since working children were expected to contribute to their family income, and schooling, albeit free, could deny the family one source of extra income. Similarly factory owners were often unwilling to subsidise such projects, since they would interfere with their production. Indeed many would refuse to allow time out of the factory for schooling and instead insisted that it be undertaken in the free time of the child, little though that may have been. Legislation in this area was usually ineffective. The provisions of the Health and Morals of Apprentices Act (1802) which 'laid down that the millowner was to provide schoolroom and paid teacher' or the 1833 Factory Act which placed a responsibility for the education of non-apprenticed children on mill-owners proved difficult to enforce or was simply ignored (Henriques, 1979).

The most significant step taken by the nineteenth-century state in the establishment of a national system of education was that embodied in the Education Act of 1870. As a result of this Act, local School Boards were to be established 'where there was clear educational need' to provide 'non-denominational elementary schools financed out of the rates in addition to Government grants' (Fraser, 1976). The aim of the Act was to permit local authorities to act to improve the attendance of working-class children in some form of schooling and to try to overcome the religious bickering that had engulfed the education debate for the previous half century. Although the Act did not establish a national education system it did lay down a more systematic role for the state in the provision of education, the culmination of which was a national education system based upon free and compulsory education up to age 14.

REACTION TO THE WELFARE OF THE STATE

Whilst it has been popular to view the development of a welfare state as necessary, desirable and inevitable, a view reflected in the writings upon which we have relied in the preceding section, other writers point out the level of discord which greeted successive attempts to secure state involvement in the provision of welfare services. It is by no means certain that such changes, which preceded the more comprehensive pattern of state welfare that developed in the first half of the twentieth century, received universal or even popular acclaim. There was, as many writers indicate, a strong ethos among the working poor of self-help and self-reliance and often a deep and bitter distrust of what the state tried to do (Johnson, 1985; Finlayson, 1994; Thane, 1996).

Mistrust of the motives of the state in extending its welfare role stems from the punitive and often brutal experiences of working people at the hand of local Poor Law Guardians. Family and community resources would usually be available to a family falling on hard times and returned to others in better times. If such resources were either not available or had been exhausted the mercy of charity was to be preferred to the workhouse (Thane, 1996). Alongside the mass of, frequently undocumented, charitable activity was the broad range of working-class self-help ranging from informal insurance and savings clubs to the more formal insurance schemes provided by friendly societies and trades unions. Membership of such societies was widespread though often the vagaries of employment would mean that individuals would enter and leave such societies as they were alternately in and out of work. But such schemes proved popular in providing insurance to cover illness, death or, less frequently, unemployment. Membership of such societies has been estimated at around a million by the end of the century (Thane, 1996).

Also increasingly common as a form of self-help during this period were co-operative arrangements for the purchase or construction of homes – the building society. Many of the building societies would be short-lived and terminate their activities when each of their members had built or bought their own home. From the middle of the century the move towards permanent building societies was underway which would provide longer-term opportunities for members to borrow and invest but which also marked a move 'away from working-class participation ... the movement also became commercial' (Finlayson, 1994).

There is therefore evidence of widespread working-class self-help across the range of social policies for which the government was beginning to take responsibility. Such self-help sat well with an economic and social doctrine of laissez-faire which dominated political thought in Victorian Britain and which preached that the proper role of the state was residual. However, there was at the same time a mood of change. Most of the self-help provision was attractive to, and in many ways restricted to the better-off working class and those for whom steady and regular employment was available. Large numbers of unskilled workers found themselves either unable to take advantage of mutual society membership or found that their benefits were as temporary as their work. With organised self-help apparently the preserve of a labour aristocracy, it appeared as though numbers of working people would, however diligently they may try, continue to be unable to provide for themselves. To a growing number of 'Benthamites', followers of the utilitarian thinking of Jeremy Bentham, such a situation was inefficient and wasteful of human resources. Herein lay the ideological justification for an expanded state role that allowed the market its free hand but would temper its worst effects by (collective) state action (Pearson and Williams, 1984).

Towards the end of the century concern grew for the position of working people who, though not indolent or lazy, suffered from the effects of poverty for reasons that were perceptibly outside their control. Concern most frequently fell on the elderly who were poor by virtue of their inability to continue to work, often caused by their ill health. After a lifetime of work the elderly appeared to be only able to rely on either charity or the workhouse in circumstances for which they appeared free of blame. Pressure grew then, particularly following the studies conducted by Charles Booth, to do something about the aged poor for whom reliance on the Poor Law appeared as a final indignity at the end of a life of privation. The political mood then was in the process of change, partly motivated by a change in ideas away from laissez-faire towards a 'new liberalism' and by a realisation that the effects of state intervention might not be as damaging as first thought. Such acceptance of a wider role for the state in social policy was to lead, at the end of the century, to a view that the state 'should be used as a vehicle for social reform, to improve the condition of the weakest and the poorest' (Clarke, Cochrane and Smart, 1992). This change in mood was to receive legislative elaboration in the Liberal reforms of the first decade of the twentieth century.

Our brief examination of an expanding state welfare role in nineteenth-century Britain indicates a polity itself unwilling to commit the state to widespread activity and cautious of the opposition such concerted action might bring. The government in each of these areas of poor relief – sanitation, employment regulation and education – took, at each stage, unsteady and faltering steps towards welfare reform. But what these tentative steps did do was to provide the justification to build upon and engage in further activities in the future. Slowly then, the state adopted and accepted, though never unequivocally, an ever-wider role in the regulation and provision of social welfare.

THE WINDS OF WELFARE CHANGE

The final decades of the nineteenth century proved to be something of a political watershed in the development of the role of the British state in welfare provision. The economic doctrine of laissez-faire was gradually giving way to a collective ideal embodied in what was termed 'New Liberalism' which envisaged 'a positive role for the state in the amelioration of social problems' (Pearson and Williams, 1984). The legislative developments of New Liberalism is something to which we turn in the next chapter; however, it is useful here to review the political and social environment within which New Liberalism developed.

One factor often cited in the creation of a new 'social' ethos for the Liberals was their changing political fortune. Working people had, and were continuing, to gain the electoral franchise which also heralded the development of a working-class politics. The establishment first of a 'new unionism' and later the Labour Party posted a not inconsiderable electoral threat to the Liberal Party which had to be addressed. Similarly there was a change in attitudes towards social issues. The studies by Booth in London and Rowntree in York indicated that poverty might not be simply down to laziness within the labouring classes. Instead the economic operation of society, the unfettered free market might, it was suggested, be the cause of poverty which in turn 'could be the cause of people being unable to live freely' (Clarke, Cochrane and Smart, 1992).

The studies by Booth and Rowntree contributed to a debate about how society might attempt to measure poverty objectively and how minimum social standards might be defined and achieved. Rowntree's study talked of a minimum necessary to maintain physical efficiency whilst Booth spoke of a 'line of poverty' below which were grouped classes of people who had only casual, intermittent or small but regular earnings. 'By the word "poor" I mean to describe those who have a sufficiently regular though bare income, such as 18s to 21s per week for a moderate family, and by "very poor" those who from any cause fall much below this standard' (Booth, 1892). Rowntree refined this in his attempt to define conditions of primary and secondary poverty wherein those suffering primary poverty were 'families whose total earnings were insufficient ... for the maintenance of merely physical efficiency' (Rowntree, 1902). The conclusions reached by these two surveys, though not universally accepted, were that around 30 per cent of the population were living in poverty (Booth suggested 30 per cent and Rowntree 28 per cent). Rowntree went further in his analysis by suggesting that there existed a cycle of poverty throughout the lives of the labouring poor. The years of childhood, early marriage and old age were those in which poverty was highly likely and often for reasons that were beyond the control of the individual concerned, but as a result of 'complex economic and social factors' (Fraser, 1984).

Such surveys, themselves groundbreaking in the development of social research, together with a changing and turbulent political climate altered fundamentally the basis of debate about social policies and the proper role of the state in providing welfare. We will go on to see that the first two decades of the twentieth century, rooted as they were in the changes of the nineteenth, laid the foundations of a formally organised welfare state which would not become a reality for another half century.

CONCLUSION

What we have concerned ourselves with in this chapter has been the foundations of our late twentieth-century welfare state. Clearly the welfare state was not established by, nor did it develop from the publication of the Beveridge Report. Many of the principles of welfare, ideological, political and philosophical have been with us for many centuries. The changes in state welfare introduced and developed in the nineteenth century that we have discussed in this chapter represent an attempt to place those principles in a legislative and structural framework. Similarly many of those principles remain with us today, in the rules and policies adopted by our modern welfare state.

REFERENCES

Barker, P. (ed.) (1984) *Founders of the Welfare State*, London: Heinemann.

Booth, C. (1892) *Life and Labour of the People in London* (Vol. I).

Clarke, J., Cochrane, A. and Smart, C. (1992) *Ideologies of Welfare: From dreams to disillusion*, London: Routledge.

Finlayson, G. (1994) *Citizen, State and Social Welfare in Britain 1830–1990*, Oxford: Oxford University Press.

Fraser, D. (ed.) (1976) *The New Poor Law in the Nineteenth Century*, London: Macmillan.

Fraser, D. (1984) *The Evolution of the British Welfare State*, London: Macmillan.

Henriques, U. R. Q. (1979) *Before the Welfare State: Social administration in early industrial Britain*, London: Longman.

Hobsbawm, E. J. and Rudé, G. (1969) *Captain Swing*, London: Lawrence & Wishart.

Johnson, P. (1985) *Saving and Spending: The working-class economy in Britain 1870–1939*, Oxford: Oxford University Press.

Marshall, J. D. (1985) *The Old Poor Law 1795–1834*, London: Macmillan.

Pearson, R. and Williams, G. (1984) *Political Thought and Public Policy in the Nineteenth Century: An introduction*, London: Longman.

Pollard, M. (1984) *The Hardest Work Under Heaven: The life and death of the British coal miner*, London: Hutchinson.

Rowntree, B. S. (1902) *Poverty: A study of town life*, London: Macmillan.

Slack, P. (1995) *The English Poor Law 1531–1782*, Cambridge: Cambridge University Press.

Thane, P. (1996) *Foundations of the Welfare State*. London: Longman.
Vincent, C. (1991) *Poor Citizens: The state and the poor in twentieth century Britain*. London: Longman.

ANNOTATED READINGS

Perhaps still the most comprehensive and accessible account of legislative change across the range of social policy, particularly in the nineteenth century, is to be found in D. Fraser's *Evolution of the British Welfare State* and a further useful source is Henriques' *Before the Welfare State*. The most accessible account of the later nineteenth century and the Liberal welfare reforms before the First World War can be found in Thane's *Foundations of the Welfare State*.

Discussion and analysis of the area we might usefully refer to as non-state welfare has been growing in recent years. Johnson's *Saving and Spending* gives perhaps the fullest account of the working-class economy during the industrial revolution whilst Finlayson's *Citizen State and Social Welfare in Britain 1830–1990* explores the development of self-help and mutual aid as alternatives to the 'state-led' notion of welfare reform.

For an exposition of the ideas and ideals and the political debates behind the welfare reforms of the day and the controversy over the right role for the state in promoting public welfare, see Pearson and Williams *Political Thought and Public Policy in the Nineteenth Century*. Clarke, Cochrane and Smart's *Ideologies of Welfare: from dreams to disillusion*, explores similar territory whilst an interesting biographical detour may be found in Barker's *Founders of the Welfare State*.

3 The welfare state years: Consensus and conflict

OBJECTIVES

- To describe the institutional development of the British welfare state through the first half of the twentieth century.
- To explore the existence of consensus in British social policy.
- To introduce and examine the idea of a crisis of the welfare state.

INTRODUCTION

As we indicated in the preceding chapter, it may be tempting to lay the foundation of the British welfare state with the publication of the Beveridge Report in 1942. However, as we have seen, many of the principles embodied within the welfare state have their roots in the often pioneering work of social reformers in the nineteenth century. Similarly we can identify, in the structures of the welfare state, an earlier ancestry. In particular we can suggest that the modern structures of British welfare are those laid down in the reforms introduced under the Liberal government in the first decade of the twentieth century.

We begin by examining these reforms and go on to suggest that the introduction of measures such as school meals, old age pensions and later the principle of insurance-based social security were the basis of many, if not most, of the welfare principles upon which we rely today. The impact of Fabianism, as a coherent set of ideas, together with the impact of war combined to lend legitimacy to the idea of widespread and formalised state action across a wide range of social and economic activities. Such was the effect of this new state activity that the notion of a welfare consensus, a broad acceptance of the role of the state in many areas of public and private life, developed in the post-war decades. This notion of consensus on social policy we explore in the latter part of this chapter, whether the term is itself meaningful and what the nature of that consensus might be.

LIBERAL SOCIAL POLICY

In January 1906 the Liberals under Campbell-Bannerman won a landslide general election victory, ending almost 20 years of Conservative rule, and, though social reform was not high on their list of priorities, it did benefit from the victory.

The presence of 53 Labour MPs was more than anything else a symbolic and powerful symbol of the aspirations of working-class men and women and of the failure of the two-party system (Sullivan, 1992; Thane, 1996). As one contemporary report put it:

> The emergence of a strong Labour element in the House of Commons has been generally welcomed as the most significant outcome of the present election. It lifts the occasion out of the ordinary groove of domestic politics and will have far wider influence than any mere turnover of party voters. (*The Times*, 30 January 1906)

In many ways the Labour presence in the House acted as a social conscience for the Liberal majority and prompted the first stirrings of welfarism.

THE EMBRYONIC WELFARE STATE

In 1908 the government introduced old-age pensions but not before being prodded into action by the back benches and activities outside the House. The government seemed to fear that a Conservative majority in the House of Lords would overturn any progressive legislation it sought to introduce. Yet a series of bad by-election results saw a succession of government seats lost to the Labour Party.

Herbert Asquith who had taken over as Prime Minister and David Lloyd-George the President of the Board of Trade were to be powerful movers in the introduction of new pension legislation. The Bill proposed that old-age pensions be non-contributory and that they be introduced to offer relief to aged paupers and relieve the strain on the Poor Law, which was itself under consideration by a Royal Commission. Lloyd-George proposed the introduction of a pension age of 70 years, and so it was, with the successful passage of the legislation, that pensions were introduced from 1 January 1909. The new pension was paid as a right and by this measure reformers hoped to remove the stigma that had been associated with the Poor Law. As a result the numbers who applied far outstripped expectations, suggesting, in Lloyd-George's words: 'a mass of poverty and destitution which is too proud to wear the badge of pauperism'.

Lloyd-George was to ensure his name in welfare history by his next intervention into the realm of social reform. As Chancellor in 1909 he was faced with a projected budget deficit of £16 million and he decided that the solution to his financial dilemma was to be by the introduction of his 'people's budget'. He intended to raise revenue by increasing duty on alcohol and tobacco, but also on petrol duty and the use of motor vehicles, a levy that fell disproportionately on the wealthy. He also introduced a progressive form of income tax which Lloyd-George described as:

> A War Budget. It is for raising money to wage implacable warfare against poverty and squalidness. I cannot help hoping that before this generation has passed away we shall

have advanced a great step towards that good time when poverty and wretchedness and human degradation which always follow in its camp will be as remote to the people of this country as the wolves which once infested the forests. (*Hansard*, 29 April 1909)

So radical were these proposals for their day that the House of Lords rejected them and brought the two Houses of Parliament directly into conflict with one another. Lloyd-George warned that the Lords 'five hundred men chosen accidentally from among the unemployed' would not frustrate the will of the democratically elected government. The conflict prompted a constitutional crisis over which two general elections were fought in 1910; the first confirmed the people's budget and the second caused the reform of the constitutional powers of the House of Lords who would from then on no longer be able to thwart the will of the Commons.

One of the most important structural principles of the British welfare state, which remains an important pillar today, was the introduction of social insurance to cover the interruption of earnings. Lloyd-George proposed the introduction of a tripartite scheme into which contributions would be paid by employee, employer and the government itself. The contributions would insure the worker against the 'accidents of life', such as ill-health or death of the breadwinner, which had been recognised as major causes of poverty and destitution, and which would bring destitution on to whole families. The insurance principle was extended during and after the First World War to include periods of casual unemployment due to temporary recession – which itself formed a cornerstone of the Beveridge proposals 30 years later.

The years between the two world wars, during which time the Labour Party gradually replaced the Liberals as the 'natural party of opposition', were also years during which Britain itself moved from welfare scepticism to welfare collectivism. Early attempts at state intervention in individual welfare had often been viewed with suspicion, as a threat to the attempts of working-class people to better their lives (Pelling, 1984; Sullivan, 1996; Thane, 1996). Early Labour response was to oppose the extension of state power implicit in the Liberal welfare reforms; it was the state after all, whose welfare of the Poor Law was the most hated. Working-class experience of the welfare 'state' had been unequivocally oppressive, and it is unsurprising therefore that the working classes viewed Lloyd-George's reforms as some attempt to extend the workhouse solution to poverty (Pelling, 1968).

It was not only in the attempts at the relief of poverty, however, that there was suspicion. Experience in both education and housing policies suggested that welfarism would be nothing more than another burden. The construction of homes for working people, in the aftermath of slum clearance at the end of the nineteenth century, by charitable organisations was frequently the cause of resentment. Large well-ventilated rooms might be congenial to the health of large working-class families, but were also impossibly expensive to heat and the rules and regulation of behaviour that went with such charitable tenancies were felt to be an unwelcome incursion into people's liberty and life style. The Labour movement itself sought to redress the balance by the construction of 'model' working-class housing in the inter-war years, such as those of the Co-operative movement or the Tolpuddle Martyrs Memorial Cottages, and such a move might indicate a guarded welcome for municipal housing projects.

Interventions into the field of education raised similar worries and feelings of hostility amongst working people. One of the most ardent objections was the potential loss of earnings for a working-class family that compulsory education implied. Many families were in fact dependent for their very survival on the earnings from their children's employment. The progression of education reforms, which has continually increased the element of compulsion, alongside moves to restrict the hours worked by children, remained substantially unsupported by ordinary working people in the late nineteenth and early twentieth centuries. Their fears were grounded in an anti-statist philosophy which regarded the state as something which worked for and protected the interests of the wealthy (see Pelling, 1968). Likewise, the welfarism of the state, as expressed by the Liberal welfare reforms of the first decade of the twentieth century, was viewed as something antithetical to the alternative forms of working-class welfare provision already in place (Johnson, 1983; Finlayson, 1994; Thane, 1996). The clearest statement of an alternative form of welfare was the widespread existence of the Friendly Society whose central concern was mutual insurance against sickness and unemployment. Strong within such societies was the belief that mutual self-help was socially and morally preferable to redistributive provision implemented by state functionaries, whose activities would inevitably involve intrusion into the private lives of citizens (Thane, 1996).

THE FOUNDATIONS OF THE FABIAN LEGACY

The reasons for the gradual acceptance of welfarism within the Labour movement and the wider working classes has much to do with the development of the ideas of Fabianism. The Fabian Society, led by the indomitable Sidney and Beatrice Webb who themselves played a crucial role in the production of the Minority Royal Commission Report into the Poor Law, held that socialism in Britain was entirely compatible with the institutions of the state and could, and should, be realised through a parliamentary route. The state itself, they held, could be harnessed to promote the collective good and act as a neutral umpire between the demands of different interests. This view of the state, and its role in the promotion of welfare and the collective good, was to form the backbone of 'social administration', the forefather of today's 'social policy' (see chapter 1). Put simply, the election of a Labour government would give the working class control of the state machinery of Westminster and Whitehall.

Social democracy in Fabian eyes, then, required not the 'withering away' of the state, but that it be fashioned into an instrument of social change and that the *expert administrator*, the civil servant, under the guiding hand of the elected parliament, become the tool for the implementation of (gradual) social change.

Inherent in the notion of gradual social change was the concept of ethical socialism apparent in the writings of theorists such as Tawney and Marshall. Within their writings was a notion of equality which emphasised self-esteem and dignity. Unevenness was acceptable but not the grotesque and blatant exploitation that they said characterised British capitalism, equality was to be a concept consistent both with individual difference and economic growth – ideas resonant of modern Labour thinking. Social policy within this ethical socialism would be used to diminish artificially created differences (Tawney, 1952).

WAR-TIME WELFARE

It is, of course, also right to view the collective experience of the Second World War as a seed bed for the post-war welfare state. The nationalisation of hospital services and the development of an education policy that would make secondary education a right for all children played their part in creating a political climate in which post-war welfare measures would flourish. Several factors came together to create the climate of collective suffering; personal income was taxed at a high level, wage rates overtook inflation and unemployment was virtually abolished as both men and women joined either the armed forces or the home front services working in munitions or the Land Army (Jones, 1991; Addison, 1992). The social and economic planning of the war years led to a real and apparent redistribution of resources and may then be viewed as a 'dry-run' or prototype of post-war welfare state planning (Titmuss, 1950).

Thus it might be claimed that these factors, together with the shared danger of war time, created a greater sense of social solidarity in British society than had hitherto been the case. Conscripts from different walks of life and social classes were thrown together and formed close bonds of comradeship. Dockers and doctors shared the security of air-raid shelters in the major cities, and rural, often middle-class, families provided homes for evacuees, which for one commentator was the nearest British society came to socialism (Foot, 1983).

By 1945 and the landslide general election, the hostility of the labour movement to state social welfare appears to have evaporated. The experience of crushing poverty and privation in the depressions of the 1920s and 1930s left many with the feeling that something had to be done and that the state may, after all, be the obvious solution. The experience of the war years, of collective deprivation and a collective, state, response, reinforced that feeling. The calls by Keynes and Beveridge for a twin pillar approach of full employment and a welfare state looked increasingly attractive and the Labour Party became identified with the crucial social issues of the day. All of these factors then, we might say, set the seal on the post-war orthodoxy of social reform and welfare statism.

WELFARE CONSENSUS?

One important outcome of the collectivism of the war years was the creation of what was to become to be described as the 'post-war consensus' on welfare and the welfare state. Much of the post-war period is said to have been characterised by broad agreement in political debate about the role of the state in civil society. There was, it seemed, a continuity between the domestic politics of the Labour and Conservative Parties and a substantial degree of agreement, in principle, about the need for government intervention to ensure economic growth, full employment and the provision of more or less comprehensive welfare services (Middlemass, 1979, 1986; Greenleaf, 1983).

The assumed nature of the welfare state was summed up in the oft-quoted phrase 'from cradle to grave', or 'womb to grave', in which 'life ... is monitored by, or is dependent upon, a vast network of state social legislation and provision' (Jones and Novak, 1980). The welfare state itself became regarded as a creature of consensus politics which, irrespective of their objective success or failure in meeting social need, was to be fostered, defended and extended as the mark of a civilised society. We shall, in the rest of this chapter, aim to untangle the conflicting arguments about the existence, nature and scope of the post-war British consensus.

The consensus, so it was said, evolved from the aping, by the Conservative Chancellor of the Exchequer, Butler, of the economic policies of his Labour predecessor, Hugh Gaitskell. So clear was the belief in the consensus that it acquired its own identity in the phrase 'Butskellism'. That the consensus existed appears to be in little doubt, since we are told that from the early 1970s, it came under increasing strain in the austere economic climate of the day. Indeed we are further told that the consensus was responsible for many of the social problems visible in Britain in the 1970s and early 1980s.

But the roots of this apparent consensus can be traced back to the inter-war years. The privations, at least for working people, of the 1920s and 1930s and the clearly polarised, along class lines, response of the government to that period of economic crisis, which sought to protect the owners of finance capital, were still clear in the post-war memory. In addition, the minority Labour governments of 1923 and 1929 appeared powerless to break free from the drive for profit of British capitalism. It was in this environment that the idea of a negotiated settlement between labour and capital, which would ensure steady economic growth but also alleviate the suffering of many, gained currency (Addison, 1975; Sked and Cook, 1979; Briggs, 1983).

The range of policies which made up the post-war consensus are those stemming from the economic philosophy of John Maynard Keynes and the social philosophy of Sir William Beveridge in what has come to be called the Keynesian Welfare State (KWS) (Burrows and Loader, 1994). Keynesian policies were ones which assumed, or were consistent with, the intervention of government through fiscal and monetary techniques to regulate demand and encourage full employment. Beveridgian social policies were intended to contribute to the development of comprehensive welfare services, access to which would confer a sort of social citizenship. Accordingly, Keynes plus Beveridge were seen to equal Keynesian social democracy, or welfare capitalism or consensus.

The elements of that consensus can be conceptualised in the following way. In the first place the settlement represented a political turnabout. The inter-war years had been dominated by one political party at the helm of government. Although Labour formed two short-lived administrations, the Conservative Party, on its own or in coalition with the rump of the other parties, monopolised the politics of policy making in government. The formation of a genuine coalition government, a political expedient for Churchill as wartime Prime Minister, was the first step in this turnaround. The landslide of the 1945 general election completed the transformation. A new two-party system emerged in which both parties, now Conservative and Labour rather than Liberal, enjoyed relatively stable and relatively equal support (see Butler and Stokes, 1974, for an analysis of post-war 'consensus' voting patterns).

The second element of the new political consensus was that the policies said to characterise the years of consensus could be clearly distinguished from those of the inter-war years. The post-war settlement which included the social security plans of the Beveridge Report, the establishment of the National Health Service, the introduction of compulsory free secondary education and the pursuit of full employment as a policy goal, represented to many the creation of new 'rights' of citizenship (Parker, 1972; Gamble, 1987; Sullivan, 1989). Indeed, as a 'sustained attempt to reduce inequality through public action' (Gamble, 1987).

The third element of the post-war settlement is often seen as foreshadowing what was to happen in later years in both the politics of industrial relations and the politics of social policy making. That is, in accepting the trades unions, who had fought through the inter-war years for their right to be consulted and even incorporated into the decision-making processes of government, powerful state and private interests were embarking on a momentous change in direction from inter-war practices and principles. Of special significance is the legitimation of a tripartite structure of decision making in industry (and wider economic planning), in the form of the National Economic Development Council, and in social policy making. The introduction of this 'corporatist' format of decision making reached its zenith with the negotiation of the Social Contract between the Labour administration and trades unions in the mid-1970s. It is this policy-making change which is said to most epitomise the years of consensus in which successive Labour and Conservative administrations showed themselves willing to continue the policies of their predecessors. One of the clearest examples of policy consensus may be said to be the advent of comprehensive education in the 1960s, continued and consolidated under Margaret Thatcher's tenure as Education Secretary (Weeks, 1986; Reynolds and Sullivan, 1987; Sullivan, 1992).

Some commentaries point to the issue of nationalisation, and the apparent disagreement over the state's role in the direct management of industry, to suggest a lack of consensus. The post-war Labour government had established a mixed economy in which public and private corporations would coexist. In pursuit of this strategy the Attlee government had nationalised a number of major industries including coal and steel. The following Conservative administration, from 1951, returned steel to private control but retained most of the others under state control, though arguably remained lukewarm towards them. Those industries that remained in public control were encouraged to operate as though they were private enterprises and brought in private sector businessmen to senior positions (Greenleaf, 1983; Blake, 1985). The Conservatives then appeared to accept major elements of Labour's post-war settlement, such as full employment and the welfare state, as both evolutionary and desirable.

There are of course, as we indicate above, differences in emphasis between the parties but much of the evidence seems to attest to the existence, over almost 30 post-war years, of a *de facto* political consensus on a mixed economy, full employment and a welfare state. The notion of consensus appears stronger when contrasted to the politics of conflict which characterised the inter-war years, rather than agreement at the level of individual policy in the post-war years. Whether or not we accept the existence of a consensus in British post-war politics, what does seem clear is that the ideas embodied in Keynesianism about economic management and in Beveridge's social philosophy acted as midwives to a relatively durable form of welfare capitalism.

The nature of that welfare capitalism is perhaps nowhere better analysed than in Marshall's seminal essay *Citizenship and Social Class* (1963), which identifies the foundations of consensus not so much in the pursuit of particular policies or the formation of particular political structures, but in the establishment of wider and deeper social rights for citizens. These rights, including access to welfare, in the famous phrase 'free at the point of delivery', and full employment are important elements of the post-war consensus. They were viewed as the culmination of a process which delivered a wider package of social rights, which included the civil and legal rights already won. According to Marshall, these rights were important to the development of capitalism, since although they promised greater access to material wealth they also attempted to incorporate potentially disruptive individuals or groups into the value structure of capitalism (Marshall, 1963). The significance of the consensus, that Marshall believes to have been created by the addition of social rights, was that it altered the emphasis of twentieth-century British capitalism without altering its organisation and power.

Other commentators, whose views were held to be peripheral and minority views, took a rather different approach. This group, latterly referred to as neo-liberals or the radical right, acknowledged the creation and operation of a post-war political consensus, yet perceived it not as a boon but a back door tyranny. Their views, which over the past 20 years gained the status of political orthodoxy, suggested that:

(i) the development of state intervention in the advanced nations of the twentieth century represented an embryonic state socialism and is one step on the 'road to serfdom' (Hayek, 1944) and the loss of individual freedom;

(ii) the development of welfare states and protective legislation removed the responsibility for behaviour from individuals. Welfare states, as a consequence, have created irresponsible societies (Boyson, 1971) in which individuals and families and communities look to the state for the provision of resources, cash and services which they ought to provide for themselves.

The welfare consensus, or so it is believed, was the creation of misguided, though possibly genuine, political reformers. They legitimated wide-ranging interventionist activities for the state in areas of the economy, in industry and in issues of personal welfare. As a result they distorted the true and historic independent status of the individual and the role of the 'natural' operation of the market in the allocation of resources. Instead of engaging in unregulated exchange relationships with employers, sellers of goods and other individuals, citizens were made the servants of the state. Instead of promoting social rights, consensus politics conferred the status of serfdom on citizens whose actions were circumscribed by the all-pervasive regulatory actions of the state. One of the consequences was to place the state in the role of family head or *pater familias*. (The New Right's views on the consensus and the need for its destruction are explored in greater depth in chapter 7 of this volume.)

What neo-liberalism is in no doubt about is that the development of the post-war consensus led to a transformation in the nature of and relations between the state and the market. The state changed from its minimal predecessor, with residual economic and social functions, to a collectivist state exhibiting extensive central planning functions in the economy and in welfare (Hayek, 1960).

The orthodox understanding of post-war British politics is one that seldom doubts the reality of consensus as a guiding political principle and practice in which the bipartisan administration of a shared set of policy frameworks was a political reality. However, one dissenting voice is apparent in the works of historian Ben Pimlott who seeks to dissect what he regards as the 'myth of consensus'. His scepticism is founded in the overtly conflictual politics of the Thatcher era against which earlier politics indeed appear consensual in nature. He further argues that if consensus existed it remained a well-kept secret from the political actors of the day.

Indeed he regards the Beveridge Report, which provided the rationale for the welfare settlement, as less than unanimously accepted. The Conservative wartime leadership felt the proposals to be expensive and potentially divisive. He also cites a widespread lack of enthusiasm from amongst Labour Ministers, especially Ernest Bevin, who felt that Beveridge's proposals would not allow a future Labour government sufficient flexibility in the introduction of social welfare and social security policy. Bevin also clearly believed that the proposals would weaken the ability of trades unions to secure adequate wage settlements because of the implicit adoption of a 'social wage' (see also Bullock, 1967; Harris, 1981; Morgan, 1990).

Pimlott also cites the clear hostility of the medical profession to the introduction of a National Health Service (NHS) which implied limitations to the professional power of doctors. The Conservatives also opposed the introduction of the NHS, and Bevan's concessions to the doctors might be seen as further evidence of conflict – 'I choked the doctors' throats with gold' – rather than as a manifestation of political consensus. Similarly there was continued hostility towards comprehensive schooling, before and after its introduction, until a Labour government forced the issue with the passage of the 1976 Education Act (repealed by the Conservatives within five years).

Whether or not we accept the advent of consensus between the governments of post-war Britain as a broad agreement over elements of policy, or a broad agreement within which there was room for diverse political opinion (Kavanagh, 1987), or indeed we reject the notion of consensus as a more hopeful than realistic analysis, one thing we can be sure of is the upheavals in British politics and policy which came to be known as the end of consensus. It is to this that we shall turn in our next chapter.

REFERENCES

Addison, P. (1975) *The Road to 1945*, London: Quartet.

Addison, P. (1992) *Churchill on the Home Front*, London: Cape.

Blake, A. (1985) *The Conservative Party from Peel to Thatcher*, London: Fontana.

Boyson, R. (1971) *Down With the Poor*, London: Churchill Press.

Briggs, A. (1983) *A Social History of England*, London: Weidenfeld & Nicolson.

Bullock, A. (1967) *The Life and Times of Ernest Bevin*, London: Heinemann.

Burrows, R. and Loader, B. (1994) *Towards a Post-Fordist Welfare State?*, London: Routledge.

Butler, D. and Stokes, D. (1974) *Political Change in Britain*, London: Macmillan.

Finlayson, G. (1994) *Citizen, State and Social Welfare in Britain 1830–1990*, Oxford: Clarendon Press.

Foot, M. (1983) *Loyalists and Loners*, London: Collins.

Gamble, A. (1987) *The Free Economy and the Strong State: The politics of Thatcherism*, London: Macmillan.

Greenleaf, W. H. (1983) *The British Political Tradition, Vol. 3: A much governed nation*, London: Methuen.

Harris, J. (1981) 'Social Policy Making in Britain during the Second World War', in Mommsen, W. (ed.), *The Emergence of the Welfare State in Britain and Germany*, London: Croom Helm.

Hayek, F. (1944) *The Road to Serfdom,* London: Routledge (reprinted 1993).

Hayek, F. (1960) *The Constitution of Liberty,* London: Routledge & Kegan Paul.

Johnson, P. (1983) *Saving and Spending: The working class economy in Britain 1870–1939,* Oxford: Oxford University Press.

Jones, C. and Novak, T. (1980) 'The Welfare State', in Corrigan, Philip (ed.), *Capitalism, State Formation and Marxist Theory,* London: Quartet.

Jones, K. (1991) *The Making of Social Policy in Britain, 1830–1990,* London: Athlone Press.

Kavanagh, D. (1987) *Thatcherism and British Politics,* Oxford: Clarendon Press.

Marshall, T. H. (1963) 'Citizenship and Social Class', in *Sociology at the Crossroads,* London: Heinemann.

Middlemass, K. (1979) *Politics in Industrial Society,* London: Andre Deutsch.

Middlemass, K. (1986) *Power, Competition and the State, Vol. 1: Britain in search of balance,* London: Macmillan.

Morgan, K. O. (1990) *The People's Peace,* London: Oxford University Press.

Parker, J. (1972) *Social Policy and Citizenship,* Oxford: Martin Robertson.

Pelling, H. (1968) *Popular Politics and Society in Late Victorian Britain,* London: Macmillan.

Pelling, H. (1984) *The Labour Governments 1945–51,* London: Macmillan.

Pimlott, B. (1988) 'The myth of consensus', in Smith, L. (ed.), *The Making of Britain: Echoes of greatness,* London: Macmillan and London Weekend Television.

Reynolds, D. and Sullivan, M. (1987) *The Comprehensive Experiment,* Brighton: Falmer Press.

Sked, A. and Cook, C. (1979) *Post War Britain: A political history,* Harmondsworth: Penguin Books.

Sullivan, M. (1989) *The Social Politics of Thatcherism: New conservatism and the welfare state,* Swansea: University of Wales.

Sullivan, M. (1992) *The Politics of Social Policy,* London: Harvester Wheatsheaf.

Sullivan, M. (1996) *The Development of the British Welfare State,* London: Prentice Hall/Harvester Wheatsheaf.

Tawney, R. H. (1952) *Equality,* London: Allen & Unwin.

Thane, P. (1996) *Foundations of the Welfare State,* London: Longman.

Titmuss, R. (1950) *Problems of Social Policy,* London: HMSO and Longman Green & Co.

Weeks, A. (1986) *Comprehensive Schools: Past, present and future,* London: Methuen.

ANNOTATED READINGS

There are a number of useful historical descriptions and analyses of the development of the post-war welfare state in Britain. Readers may find those by Lowe (1993) *The Welfare State since 1945,* Hill (1993) *The Welfare State in Britain: A political history since 1945* and Glennester (1995) *British Social Policy since 1945* particularly informative.

For discussions of the changing political economy, the welfare consensus and its demise, Sullivan's (1992) *The Politics of Social Policy* and Deakin's (1994) *The Politics of Welfare: Continuities and Change,* are both thorough and insightful, while the rise of Thatcherism may be explored in Gamble's (1987) *Free Economy and the Strong State* and Kavanagh's (1987) *Thatcherism and British Politics.*

Concluding comment to Part I

In this part we have introduced and explored some of the background to and historical development of social policy in Britain over the nineteenth and twentieth centuries. From within such an historical overview we can point to a number of features that remain important to the development of modern social policy.

The deserving and the undeserving, the distinction first drawn in Elizabethan legislation, between those who suffer poverty as a result of external factors perhaps beyond the control of an individual and the lazy or indolent poor who would rather beg than work, is one we still make today. The 1990s debate over the existence, or persistence, of an underclass, trapped in poverty and following different, and therefore anti-social, codes of conduct is clearly resonant of an earlier age. Similarly the revulsion and panic induced by the pitching of travellers' caravans on vacant land across the nation reminds us of the fortress mentality adopted by many parishes under the old Poor Law system.

The New Poor Law, as we have seen, brought to us a new vocabulary and new ideas, again which inform the course of policy today. The deterrent effect introduced by the doctrine of less eligibility and the workhouse system of duty to those who provided for one's welfare have survived through successive generations of welfare policy. The twin notions of duty and responsibility mirroring the language of rights, that has grown up in social policy, have been revived for the 1990s in the New Deal which stresses that claimants must be prepared to undertake training or community-based work within the environment task force if they are to go on receiving benefits.

Developments begun in the nineteenth century in the creation of environmental, as opposed to medically based health services, and of non-denominational state-funded education again remain with us today, essentially unchanged. Both services when created were rooted in a tradition of local government which itself dates back to the Elizabethan Poor Law and is jealously guarded and frequently the source of conflict.

The later years of our historical overview witnessed the development of a welfare state built upon principles of insurance, introduced by the Liberal legislation of the first decade of the twentieth century, and later upon the twin pillars of steady economic growth and full employment. The building blocks of the welfare state added in the Beveridge era, that government and the welfare state were vital to successful economic management, themselves created the foundations of a welfare and economic crisis that were to be part of British political culture until the dark days of economic recession in the 1970s and 1980s. These years of development also built into the welfare state an institutionalised gender and ethnic imbalance that we are only in the later twentieth century attempting to effectively deal with.

Part II

THE CONTEMPORARY CONTEXT

Introduction to Part II

In this part we turn to the contemporary social policy environment and to three aspects in particular. The climate for much government activity, and more especially social policy, has since the middle of the 1970s been one of great turmoil. The welfare state in Britain has undergone a crisis of confidence, brought about largely by external factors. This has led to a reassessment of its own position within the British polity, including revision of the role of government itself and a reevaluation of how governments finance and deliver public services.

The first chapter in this part explores the idea of the crisis of the welfare state and the end of the golden years of welfare consensus that were thought to have developed in the decades following the Second World War. The notion of crisis is explored from four different perspectives: economic, political, social and from that of internal contradictions within the welfare state itself. The upshot of this crisis has been a rethinking of the proper role of the state in providing welfare and in particular of its role in financing welfare.

These two themes are taken up in the following two chapters which go on to examine, first, the policy process. That is how policy is made, who is responsible for the initiation, implementation and evaluation of policy, generally, and of welfare policy more particularly. Chapter 5 also explores various attempts to modernise the state and to bring the process of policy making out of the nineteenth century, concluding with a brief examination of the proposals of the present Labour government to shake up the British constitution for the next millennium.

The final chapter of this part examines two inter-related questions: how are we to pay for our welfare services, and have they become an expensive luxury in an era where individuals are more able to take greater responsibility for their own welfare? Secondly this chapter looks at spending on welfare services and the pattern of spending devoted to social policy as opposed to that of general public spending.

4 The welfare state in crisis

OBJECTIVES

- To introduce and examine the concept of a crisis of the welfare state and the 'end of consensus' debate.
- To explore the crisis of welfare from the perspectives of economic crisis, political crisis, social crisis and the crisis of internal contradiction.
- To describe and assess the changing political environment of welfare through the 1980s and 1990s.

INTRODUCTION

This chapter seeks to examine the idea that, developing out of the economic recessions of the 1970s and 1980s, the welfare state found itself in crisis, which was to herald the end of the post-war consensus and may have marked the beginning of the end for the welfare state.

We suggest, however, that the crisis faced by the welfare state was not simply a product of economic recession, although many of the questions asked of state welfare centred themselves around the notion that the welfare state was no longer affordable. Instead we argue that the welfare state crisis was made up of four inter-related themes: a crisis of economics and affordability, a political or ideological crisis, a social crisis and a crisis prompted by apparent internal contradictions within the welfare state itself.

The idea of an economic crisis is based upon evidence that suggested two things. First, that within any advanced western society the demand for services, and increased and better service provision, will always outstrip available resources, particularly financial. Secondly, the shifting demographic patterns of western nations, the increasing numbers of the dependent elderly alongside dwindling numbers of people of working age, reduce the tax base out of which any welfare state can be financed.

A political crisis is argued to have emerged out of a number of factors. Ideologically, increasing numbers of commentators questioned whether a welfare state was any longer desirable since it appeared unable to provide what it promised and instead appeared to cause positive harm, particularly to notions of individual responsibility. The political crisis also suggested that the political institutions were in a process of decline which questioned their legitimacy in ruling over society and that such a crisis manifested itself in declining electoral support for the main political parties. The political crisis was also said to be reflected in the bureaucratic control over the welfare state, by which welfare bureaucracies would expand without regard to the efficient provision of services.

The idea of a social crisis finds its validity in the apparent consequences of welfare policy, many of which are unintended. Here it is suggested that social policies have failed to address the very social problems that they were established to deal with. Instead, state social policy has created new social problems or made worse those already in existence. The apparent development of an underclass and a culture of dependency that has developed within the language of welfare rights, together with the decline of the traditional family, the increase in divorce, illegitimacy and lone-parenthood are all cited as clear evidence of such a social crisis of welfare.

Finally the chapter explores what may be the most damaging of the aspects of welfare crisis, that of internal contradiction. Internal contradiction may be said to be the most damaging because the welfare state has been unable to address the very issues outlined at its inception. The 'Big Five' pinpointed by the Beveridge Report (Beveridge, 1942) – disease, ignorance, idleness, squalor and want – can be said to be still with us only in new forms of social exclusion, persistent poverty, illiteracy and innumeracy and urban decay. Such issues are set against ever-increasing resources dedicated to the solution of society's problems.

THE NATURE OF THE CRISIS

a point in the development of a system where incremental evolution is no longer possible and where fundamental changes are required to ensure survival and prevent collapse and disintegration. (Baldock, 1989)

During the latter part of the 1970s and the following decade much literature emerged in which it was suggested that the welfare state, as conceived in the post-war economic and social settlement of Keynes and Beveridge (the Keynesian Welfare State or KWS), was in crisis. Whether the nature of this crisis implied that the welfare state was terminally ill or whether it implied that radical and fundamental changes in the structures and principles underlying the welfare state were needed was not entirely clear in this literature, but often the former scenario was preferred. Particularly important at this time were a number of reports (OECD, 1980, 1985, 1988) which were extremely influential in setting the parameters of the debate on the 'welfare state', which it was suggested required root and branch reforms if it was to survive, in any recognisable form, the economic, social and demographic pressures being visited upon it.

The picture painted of the apparently fatalistic scenario was: social expenditures had experienced a period of rapid growth in the years following the end

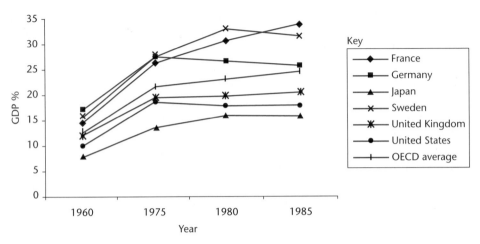

Fig. 4.1 The rise in social spending (selected OECD countries)

Source: Adapted from OECD (1988) *The Future of Social Protection.*

of the Second World War, indeed their growth had consistently outstripped the growth in GDP over the same period. But this had been possible because, according to the tenets of economic and social settlement, such growth was accompanied by strong economic growth and high levels of employment. From the mid 1970s, following the economic crisis brought about largely by the oil price rise of 1973, western economies began to experience slowing growth, rising unemployment and declining public revenues, and to experience rising pressures from increased demand on social services (Schmidt, 1983) (see figure 4.1). Therefore the ability of welfare states to continue funding expanding social programmes was increasingly and widely questioned as rates of growth slowed, rapidly in many cases (see figure 4.2).

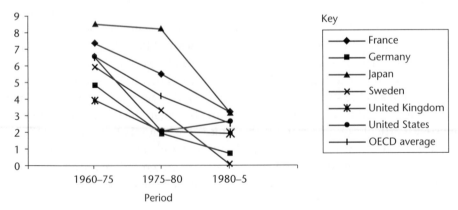

Fig. 4.2 Growth of real social expenditure (selected OECD countries)

Source: Adapted from OECD (1988) *The Future of Social Protection.*

The second part of the picture was to suggest that demographic changes, both current and in the future, would place social expenditures under unsustainable pressure which would eventually cause collapse. In particular the problem was identified as one of the ageing of populations; ever larger numbers of people, living longer and healthier lives, paradoxically because of the success of the welfare state, would retire from employment earlier in their lives and place ever-greater demands on, especially, income support, health and personal social services. This forecast problem would be further compounded by a marked decline in fertility rates, such that, in some advanced economies, falling birth rates would eventually lead to an overall population decline. These two factors taken together, so the theory ran, would increase dependency ratios whereby people of working age, and thus paying tax revenues to governments, became an increasingly smaller proportion of the overall population. The situation facing governments would thus be one of a declining income base to fund social systems placed under increased pressure and demand (OECD, 1988, pp. 7–16).

The notion of a developing crisis within the welfare state, as we have seen, has its origins in the successive economic crises which befell Britain from the early 1970s. In a period of rising unemployment coupled with high rates of inflation, falling levels of production and high levels of government spending (and public borrowing) the British economy entered what came to be regarded as a period of 'stagflation'. As Mishra suggests 'the key postwar supports of Keynesian economics and the Beveridgean welfare state had been seriously weakened'. In particular the economic rationale of the welfare state had all but collapsed and on the social side the gap between 'promise and performance' was too wide to be ignored (Mishra, 1984, pp. 18–21). Disillusionment with the post-war welfare consensus was according to some triggered by the collapse of fixed exchange rates and therefore 'preceded the Arab–Israeli conflict of 1973, it is clear in retrospect that it was fuelled by the economic factors which followed that event' (Gamble, 1994; Gould, 1993, p. 4).

> By the mid-1970s ... post-war prosperity was under threat. The oil crisis, stagnant economic growth, increased labour activism, inflation, capital flight, deindustrialisation, falling productivity and other economic problems were impeding the ability of governments to satisfy rising expectations. (Midgley, 1991, p. 10)

Gradually the consensus norms of economic management and full employment were dropped as the government slowly but surely abandoned any notion of maintaining a budget deficit to ride the worst of the economic storm in favour of strict housekeeping in the form of monetarism.

The crisis of welfare which had developed from the crisis of the economy manifested itself in four distinct but overlapping ways. First, an economic crisis of welfare which suggested that economies undergoing such rapid and seemingly permanent transformations could no longer support high levels of welfare spending. Secondly, there developed a political crisis which suggested that the state itself had become too large and the logic of state bureaucracy was that the state would grow ever larger. That crisis was fought out as the British electorate returned successive governments committed to reducing levels of public spending and to reducing the intrusive nature of government itself (to roll back the state) – the welfare state was perceived, especially by those employed within it, to be under attack. Thirdly, a theory of social crisis of welfare developed which argued that welfare itself undermined 'traditional' social values, in particular in relation to the institution of the family and marriage, and created a 'dependency culture' or 'nanny state'. Finally, and perhaps most seriously, the British welfare state developed a crisis based upon its own apparent internal contradictions; that is the state, with its welfare safety net, had signally failed to achieve its own stated goals, resources were frequently distributed in a way which benefited those in least need so that in the 1960s persistent poverty was 'rediscovered'. This then represented a crisis of cultural and ideological norms upon which the welfare ideas had been founded (Schmidt, 1983).

For much of the 1980s social policy discussion was premised on the basis that the welfare crisis had happened and that the welfare state was about to breathe its last. Lately, however, commentators have come to recognise the persistence of welfare state regimes demonstrated by continuing high levels of government spending on welfare though often within a set of radically altered welfare institutions and radically altered sets of goals and priorities.

The economic crisis of welfare

Under the rules of the post-war consensus 'social policy in Britain has been dominated by the assumption that government must be the chief architect of welfare provision' (Taylor-Gooby, 1991). The apparent logic of this consensus was that the state should be responsible for both income and for expenditure on welfare and should have the final say over the structure and pattern of policy delivery within the welfare state. Within this arrangement the economy and welfare state would enjoy a symbiotic relationship, each unable to survive without the other.

Over the period from the mid 1960s onwards much literature has been devoted to providing an analysis of the causes of Britain's economic problems and Britain's economic decline – the 'British disease'. The need for a solution to Britain's economic crisis gained even more urgency following rapid and successive economic failures which most clearly questioned the post-war consensus. The perception 25 years on is one of overnight oil price rises on the part of OPEC countries as a result of the middle-east conflict, followed swiftly by the miners' strikes of 1972/4 and the 'three-day week', which led to the fall of the Heath government, and culminated in the need for the Labour Chancellor, Denis Healey, to take a loan from the International Monetary Fund, reducing Britain's status to that of 'third world debtor'. It was, then, the coming together of the above events which brought the debate surrounding the crisis of welfare most sharply into focus.

The underlying premise of the economic crisis of welfare was that Britain, and by analogy other advanced western economies, could no longer afford to support a welfare state. The assumption was that the 'deterioration in economic performance and increases in government's share of the economic product ... are causally related' (Cameron, 1985, p. 9). Indeed, the welfare state came to be regarded as a brake on economic growth and capital accumulation, in short the welfare state, as it had developed, was economically harmful (Plant, 1985). The economic dysfunction caused by a government overburdened by welfare spending was an argument which found favour in a number of circles, both political and academic.

On the political right it was both increasingly and convincingly argued that the welfare state had become more 'ambitious, inflated and expensive until it had become a social problem in itself'. Critiques of post-war economic policy argued that the Keynesian notion of demand management could only create inflation within an economy which in turn would damage productivity and growth and create a government deficit. The electoral promises made by politicians, on both sides of the consensus, to both increase service provision and to reduce taxation create an impossible burden on the 'productive' economy. The outcome is one of 'excessive government regulation, high tax burdens and reduced profits which combine to stifle investment growth and wealth creation'. The solution to this economic problem is to roll back the state (Mishra, 1984, pp. 42–5).

The Bacon and Eltis thesis

According to the Bacon and Eltis thesis (Bacon and Eltis, 1976) the root of British economic problems is the pre-eminent position of the welfare state. As that part of the British state has grown so it has denied resources to those 'productive' sectors of the economy. The common currency of the economic argument is that the welfare state, and much public expenditure, is *de facto* unproductive, or in the terms used by Bacon and Eltis, represents non-marketed outputs. The welfare state has, according to this proposition, denied labour resources to those productive sectors of the economy through the rapid growth in the numbers of state employees, or in their words 'the fall in industrial employment in relation to non-industrial employment in what has caused Britain's economic difficulties' (Bacon and Eltis, 1976, p. 20).

Secondly, as welfare spending as a proportion of national wealth has continued to rise, financial resources for investment are denied to the productive sector so denying the possibility of improving economic productivity. Additionally, company profits, which they may use for investment, are diminished by the increasing burden of labour costs brought about by a combination of trades union wage demands and government employment taxes. The response of the KWS is to increase government employment, so as to boost purchasing power in the market place, but for which it needs to further increase the burden of taxation which in turn depresses company productivity and profits. The net effect therefore is that the state sector succeeds in 'crowding out' the private entrepreneur and ensures continued low productivity as the economy enters a spiral of decline, leading to total economic collapse.

The consequence of this process of economic crowding out is that the welfare state provides the seeds of its own destruction. Low and falling productivity coupled with high and increasing levels of unemployment deny tax incomes to the government as fewer workers means a reduction in direct taxation on income. Additionally high levels of government spending, in reducing the productivity of the economy, will reduce the incomes of those in employment and therefore reduce both direct taxation on income and indirect taxation on spending. If government is to maintain the position of its services within the economy it must therefore increase levels of taxation, both direct and indirect, which in turn will further crowd out and reduce economic efficiency. The problem of economic productivity may be further exacerbated by an increasingly aged population and reductions in the common age of retirement from work which will further reduce government incomes whilst placing increasing demands on government expenditures. High levels of state spending and of taxation will therefore, in the end, destroy the welfare state since there will no longer be sufficient resources within the economy to support welfare expenditures. The result will be, as witnessed in Italy in 1994, that government have cut the value of state pensions and other welfare provision, since there will no longer be sufficient numbers of people in employment to finance those dependent upon welfare.

One further aspect of the economic theory of crisis is that in order to maintain a welfare state, government must increase levels of taxation, which in itself will prove a disincentive to work. As tax levels rise so it will become inefficient and economically irrational for individuals, particularly those paying higher levels of marginal taxation, to work at all, so denying further resources to an already over-stretched economy. The solution according to Bacon and Eltis is one which now sounds familiar in British political circles, to cut government spending and particularly spending on the non-market sector of the economy.

Such economic arguments as those outlined above may be more commonly associated with writers of the political right. But a similarly effective argument for the economic dysfunction of the welfare state has been proposed by the left. Evidently dismayed by the rapid expansion of state activity they propose that the state and its welfare derivative are nothing more than a superstructural arm for the control of the means of production. These ideas, most often associated with the writings of Offe, Gough, O'Connor and Ronge, first argue that the creation of consensus was a denial of the right and historical place of the working class. The welfare consensus itself represents compromise between labour and capital and, in a form of institutional arrangement, the corporatist elements of consensus, guarantees the primacy of capital over labour. The political and trades union representatives are then doing little more than collaborating with capital to blunt and thwart the radical demands of the working class. Secondly, they argue that the welfare state is the 'handmaiden of capitalism'. Thus the function of the welfare state is to increase capital accumulation by improving worker productivity and reducing class conflict. The creation of comprehensive services of health, welfare, education and social services is for the explicit purpose of the maintenance of a fit, educated, disciplined and flexible workforce.

Inherent within this institutional arrangement is a contradiction; the welfare state is attempting to support a structure which allows capitalism to better fulfil its own function of accumulation (i.e. profit), but at the same time is forced to concede some of the demands, albeit toned down, of the working class for greater value of benefits and range of services. Its attempt to fulfil such demands reduces some of the surplus value available to capital and so denies the accumulation function and creates an 'accumulation crisis' (O'Connor, 1973). The contradictions posed by the creation of a welfare state, with the explicit purpose of accelerating capital accumulation while at the same time attempting to pacify the demands of labour, will in turn create a legitimation crisis. The factors which make up this legitimation crisis are then: pressure to 'maintain a viable economy and the conditions of capital accumulation at the same time as retaining electoral legitimacy with voters who expect certain levels of social provision which demand relatively high levels of government expenditure' (Bryson, 1992, p. 11). Ultimately the welfare state can only ever reflect those economic contradictions which are an inevitable part of a capitalist economy.

Marxist theorists argued alternatively that the welfare state fulfilled the necessary functions of capitalism. On the one hand, it aided the productive function by providing a healthy, educated workforce and, on the other, it acted as a form of social control which helped to maintain social peace (Mishra, 1984, p. 67). Marxists, like their neo-liberal counterparts, argued that the welfare state in particular, and the capitalist state in general, were approaching a crisis because liberal-capitalist economies which had, at the end of the Second World War, adopted Keynes–Beveridge economic and welfare principles would no longer be able to afford an expansive welfare state at a time of economic retrenchment. In short, the welfare state has a long-term debilitating effect on the capitalist economy (Mishra, 1984, p. 69). However, their arguments are developed from their own particular ideological perspective. That is that welfare and the welfare state occupy a position within the inherent contradictions faced by any capitalist economy and that the welfare state, whilst offering possibilities for the legitimation of the capitalist order, also threatens the production and, most particularly, the accumulation functions of capitalist economies.

The theory of economic crisis facing the welfare state then proposes that the internal contradictions of a large and expansive welfare state, either in terms of crowding out the market and productive sector or in terms of a legitimation crisis, will be the seeds of its own downfall. Government and the economy will no longer be able to support the levels of welfare demanded and the welfare state itself is therefore in danger of collapse and disintegration. For neo-liberals the essence of the problem is one of the crowding-out of the productive sector of the economy, whereas for Marxist writers the welfare state can only succeed in postponing the inevitable crisis and collapse of capitalism as it enters a stage of 'fiscal-crisis'. On the surface, then, the arguments appear to be saying the same thing, that the modern state could no longer afford its over-generous welfare provision in which society demands ever higher levels of welfare spending combined with decreasing levels of taxation.

The political crisis of welfare

Whilst the notion of an economic crisis of welfare is undoubtedly the most important for our discussion of modern social policy and indeed underpins much of the discussion of welfare crisis, it is not the only aspect of importance. The idea of a developing political crisis of welfare focuses largely around the debate about the role of the state and on theories of how the state operates in practice. In particular questions were raised regarding the responsiveness of bureaucratic welfare services to social needs, whether they be defined in relation to consumers, clients or citizens (Weale, 1985). Emphasis here is placed particularly upon the role of the politician and the role of the bureaucrat in the provision of welfare and is central to the debate regarding the right role for the state in a modern democracy. The debate stresses that the state itself is too big and its tendency is one of expansion, which in turn means that the state will always be intrusive and invasive. The solution must be therefore to reduce the role of the state, particularly with respect to its paternalistic welfare roles.

Economic theories of bureaucracy emphasise the importance of the bureaucrat whose indicators of success are provided by reference to the agency or bureau. Such theories in particular note the tendency of bureaucrats and managers to pursue incremental and annual increases to their departmental budget and to extend the powers of their department. This process of 'empire building' within government departments is regarded as a good indicator of performance within the organisation but one which is pursued without reference to the parameters of the policies pursued by that department. Bureaucracies may therefore be regarded as good performers without any improvement in the quality of the services offered. Less damning criticism points to the preference of professionals in welfare services to pursue the interesting, prestigious and fashionable over the mundane, ordinary and unfashionable (Weale, 1985, p. 156). Nevertheless bureaucracy may be said to be following an agenda within which the pursuit of optimum policy outcomes may not obtain.

The idea of bureaucratic empire building is reinforced by the notion of the 'vote motive'. This suggests that politicians, whose prime motivation is to secure office, will engage in a kind of public auction promising the electorate ever-increasing levels of spending and expansion of services, often without regard to the question of raising the extra revenue this entails. Politicians of different hues therefore attempt to outbid one another in the competition for votes, without regard to what has been called the economic consequences of democracy (Brittan, 1977). In this model of the political process rational politicians attempt to maximise their vote and bureaucrats their bureau which together generate excessive expectations among the electorate, who, as we have seen, remain unwilling to shoulder an increasing tax burden.

Once in office politicians, in the knowledge that for the lifetime of their political office they may never be accountable for their spending decisions, attempt to keep those electoral promises and are bound to argue in Cabinet for expansion of their departmental budget. They are supported in this endeavour by civil servants whose aim is also to expand their departmental budget. We might not consider such a situation as problematical were it not for the monopoly or near monopoly position occupied by welfare services which makes for inefficiencies because there is no incentive within such a system for efficiency or effectiveness (Sullivan, 1996, p. 263).

Other writers have identified the growth of a big and cumbersome government as the source of the crisis of politics and political legitimacy. Rose (1980) points to the growth of big government and suggests that its unresponsiveness may lead to problems of ungovernability and political bankruptcy as governments lose popular consent. Political scientists point to the decline of traditional class-based patterns of voting at general elections (class dealignment) and an overall decline in traditional political participation, particularly for the two main parties (partisan dealignment), as factors in the decline of political legitimacy. We may also observe the rise in the fortunes of third parties (traditionally regarded as protest voting) and the rise of so-called 'single-issue' politics, such as the participation of Sir James Goldsmith's Referendum Party in 1997 or issues such as nuclear disarmament and the environment as further factors contributing to a political crisis.

Others point to the increasing complexity of contemporary political life and the increased prospect of policy failure to suggest that government can no longer respond effectively to new or continuing social problems. We need only glance at the proliferation of political memoirs over recent years to conclude that government Ministers, even with their armies of civil servants, have no realistic prospect of managing the highly developed super-departments that have been visible on the political landscape since the 1960s. Indeed it is often suggested that the huge quantity of resources consumed by these departments to administer welfare services, can only damage the quality of service provision (Seldon, 1985). What we may suggest is that state-led endeavours, especially when organised by large bureaucracies who may pursue their own political or administrative agenda and thus be unable or unwilling to respond to new demands, have for some years now had a question mark over the effectiveness of their operation. Not only are the poor not benefiting from welfare policies – they may be positively repressed under a massive welfare bureaucracy.

Social crisis

The concept of a social crisis of welfare is based upon the persistence of social problems and upon the emergence of 'new' social problems the cause of which may be attributable to the welfare state itself. Central to this concept are the notions of the 'nanny state', which attacks individual responsibility, or the emergence of an underclass, which itself develops a set of social norms outside, and therefore in conflict with, those of the rest of society.

The picture painted of modern society is one wherein dependency is endemic and has been encouraged by the permissiveness of the welfare state which has, over the decades, emphasised welfare 'rights' without a corresponding emphasis on the obligations of citizenship. The generosity of the welfare state, and especially that of cash benefits, is said to have damaged the key basis of the capitalist economy, the work ethic. Therefore the poor, acting in an economically rational manner, are given an incentive, in the form of 'outdoor relief', to avoid regular and long-term employment. In turn, this incentive effect may be said to be transmitted across generations of poor families in the creation of what has been termed a 'culture of poverty'. This culture then, most damagingly, begins to undermine the moral fibre of society and in particular the role of the family.

We begin, as writers such as Murray have argued, to see the emergence of an underclass (or residuum) of poor who have rejected the moral and cultural values of their fellow citizens in their acceptance of a counter culture. Evidence for this may be found, not only in levels of benefit dependency, but in other social indicators; thus we see rising numbers of single-parent headed families, rising rates of divorce and family breakdown, rising rates of illegitimate births and rising rates of crime, including benefit fraud. Thus divorce and single parenthood are said to be encouraged by the wealth and generosity of welfare benefits together with the more general availability of contraception and the easing of divorce laws. Crime and benefit fraud have become legitimised and accepted within society at large and more pertinently have become accepted as an alternative way of life in the developing underclass within which (regular) employment is no longer the norm. Illegitimacy and single parenthood is said to compound these social problems as the continued inter-generational lack of a male role model or father figure further legitimates such amoral and asocial behaviours (Murray, 1990). And, although actions to deal with such emergent social problems have been associated with the political right and the policies of the governments of

Margaret Thatcher and John Major in Britain, the centre and social democratic left politically are keen to show themselves to be tough on the causes of social problems.

At perhaps a more philosophical level, the existence of the welfare state system has, it is argued, fundamentally damaged the framework of society in its threat to freedom. The origins of this arm of the crisis of welfare may be located within the writings of Friedrich Hayek (*The Road to Serfdom*), ideas which although formulated at the birth of the welfare state, did not gain political acceptability until the 1970s. Hayek's concern is with the effect that a welfare state has upon individual freedom and which draws parallels with the totalitarian centralist states then developing in the east of Europe and already witnessed in the fascism of Italy and Nazism of Germany. The essence of the problem for the welfare system is that the Keynes–Beveridge notion of a managed economy in which the welfare system is in productive harmony with the economic system is a centrally controlled and planned economy. Whilst the methods employed may not be the same, at least on the surface, as those of totalitarian regimes, they both employ a false notion of freedom, one which denies liberty and which relies upon coercion to achieve its goals (Hayek, 1993).

In such a centralised and planned system the role of the individual is severely undermined by the state to the point that individuals come to rely wholly on the state. The ideology of welfarism employed by the KWS, which seeks to pursue noble ideals such as freedom from want and of equality, says Hayek, is misguided and the true notion of freedom is 'lack of coercion'. As such, when individuals and families find themselves facing economic or social hardships they will, almost as a habit, turn to the state and demand its help and support without attempting to deal with those hardships. In short, people will become dependent upon welfare and this dependency is, of itself, harmful to the notion of individualism upon which society is truly founded.

Over generations, the negative effects of welfare develop into a culture of dependency within which individuals are unable to help themselves. In Charles Murray's analysis this culture leads to the creation of an underclass characterised by long-term unemployment and poverty, a culture of (unmarried) lone parenthood and of crime. The phenomenon is particularly observable in ghettoised inner-city areas which in the United States is most often populated by minority ethnic communities but in Britain may be observed in decaying and often isolated (geographically and socially) council housing estates. The activities of the welfare state, therefore, have, in this analysis, created a new class of undeserving, indigenous poor who lack the incentive for self-improvement.

The pervasiveness of the welfare state, and especially the notions of comprehensive and universal services, further undermines the individual by destroying the charitable ethics of the better off elements within society. The social duty of the nineteenth century to care for those less well off than ourselves, and characterised by charitable giving, has been destroyed by high levels of individual taxation. Taxation both reduces the amount of available cash that individuals are able to donate to charity and the very concept of taxation makes charitable giving redundant. The government itself becomes the agency providing for those in need thus making charities and donations to charity unnecessary. Therefore, in both the coercive imposition of taxation to finance welfare and in the paternal delivery of welfare through state bureaucracies, the welfare state can be shown to be essentially harmful and maleficent.

INTERNAL CONTRADICTIONS OF THE WELFARE STATE

The final element of the crisis of welfare is the notion that the welfare state faces fundamental and internal contradictions which undermine its own claim to legitimacy. In the British example this is reflected in the failure of the welfare state to successfully tackle the 'Big Five' identified in the Beveridge Report and which it set out to eliminate. This provided some of the parameters within which the post-war welfare state was to operate, but also in the form of an ideological crisis which questioned the ideals of collectivism upon which the welfare state was based.

The strongest strand of this argument is that developed by those writers proposing a 'rediscovery of poverty' from the 1960s onwards. Beveridge's promise to eliminate want by the dual provision of an insurance-based benefits system supported by the safety net provided by national assistance was, suddenly it seems, discovered to have failed. The welfare state had done little, if indeed anything, to redistribute income and wealth from rich to poor and more seriously the welfare state seemed to benefit those people least in need. Middle-class families were more able to exploit the myriad of welfare state systems that had grown up, and much of the workforce of the agencies of welfare was itself middle class.

As Johnson summarises, in 1962 Titmuss showed that the operation of the welfare state had achieved little by way of income redistribution from rich to poor. Indeed rather than redistribute from rich to poor (vertical redistribution) the welfare state tended to redistribute within classes and particularly from those in to those without employment (horizontal redistribution). Furthermore, in 1965 Abel-Smith and Townsend rediscovered poverty among the affluence of a modern and prosperous welfare economy. These studies were compounded by claims from groups such as Shelter and the Child Poverty Action Group which pointed to policy failures and by official publications such as the Plowden and Newsom reports which showed little progress in educational equality and the Black Report which highlighted the persistence of health inequalities (Johnson, 1987). What successive reports and interest groups showed was that across the whole range of life chances – economic, health, education or public housing – the welfare state was having little significant impact.

Furthermore, it was now being successfully shown that the welfare state, as an institution, reflected not the desires of a progressive nation towards greater social equality, but the vested interests and prejudices of that society. The welfare state was a slow and ponderous set of organisations that responded poorly to either criticism or changes in its social and cultural foundations. Feminist writers began to point to the failure of the state to even recognise the existence of women and the persistence of a welfare model based upon full (male) employment which simply reinforced traditional oppressions. So too the welfare state, like much of society, ignored a generation of inward migration and the changes brought about by the creation of a multi-cultural society. Supporters may point to the advent of anti-discriminatory legislation as proof of the welfare state's durability and adaptability (The Equal Pay Act 1970, Sex Discrimination Act 1975 and Race Relations Act 1976), yet 30 years on in some sectors equal pay still appears a chimera whilst in others sexual and racial bullying (most publicly in 1997 in the police and armed forces) continues apparently unchecked. Indeed it was only at the end of the 1980s that equality of treatment for benefit claimants became, on paper, a reality.

Further damning evidence was produced in 1987 (Le Grand, 1987) which reported that 'most public expenditure on the social services ... favours the higher social groups' and that across the range of publicly subsidised services, in health, education and housing, the social services had not achieved equality in any of its interpretations (Le Grand, 1987, pp. 137–78). Thus poor housing, poor health, educational failure and increasing unemployment continued to affect the same social groups that had always suffered, but in ways that were now compounded by the actions of welfare provision. Inner-city 'back to back' slums had been replaced by suburban slum estates, the health and life expectancy of the poorest within society was often no better than the peoples of many so-called 'third world' countries and the educational experiments of the 'loony left' in Britain's town halls and the teaching profession, had by many accounts turned Britain into a backward nation. Indeed a new social phenomenon was stalking the land, one which suffered the combined failures of the collectivist welfare dream, in short the welfare state had created and was maintaining a class of dependent poor, the so-called underclass (see chapter 10 for further discussion). We can therefore see how the four elements of the crisis we have identified are closely related, since it was the apparent internal and unchecked contradictions of a welfare state which promised so much, that laid the foundations of the crisis of legitimacy.

CONCLUSION

The four elements of the crisis discussed above may on their own have represented little threat to welfare, but the convergence and inter-relationship of these four factors from the mid 1970s onwards convinced many of the imminent demise of the welfare state. But despite much political rhetoric, many writers now are beginning to point to the persistence of welfare, wherein the bulk of welfare spending continues to be financed from general taxation albeit within a radically different set of institutional arrangements, that of the 'internal market'. Others, however, insist that the longer-term intentions of the present government remain the disestablishment of the welfare state and that the present arrangements are little more than a 'creeping privatisation'.

REFERENCES

Bacon, R. and Eltis, W. (1976) *Britain's Economic Problem: Too few producers*, Basingstoke, Macmillan.

Baldock, J. (1989) 'United Kingdom: A perpetual case of marginality', in Munday, B. (ed.), *The Crisis in Welfare: An international perspective on social services and social work*, Hemel Hempstead: Harvester Wheatsheaf.

Beveridge, W. (1942) 'Social Insurance and Allied Services', Cmnd 6550, London: HMSO.

Brittan, S. (1977) 'The Economic Consequences of Democracy', *British Journal of Political Science*.

Bryson, L. (1992) *Welfare and the State*, Basingstoke: Macmillan.

Cameron, D. (1985) 'Public Expenditure and Economic Performance in International Perspective', in Klein, R. and O'Higgins, M., *The Future of Welfare*, Oxford: Blackwell.

Gamble, A. (1994) *The Free Economy and the Strong State: The politics of Thatcherism*, second edition, Basingstoke: Macmillan.

Gould, A. (1993) *Capitalist Welfare Systems: A comparison of Japan, Britain and Sweden*, London: Longman.

Hayek, F. A. (1993) *The Road to Serfdom*, London: Routledge.

Johnson, N. (1987) *The Welfare State in Transition: The theory and practice of welfare pluralism*, Hemel Hempstead: Harvester Wheatsheaf.

Le Grand, J. and Winter, D. (1987) *The Middle Classes and the Welfare State*, London: Welfare State Programme, LSE.

Midgley, J. (1991) 'The Radical Right, Politics and Society', in Glennerster, H. and Midgley, J., *The Radical Right and the Welfare State: An international comparison*, Hemel Hempstead: Harvester Wheatsheaf.

Mishra, R. (1984) *The Welfare State in Crisis: Social thought and social change*, Hemel Hempstead: Harvester Wheatsheaf.

Murray, C. (1990) *The Emerging British Underclass*, London: Institute of Economic Affairs.

O'Connor, J. (1973) *The Fiscal Crisis of the State*, New York: St Martins Press.

OECD (1980) *The Welfare State in Crisis*, Paris: OECD.

OECD (1985) *Social Expenditure 1960–1990: Problems of growth and control*, Paris: OECD.

OECD (1988) *The Future of Social Protection*, Paris: OECD.

Plant, R. (1985) 'The Very Idea of a Welfare State', in Bean, P., Ferris, J. and Whynes, J. (eds), *In Defence of Welfare*, London: Tavistock Publications.

Rose, R. (1980) *Challenge to Governance: studies in overload politics*, London: Sage.

Schmidt, M. (1983) 'The Welfare State and the Economy in Periods of Economic Crisis: A comparative study of twenty-three OECD nations', *European Journal of Political Research*, 11: 1–26.

Seldon, A. (1985) 'The Idea of the Welfare State and its Consequences', in Eisenstadt, S. N. and Ahimeir, O. (eds), *The Welfare State and its Aftermath*, Totowa, NJ: Barnes & Noble.

Sullivan, M. (1996) *The Development of the British Welfare State*, Hemel Hempstead: Prentice Hall/Harvester Wheatsheaf.

Taylor-Gooby, P. (1991) *Social Change, Social Welfare and Social Science*, Hemel Hempstead: Harvester Wheatsheaf.

Weale, A. (1985) 'Why are We Waiting?: The problem of unresponsiveness in the public social services', in Klein R. and O'Higgins, M. (eds) *The Future of Welfare*, Oxford: Basil Blackwell.

ANNOTATED READINGS

The notion of welfare state crisis may be explored, as we have seen, from a number of different perspectives. The idea of an economic crisis is explored in Bacon and Eltis's work, *Britain's Economic Problem*, and in the article by Sam Brittan, *The Economic Consequences of Democracy* or from a Marxist perspective in O'Connor's *Fiscal Crisis of the State*. The ideas exploring political crisis may be read in Andrew Gamble's *Free Economy and the Strong State* and in Mishra's *Welfare State in Crisis*. Other volumes worth consulting include Murray's work on the British Underclass together with that by Seldon (*The Idea of a Welfare State*) and Le Grand (*The Middle Classes and the Welfare State*).

5   Making policy

OBJECTIVES

- To outline the political and policy environment within which social policy is developed and implemented.
- To explore the roles of central and local government in the development of social policy.
- To outline the prospects for further change in the social policy making environment.

At its most basic level the policy process has been described as a 'black box' into which are entered 'inputs' and from which emerge 'outcomes'. Thus a typical input would be represented by the policies of an elected government and outcomes would be those policies as received by a population. Diagrammatically this might appear as shown in figure 5.1.

This is the policy process at both its most simple and at its most uninformative. Such a description merely tells us that there are demands made upon governments who respond with policies and tells us nothing of what is going on inside the 'black box'. In such a model the policy process is assumed to be a neutral and impartial arbiter of policies devised by a government, whatever the political shade of the party in power. Such a model therefore tells us little or nothing of the values and ideas which help to shape and form policies and the direction they take once implemented (see Ham and Hill, 1993).

POLICY MAKING AT THE CENTRE

Within the parameters of the British state, the central state may be considered to be crucial since it is within the centrally based 'corridors of power' that many decisions

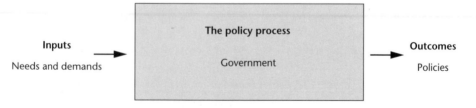

Fig. 5.1 The black box approach to policy making

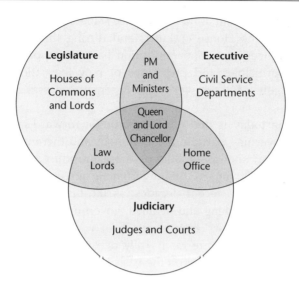

Fig. 5.2 The making of policy

Source: Adapted from B. Jones *et al.* (1994) *Politics UK.*

are made. Constitutionally, Britain operates a tripartite division of powers between the legislature (Parliament), the judiciary (Judges, Courts and Tribunals) and the executive (the Civil Service and the departments wherein they work). This remains something of a constitutional fiction, however, since there is a great deal of interplay between the three arms of the constitution. Crucial to this interplay is the role of the Prime Minister and the Cabinet which has developed over the past two centuries and is today pivotal in the making of policy. The Labour government of Tony Blair signalled the importance of the Cabinet by establishing within it the Social Exclusion Unit and with it the central planks of that government's programme.

This type of representation illustrates the different constitutional functions of the various arms of the separation of powers. Thus the job of the legislature is to debate and consider the introduction of new laws, to consider the effective operation of existing policy and to oversee the efficient running of government departments. Members of Parliament exercise this power through the system of Parliamentary committees (both Standing and Select Committees) where they are able to question Ministers and senior Civil Servants. MPs are also able to inter-rogate Ministers, including the Prime Minister, via the system of MPs questions and a weekly 30 minute Question Time with the Prime Minister. Private indivi-duals may also be summoned to give evidence to Select Committees, notably in recent years at hearings to consider the Mirror Group pensions case and the selling of arms to Iraq and the collapse of the Matrix Churchill company.

New legislation passes through the apparently laborious process of First, Second and Third Readings in the House of Commons interspersed with detailed discussion of a Bill's content at the Committee stage. A Bill will then also receive consideration from the House of Lords and during this whole process MPs and Lords from government and opposition have the opportunity to question and debate the principles and provisions of new legislation and to suggest amendments. Finally a Bill receives Royal Assent and passes into law as an Act of Parliament.

Most legislation today is that which is brought forward as part of the programme of the governing party in the Commons and there is usually little time to debate opposition sponsored Bills or those introduced by individual MPs (Private Members Bills) unless the government agrees to make room within Parliament's schedule. In recent decades, as the business of government has become more time consuming and detailed, governments have resorted more to the introduction of Statutory Instruments (SIs) which amend and change the provisions of legislation but are rarely fully debated on the floor of the House. This technique has been pursued on the basis that it will make Parliament more efficient but has also brought with it charges that governments use SIs to introduce controversial new laws without the opportunity for proper debate and scrutiny.

Because most debate in the House of Commons concerns government business, and this is a tendency that has mushroomed during the twentieth century, increased significance and power has been accorded to government Ministers and most notably to those Ministers occupying seats within the Cabinet, and, of course, most importantly to the Prime Minister. This has led to charges that Britain is becoming a nation of executive government and is therefore losing its democratic legitimacy. Ministers, as MPs, participate in the legislative process outlined above, but occupy a special position as senior, long-serving and experienced members. But Ministers also occupy an executive role as titular head of a government department and are so charged to fight for the interests of their own department within both Cabinet and Parliament. This creates a potential conflict of interest as one agenda for action within the executive comes into conflict with the policy agenda of government.

We turn next to examining where policy is made and describe the structures and functions of central government departments, such as the Department of Health or Department for Education and Employment, or describe the structures of government at a local level, for example regional or local government. Such an approach would provide us with a picture or plan of government and we might be able to discern which individuals, government Ministers, civil servants or local government officials are responsible for making policy at different levels of government. An example, illustrating the structure of the National Health Service following the NHS and Community Care Act is given on p. 61.

Here we face additional questions regarding the policy process. Figure 5.3 only really shows us the structure of a central government department where in fact much of the delivery of health policy is conducted at a local level, whether by

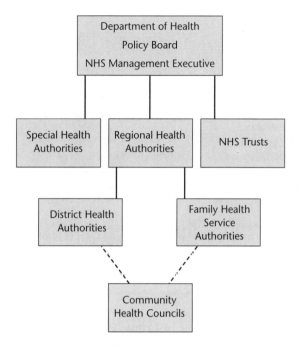

Fig. 5.3 The departmental structure of the health service

Source: C. Ham (1992) *Health Policy in Britain*. Reproduced by permission of Macmillan Press Ltd.

NHS Trusts, GPs, dentists *et al.*, or by other agencies. For example, some health policy remains a function of local government, public or environmental health, or of the privatised utilities in the supply of clean water and treatment or disposal of sewerage and waste. It also remains, as governments have often shown, a relatively easy task to alter and reform the structures and institutional arrangements of government, without, apparently, affecting the policy-making process, at least as perceived by service users who may care little for how policy is made. Such a diagrammatic representation also tells us little of how the non-government sector, the commercial, voluntary and private sectors of welfare, fit into the policy process. We might therefore be led to believe, by such representations, that social policy only involves the activities of government or a particular department of government. Indeed as Tony Butcher clearly illustrates, much of the assumptions behind the establishment of the post-war welfare state evolved from the notion that government should both provide and fund welfare services (Butcher, 1995).

A further, more detailed, examination of the executive role of government might then go on to explore the role of the Prime Minister and the Cabinet, the upper reaches of the civil service and even the role of the monarchy. Any examination of the British constitution in the latter part of the twentieth century must

Exhibit 5.1

The government in Cabinet

Prime Minister	Tony Blair
Home Secretary	Jack Straw
Chancellor of the Exchequer	Gordon Brown
Foreign Secretary	Robin Cook
Secretary of State for Health	Alan Milburn
Secretary of State for Environment	John Prescott
Secretary of State for Education and Employment	David Blunkett
Secretary of State for Defence	Geoffrey Hoon
Secretary of State for Northern Ireland	Peter Mandelson
Secretary of State for Social Security	Alastair Darling
Lord Chancellor	Lord Irvine

The main offices of state. Other members of a government's Cabinet would include Ministers for Transport, Scotland, Wales and Northern Ireland and other junior ministerial positions which may at times be included in the Cabinet or even non-government posts such as the chairperson of a political party.

surely conclude that the joint roles of Prime Minister and her/his Cabinet are pivotal in the creation, passage and implementation of policy. The PM and Cabinet (see exhibit 5.1) represent a central core in the policy process which is supported by an array of Cabinet Committees and a small army of (theoretically) 'neutral' civil servants and politically appointed advisors, the most celebrated of which in recent times has been Mrs Thatcher's economics advisor Sir Alan Walters and her press officer Sir Bernard Ingham. Or more formally we might point to the role of the committee of 'wise persons' appointed to advise the Treasury over the conduct of economic policy. The latter do not represent a formal, constitutional part of the government machine but are nonetheless of vital importance in the creation of policy.

The civil servants of the Cabinet Office and political advisors exist to support the roles performed by Cabinet Ministers. Even a cursory reading of the diaries of any of our recent political luminaries will illustrate the volume of work they faced as individuals whilst in office, a volume of work impossible to maintain without the aid of advisors who work on policy papers, prepare departmental briefings or press releases (see for example the various diaries of Richard Crossman, Barbara Castle, Tony Benn, Margaret Thatcher, Nigel Lawson or Bernard Ingham). Constitutionally, at least, Britain employs a doctrine of ministerial responsibility by which a Minister is held to be responsible for all the actions of their department and its civil servants, and although little can be done to enforce such a doctrine, which we may suggest in any case is outdated and in need of replacement, much of a Minister's time in the House of Commons is spent answering questions about the activities of their department. In practice a Minister will seldom resign over what might be considered the minor misdemeanour of a junior civil servant and recently there is the tendency to devolve departmental functions to agencies whereby some organisation other than a central government department delivers a service but is responsible to its manager rather than a Minister. We might argue that the creation of a benefits agency to deliver income maintenance benefits under the control of a chief officer or senior manager, more along the pattern adopted by a privately constituted company, damages the process of democratic responsibility to the Commons.

The final arm of the tripartite division of state power is collectively referred to as the judiciary and comprises the system of courts and the role of the judges (who also of course play a role in the creation of policy since they sit in the House of Lords as Law Lords) in interpreting policy and arbitrating in disputes over the principles or implementation of an Act of Parliament. So too we can count here the vast array of semi-judicial tribunals, which sit within the executive arm of government, such as Industrial Tribunals or Social Security Appeal Tribunals. Judgments made in Courts, and those of higher-level tribunals, such as the Social Security Commissioners, are said to set legal precedent and to bind lower courts and tribunals. In this sense the judiciary may also be said to make policy and not simply interpret legislation since their decisions may change the way in which policy is delivered by departments and may even operate counter to the intentions of the original legislation.

Since 1973 an additional court has appeared in the hierarchy of the judiciary, the Court of the European Union, which is able to make decisions over the interpretation of Union legislation or the breaching of such legislation by member governments. Such decisions, in their turn, are binding on governments and the legal systems of the European Union. Thus the British government was forced to amend its own legislation following a 1986 European Court decision over the equal treatment of men and women in the claiming of Invalid Care Allowance (ICA).

The very brief sketch presented above gives us only a snapshot of the constitutional arrangements of government at the centre. However, how much does this really tell us about the making of policy in Britain today? For example, following the implementation of the Next Steps Report (Improving Public Management in Government: The next steps) the Department of Social Security has a core staff of a mere 2,000 based in Whitehall (Ling, 1994). The bulk of department staff are now employed by agencies (the Benefits, Contributions and Child Support Agencies are the largest) and not directly by the DSS and these staff are employed in local offices where policy can be said to be 'delivered'. A similar pattern may be discerned in all government departments with the majority of staff employed at a local level whether in District Health Authorities or NHS Trusts in the health service, by local authorities or schools, colleges and universities in the education service. It is for this reason that we now turn to the local dimension of policy making.

POLICY MAKING AT THE PERIPHERY

The most obvious place to begin looking at the local dimension of policy, particularly social policy making, is to examine the role of the local authority. Local authorities are charged with responsibility, although this may be mandatory or discretionary, for implementing a range of centrally determined policies. Specifically they may be responsible for education, personal social services and housing in the field of social policy, and for a range of other services, such as environmental and leisure services, as well as for making contributions in the delivery of local health, police and transport policies. Often, however, local authorities have little or no independent function in determining policy and may be limited to enacting the provisions of an Act of Parliament. Increasingly commonly, local authorities exercise a strategic role in the planning of services for their particular areas, services which are provided by other agencies, such as schools or bus companies, or they may hold a supervisory role in overseeing the working of policy implemented through private or voluntary agencies, such as is developing in the delivery of community care policy.

In organisational terms many local authorities mirror the structures found in Whitehall having specific service departments with an elected councillor playing the role of Minister and serving with other councillors on a Cabinet-like policy committee. Likewise departmental committees, comprising councillors and local government officials, the civil service of local authorities, deliberate new policy measures. However, there exists far greater variation in local policy making; for instance there are different tiers of local authority with different functions, there is far greater variation in the political make-up of local authorities with Liberal Democrats often ruling local council chambers and numbers of 'independent' councillors serving as individuals rather than following a party line. Many councils are recorded as 'hung' with no party having overall control and although these factors may possibly be witnessed in parliament they are far more common at a local level. Yet variation in policy has been far less common across authorities in recent years as central government, which after all controls the purse-strings of local government finance, has sought to exercise its authority and to ensure that nationally standards in the delivery of services are comparable. Thus in education, the pursuit of national standards in literacy and numeracy, and the perceived need for Britain to catch up in the education of its children, has led to the introduction of a national curriculum and nationally established standards to be monitored by attainment tests.

However, local authorities are not the only local arm of the policy structure. As we have already indicated much central government business is conducted not by departments based in Whitehall, but in the local offices of those departments, their agencies or semi-autonomous organisations. We must therefore also consider the roles of the regional and sub-regional arms of government such as District Health

Authorities (DHAs) and the roles of the so-called opted-out sectors, such as NHS Trusts and Grant Maintained Schools, together with the greater degree of autonomy granted to other providers. Thus the devolution of decision-making powers, within nationally set guidelines, can be seen in a range of social policy providers, such as local benefit offices, locally managed schools or the privatisation of public utilities, such as the gas, electricity and water industries. We can also see the creation of other formally independent organisations, which may be funded by government or privately run, such as local development corporations or the incorporation of polytechnics and local colleges of further education, removing them from the control of local authorities.

The 1990s have been defined by the governments of the 1980s and early 1990s as the decade of enabling. No longer will government, at whatever level, be regarded as the funder and provider of services but instead will have a supervisory or strategic role in the delivery of services. The various roles of local authorities have been curtailed in a range of ways with central government more prescriptive than ever before in determining what a local authority may do and how it may raise funding and spend its finances. At the same time government has attempted to widen the policy-making process and undermine what it saw as the creation of Labour controlled fiefdoms, especially in the inner-city authorities. Its most public attempt, and public failure, to control local authorities was the aborted introduction of the community charge or poll tax, but in many other ways local authorities find their hands tied. There has been an attempted privatisation of the policy process in local government by the introduction, and sometimes imposition, of appointees over locally elected councillors. For example we have seen the abolition of Municipal Counties in 1986, with many of their functions taken on by quasi-autonomous boards populated by appointees of the Secretary of State, and a decline in the role of local councillors (and local party appointees) in the running of schools as the government has pressed home the ideal of parent power in the form of parental choice and the election by parents of parent governors. This has gone hand in hand with the devolution of decision-making powers and management away from the local education committee to the head teacher.

The debate about such changes and their contribution to democracy continues to rage as the government argues for an end to political control of many of our social services which they say makes those services nearer and more responsive to service users, and opponents of these changes argue that the proper forum for local democracy is a locally elected authority. But it is clear that such reforms are bringing fundamental change to the formulation and implementation of policy. However, the type of policy-making model set out above describes a set of constitutional arrangements, and, whilst it may tell us the layout of the policy map, it gives us little information about how policy is made or implemented and what influences the creation and success or failure of social policy. We need now to turn to the vexed question of 'who makes policy?'.

Who makes policy?

As we have already indicated, the formal passage of legislation, that is the making of laws and Acts of Parliament, takes place within the confines of the Houses of Commons, the Lords and the system of Select and Parliamentary Committees. We may therefore choose to examine the passage of legislation through the Houses of Parliament and seek to explore the importance of debates or of Second Readings and the Committee Stage for a particular piece of legislation. We would then have built up a reasonably detailed picture of one part of the institutional arrangements for the creation, passage and implementation of new policy. However, we have already indicated that much, possibly as much as 95 per cent, of the business of Parliament is taken up in the debate of government-sponsored legislation and government policy.

We might next turn to the government, as chief initiator of policy, to ask again who makes policy? We have stated above that the Cabinet and Prime Minister occupy a crucial position in the policy machine since they are, technically at least, responsible for the initiation and implementation of policy; thus we could turn to the operation of Cabinet and its committees. But again, as we have already noted, Cabinet Ministers rely heavily upon their civil servants for information and advice, an individual would after all be unable to retain the sum of information relating to all the work of a department. The Cabinet meets once or twice per week for a morning and clearly would be unable, even as a group of 20 senior government members, to consider the breadth and depth of policies within its remit.

The role of civil servants may in turn suggest to us that it is they who, in controlling the flow of information between a Minister and department, are able to set and maybe even to manipulate the policy agenda. They may for instance, if it is not too conspiratorial, present to a Minister a set of 'preferred' policy options and thereby exclude more radical solutions to policy problems, so leading politicians to amend, and perhaps abandon, their ideologically motivated plans. Such a scenario would suggest that the policy process is inherently conservative and restricts itself to slow and incremental change (Ham and Hill, 1993).

But such a description of institutions and the way in which they operate does not seem to be sufficient for our needs. Such a study does not explain to us 'why' a particular piece of legislation is created, 'how' that policy is being implemented or its impact on the well-being of citizens. Thus we might go further than the descriptive study outlined above and seek to examine some of the factors that influenced the creation and formulation of new policy. We could, for instance, look at the role of political parties in promoting policy as part of their electoral manifesto, which when in government they seek to implement. We need to know how, for instance, parties arrive at their manifesto, how proposals are discussed internally, the role of the party conference for example. In turn we can consider the role of the media in examining those policy proposals and the impact of the various pressure groups who pursue their own agenda and add their comments to party political manifestos. We can by this means create, as Mullard (1995) suggests, a policy hierarchy which has at its head an elite represented by Westminster and Whitehall, the so-called corridors of power, followed by the political parties and range of interest and pressure groups whose role is to engage in political debate and dialogue over ideological principles. That debate is said to resolve itself within the electoral process with the victor claiming a mandate from the people for their principles and policies. The next strata in this hierarchy is that of the grassroots (party or pressure group) activist whose perspective and interpretation of policy will often differ from that of their leadership followed by the public/electorate who remain often the least well informed about policy and the policy process.

However, public debate over policy rarely considers the detail of policy and often seems to consist purely of 'the media soundbite'. Additionally, what public debate there may be over policy may often not concern social policy but any of the other areas with which government may be involved and most frequently revolves around questions of the economy which often dominates a domestic political agenda. The end point for such an analysis is to examine the role of the electoral process in the making of policy and the pursuit of power by political parties. Democratic theory would suggest, at its most ideal, that what we have is a system of government by the people for the people, and that our MPs are nothing more than our representatives in Parliament. But clearly MPs have a number of different pressures which affect the way in which they vote: they are representatives of their constituents. They are also representatives of their party, which is enforced with party whips whose job it is to ensure that MPs are present and vote the 'right way'. But MPs are more than just constituency and party representatives; each swears allegiance to the monarch and thus also serves the 'national interest', however that may be defined, and finally an MP always has to consider his or her conscience in voting in the Commons.

What we are suggesting here is that we cannot, with any degree of credibility, identify which actor within the policy system is responsible for making policy. There is, in reality, no hierarchy of decision making by which policy can be made at central government and passed down into implementation by the bureaucracy. Policy is more of a web of different interests, influences and actors all interlinked to one another in such a way that those linkages change over time and with different issues. This might suggest that a pluralist policy structure exists, but we may also be able to identify policy elites which are capable of exerting greater pressure or influence than other groups and occasionally disproportionate pressure or influence. We would therefore agree with Rhodes' suggestion that a model of policy communities provides a useful way of examining policy making in the British context (Rhodes, 1988).

The overriding problem with the institutional method of analysis has been that the process itself has often remained at best hidden and at worst assumed to be obvious. More recent, institutional, change, such as the development of closer links at a European level following the Single European Act (1986) and the Maastricht Treaty (1992) or the shifting pattern of relationships between Ministers and their departments (or agencies of a department), does appear to be changing at a more fundamental level the process of making policy.

The policy process, as we have seen, is more than simply the sum of its parts. There is clearly more to making policy than we can determine by outlining and describing the nuts and bolts of the policy machine. An example might illustrate this point. If asked to talk about motor racing we could draw an accurate picture of a racing car, its engine, aerodynamics or design. But that would not tell us how to drive such a machine or about the psychological thrill we might derive from driving it. Similarly, to describe the policy process in terms of its mechanics is insufficient as it tells us little of how to make policy or why some people are attracted to become policy makers, that is: what makes the machine and its driver tick?

Spicker (1995) argues that social policy making in particular and the wider policy process in general are very much to do with power and the values of those engaged within the policy process (see chapter 7). We could equally suggest that the community or environment within which policy is made is of crucial importance and, in the era of globalisation, those factors external to and beyond the control of our domestic policy environment assume ever greater relevance (see chapter 18).

We have already suggested above that the institutional structures are in a continuous process of flux and change and that the relationship between central policy making and what goes on at the local level, including the delivery of policy informs the way in which policy is made and implemented. Thus we have a number of interesting and useful avenues to explore which might give us greater insight into the making of social policy.

CONSTITUTIONAL REFORM

At the time of writing the policy-making structures of the United Kingdom are about to undergo fundamental and far-reaching change. In 1998 ballots in Wales, Scotland and Northern Ireland have confirmed proposals for constitutional reform. Wales is set to establish a directly elected Welsh Assembly whilst Scotland is to obtain its own Scottish Parliament, with limited tax-raising powers. In Belfast, after the Good Friday Agreement, a new Assembly, again with direct elections, has been established. And, although the social problems of Northern Ireland have their own dimension flavoured by what has been euphemistically termed 'the Troubles', each of these constitutional changes offer the prospect of change to the social policy-making process. Powers currently held and administered through the Northern Ireland, Welsh and Scottish Offices may themselves be devolved to the newly constituted Assemblies. We may therefore witness the development of a distinct Northern Irish, Welsh and Scottish social policy, with less direction from Whitehall than is currently the case.

REFERENCES

Butcher, T. (1995) *Delivering Welfare: The governance of the social services in the 1990s*, Buckingham: Open University Press.

Clarke, J., Cochrane, A. and McLaughlin, E. (1994) *Managing Social Policy*, London: Sage.

Elcock, H. (1994) *Local Government*, London: Routledge.

Ham, C. (1992) *Health Policy in Britain*, London: Macmillan.

Ham, C. and Hill, M. (1993) *The Policy Process in the Modern Capitalist State*, Hemel Hempstead: Harvester Wheatsheaf.

Hill, M. (1993) *The Policy Process: A reader*, Hemel Hempstead: Harvester Wheatsheaf.

James, S. (1997) *British Government: A reader in policy making*, London: Routledge.

Jones, B. *et al.* (1994) *Politics UK*, Hemel Hempstead: Harvester Wheatsheaf.

Levin, P. (1997) *Making Social Policy: The mechanisms of government and politics and how to investigate them*, Buckingham: Open University Press.

Ling, T. (1994) 'The New Managerialism and Social Security', in Clarke, J., Cochrane, A. and McLaughlin, E. (eds), *Managing Social Policy*, London: Sage.

Mullard, M. (ed.) (1995) *Policy-Making in Britain: An introduction*, London: Routledge.

Rhodes, R. A. W. (1988) *Beyond Westminster and Whitehall*, London: Unwin Hyman.

Spicker, P. (1995) *Social Policy: Themes and Approaches*, Hemel Hempstead: Prentice Hall.

ANNOTATED READINGS

For an expanded description and discussion of the institutions and structures of the British policy machinery, readers should consult B. Jones *et al.*, *Politics UK* (Harvester Wheatsheaf). For a wider examination of the policy process within the structural framework, S. James' *British Government: A reader in policy making* illustrates a number of useful points, similarly M. Mullard's *Policy Making in Britain: An introduction* (both published by Routledge) offers some useful case studies of different aspects of the policy process. The most comprehensive thematic approach is provided by Ham and Hills, *Policy Process in the Modern Capitalist State* (Harvester Wheatsheaf). Description and analysis of local policy-making institutions and procedures may be found in H. Elcock's *Local Government* (Routledge) whilst recent developments in social services in particular are examined in T. Butcher, *Delivering Welfare: The governance of the social services in the 1990s* (Open University Press). More specific analysis of policy making for social policy may be found in Peter Levin's *Making Social Policy: The mechanisms of government and politics and how to investigate them* (Open University Press) which gives an interesting case study approach to different social policies pursued during the 1980s and 1990s, whilst a more detailed analysis in the management of social policies and their departments is offered in J. Clark *et al.*, *Managing Social Policy* (Sage).

6 Paying for welfare

OBJECTIVES

- To outline the role of government in funding and providing social services via general taxation.
- To examine the size and scope of the welfare state and spending on welfare services.
- To introduce changes in the patterns of funding and management in the welfare state.

This chapter is concerned with two issues which we can conveniently term the economics of welfare. The first question we consider in this chapter is that of the financing of welfare services and in particular the source of welfare spending, i.e. the range of financial measures employed by the government to raise money for the welfare state. But we have to bear in mind too that much welfare is financed not by governments but by individuals, private and charitable funding, but the focus of this chapter is not to be the wider notion of 'welfare finance' but the more narrowly defined financing of 'social services'. The second question is to consider how, by what mechanisms, the government seeks to prioritise its welfare spending and the allocation of resources. In essence they represent two sides of the same coin in a system in which government both raises and then distributes resources.

An important point to bear in mind regarding the financing of welfare is that, although we will consider government funding and financing of social services, it does not follow that we will consider the government provision of welfare services. Over recent years this distinction has become more clearly made as government has financed devolved and semi-autonomous provision for example in the education and health services. However, whether we consider direct government provision of services or the more indirect financing of private, charitable or semi-autonomous state services, the fact remains that the great bulk of welfare services are financed out of government funds and therefore from general taxation.

Nominally the figurehead of public spending is the Chancellor of the Exchequer who presents annual tax raising and departmental spending proposals in a Budget speech normally in November each year. Tradition had dictated that spending proposals for the forthcoming financial year were presented in an Autumn statement whilst tax raising was left to a Budget speech in March the following year. This process was temporarily ended by a White Paper of 1992 which proposed a unified budget the first of which was delivered on 30 November 1993 (Glennerster, 1997). The task for the Chancellor in delivering the Budget speech and the subsequent Finance Bill is to review the performance of the nation's economy, to announce government plans for spending over the coming years and to indicate how the revenue to enable that spending is to be raised. This was, however, to be short-lived as the incoming Labour Chancellor, Gordon Brown, returned the budgetary process to its dual Autumn and Spring format.

Exhibit 6.1

British Chancellors since 1945	
Chancellor	Government
Hugh Dalton	Labour 1945–51
Sir Stafford Cripps	
Hugh Gaitskell	
R. A. Butler	Conservative 1951–64
Harold Macmillan	
Peter Thorneycroft	
Derick Heathcoat Amory	
Selwyn Lloyd	
Reginald Maudling	
James Callaghan	Labour 1964–70
Roy Jenkins	
Iain Macleod	Conservative 1970–4
Anthony Barber	
Denis Healey	Labour 1974–9
Sir Geoffrey Howe	Conservative 1979–97
Nigel Lawson	
John Major	
Norman Lamont	
Kenneth Clarke'	
Gordon Brown	Labour 1997–

The Chancellor's job, however, is much wider than this simple process suggests; the Chancellor having attained over many decades the overall responsibility for the running of the British economy, its regulation and maintenance. Thus the control of inflation, stimulation of private spending or saving, the often rapid fluctuations in the housing and retail spending sectors, all fall within the purview of the Chancellor, although an important and significant change introduced by the incoming Labour government in 1997 has been to place responsibility for decisions over bank base rates and explicitly the control of inflation in the hands of the Bank of England rather than the Treasury.

At the centre of the public finance and spending institutions sits the Treasury 'that fat old spider lurking with undiminished appetite at the centre of the public policy web'. It is the Treasury which retains control of overall government spending and the raising of finance but which also maintains a day-to-day interest in the spending patterns of individual departments and 'invokes a persistent claim to exercise continual close control over the totality (as well as the detail) of expenditure' (Page and Deakin, 1993, p. 2).

The Treasury's task is to collect revenues which may be in the form of direct taxation such as income tax, which is the most easily recognised, but also other forms of direct taxation such as corporation tax, capital gains or inheritance tax. Direct taxes it may be argued are inequitable since they tax individuals at the same rate, regardless of their income and thus represent a far larger proportion of the income of poorer earners. Yet we may also argue that this is the fairest form of taxation since an equal portion of income is taken from each individual. Rarely, however, do we find a simple basic rate tax system in operation and much more commonly we find some form of 'progressive' system which imposes a higher rate of income tax as an individual's level of income rises.

Alternatively the government may raise taxes indirectly, for example taxes on consumption and spending, such as value added tax (VAT), or duties on goods, such as cigarettes, alcohol or fuel. This form of taxation raises funds directly from those people who consume certain goods, thus the more an individual consumes the more tax they pay. At face value then this form of taxation is fairer since tax is paid on the amount of a good consumed, but equally such taxation may be deemed unfair if it means that those individuals with incomes considered marginal may find that the imposition of such a tax makes those goods unaffordable. Thus VAT on fuel introduced by the last Conservative government was criticised for creating fuel poverty and creating luxury goods out of basic amenities such as electricity and gas. Thus, although we may say that the task of the Treasury is to raise revenue, it is rarely simple and a fine line is often sought between the type and rate of taxation with due consideration given to its effects on the wider economy.

Successive Conservative governments, for example, between 1979 and 1997 regarded National Insurance as a taxation on employment which damaged the prospects for economic recovery and restricted the availability of investment funds; similarly they regarded high rates of income tax as a disincentive to economic prosperity and enterprise. The balance of taxation sought by those governments was therefore altered towards more indirect taxation on consumption, such as VAT, with the top rate of income tax reduced to 40 per cent (from 80 per cent) with similar but smaller rates of reduction at the lower levels of income tax (down from 33 per cent in 1979 to a standard 25 per cent, but 23 per cent for the first £2,000 earned).

The second principal task of the Treasury, though no less simple, is the distribution of funds to the spending departments, direct to service providers (state enterprises such as hospital trusts), direct to households in the form of tax relief or to third parties, such as local government or charitable organisations who themselves provide welfare services. The process by which such reallocation takes place has become known as the Public Expenditure Survey (PES) 'a series of "bilaterals" involving small groups of Treasury officials in continuous dialogue with their opposite numbers in the spending departments, with ad hoc ministerial intervention in the final stages' (Deakin and Parry, 1993, p. 31). This process, which takes place over a 15 month cycle, seeks, first, to analyse the previous spending round from which guidelines are issued; secondly, the spending departments submit their bids for funds for the coming spending round which are then scrutinised by the Treasury who enter bilateral negotiations with each department to determine totals. The final stage of the PES process is one of negotiation, between Ministers responsible for different departments, and is ultimately resolved in Cabinet. The climax is the annual Chancellor's Budget speech. (For a more detailed discussion of the PES system see Glennerster (1992, chapter 4) and Levin (1997, chapter 8) from which the following table is derived.)

Exhibit 6.2

The Annual Public Expenditure Survey to 1996	
January	Three year spending plans published in White Paper.
March	Treasury informs spending departments of its economic 'assumptions' – rate of inflation, economic growth, etc.
April	Spending baselines from previous period agreed between Treasury and departments.
May	Departments submit their spending proposals to Treasury followed by more detailed 'bids' for their programmes.
June, July and September	Bilateral negotiations between departments and Treasury attempt to reach agreement on spending proposals. Cabinet takes outline decision on overall spending via EDX Committee.
October	EDX sets final figures for each department. If agreement is outstanding the 'Star Chamber' is convened to make recommendations to Cabinet.
November	Final Cabinet decision and Budget speech by Chancellor.

In the context of this book, however, we are less concerned with the overall pattern of government income and expenditure and government's role in economic management but with what is regarded more directly as spending on social policies and perhaps more importantly with how our society sets priorities in the way in which we spend government revenues. Despite much rhetoric over the past two decades suggesting that welfare spending has been reduced and that the welfare state has been under attack from government, an examination of public expenditure shows that instead of falling, public spending has remained steady, although its rate of rise has been checked. What governments have done in that time has been to re-prioritise welfare spending, necessarily, in the face of declining economic performance and, as some writers still suggest, no post-war government has seriously contemplated the question of whether we need a welfare state and its attendant expenditures. Those who portray themselves as welfare radicals still regard public expenditure as 'excessive, wasteful and economically damaging' (Marsland, 1996, p. 67), but they appear to have made little headway within the corridors of power. Those who search for a residual state have been disappointed to see government spending remain stubbornly high as a proportion of national wealth at around one quarter of GDP. Yet we will not be surprised to learn that the picture of overall government spending is somewhat more complex.

Over the past 20 years governments have and continue to question the priorities of welfare spending and the propriety of a system in which governments both finance and provide welfare services. We have developed instead a much more mixed economy of welfare in which government continues to play a major role in financing welfare services but those services are provided by a range of different agencies, public, private and personal. So too government has sought to redefine the way in which we as a society think about welfare and to make individual provision, rather than state intervention, the normal form of provision in the first instance. Thus the wider use of the means test rather than universal provision, the targeting of welfare services to those 'most in need' (however that is defined) and tightening of penalties for welfare fraud have attempted to narrow the basis upon which the welfare state is founded. That such a narrowing has not led to a concomitant reduction in the burden of public expenditure may be attributed to a number of factors: for instance, persistently high levels of unemployment, an increasingly aged population or the assumed tendency of bureaucracies to avoid spending reductions and to maintain or increase their budget.

Whatever the reasons behind such a change, the depth of that change is clearly illustrated by the 1997 Budget speech of the Chancellor of the Exchequer, Gordon Brown, in the new Labour administration which had, before its election, promised to stay within public spending targets. Brown's speech stressed financial sustainability in which government would only borrow in order to invest, with current (revenue) spending met directly from taxation; public debt, he said, would be prudent and stable. Government fiscal policy would emphasise the control of inflation and a plan to reduce the overall public deficit was introduced in an attempt to induce a balanced and lasting recovery. The speech was backed by a pre-election promise to maintain the two year public expenditure targets introduced by the previous Conservative administration. It was in many ways a speech reflecting the style of 'household' economic management introduced by

Exhibit 6.3

Public expenditure on welfare			
	1986–7		1997–8
Total public spending		163,400	315,000
Social Security		44,293	95,500
Pensions	18,724		
Invalidity	2,617		
Sickness	123		
Unemployment	1,618		
Supplementary benefit	7,264		
Child benefit	4,573		
Disablement benefits	1,533		
Housing benefit	3,154		
Other	1,468		
NHS		20,017	36,500
Education		17,508	38,200*
Housing		3,904	3,800

Source: Welfare spending (1986 figures adapted from Barr).
*UK figure.

Mrs Thatcher and her Chancellors, Howe and Lawson, rather than that of 'old' Labour Chancellors who, it was said, sought to spend their way out of a crisis.

Labour's first budget for 18 years was, however, much more than the wholesale adoption of the political ethos of the previous government which had the Conservative peer, Lord Archer, declaring that Tony Blair had stolen Mrs Thatcher's handbag. It marks the climax of a process of fundamental reconsideration of the welfare principles society should adopt, without simply reverting to a mythical golden age in which residual welfare and minimal government intervention was of paramount importance. Underlying that Budget we can discern a number of theoretical strands promoting not only welfare 'rights' but also welfare 'obligations'; without readopting the principle of full employment as the first strand of government economic policy, Brown strongly reasserts the work ethic over welfare dependency and promises benefit cuts for those, particularly the young unemployed, who refuse opportunities to undertake work or training. But this principle is not confined to the young but extended to lone parents who are to be encouraged to find work through the greater availability of childcare and after-school clubs together with a greater disregard of childcare costs in benefit calculations. The finance for these proposals, in light of the promise to retain government spending targets in the short-term and the introduction of a deficit reduction programme in the longer term, is to be found in the much vaunted 'windfall tax' on the privatised utilities and the reprioritisation of

National Lottery spending. Whether this can be sustained long term remains to be seen, but it does place the government in the precarious position of waiting to reap the rewards of their welfare-to-work programme.

The wider welfare state has seen the headline injection of funds into the National Health Service (£1.2 billion allocated from reserves to improve patient care, with a further £300 million to address the expected winter crisis in the 1997–8 period) and into education (£1 billion allocated from reserves plus a £1.3 billion capital investment programme). In addition the government hopes the NHS will save substantial administrative costs from the abolition of the internal market mechanism and intends to recoup the costs of treating the victims of road accidents directly from insurance companies, which some may argue amounts to private health insurance.

In higher education the announcement of extra funding has been tempered by the introduction of tuition fees, which many fear will reduce applications to University therefore reducing University funds, but more fundamentally will restrict access to universities to those most able to afford the privilege. Here too, however, the initial cash injections depend on the one off windfall tax and the National Lottery and its long-term success is, at the time of writing, difficult to gauge. Additionally, the Chancellor announced: widening the scope for 'green' taxes and increased spending to improve house insulation; the phased release of local authority capital receipts and the relaxation on local authority borrowing; a further reduction in tax relief on mortgage interest payments and increased penalties for tax avoidance.

It is at this early stage difficult to place the policies of the new administration into a wider political and historical context. We may, on the one hand, suggest that the new government is adopting and continuing the policies of the previous government and that this shows how far reaching and pervasive have been the ideas propagated by the new right, but, on the other, we may argue that new Labour has reassessed its policies and priorities for the 1990s and into the new century.

SPENDING ON WELFARE AND THE WELFARE STATE

We may distinguish three elements when considering paying for welfare and more specifically the welfare state. Glennerster refers to these as taxes, charges and fees and charitable spending, although the actual pattern of spending on services is more complex than this simple categorisation may in fact suggest (Glennerster, 1992; Alcock, 1996). Taxation, as we have already seen, is a compulsory system of fundraising employed by the state in order to fund government policies and falls into two broad categories, direct taxation (income tax or National Insurance Contributions, for example) and indirect taxation, for instance consumption taxes (VAT, for example). As we have already noted, although the overall burden of taxation has changed little, the balance between direct and indirect taxes has shifted markedly and, for much of the past two decades, fiscal policy which has reduced income taxes has favoured the better off.

National insurance, although termed insurance, is in actuality a form of direct taxation. Insurance payments, for instance those expended for retirement pensions or life insurance, may be most commonly regarded as a form of long-term savings scheme in which contributions plus interest earned, are paid back in the form of either a lump sum or as a periodic (weekly or monthly) income. National insurance has, however, since 1957, when its actuarial principle was abandoned, been a fund used to finance current expenditure. In essence, today's NI contributors pay for today's pensioners and are not saving for their own retirement (Lowe, 1993).

However, taxation in all of its forms is rarely sufficient to fund all the programmes that government intends to pursue and the shortfall is made up by borrowing, what is usually referred to as the Public Sector Borrowing Requirement (PSBR). The PSBR fluctuates over time and often rises dramatically particularly in times of crisis, for instance to finance military needs in time of war; but in the past decade government has sought to reduce and even to eliminate public-sector borrowing as a significant element of public financing. In 1996/7 the PSBR was estimated to be £22.7 billion but forecast to fall to £10.9 billion in 1997/8 and to £4 billion for 1998/9 but we should remember that this reduction has been achieved whilst the government has enjoyed 'one-off' sources of funds from privatisation and the windfall tax. One should also remember that the recourse to borrowing to finance government spending imposes costs, so that in 1996/7 debt interest will amount to an estimated £22.5 billion (Cocks and Bentley, 1996). The previous Conservative administration regarded the PSBR as both a drain on public resources which denied those resources to other publicly financed programmes and as an unacceptable burden on the taxpayer, a burden which had largely been created by the profligacy of earlier governments and their policies of welfare state expansion.

The raising of revenue from taxes, direct and indirect, national insurances, council tax and business rates together with other incomes in the form of trade surpluses and the proceeds of privatisation and public borrowing (£22.7 billion) will for 1996/7 create a total government budget of some £307 billion. This represents around two-fifths (41 per cent) of national wealth as GDP is estimated at £752.2 billion whilst for the same year the PSBR represents 4 per cent of GDP but is set to fall, according to the government's published targets, to around one-quarter of GDP.* At the same time government revenue from (direct) taxation

---

* The reader must also note here that the method of calculating government expenditures is set to change following the introduction of new accounting criteria as a result of the operation of the Maastricht Treaty. Should the government of the day opt to join the European Single Currency, accounting practices will be set to change further still.

looks set to fall further as government attempts to continue the process of reducing income tax rates. Clearly, as we have already noted, government will expect its indirect taxation revenue to rise as it continues to target consumption and we may expect that this will meet some of the reductions in direct taxation revenue. But we may also expect that the range of fees and charges for welfare services will increase dramatically as they have in the last decade and a half, and it is to this that we now turn.

We can regard the fees and charges levied for state welfare services (for instance charges for prescriptions, dental or ophthalmic services or charges for residential care for the elderly) as a form of indirect taxation, since they represent a government regulated charge for the consumption of a particular service. To some writers such a move represents a process of terminal decline for the welfare state, since such charges undermine the principles of universality upon which the welfare state is said to be founded. We should note here, too, that the more general introduction of fees for state services may in turn exclude poorer members of society from what we may consider 'basic' welfare provision, such as regular optical and dental examination. Such charges also therefore undermine the notion of equity, that across the population and across the nation there should be some measure of equality of access and quality in welfare services. And, as Alcock notes, though there may be rebates in place to encourage people not to forgo such services, such rebate systems are rarely simple and may exacerbate the problems associated with lack of use of welfare services, such as accentuating the 'poverty trap' or causing a decline in health standards (Alcock, 1996).

Supporters of fees as an effective method of regulating and rationing services stress that people should be encouraged to contribute to their own welfare, on the grounds of individual responsibility. Such responsibility they argue leads people to value the welfare services and is not a simple symbol of neo-liberal thinking of Cabinet Ministers, such as Frank Dobson and Frank Field (respectively Health Secretary and Minister with responsibility for a review of the welfare state) both adopting a 'welfare rights/welfare responsibility' theme in the early months of the new Labour government. Implicit in such thinking is perhaps a more long-term view of the welfare state than we have been used to from our politicians, but a view brought about by a pragmatic response to an impending crisis.

The nature of this crisis has its roots in the long-term demographic changes throughout the world which sees at one end of the age scale people living longer and at the other fertility rates declining. Welfare states are therefore faced with the prospect of an increasingly elderly population, living well beyond retirement age and possibly increasingly frail, often portrayed as an increasing burden on the state. At the same time, falling birth rates present the prospect of a shrinking workforce and therefore shrinking revenue base. We should not be surprised then to see an increasing commitment of public funds to the care and treatment of the frail elderly: in 1996/7 £2.1 billion of the budget for hospitals was spent on geriatric care (10 per cent), £1.5 billion of the community health services budget (almost 30 per cent) and £4.6 billion of the personal social services budget (47 per cent) (Cocks and Bentley, 1996). The extension of fees and charges for welfare services is thus dominated by the prospective crisis in the care of the elderly and is often highly controversial, such as the recuperation of residential fees from the estate of an individual, often after their death or by the sale of their home which is regarded as 'notional capital'. But the attempt to restructure the long-term future financing of welfare is not restricted to the elderly; severe restrictions in the coverage of mortgage housing costs for social security claimants has led to an explosion of private mortgage insurance schemes alongside such schemes for healthcare and eldercare. Critics of such policies point to the reduced coverage they provide and to the restricted access for those on low incomes or in temporary employment when compared to the coverage they formerly received, and it seems that as government moves towards a reduced role in the provision of welfare it unfortunately lags behind in the careful regulation of such alternatives.

In addition most privately provided welfare services (for instance so-called alternative therapies such as aromatherapy or osteopathy) are paid for by direct charges, frequently at the point of consumption. However, some private welfare services are paid for by means of insurances taken out in addition to government levied taxes and insurance contributions, the most common of these is perhaps private health insurance provided by companies such as BUPA or PPP. It is important to note here that such private fees for welfare services are often regarded as luxuries, since such expenditure is voluntarily entered into and may be for welfare services that are unavailable to much of the population. But for those individuals able to take advantage of such additional services, we should also remember that they pay additional charges, above government taxation.

Private welfare provision (or its privatisation), as we have alluded to above, embodies a multi-billion pound sector which is often difficult to navigate. In addition to the army of private providers, government has sought to deliver much of its own welfare, we might say, at arm's length. That is through the creation of complex 'quasi-markets'. Thus the short-lived NHS internal market, the creation of private corporations to deliver further and higher education, the local management of schools or the increasingly supervisory and regulatory role of social services departments, are attempts to charge the public sector with responsibility for the efficient provision of social services. Government has sought in this context to impose 'efficiency gains' or to provide more services from a reduced unit of resource and to make providers compete for 'customers' as resources are tied more to the number of customers, for example, treated (by NHS Trusts) or taught (in Schools, Colleges or Universities). Such a market has been reinforced by the introduction and adoption of often crude league tables and performance indicators which are to provide the customer with more perfect information about the market within which they find themselves (Le Grand and Bartlett, 1993).

Charitable gifts and voluntary support, whether given as donations of cash or of kind, that is care or time given freely, forms undoubtedly the smallest but also the most diverse element in funding our welfare state. Donations may vary from those establishing educational foundations and trusts which provide funds to support pupils and students both in school or higher education, regular company donations which attract government tax concessions right down to the stalwarts who regularly collect public donations for good causes such as the Royal British Legion's annual collections for Remembrance Day in November (often referred to as poppy day). Non-cash voluntary giving may be provided by organisations such as the WRVS providing tea and refreshments in hospital waiting rooms, the carers or 'buddies' who befriend and care for the terminally ill both informally and within the hospice movement, right down to family and friends who care for sick and ill relations. The range of what we may refer to as charity or voluntary giving is therefore broad and complex and not easily quantified, especially in financial terms. The nature of the services themselves may therefore appear to be somewhat random: recipients may not know that such organisations or services exist, their provision may be more patchy than state services, access to voluntary services is often more difficult and may be more strictly means-tested or there may be conditions attached to the provision of services. In addition service users may feel a greater sense of stigma in turning to charity than they do in applying for state-provided welfare, which may deter their application altogether.

However, voluntary- and charity-provided welfare services may also have considerable advantage over those provided by either the state or 'for-profit' organisations. The Wolfenden Report (1977) pointed to the considerable flexibility that voluntary organisations have over their private and statutory counterparts, since they are not bound by formal rules and may therefore be innovative in developing new services and new forms of service delivery. The voluntary sector could also be said to fill those gaps left by private and state provision and therefore provide alternatives where the other sectors may be unwilling or unable to act. The treatment and care of HIV sufferers, for example, has largely been left to the voluntary and charity sector, given its highly controversial and sensitive nature.

It must be noted, however, that many voluntary organisations have become almost totally reliant upon the state for their funding, particularly the local state. Thus, for example, Citizens' Advice Bureaux, whether nationally (NACAB) or local offices, could no longer function without public funds. This is a situation which has changed dramatically since the enactment of the new community care legislation in the 1990s (NHS and Community Care Act 1991) which places many voluntary and charitable groups in a much closer relationship with, especially, local authorities. Local authorities, since that Act, have developed far greater regulatory and financial control over those local groups providing care in the community. We may conclude from this that such voluntary organisations are not truly independent and that their financial relationship with the state threatens their independence and their vitality. Yet, at the same time, such groups continue to 'bite the hand that feeds them' when Community Health Councils embrace their role as local health watchdog and feel able to criticise their local NHS Trust or District Health Authority, or a local CAB challenges its local authority on behalf of its client. Although voluntary groups appear therefore to be in a vulnerable and ambiguous position within the welfare state, especially when we attempt to quantify their contribution, they also continue to occupy a valuable and recognised place within the welfare mix.

REFERENCES

Alcock, P. (1996) *Social Policy in Britain: Themes and issues*, Basingstoke: Macmillan.

Cocks, R. and Bentley, R. (1996) *£300 Billion Pounds: Government spending: the facts*, Reading: Databooks.

Deakin, N. and Parry, R. (1993) 'Does the Treasury have a Social Policy?,' in Page and Deakin (eds), *The Costs of Welfare*, Aldershot: Avebury.

Glennerster, H. (1992) *Paying for Welfare: The 1990s*, Hemel Hempstead: Harvester Wheatsheaf.

Glennerster, H. (1997) *Paying for Welfare: Towards 2000*, Hemel Hempstead: Prentice Hall/Harvester Wheatsheaf.

Le Grand, J. and Bartler, ed. (1993) *Quasi Markets and Social Policy*, Basingstoke: Macmillan.

Levin, P. (1997) *Making Social Policy: The mechanisms of government and politics and how to investigate them*, Buckingham: Open University Press.

Lowe, R. (1993) *The Welfare State since 1945*, Basingstoke: Macmillan.

Marsland, D. (1996) *Welfare and Welfare State: Contradictions and dilemmas in social policy*, London: Macmillan.

Page, R. and Deakin, N. (1993) *The Costs of Welfare*, Aldershot: Avebury.

ANNOTATED READINGS

Writings in this area easily overlap with economics texts and are not necessarily written with a social policy audience in mind. However, some of the most accessible work for social policy students is that written by Howard Glennerster, *Paying for Welfare*. A useful text arising from the proceedings of a 1992 Social Policy Conference is the edited collection by Deakin and Page, *The Costs of Welfare*. For an interesting venture into the changing pattern of welfare spending and management a useful source is Le Grand and Barlett's *Quasi Markets and Social Policy* or Levin's *Making Social Policy*.

Concluding comment to Part II

This part has attempted to establish the contemporary environment within which social policy is currently made. We have examined the ideological, structural and financial realms within which social policy is formulated, implemented and against which it may be evaluated.

As we have suggested this is an environment in a process of continuing flux and change. The prospects for devolution in policy making to Welsh, Scottish and Northern Ireland Assemblies, together with devolved tax-raising powers for some or eventually each of these assemblies, promises to change forever the contemporary policy environment. Similarly in 1999 Britain held direct elections to the Scottish and Welsh Assemblies, elections to the Northern Ireland Assembly were held in 1998, and will hold direct elections to the European Parliament, for the first time in Britain, using proportional representation.

The Blair government is proposing further constitutional change involving the wider and more regular use of proportional representation in British local and general elections. So too they are currently debating methods of strengthening the election of public officials in local government and are considering measures such as the direct election of Mayors and citizens' panels. The change of administration at Westminster, it seems, has opened debates on a wider range of possible changes to the way in which policy is made.

Change at the centre is also either proposed or has already come into operation. So the legislative function of the House of Lords, or at least its hereditary side, is currently under debate as is the role of the Monarchy in twenty-first-century. Britain and the possibility of what appears to be a more republican constitutional settlement is seriously considered with the introduction of government at regional level, that is within England as distinct from the Assemblies mentioned above. Already in financial management the Chancellor has introduced a range of fundamental changes that will alter the making of policy itself. Control of interest rates passed early in the life of the new administration out of the hands of the Treasury into that of the Bank of England and its governor. Further, government is to switch from the annual financial planning cycle described above to a three-year cycle which is intended to provide greater surety and stability in budgeting for public services.

Part III

THEORY AND SOCIAL POLICY

Introduction to Part III

Social policy as a discipline increasingly draws on a range of theoretical perspectives in order to explain not only who gets what in a range of welfare situations, but also how welfare states arise and what explains changes in welfare over time. The three chapters in this part introduce you to ideas about social policy and to the most frequently used theoretical approaches in the study of welfare.

Chapter 7 introduces the basic ways in which we might understand theory – what are the fundamental principles and concepts which are important in analysing social policy, what ideas do theories use and how do theories differ in their use of these concepts. We will also look at how to judge a theory – how can theories be tested or measured?

The next two chapters then outline the basic theoretical approaches used in the study of social policy. Chapter 8 is concerned with the more traditional theories of welfare – those which have been developed over a relatively long time – often being added to and refined after the introduction of welfare systems. Chapter 9 then looks at some of the more recent theoretical developments and outlines the major strands of newer theories of welfare.

This is difficult material to absorb – particularly in one sitting. The best way to make progress is to read these chapters alongside those on different sectors of social policy, which follow in part IV. Then return to part III and the chapters here with some specific questions in mind. Ask yourself how Marxist approaches would explain the development of the National Health Service or universal education. How would feminists view recent developments in the social security system? How would anti-racist theory explain family policies in Britain?

In addition, there is a guide to further reading at the end of each chapter and this should be used to help you to develop your understanding of each theory, as well as the ways in which theories in general are used in social policy. Understanding theory is difficult – but it is also the tool which equips the student to go beyond description to critical analysis and explanations of social policy.

Theoretical principles and concepts

by Judith Carlson

OBJECTIVES

- To examine the importance of theories and political ideologies in explaining the development and outcomes of social policies.

- To explore the principles that might guide the development of social policies such as need and equality.

- To consider the role that social policies play in the pursuit of social justice and greater social equity.

- To consider the value of competing social theories in explaining social policy.

INTRODUCTION

It is difficult to achieve an adequate understanding of social policy in the absence of theory. This is because social policies usually originate in and are shaped by the belief systems of those who initiate them. Whilst some social policy text books call these belief systems 'ideologies of welfare' (George and Wilding, 1976, 1985 and 1994; Clarke *et al.*, 1987), they can also be regarded as theoretical perspectives. Some key examples of the importance of such ideologies or theories in shaping welfare policies include the influence of classical liberalism on Victorian social policies, the influence of Fabianism on the social democratic welfare state and the influence of the New Right on the new or reconstructed welfare state of the 1980s and 1990s. Other theories have been less important in influencing actual policy agendas but offer useful perspectives on mainstream approaches and point the way to alternative ways of organising social policy. Theory thus lends coherence to social policy as a critical discipline.

WHAT IS THEORY?

An analogy may be drawn between social theories and road maps: just as we need maps to negotiate our spatial environment, so we also need maps which show us how society is structured to enable us to analyse, discuss and intervene in social processes (Best and Kellner, 1991). Maps and social theories each help us to chart the territory be it a labyrinth of roads and landmarks, or a network of social institutions and social processes. However, maps are purely descriptive: they show us *how* factors interrelate, but they fall short of explaining *why* things are structured in this way. In contrast, while describing social processes is as a preliminary stage in theory building, theory proceeds to analyse and explain why social institutions, social processes and social interaction take the form that they do. Four elements of theory can be elaborated as follows (Spicker, 1995):

Description

This element is usually concerned to produce classifications to make comparison easier, or to show inter-relationships between cases. Feminist perspectives use categories based on gender and seek to describe basic differences in material conditions of men's and women's lives. Marxists use social class in a similar way.

Analysis

This element moves beyond the descriptive, to ask *why* relationships between social phenomenon take the form that they do. For example, feminists may first describe or map differences in patterns of poverty between men and women. They may then proceed to explain this by reference to underlying differences between men and women. So, women's heightened vulnerability to poverty may be explained by the tendency for them to be financially dependent upon men. Women's dependence has been used as justification for inferior pay and social security provision for women. But the consequences of this are that if men fail to share their income with women, or if women set up independent households, then women are at risk of poverty.

Normative examination

The practice of social policy is not neutral but laden with values. In other words it is a practice underpinned by ideas about how society *ought* to be organised. One of the purposes of theory is to make it possible to examine these underlying principles. This chapter reviews some of the key concepts which contribute to this normative dimension (e.g. equality and social justice) but the normative content of social policy extends beyond this to incorporate broader attitudes towards the role of men and women, issues of rights and responsibilities and questions around sexuality. Thus, another way in which feminists might explain women's greater vulnerability to poverty is by examining the value base or normative assumptions which underpin social policy. Many feminists have argued that these assumptions are patriarchal in nature.

Normative prescription

Social policy is concerned with practical solutions to practical problems (Spicker, 1995) hence it contains a heavy element of prescription. Those theoretical perspectives which are explored here can all be characterised as normative or prescriptive. What this usually means, in relation to social policy, is that these theories put forward practical proposals for reform: for how policies *ought* to be organised. This is sometimes done by suggesting an ideal or putting forward a utopian vision which allows us to see what social policy would look like and how welfare would be delivered in the theorists' ideal society. However, not all theoretical perspectives are prescriptive in the utopian sense. Postmodernists, for example, feel that norms suppress difference and so offer no utopian vision. They emphasise self-defined need, generated from the bottom up, and seek to promote democratic and inclusive modes of policy making, but they have no desire to see their own utopias imposed upon others from the top down.

CLASSIFICATION OF THEORETICAL PERSPECTIVES

The majority of social policy textbooks (e.g. George and Wilding, 1976, 1985, 1994; Room, 1979; Mishra, 1981, 1984; Taylor-Gooby and Dale, 1981; Forder, Pontin and Walklate, 1984; Clarke, Cochrane and Smart, 1987; Williams, 1989) have focused on recognisable theoretical perspectives and attempt to divide these into categories. George and Wilding's (1976) text has been seen as a turning point in the field of social policy. Previously, debates had taken place in a theoretical vacuum, but George and Wilding's text represented a rediscovery of the long-standing links between welfare, politics and ideologies (Clarke, Cochrane and Smart, 1987).

Table 7.1 is intended as an aid to understanding the relationship between different systems of classification which have been used in welfare theory textbooks and the relationship between different theoretical perspectives in terms of political orientation. You should not expect to fully understand table 7.1 at this stage but it will be useful to refer back to it while reading chapters 8 and 9, and will guide you in your reading of other texts on welfare theory. Our typology uses the existing convention of thinking of political approaches and theoretical perspectives as a continuum between two poles identified as 'left' and 'right'.

The next table, table 7.2, shows left–right orientations towards four key dimensions: attitude towards social change, approach to social justice, attitude towards state intervention and view of human nature.

The first two dimensions in the typology must be understood in relation to the historical context of the terms left and right which originate as a description of seating arrangements in the French parliamentary chamber in 1789 during debates on the King's right of veto. Those seated on the right supported the continuation of the royal veto, while those on the left called for its abolition and those in the centre for compromise (Bullock, Stallybrass and Trombley, 1988). The term 'right-wing' thus once denoted a desire to conserve the privileges attached to traditional modes of status and authority. But it has also come to be associated with a form of liberalism which is interested not in the preservation of status, but in the promotion of reward on the basis of 'desert'. This liberal element is

Table 7.1 Classification of theoretical perspectives and approaches in social policy

	Left		Centrist reformist		Right	
	Revolutionary	Reformist	Left	Right	Radical	Conservative
Marxist	Marxist	Socialist Radical Social Administration Social Democratic	Fabian socialism	New liberalism Reluctant collectivism Middle way Non-socialist welfare collectivism	Classical liberal Laissez-faire Anti-collectivism	Conservative Authoritarianism
Political economy				Communal liberalism	New Right	
Feminist perspectives Radical		Socialist		Liberal	Neo-liberal	Neo-conservative
Anti-racist perspectives Marxist		European/Internationalist		Race relations		
Greenism			Environmentalism			
		Soft postmodernism Radical pluralism			Individualism	
		Structuralism Marxism and functionalism				
		Reformism Idealism				

Sources: George and Wilding, 1976, 1985; Taylor-Gooby and Dale, 1981; Mishra, 1984; Clarke *et al.*, 1987; Williams, 1989; George and Wilding, 1994; ISP, 1997.

Table 7.2 Political orientations in social theory

Dimension	Left	Right
1. Attitude towards change	Radical (promotes change)	Conservative (preserves social status quo)
2. Approach to social justice	Egalitarian (needs)	Inegalitarian (status + desert)
3. Attitude towards the state	Statist/collectivist/interventionist	Anti-statist/anti-collectivist/laissez-faire
4. Attitude towards human nature	Humans are co-operative + altruistic	Humans are selfish + individualistic

more radical than the conservative element but both are to the right of centre and left approaches in the continuum.

The third dimension in the typology, attitude towards the state, is particularly associated with nineteenth- and twentieth-century developments when the left and the right came to be associated with different attitudes towards the role of the state. Thus classical liberals adopted a laissez-faire approach while Fabians were committed to a significant role for the state in social and economic planning. This dimension is the primary logic underpinning most classifications of welfare theory (see Lee and Raban, 1983; Williams, 1989; George and Wilding, 1994).

The fourth dimension, attitudes to human nature, has long-standing links with political ideologies and directly informs attitudes towards criteria for social justice, the second dimension (George and Wilding, 1994).

These then are the basic orientations associated with left and right. However, the world is not a tidy place, and we can identify two key areas of difficulty:

The typology over-estimates the coherence within the perspectives and the differences between them

There will always be important exceptions to any rule and students of social policy will come across many examples of overlap between apparently disparate social theories. For example, many conservatives have a paternalistic outlook which promotes status in the form of hierarchical and unequal social relations but which does not have an individualistic stance on human nature. Instead, there is a strong sense of community and mutual co-operation which includes a duty to support the poor. Some paternalistic conservatives believe that this can be achieved via private philanthropic activity while others see a significant role for the state. So not all conservatives adhere to individualism and anti-statism/anti-collectivism.

An important example from the other side of the left–right continuum is libertarian socialism (for example, utopian socialism, guild socialism and ethical socialism). The libertarian socialist tradition has a deep-seated suspicion of state intervention and preference for mutual aid in a community of equals (Lee and Raban, 1983). So, although anti-statism has been identified as a right-wing political orientation, in practice it is not the preserve of the right.

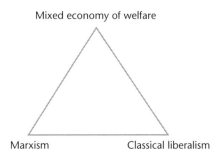

Fig. 7.1 Three models of social welfare

Source: Pinker (1979), chapter 12.

The left–right continuum fails to adequately characterise the middle ground

Pinker (1979) argues that the middle ground is something more than a compromise between the two extremes and asserts its existence as an independent 'third way'. The third way might be better represented as part of a tripartite typology in which the continuum is seen as triangular rather than linear (see figure 7.1; Pinker, 1979; Lee and Raban, 1983).

It is also important to appreciate that the work of individual theorists tends to develop over time. In chapter 8, for example, Peter Townsend is identified as a Fabian, whilst in chapter 9 the importance of his recent work to the international strand of anti-racist theory is recognised. There are also a number of theorists who have moved on from espousing broadly Marxist perspectives to adopt a soft postmodern position.

These difficulties suggest that there may be a case for using an alternative approach to exploring welfare theory which focuses upon the underlying principles and concepts as discrete elements. Before George and Wilding's (1976) pioneering text this was in fact the more usual approach (see, for example, Pinker, 1971; Forder, 1984). Spicker (1988, 1995) has continued to use this approach. However, he acknowledges that principles are not formed randomly but arise in relation to ideologies or theories (1988). It is, however, useful to review some of the major issues in theoretical debate in social policy and to highlight some of the most important principles which underpin theoretical perspectives, before we examine individual perspectives. This will help in an understanding of the differences between theoretical approaches.

NEED

The way in which human needs are defined has important implications for policy interventions. We can distinguish between different approaches by considering three questions: what is included as a need; how is need measured; who defines needs?

What is included?

There have been two major approaches to the question of what is to be included. Classical liberals and the New Right insist that need be defined in absolute or subsistence terms as the bare minimum necessary to secure physical efficiency; Fabians such as Peter Townsend, on the other hand, have supported a relative needs approach which stresses the importance of participation or an ability to share the customary standards of the society in which one is living.

How should need be measured?

The question of how need should be measured has been an important one for feminists who criticise mainstream approaches for failing to look inside the household. Need is often measured by looking at the resources of the household as a whole but there is no guarantee that all individuals living in that household have equal access to those resources.

Who defines need?

Finally, the question of who should decide what needs are has prompted much debate in social policy. The Fabian approach placed great faith in experts and the scientific definition of need but this has been criticised as undemocratic and for failing to take into account the felt needs of welfare consumers. Mack and Lansley (1985) developed a consensual approach to need definition which asked ordinary citizens to determine the necessities of life. Postmodernists prefer to emphasise self definition by individuals or communities. Recently a new technique called community profiling has been developed which seeks to combine the insights of experts and communities (for example, Percy-Smith and Sanderson, 1992).

EQUALITY

Chapters 8 and 9 discuss some radically divergent approaches to the concept of equality. The basic division is between *formal* equality and *substantive* equality. This division is in turn underpinned by divergent conceptions of freedom. *Formal* equality is associated with a negative view of freedom and advocated by those adopting a broadly liberal position (for example, classical liberals, New Right). Here every individual is equal before the law. This means that everyone has the right to pursue their own ends and desires within the context of a formal but limited legal framework. The framework is designed to prevent one person's choices from impinging on the *formal* equality enjoyed by everyone else. Those who prefer *formal* equality usually do not anticipate equality of outcome. Indeed they often see inequality as beneficial to society because it constitutes an incentive system which combines the stick of extreme poverty and the carrot of extreme wealth.

In contrast, arguments for *substantive* equality focus upon the significance of material constraints in inhibiting freedom (Weale, 1983). Inequality is seen as divisive and inefficient. Proponents of *substantive* equality thus adopt what is termed a positive approach to freedom. This entails a degree of resource equalisation or distributive justice because a levelling effect is desired in order to overcome the threat to liberty posed by poverty and inequality. This does not necessarily imply full equality of outcome. Adherents to this approach tend to adopt a broadly social democratic position (Fabians, for example).

Opponents of *substantive* equality complain that it implies discrimination and coercion and is therefore in conflict with *formal* equality (Hayek, 1944; Deakin, 1994). For example, redistributive taxation is seen as coercive. Similarly, in order to produce equality of outcome in education, it is necessary to exercise positive discrimination and to concentrate resources on the less-able students. This may disadvantage other students who are left with a smaller share of educational resources. In the case of both equality of outcome in education and in income redistribution, the egalitarian effects thus generated are characterised in terms of a levelling down of standards to an inefficient and uniform mediocrity, a ceiling on opportunity in relation to education and a cap on incentives in relation to income.

Supporters of *substantive* equality dispute this and assert that a positive, proactive approach promotes efficiency by supporting individuals and providing them with the security that they need to function effectively in their social roles as workers, parents and citizens. The use of positive discrimination in education is justified as compensation rather than discrimination because the intellectual development of some students has been inhibited by their environment. Such policies are thus concerned to redress the systematic inequalities which arise out of existing modes of social and economic organisation (Spicker, 1988, 1995). In short, treating people as equals means recognising their differences, because the capacity of individuals stems from their membership of groups which are in turn disadvantaged for arbitrary reasons (O'Connor, 1993).

EQUITY AND SOCIAL JUSTICE

The conflicts between the two positions discussed above can be elaborated further if we consider them in relation to debates over equity or social justice. In social policy the term 'social justice' has been adopted by the Social Democratic and Fabian approaches where it has been given a particular meaning – namely welfare or need – and used in an attempt to justify interventionist and institutional approaches to social policy (Hewitt, 1992). But in fact it can be judged in relation to several criteria: welfare or need is one possible criteria, but we might also consider status and property rights, together with 'desert' – meaning the rewards which people deserve to receive based on contributions they have made or the results they have achieved (Miller, 1976, cited in Forder, 1984; Spicker, 1988).

Table 7.3 Social justice and political orientation

Theoretical perspective	Primary principle of social justice	Political orientation
Classical liberal	desert	liberal
Marxist	need	socialist
Fabian	need	socialist
New Right	desert + status	liberal + conservative
Feminist	need, desert	socialist, liberal
Anti-racist	need, desert	socialist, liberal

Sources: Runciman, 1965, 1966; Miller, 1976.

Social justice is currently decided with reference to a mixture of these three criteria. Whether or not this arrangement is viewed as equitable depends upon the theoretical position one follows. Three approaches to social justice can be identified as socialist, conservative and liberal (Pinker, 1971; Forder, 1984). For example, in classical liberal and New Right theory, an emphasis on need might be seen as inequitable or socially unjust: this is because need implies a redistribution of income and wealth and contravenes their preferred criteria of desert and property rights. In contrast, Marxist, feminist and anti-racist theorists would point to the historic injustice inherent in stressing status and property rights, giving preference instead to need and desert. Feminists also insist that the way in which desert is currently understood must change to include a recognition of the contribution which women make in the home (Pateman, 1989).

The view adopted in relation to equality (formal or substantive) and the approach taken in relation to social justice (status, desert or need) will have significant implications for approaches to social welfare. For example, in spite of their refusal to see social justice based on need, there are few classical liberal and New Right thinkers who would abandon the poor altogether. What they do object to is the notion of welfare rights. Hence they opt for a residual approach to welfare based on selectivity or targeting and the use of unpopular means tests. Such benefits are intended to be unattractive and provide a stigmatising safety net for the very poor which barely guarantees subsistence. The state's role is reactive in that it only responds to market or family failures.

In contrast, supporters of substantive equality and the social justice based on need will give preference to universality. This is usually associated with the state in a pro-active role which meets the welfare needs of all strata of the population and not just the very poor. Means tests are rejected and circumstances such as old age, disability, sickness, parenthood and unemployment are used as proxies for need.

In Fabian and social democratic approaches to social policy, universality has been linked with social insurance. But this has proved controversial because social insurance tends to reinforce existing social divisions and because, although insurance benefits are based on contingency rather than means, this has not proved to be a sufficient guarantee of universality. Feminists have been particularly critical because historically the insurance approach has tended to exclude women. Occupational segregation means that women are concentrated in part-time and low-paid segments of the labour market. Because of this many women fall below the threshold for making national insurance contributions. Hence when women experience unemployment they are much less likely to qualify for unemployment benefits (Jobseekers Allowance). The insurance approach is also problematic in relation to pensions because women are much more likely to take career breaks to care for dependants, and at that time would not be contributing to pension schemes.

POWER AND THE STATE

Most theoretical perspectives are interested in the distribution and exercise of power in society, focusing on questions of how power is obtained, maintained and wielded, and questions of who has power and why. There are a number of different models of the distribution of power in society and a majority of these models refer to the role of the state in relation to the distribution of power. Power can be conceived in both macrological and micrological terms (see exhibit 7.1 below). The former approach involves a focus upon key social institutions, such as the state and capitalism or corporate interests (this is sometimes termed the objective dimension), while the latter focuses on the local level of interpersonal relations (the subjective dimension). The two approaches are not mutually exclusive, but many theoretical perspectives have tended to give emphasis to one or other, a problem which we shall be returning to later on when we consider ways of evaluating theory. The four basic positions regarding the power and the state are summarised in table 7.4 and are discussed below.

Exhibit 7.1

Criteria for an adequate theoretical perspective	
• macro-theoretical	• micro-theoretical
• objective	• subjective
• social structures	• human actors
Source: Williams, 1989, chapter 2.	

The state is neutral

This view of the state underpins classical liberalism, liberal feminism and race relations. It comes from liberal pluralism where power is seen in positive terms, not as coercion but as a capacity to influence policy agendas (Dahl, 1961). The

Table 7.4 Models of power and the state

	Liberal pluralism	*Marxism*	*Feminism*	*Postmodernism*
Nature of the state	Neutral arbiter/ interest broker	Instrument of capitalism	Instrument of patriarchy	Fragmented; incoherent; an effect of wider power relations
Distribution of power in society	Dispersed, interest groups	Concentrated, capitalist	Concentrated, male	Dispersed, network
Model of power relations	Pluralistic (interest groups)	Binary (capitalists vs workers)	Binary (men vs women) or dual systems (capitalism + patriarchy)	Radical pluralism (new social movements, alliances)
Power works via . . .	Influence	Coercion	Coercion	Negotiation
Power emanates from . . .	Top-down	Top-down	Top-down	Bottom-up
Macro/micro?	Macro	Macro	Macro + micro	Macro → micro

policy process involves a competition for influence between interest groups and is entirely open, with the state adopting a neutral function as arbiter of rival demands and always seeking the fairest possible outcome (McLennan, 1984). There is no possibility of any one interest group dominating the political process or capturing the state. Initially, liberal pluralists failed to recognise systematic structures of power at the macro-level, but later pointed to the capacity of some social groups to set agendas and achieve ideological control (Bachrach and Baratz, 1963; Lukes, 1974). However, liberal pluralists continue to see the state as potentially neutral, and that, although 'up to now the state has been male', the potential for altering this is within our grasp (Eisenstein cited in Allen, 1990).

The state is capitalist

Orthodox Marxists tended to see the state as an instrument of capitalism. They argued that interests in society were split between capitalists and workers and that social policy worked coercively as a mechanism of social control securing labour discipline. More recently, there has been recognition that welfare measures are in part the product of working-class struggles against exploitation: the state grants social reform in an attempt to secure ongoing legitimacy for the capitalist system, but the emphasis is on co-opting workers rather than coercing them.

The state is patriarchal

This view of the state is supported by radical and socialist feminists. Radical feminists conceive the state as a bastion of male power which will consistently act to promote the interests of men. Socialist feminists prefer a dual systems theory in which women's status and function are jointly determined by their dual roles in relation to production and reproduction. Here the state represents the combined interests of men as capitalists and men as men. In this case there is some potential for a conflict of interests. For example, it may be in the interests of men as capitalists to incorporate women into the labour force, while it may be in the interests of men as patriarchs to exclude them.

'The state' is fragmented

This view is associated with postmodernism. The postmodern view of power starts from a pluralistic position in which power is conceived as dispersed. No one group possesses power to the exclusion of others. Rather power is relational, being exercised from a plurality of points within a network. 'The state' does not exist in the form proposed in the Marxist and liberal pluralist models, both of which view it as a sovereign entity ruling society from the top down. Post-modernists argue that the state is simply an effect or by-product of power relations which prevail at the micro-level in society as a whole. The state cannot be controlled by any one group because power relations are far too dynamic and pluralistic. As a result the state is not seen as coherent: it is not capitalist or patriarchal but full of contradictions and inconsistencies. Policy may be pushed in progressive directions through the political struggles of radical new social movements like feminism and anti-racism.

EVALUATING THEORY

Since theories are about values it is extremely difficult to evaluate them in a value free or objective way. But there are, nevertheless, a number of ways in which we assess the validity of particular perspectives. First, we might adopt an explicitly subjective approach in which we either measure validity in relation to our own set of normative yardsticks, or in which we compare and contrast two or more theoretical perspectives using one set of norms to inform our appraisal of another. Secondly, we might examine the adequacy of the methodological framework which they use. Finally, we might adopt an entirely empirical approach which rests on an examination of the fit between the theoretical perspective and social reality.

Normative comparison

In the introduction to this chapter we established that one of the four key purposes of welfare theory is normative examination. Individual theories can be used to evaluate existing welfare arrangements, but we might also use a particular theoretical perspective to evaluate another. Alternatively, we could define our own set of normative yardsticks and use them to measure the adequacy of a variety of theoretical perspectives.

Methodological adequacy

There are two major methodological approaches in social theory: *individualism* focuses on the role of human actors in shaping their environment and life chances; while *structuralism* conceives of life chances as being determined externally by socio-structural factors (see table 7.1 above). It is commonly recognised that the key social structures which serve to constrain human actors can be grouped under the headings of capitalism, imperialism and patriarchy. The major axes of oppression can thus be identified in terms of class, race and gender – although, clearly, this does not represent an exhaustive list. These two approaches follow the micro- versus macro-logical or subjective versus objective distinction suggested above in the section on power and the state (and see exhibit 7.2). Theoretical perspectives can be regarded as methodologically adequate only if they are able to supply an account of both dimensions of power and social change (Williams, 1989).

Exhibit 7.2

Definition and examples of determinism

- **Economism, economic determinism, economic reductionism**: social phenomenon like the welfare state are explained as instrumental to the needs of the mode of production (e.g. capitalism).
- **Functionalism**: a more generic term which can include economism. Social phenomenon are explained as instrumental to the needs of the dominant power bloc (e.g. patriarchy, capitalism).
- **Technological determinism, technological reductionism**: social phenomenon are determined by available technologies or by the technological base (e.g. industrialism, post-industrialism).
- **Biological essentialism, biological determinism, biological reductionism**: social relations are determined by genetic or biological characteristics. For example: the persistence of inequalities between social classes or 'racial' groups might be explained with reference to differences in innate intelligence or physical robustness; the sexual division of labour with reference to natural differences in aptitude between men and women.

It can therefore be argued that individualism, the preferred methodology of the New Right, is inadequate because it denies that social structures and institutions have any role in shaping people's ideas and actions. The claims made by orthodox Marxists are equally problematic but here the methodology leans too far in the other direction and allows too little room for the role of human actors in negotiating their socio-economic environment. For example, orthodox Marxist explanations of racism suggest it is an ideology produced by the capitalist class, as part of a functional strategy of divide and rule. The absorption of racist ideology by the working classes is termed 'false consciousness'. This underplays the complexities of racism at the interpersonal level and implies that if the demise of capitalism can be secured then racism will disappear alongside it.

It is important to maintain a critical awareness of the difficulties associated with such crude and conspiratorial perspectives. Such approaches are criticised for what is termed reductionism or determinism because they reduce the explanation to a single determining factor and fail to capture the complexity of social reality. In addition they stress the objective at the expense of the subjective; thus, it appears that human subjects lack freewill and the ability to control the shape of their lives and environments. We can identify a number of different modes of determinism; these are summarised in exhibit 7.2.

Neo-Marxist theory seeks to avoid determinism by adopting a materialist framework which marries the mode of production and working-class agitation in its account of the origins of welfare states. But in spite of this Marxist theory does have a tendency to give undue emphasis to structural factors. In contrast, soft postmodernists may be sympathetic to the materialist approach but still have difficulty in providing an adequate account of the role of structural factors. It is crucial that a balance is maintained between macro- and micro-approaches. Fiona Williams argues that a theory should fall into neither:

the trap of economic reductionism on the one hand, where everything is analytically reduced to the needs of capitalism, or into the trap of sociological pluralism on the other, where society is analysed in terms of different counterbalancing forces – whites, blacks, women, men, bosses, trade unions and so on [each of which takes on] a free floating and independent form. (Williams, 1989)

In practice there may not be a single theoretical perspective which entirely satisfies the criteria of methodological adequacy. As a solution to this problem Williams proposes a multifaceted approach which draws upon several theoretical perspectives simultaneously, specifically in order to combine macro and micro theoretical elements and to ensure that class, race, gender and other significant social divisions are all included (Williams, 1989, 1992; Best and Kellner, 1991). This is not, however, a question of adopting an indiscriminate pick-and-mix approach, as there would need to be some degree of consistency in terms of the underlying values which have been explored in this chapter.

Empirical adequacy

The third approach to evaluation rests upon empirically testing the fit between social theory and social reality. It rests on looking at the theoretical perspective to see if there are some instances which it fails to explain adequately. So theoretical perspectives can be discarded or accepted on the basis of an appeal to the empirical evidence. For example, Marxist perspectives might be criticised for their concentration on class-based dimensions of power and privilege and their failure to explain inequalities associated with race and gender. In contrast, postmodernists have been criticised for their neglect of class. In addition, a number of theoretical perspectives might be challenged for failing to supply an adequate description of the distribution of power in society and the nature and role of the state (e.g.

New Right, Fabianism). In practice it may always be possible to select empirical evidence which appears to support a particular theoretical perspective. For this reason, some commentators reject this method of evaluating theory (e.g. Lee and Raban, 1983).

To evaluate theory we may use some combination of the three approaches outlined above. The key question which needs to be answered is whether the perspective enables us to see, understand and reflect upon social reality, or does it obscure and confuse the issues.

CONCLUSION

We need to consider the ways in which different theoretical perspectives offer different understandings of social policy – how it is made, why certain policies have been designed as they have, and what the implications are for particular social groups. How a theoretical perspective responds to these questions is dependent on the claims which are made about power, the role and nature of the state and on the approach to social justice. There is no 'right' or 'wrong' theoretical perspective. Whether a theory is appropriate and applicable depends on the context and the value system of those doing the analysis. In the following two chapters we explore a range of theoretical perspectives, beginning with those described as 'traditional', in chapter 8, before going on to consider relatively recent developments in theoretical approaches to social policy in chapter 9.

The relatively systematic arguments presented within each of the theoretical perspectives explored in the next two chapters have provided the major organising positions or frameworks for political activity and conflict around welfare since the early nineteenth century. Fabianism and New Right theories in particular have resulted in relatively coherent policy programmes and many of the ideas put forward by Fabian and New Right thinkers have been directly implemented or else have had a more indirect influence on social policy. Other theoretical perspectives such as feminism, anti-racism and postmodernism have tended to be more marginal. But this does not mean that they have been totally submerged: for example, state organisations have been set up to oversee equal opportunities and 'race relations'.

REFERENCES

Allen, J. (1990) 'Does Feminism Need a Theory of "The State"?', in Watson, S. (ed.), *Playing the State: Australian feminist interventions*, London: Verso.

Bachrach, P. and Baratz, M. (1963) 'Decisions and Non-Decisions', *American Political Science Review*, 57.

Best, S. and Kellner, D. (1991) *Postmodern Theory: Critical interrogations*, London: Macmillan.

Bullock, A., Stallybrass, O. and Trombley, S. (eds) (1988) *The Fontana Dictionary of Modern Thought*, 2nd edition, London: Fontana.

Clarke, J., Cochrane, A. and Smart, C. (1987) *Ideologies of Welfare: From dreams to disillusion*, London: Routledge.

Dahl, R. (1961) *Who Governs?* Yale: Yale University Press.

Deakin, N. (1994) *The Politics of Welfare: Continuities and change*, Hemel Hempstead: Harvester Wheatsheaf.

Forder, A. (1984) 'Two Theories of Social Justice', in Forder, A. *et al., Theories of Welfare*, London: Routledge & Kegan Paul.

Forder, A., Caslin, T., Pontin, G. and Walklate, S. (1984) *Theories of Welfare,* London: Routledge & Kegan Paul.

George, V. and Wilding, P. (1976) *Ideology and Social Welfare,* London: Routledge & Kegan Paul.

George, V. and Wilding, P. (1985) *Ideology and Social Welfare,* 2nd edition, London: Routledge & Kegan Paul.

George, V. and Wilding, P. (1994) *Welfare and Ideology*, Hemel Hempstead: Harvester Wheatsheaf.

Goodin, R. and le Grand, J. (1987) *Not Only the Poor*, London: Allen and Unwin.

Hayek, F. (1944) *The Road to Serfdom*, London: Routledge (reprinted 1993).

Hewitt, M. (1992) *Welfare Ideology and Need: Developing perspectives on the welfare state*, Hemel Hempstead: Harvester Wheatsheaf.

Lee and Raban (1983) 'Welfare and Ideology', in Loney, Boswell and Clarke (eds), *Social Policy and Social Welfare*.

Lukes, S. (1974) *Power: A radical view*, London: Macmillan.

Mack, J. and Lansley, S. (1985) *Poor Britain*, London: Allen & Unwin.

McLennan, G. (1984) 'Capitalist State or Democratic Polity? Recent developments in Marxist and Pluralist Theory', in McLennan, G., Held, D. and Hall, S. (eds), *The Idea of the Modern State*, Milton Keynes: Open University Press.

Mishra, R. (1981) *Society and Social Policy*, London: Macmillan.

Mishra, R. (1984) *The Welfare State in Crisis: Social thought and social change*, Hemel Hempstead: Harvester Wheatsheaf.

O'Connor, J. S. (1993) 'Gender, Class and Citizenship in the Comparative Analysis of Welfare State Regimes: Theoretical and methodological issues', *British Journal of Sociology*, 44(3): 501–18.

Orloff, A. S. (1993) 'Gender and the Social Rights of Citizenship: The comparative analysis of gender relations and welfare states', *American Sociological Review*, 58: 303–28.

Pateman, C. (1989) 'The Patriarchal Welfare State', in Pateman, C. (ed.), *The Disorder of Women*, Cambridge: Polity.

Percy-Smith, J. and Sanderson, I. (1992) *Understanding Local Needs*, London: Institute for Public Policy Research.

Pinker, R. (1971) *Social Theory and Social Policy*, London: Heinemann.

Pinker, R. (1979) *The Idea of Welfare*.

Room, G. (1979) *The Sociology of Welfare*, Oxford: Blackwell.

Spicker, P. (1988) *Principles in Social Welfare: An introduction to thinking about the welfare state*, London: Routledge.

Spicker, P. (1995) *Social Policy: Themes and approaches*, Hemel Hempstead: Prentice Hall/ Harvester Wheatsheaf.

Taylor-Gooby, P. and Dale, J. (1981) *Social Theory and Social Welfare*, London: Arnold.

Weale (1983) 'Issues of Value and Principle in Social Policy', in Loney, Boswell and Clarke (eds), *Social Policy and Social Welfare*.

Williams, F. (1989) *Social Policy: A critical introduction*, Oxford: Polity.

103

Williams, F. (1992) 'Somewhere Over The Rainbow: Universality and diversity in social policy', in *Social Policy Review*, 4: 200–19.

ANNOTATED READINGS

Paul Spicker's *Principles of Social Welfare* systematically explores the major principles and concepts underpinning social policy. Spicker includes chapters on democracy, power, inequality, equality and social justice. Another useful text, though rather more advanced, which links some of the major principles and concepts to Fabian and New Right perspectives on the welfare state is R. Goodin's *Reasons for Welfare: The political theory of the welfare state.*

8 Traditional theories of welfare

by Mike McBeth

OBJECTIVES

- To explore the development of classical liberal political theory as a foundation for the creation of the British welfare state and its justifications for state involvement in welfare provision.

- To outline the Marxist critique of nineteenth century British capitalism and to explore the position of that critique in the development of British welfare.

- To examine the roots of the Beveridgean welfare state of the twentieth century and its Fabian parentage – the development of social administration and the advent of social policy.

INTRODUCTION

This chapter focuses on what might be termed more 'traditional' and long-standing theoretical concepts: classical liberal theory, Marxist theories and Fabian theories. A brief description of the main points of each theory is followed by a short example of the way in which the theory may be used in an analysis of the contribution of the theory to the existence of the welfare state. Such differing analyses are useful as a means to critically understand the origins and purpose of different social institutions.

As suggested in chapter 7, social theory is often used as the basis for political ideologies and party political positions. The language of social theory is, therefore, very much part of the language of everyday political discourse. However, although there are often connections between political ideologies and social theories, these should not be regarded as synonymous: for example, liberal may be used to refer to an economic or social theory that favours individualism (see below); sometimes it is used to describe permissiveness or tolerance and sometimes to refer to a political party.

CLASSICAL LIBERAL THEORY

The theoretical concept of classical liberalism combines not only theories, but ideologies and philosophies which are based on particular interpretations of personal freedom and social progress. Liberals generally interpret freedom to mean an absence of coercion rather than protection from misfortune or hardship. This contrasts with Marxist and Fabian notions of freedom which regard liberty in a more egalitarian way. Classical liberal theories and subsequent developments have become so widely accepted and unquestioned that for Anthony Forder *et al.* (1984, p. 27), 'they are treated ... as received dogma'. This poses problems assessing liberal theories, since they are so often treated as 'common sense' to analyse critically such theories might be regarded as both radical and extremist. However, when liberal theories were formulated they were controversial, since they ran counter to prevailing orthodoxies. For example, liberalism opposed the privilege of the landed aristocracy and favoured the emerging capitalist class. Liberalism was also opposed to the dominant view that one of the duties of the government was to intervene in the economy in order to protect native production from foreign competition; this protectionism typically took the form of tariffs or taxes on imported commodities. Classical liberalism may thus be regarded as providing a crucial ideological and philosophical underpinning to the development of capitalism.

The main tenets of classical liberalism originated during the eighteenth-century European Enlightenment. In this period a recognisable 'modern' society guided by rational thinking emerged. The Enlightenment followed the 'dark' or middle ages (circa fifth to fifteenth centuries), where progress and culture were thought to have stagnated following the collapse of the Roman empire. The Enlightenment was characterised by new scientific discoveries and a growing cultural relativism brought about by the discoveries of other civilisations, such as those in the Far East and South America.

An important strand in Enlightenment thinking suggested that human knowledge is neither innate nor god-given, but rather acquired cumulatively as a result of experience and observation. One of the central ideas of original liberal enlightened thinking thus became the quest for knowledge along with a questioning of traditional authority. In *The Social Contract* published in 1762, Rousseau argued against authoritarian theories of the divine right of monarchs. He proposed that government should be based on popular assent and that decisions should be founded on civil liberties. Modern democracy is therefore commonly associated with classical liberalism. Nevertheless, many early classical liberals opposed what are now regarded as essential democratic elements; for example, neither Locke nor Voltaire supported the principle of universal suffrage and both believed that the working class would not support abstracted notions, such as freedom and diversity in society. Thomas Hobbes favoured strong and even unrestrained government, arguing that the sole test of government was its effectiveness.

In Britain, liberalism was linked to utilitarianism, the philosophy propounded by Jeremy Bentham (1748–1832) and John Stuart Mill (1809–73) for example. Essentially, the utilitarian philosophy reduces human experiences to either pleasure or pain. Bentham argued that 'the greatest happiness of the greatest number is the foundation of morals and legislation'. Thus for utilitarians and many classical liberals the only legitimate functions of the state are those activities which are designed to reduce human suffering and increase pleasure. Mill wrote:

> The only purpose for which power can be rightfully exercised over any member of a civilised community, against his will, is to prevent harm to others. His own good, either physical or moral is not a sufficient warrant. (Mill, 1910)

Over time, economic issues came increasingly to dominate liberal theoretical thinking. In economics Adam Smith, David Ricardo and Robert Malthus are regarded as some of the most important classical liberal thinkers.

Adam Smith (1723–93) is often regarded as the founder of modern economics. Smith published *An Inquiry into the Nature and Causes of the Wealth of Nations* in 1776. He was among the first economic writers to seriously attempt to study the development of capital, industry and commerce. The main proposition in the *Wealth of Nations* is that the chief sources of wealth are rents, wages and profits and that the most efficient way of distributing capital is to allow the market in which goods and services are traded to operate with a minimum amount of regulation. Smith believed that all individuals within the market are motivated by a rational assessment of the benefits and costs associated with the work they do and the goods they purchase. With this in mind, people try to maximise their own happiness while minimising their discomfort. The market is thus self-regulating through the laws of supply and demand; goods which are well produced, competitively priced and relevant to people's needs will be in demand, while poorly made, overpriced and irrelevant goods will not sell. If governments pursued laissez-faire economic policies (that is, refrained from interfering in the workings of the market), then unrestrained market competition would result in a natural harmony. The importance of this proposition was that it provided a justification for the separation of economic affairs from political or moral concerns. Smith invoked the notion of an 'invisible hand' to describe how resources would be distributed:

> The rich select from the heap what is most precious and agreeable. They consume little more than the poor, and in spite of their natural selfishness and rapacity ... they divide with the poor the produce of all their improvements. They are led by an invisible hand to make nearly the same distribution of the necessaries of life which would have been made, had the earth been divided among all its inhabitants. (*Theory of Moral Sentiments*, IV, i: 10)

Two contemporaries of Adam Smith, David Ricardo (1772–1823) and Thomas Malthus (1766–1834), were also important in the development of classical liberalism. Malthus published *An Essay on the Principle of Population* in 1798 in which he argued that population will tend to increase faster than the ability of a nation to supply sufficient food to meet its needs. This generated concern among the better-off, who feared that unrestrained population growth, particularly among the poor, would exhaust the land and lead to social unrest. Ricardo developed the 'iron law of wages', suggesting that the amount of capital available to pay labour costs was finite and that wage levels are determined by the minimum amount required to maintain and reproduce the labour force. Ricardo contended that if wages were too high, then more children would be born than could expect to gain work when they grew up, thus forcing wages down as a surplus of labour competed for relatively scarce jobs. These theories helped to create a more hostile attitude towards the poor and led the way to the Poor Law (Amendment) Act of 1834.

Economic liberals tended to favour unhampered private enterprise. For example, John Bright (1811–89) opposed laws limiting working hours, arguing that such legislation violated individual liberty. The working class generally perceived that liberal ideologies tended to protect the interest of the most powerful economic groups, especially capitalists and manufacturers.

There are two contrasting views within classical liberal thinking on the role of the state. Traditional or negative liberals defend individual liberty while challenging what they perceive as the arbitrary misuse of power common to many absolute monarchies. For negative liberals, the role of the state ought to be kept to a minimum. However, positive liberals argue that the state can adopt a more constructive role in dealing with social problems. In particular, it is argued that government can assert and defend particular moral arrangements. Both positive and negative liberal thinking on the role of the state have been important influences on the modern British Conservative party.

Classical liberals are not all necessarily opposed to welfare state activities. Adam Smith, for example, supported publicly provided education, public health measures and the safeguarding of proper working conditions as maintaining the economic conditions through which capitalism can best flourish. However, modern or neo-classical liberals tend to be more directly concerned with the workings of the market and how best to distribute the products of economic growth. Neo-liberals tend to believe that an economic system that is governed by the market will ensure that wealth and property is widely distributed; this they regard as a way of preventing any concentration of power.

The welfare state as it is now conventionally understood did not exist at the time that the early classical liberals were writing. However, much classical and neo-classical liberal thinking on welfare has been developed by the new right who are attracted by its individualist tenets (see chapter 9). Classical liberal theory is normative and positivist: that is, it seeks to describe and explain both causes and remedies. Given that a welfare state is essentially concerned with the alleviation of poverty, then some analysis of the causes of poverty, according to neo-classical theory, is required. Since neo-classical and classical liberal theory establishes that the free market is the most efficient way of distributing resources it follows that intervention into the workings of the market, especially by the state, will have a distorting effect. Unwarranted state intervention will amplify social and economic problems since the market system will be less efficient and economic growth will slow. If, for example, the state tries to alleviate poverty by providing welfare, such action will inevitably make the problem of poverty worse, since slower economic growth will decrease the level of employment and reduce tax receipts. Furthermore, individual freedom is of paramount importance and any attempt by the state to provide fiscal help to the poor compromises that individual freedom in two ways: first, by requiring those who earn wages to pay extra taxes to support the poor and, second, by creating the conditions under which poor individuals and the state will have a relationship of dependency.

Classical liberals regard the causes of poverty as essentially individual rather than structural. Poverty may be traced to personal failings rather than to failings of the economic or political system. Furthermore, since individual rights must be preserved then individuals must have the 'right' to be poor. In addition, in a free market, equality is impossible to achieve and some inequality is desirable, since inequality drives people to better themselves through hard work, competition, innovation and invention and this in turn maximises economic growth.

For classical liberals, the emergence of the welfare state is explicable mainly in terms of its apparent attraction at the time of inception. Corelli Barnett (1986) argues that the welfare state was a necessary short-term benefit for the nation following the rigours of the Second World War. Barnett believes that those who supported the introduction of a welfare state did not take a long-term view of the economic needs of the country. The welfare state is thus regarded as an anachronism and no longer beneficial. A recurrent objection to the welfare state is the belief that the services provide benefit to those who do not need it. Post-sixteen education, child benefits and free health care, for example, favour the middle classes who could afford to buy services privately. Furthermore, the welfare state has created groups of professionals, such as doctors and social workers, who are dependent on the state for their own income and who have a vested interest in preserving and perpetuating state welfare.

To many of those influenced by classical liberal theories, the welfare state is a pernicious institution which causes an unacceptable level of interference into the workings of the market. State welfare represents a monopoly on the supply of certain goods and services and this lack of competition is seen as both inefficient and as concentrating too much power with the state. The welfare state is regarded as being wasteful of a nation's resources because many of the available goods and services are free at the point of use. In liberal economic theory, if the price of the goods and services is zero, then the laws of supply and demand are violated and demand will be infinite. For example, demand for free health care outstrips supply and so inefficient rationing is introduced and those most in need do not necessarily receive treatment. For the individual, welfare is also socially disruptive since it encourages people to be dependent and to assume that they have a right to welfare without directly paying for it.

Some supporters of classical and neo-classical liberal theories support welfare in certain, limited circumstances. There is some recognition that the market is imperfect and that some groups, for example the chronically sick or the mentally ill, may not be able to make provision for themselves. Generally, however, those inspired by liberal theories assume that charity and philanthropy would cater for the deserving poor. Additionally, the state might be expected to intervene in the market in order to provide essential support networks, where costs are too great for individual business, for example transport systems and other costly but essential infrastructure.

The most fundamental critique of classical liberal ideology rests on the assumptions which liberals tend to make about the nature of individualism and individual freedom. It is questionable that freedom from coercion is a sufficient mechanism for ensuring optimum happiness. Individualism can only guarantee the freedom of some (the most privileged and the more able). Individualism can also be regarded as an inefficient way of managing the economy; theories from the left suggest that people work best and achieve more when they work in co-operation with each other and have shared aims and common goals.

A further important criticism of liberalism rests on the assumptions that are made about the private market. Questions need to be asked about Adam Smith's so-called 'hidden hand'. To what extent can there ever be perfect competition; does the market truly operate freely; are individuals really rational and able to judge their own welfare needs? Do people have sufficient knowledge or foresight to make complex decisions about their future welfare needs? If welfare were left to individual free choice, then what would happen to those who had failed to adequately provide for themselves and their dependants?

Classical liberal theory has been extremely influential. It is particularly, although not exclusively, associated with the political right. The continuing attraction of this group of theories lies in their appeal to individual responsibility, self-help and personal advancement.

MARXIST THEORIES

Marxism as a set of theories grew from disenchantment with the growing inequality which was experienced through the nineteenth and into the twentieth centuries. The theories developed by Karl Marx (1818–83) and his followers have had a profound influence on the modern world, but it is important to remember that 'Marxism' is not a simple discrete set of ideas originating from one person. Rather, Marx was able to develop ideas which were current in the period before the nineteenth century. Marx has been of considerable significance to the development of left-wing ideologies since he was able to formulate a coherent theoretical framework which encompassed a wide range of ideas and helped to explain the relationship between rich and poor in society.

Since Marx's death, a diverse range of individuals have claimed that their particular interpretation or development of Marx is correct. Marxist theories have thus been used to justify a wide range of activities and it is important to understand that Marxism encompasses a disparate set of views, some of which conflict with one another. The inclusion of some theories as Marxist as distinct from 'socialist', 'radical' or 'conflict' theories is somewhat arbitrary and often such categorisations rely on the self-identification of writers rather than a more objective analysis of their ideas.

Marx attempted to develop a set of theories which would explain the persistence of inequality. However, a particular feature of Marxism is a concern to translate an analysis of social phenomena into a programme of action. Therefore Marxists are also concerned with remedying inequality and social injustice. This links with social policy and is one of the important distinctions between social policy and sociology. Marx himself said, 'The philosophers have only interpreted the world in various ways; the point is to change it' (*Theses on Feuerbach*, 1888, p. xi).

At the time that Marx was working, the economies of the major industrialising countries were growing apace and vast fortunes were being realised. Wealth was concentrated among a relatively small privileged group and Marx sought to understand this apparent contradiction: how can societies become so much wealthier while the majority of that society's members live in poverty? Marx's attempt to link the economic and the social has proved to be an important element in much subsequent sociological and social policy thinking.

Marx did not give very much formal consideration to attempts by the state to alleviate poverty. At that time state intervention was either highly punitive, such as the Poor Laws, or rudimentary, such as the Factory Acts of the same period. Marx argued that the state in a capitalist economy exists mainly to protect and advance the interests of a dominant ruling class. The state could achieve this by helping to maintain and legitimise the conditions under which capitalism can flourish, for example, by maintaining property rights. Marx was convinced that those who ran the state and had political power in society made decisions which benefited the privileged minority, not the poorer majority. For Marxists the state can act in ways which appear to benefit the poor, such as providing welfare. However, such activities are peripheral and reinforce the role of the state in legitimating capitalism either by helping to deflect criticism of the partisan nature of the state or through the 'buying off' of working-class unrest.

Marx argued that under capitalism the need to make ever-increasing profits is a guiding principle. Nonetheless, Marx argued that capitalist accumulation has not always been a dominant force. Marx traced a series of historical periods starting with primitive societies through feudal and capitalist then on to socialist and communist societies. Marx argued that societies and historical periods could be delineated by what he termed their *mode of production*, that is the way in which goods and services were organised and delivered. Within the mode of production Marx identified two constituent components: the forces of production and the relations of production.

Exhibit 8.1

Mode of production

■ Forces	■ Relations
e.g. physical resources, such as raw materials, factories, equipment, labour power and metaphysical resources such as market share, technology	e.g. the connections in terms of power or class between owners and producers

The forces of production refers to raw materials, equipment, buildings and labour power; while the relations of production are the way that those involved in making and providing goods or services are connected. Using an historical analysis, Marx argued that in capitalist societies the relations of production were based on exploitation by the owners of the forces of production.

Under capitalism exploitation is predicated on what Marx termed *surplus value*. Production costs are mostly fixed, because the price of raw materials, rent and machinery are usually outside of the control of the owner. However, labour costs are not fixed. Under capitalism, the owners of the forces of production seek to maximise profits by extracting surplus value from workers. In other words, workers are paid less than the added value of the goods or services that they produce. The surplus value is taken as profit by the owner. Workers accept exploitative working arrangements because they believe that they have no choice.

Marx believed that while most of the history of developed societies indicates that inequality between rich and poor has prevailed, such division is not inevitable. To demonstrate this, Marx pointed to certain primitive societies, where he suggested that such exploitation did not exist. This led Marx to conclude that greed and individualism were not inevitable human conditions, rather they were a result of the mode of production. Marx argued that as capitalism developed, the urge to make more profits would inevitably lead to a widening difference between those who owned capital, the ruling class, and those who only owned their labour power, the working class. This gap would lead to increasing social stress which would ultimately lead to revolution among the working class.

One of the most important contributions of Marx to modern thinking is the theory of *historical materialism* which suggests that society is not simply formed as a result of random events or the actions of great leaders, but is rather the product of observable principles based on the relations of production. Marx hoped that capitalist systems would be overthrown to be replaced by socialism and then by communism, systems which according to Marx would organise the mode of production in a fairer way.

Although social policy itself, or more accurately social administration as it was known, grew explicitly in opposition to Marxist analysis, the influence of this per-spective on social policy has been considerable and was perhaps at its strongest during the 1960s. Followers of Marx have sought to develop his theories to try to explain both the growth in state welfare provision and the apparent reluctance or failure of the working class in modern developed capitalist economies to embrace revolutionary ideals and overthrow the state.

There have been several Marxist explanations for the purpose and existence of a welfare state. Marxists often disagree as to whether or not the welfare state is of benefit to the working class. For some Marxists, the welfare state is seen as masking the true inequitable nature of capitalism and so delaying revolutionary uprising. This argument suggests that the ruling class have cynically seduced the working class with the welfare state. Thus, the welfare state uses taxes paid by everyone to provide services and to foster an illusion that the state is redistri-butive and altruistic, whilst in reality the welfare state preserves and reinforces particular norms and structural relationships which actually benefit the accumu-lation of capital.

Some Marxists argue that the welfare state is the result of working-class struggle against exploitation. From this point of view the state has been prevailed upon to provide benefits for the poorest and most vulnerable by the threat of strikes and civil unrest. This account provides some explanation for the relative lack of revolutionary ferment in Britain compared to other European countries. However, in this particular model, the welfare state is vulnerable to cutback and perhaps eventual removal. If the ruling class perceive that capitalist processes are not likely to be endangered by working-class unrest, then welfare benefits can be withdrawn. It may be argued from this perspective that during the 1980s and 1990s in Britain the ruling class manipulated the labour market by, for example, tackling the power of workers' organisations, increasing job insecurity and lower-ing wages. This weakening of workers' power might reduce social unrest and thus bring about the conditions for slimming down and possibly even abolishing the welfare state.

Other Marxists explain the welfare state as necessary for capitalism. For example, as capitalism has developed, then the kind of workforce required has changed. New technology and the introduction of more flexible working patterns have resulted in the need for a better educated and more highly skilled workforce.

Such a workforce requires training and this is a cost to capitalists. The welfare state can thus be regarded as a mechanism which coerces the entire population to help fund those items which are beneficial to capitalist accumulation. The requirement for a literate workforce which is willing to comply with instructions from superiors is aided by a state education system which, in addition to teaching specific skills, also trains people to be deferential and competitive through what is known as the 'hidden curriculum'. Furthermore, workplace training represents yet another cost for capitalists which may not be so easily shared by the welfare state. Therefore, having trained workers, capitalists will want to maximise their investment by ensuring that staff do not take unnecessary time off through illness. Thus, the welfare state provides a health service. The National Health Service may be regarded as more efficient for capitalism, since it is cheaper for capitalists to spread the costs of health-care across the entire population rather than having company funded health schemes.

Another possible purpose of welfare, according to Marxist theory, is to maintain what is known as a *reserve army of labour*: groups of people who do not typically constitute part of the labour force other than in exceptional circumstances. Since capitalism is characterised by cyclical periods of expansion and then recession, the size of the workforce changes as people enter or leave the workforce. Other factors such as war will also affect the size and characteristics of the workforce. Thus, a section of the population is generally kept out of work, but they may be called upon to join the labour market when required. Through the payment of benefits to those who are out of work or to those with children, the welfare state serves capitalism by maintaining a group of people in society who are not usually expected to be an active part of the paid workforce, but who may be drafted in to paid work at relatively short notice. This group is usually composed of women carers, the unemployed and the disabled. This account is useful because it suggests that those who have historically received less-comprehensive or well-funded welfare services, such as the chronically sick, the elderly and those with mental illness, are treated less effectively because they are not usually active in the labour market.

A further Marxist perspective suggests that welfare constitutes social control. This perspective emphasises the role of the welfare state in 'policing' society. Welfare and allied state functions such as education, health services and the legal system are said to function to maintain certain norms, values and expectations of behaviour. The welfare state presents a partial and particular way of organising society. Living within capitalist society with its hierarchies, respect for authority, ownership and protection of private property, and even the protection of the heterosexual nuclear family, is shown as somehow normal and natural. Those who do not agree with or conform to such norms are castigated as deviants and may be punished. The unemployed and those others who form the reserve army of labour are treated harshly and serve as a reminder to those who are unhappy in their work of the consequences of not working.

Critiques of Marxist theories of the development of the welfare state point to a number of problems with the analysis. In the first place, arguments which suggest that welfare is the result of working-class struggle are perhaps focusing on the British welfare state too closely. The view that welfare is contingent on working-class struggle is problematic, since some countries which have seldom experienced extensive working-class unrest – Canada, for example – may still have a developed welfare state. Conversely, countries where class unrest has been extensive – such as Italy or Spain – may not have such a developed welfare state.

In addition, welfare is not only of benefit to the 'working class'. It is possible to argue that the welfare state could not have gained such popular approval were it not for middle-class perceptions that it has significant material benefits for them. The better off gain from welfare either because they tend to make more use of services or because they utilise the premium parts of those services. So, for example, with state education the middle classes are more likely to encourage their children to remain at school after the age of 16, which is the most expensive part of the education system. In the National Health Service, the middle classes are more likely to spend longer with doctors, be referred to the best hospital and consultants and make more extensive use of elective surgery, screening programmes and preventive health. Since higher occupational groups tend to live longer (Townsend and Davidson, 1992), the costs of providing state-funded retirement pensions to the middle classes far outweighs that which is paid to the poorest. Additionally, middle-class professional groups, such as social workers and the medical profession, have gained from the development of state welfare since they are provided with enhanced job opportunities for work which has become more secure and better paid. Marxists would counter that, since such people do not own the means of production, then many apparently middle-class people actually constitute a part of the working class. A further criticism of Marxist theories is that they generally fail to outline practical alternative welfare arrangements.

Marxists have also been criticised for being overly deterministic, that is for assuming that selected events are responsible for causing certain outcomes. Asserting that events took place, such as a prolonged working-class struggle, is not the same as actually demonstrating that such events took place. In fact British history has been comparatively free of working-class unrest. In addition, the connections between circumstance and possible consequences is not always clear. To argue that there is a causal link between, say, the development of welfare and the changing needs of capitalism is to ascribe outcomes to events without providing the necessary evidence. Using the mode of production to explain almost everything else is to ignore other important influences on social developments. Fiona Williams (1989) argues that questions of gender and race have been largely absent from Marxist analyses. An analysis of power relations in society, which essentially relies on class as a determinant, does not take account of the oppressive nature of patriarchy or racism and the way that these too are forceful components which influence the dominant relationships within society.

The predictive elements of Marx's theories have also been questioned. In particular the view that capitalism would eventually collapse under the strain of increasing tension within the relations of production is difficult to corroborate. The future that Marx and many of his followers foresaw may be regarded as utopian and has certainly not been realised in practice. It is difficult to demonstrate that people can sustain co-operative working and be free from acquisitive individualism. The notion that an entire social system can be predicated on goods and services being allocated to those who need them most might therefore be regarded as unrealistic. Marx did not appear to foresee either the ways in which capitalism itself would change, such as the development of welfare systems, nor did he predict the rise of a non-capital-owning middle class. Many companies are now managed by people who are not owners; institutions now own one another and have little influence on day-to-day running of businesses.

Nevertheless, Marxism is still a powerful theory which is helpful in shaping the way society is viewed. In particular, Marxism helps to account for the existence and persistence of conflict and inequality within society.

FABIAN THEORY

Fabian theory is perhaps one of the most important perspectives for considering social policy in modern Britain. This is because the emergence of social policy as a discrete field of study is closely connected with the work of early Fabians and the simultaneous development of the discipline of social administration. What was once commonly known as social administration broadened its scope and has become more popularly known as social policy.

The foundation of Fabian theories is the result of the influence of both liberalism and Marxism. Early Fabians rejected the Marxist theory of class struggle and the revolutionary overthrow of capitalism but supported increased equality through collective ownership and democratic control. Many Fabians were middle-class intellectuals who supported the liberal view that the market was the most effective way of distributing resources, but who also believed that the unrestrained market would lead to unacceptable inequality; therefore the market should be regulated. This combination of classical liberal economics tempered by a strong sense of moral duty aimed at alleviating poverty is known as 'reluctant collectivism'.

Fabian theory can be described as a socialist theory. However, socialism is not a single unifying theory, rather it has been variously interpreted. For Karl Marx and Friedrich Engels, socialism was the name applied to a period following the fall of capitalism and the onset of communism. By the end of the nineteenth century, Marxist socialism had become the dominant ideology of many working-class political parties. In Britain Fabians argued that their distinctive form of socialism

could regulate capitalism. The management of capitalism was regarded as important for both ethical and practical reasons. First, because capitalism exploits
workers and enables the wealthy to become richer while at the same time institu-
tionalising inequality. Second, capitalism can be regarded as inefficient since it
tends to work in cycles of boom and recession, and the latter is a waste of skills
and resources. Fabian socialism also opposed liberalism, particularly those
strands of liberalism which emphasised individualism and private rights at the
expense of co-operation and collective welfare.

The Fabian Society was a socialist educational association which was founded in
1884. The society was named after the Roman general Quintus Fabius Maximus
Cunctator whose combat tactics were said to be characterised by an unwillingness
to enter into decisive confrontational battles but rather to wear down an enemy
patiently, through the use of delaying tactics and small incremental victories. In
many ways this sums up the strategy employed by the Fabians. The most notable
early supporters of the Fabian Society included Beatrice Webb (1858–1943), her husband Sidney (1859–1947); social reformers such as Annie Besant (1847–1933), a prominent exponent of birth control; the authors and political commentators George
Bernard Shaw (1856–1950) and H. G. Wells (1866–1946) and the first future
Labour Prime Minister, Ramsay MacDonald (1866–1937). The Webbs were undoubtedly the driving force behind the Fabian Society. As Fiona Williams points out:

> Fabianism was characterised by its proposals for practical policies aimed at social
> problems. It developed the method of empirical social investigation into, for example,
> the failure of the free market to mitigate poverty, which formed the basis of pamphlets
> and reports which were used to lobby and influence government officials and politicians.
> Their objective was to move gradually to socialism through the state's reforms which
> would bring about good health and freedom from destitution for the working class.
> (Williams, 1989, p. 4)

Beatrice Webb became interested in socialism and social reform when she was
working as an assistant to Charles Booth in his important early work on poverty in
London. Later, in 1895, Beatrice and Sidney Webb helped to found the London
School of Economics (LSE). Staff and students who were associated with the
Department of Social Administration at the LSE were to have an important influence on government policies. Beatrice Webb also served on the Royal Commission
on the Poor Law (1905–09) which was established to enquire into the best remedies for poverty. She profoundly disagreed with the majority of the members of
the commission, who argued that charity and philanthropy should continue to
play an important part in the relief of poverty, and published a famous Minority
Report arguing that the state should assume increasing responsibility for welfare
and that specialist government departments should be established in order to deal
with poverty. One other notable achievement of the Webbs was the foundation of
the weekly journal *New Statesman* in 1913 which was to become a powerful voice
of the newly formed British Labour Party.

The Fabians tended to argue that the ideas and influence of prominent intellectuals were more important than material forces in determining historical social processes. Sidney Webb criticised Marxists for reducing complex social relations to a materialist basis and suggested that influencing public opinion rather than 'philosophical notions' would achieve major political advances: 'it is through the slow and gradual turning of the popular mind to new principles that social reorganisation bit by bit comes' (Webb and Webb, 1920, p. 66).

The chief characteristics of Fabianism was a belief that the state is politically neutral, with mainly administrative functions which could be utilised by any group that won an election. Fabians wanted to influence the government of the day through the presentation of objective facts and policy suggestions for social improvement. Fabians therefore emphasised that a gradualist programme of social reform could be achieved through social investigation and empiricism (eschewing theory, collecting facts and presenting evidence). The Fabians developed the systematic study of discrete social problems with the aim of proposing solutions. The Fabian approach accepted the basic conception of capitalism and supposed that greater collectivism and ultimately socialism could be achieved through parliamentary reform.

The influence of Fabianism on the labour movement in general and the British Labour Party in particular has been especially significant. The Fabian Society's contribution to the drafting of the post-Second World War settlement in Britain was considerable. Such post-war reform may be regarded as one of the most important periods of welfare reform.

Richard Titmuss (1907–73), a prominent Fabian academic, suggested that a combination of changes in social values took place during the war. The population's experience of total war during the 1940s affected welfare on three levels: popular attitudes to government intervention, the availability of information concerning social problems and government responses to such problems. Harris (1977, p. 247) points out that Titmuss:

> argued that the circumstances of the second world war created an unprecedented sense of social solidarity among the British people, which made them willing to accept a great increase of egalitarian policies and collective state action. [Titmuss] claimed that the impact of bombing and evacuation had dramatically exposed certain chronic social evils that had hitherto lain concealed from the public eye – problems like child poverty, malnutrition and the gross geographical imbalance of health and medical services that prevailed at the start of the war.

Following the war there was a determination not to return to the depression of the 1930s and with a population more used to centralised direction, post-war expectations were of higher living standards, collectivism and more interventionist governments. The evacuations forced many of the better off to come face to face with inner city poverty and deprivation, especially among children. Indeed, welfare services were consolidated during the war for pregnant women and children. Conscription into the armed services affected all strata of society and within the armed forces there was more social mixing than had previously been the case. The Labour Party, committed since 1934 to a national free medical service, had been an important part of the wartime coalition government and had experienced ministers who were particularly involved in domestic affairs. Finally, the Beveridge Report on Social Insurance and Allied Services, published in 1942 (Cmnd 6404), quickly became one of the most important and widely read documents concerning post-war reconstruction.

Although Beveridge was not a Fabian, or even a socialist, his administrative and civil service background place his aspirations and his proposals very much within the tradition of a 'reluctant collectivist'. Beveridge was asked to prepare a policy document suggesting reforms and unification of the national insurance system. Beveridge included many ideas about a future welfare state, concentrating on three main policy objectives – 'prevention rather than cure', 'education of those not yet accustomed to clean careful ways of life', and 'plotting the future as a gradual millennium taking step after step but not flinching on ultimate goals' (Beveridge, 1942, cited in Harris, 1977, p. 74).

The Beveridge Report was written in populist and extravagant language; Beveridge argued that the state should attack what he termed the 'Five Giants on the road to recovery' namely: want, ignorance, idleness, sickness and squalor. Labour were trusted to implement Beveridge's proposals more than the Conservatives and this may help to explain Labour's victory in 1945. The Fabian influence on politics was therefore at its most powerful after the May 1945 general election, when more than half of the parliamentary Labour Party were members of the Fabian Society. In the government itself there were a large number of Fabians, including Clement Attlee, the Prime Minister, and nine other Cabinet Ministers. By 1948, the welfare state in more or less its present guise had been established. The Conservative Education Act in 1944 was followed by a series of achievements which seemed to many at that time to be almost revolutionary. The Labour government under Attlee acted on the Fabian principles of incremental changes regulating the market economy. In addition, the government was committed to managing the economy according to the principles of John Maynard Keynes (1883–1946). Keynes advocated high government borrowing in order to fund public spending on such activities as job creation during periods of economic recession which could then be repaid through increased tax receipts once recession was over. The main post-war changes included comprehensive national insurance and national assistance; a new system of family allowances; higher universal pensions; industrial injuries compensation and the creation of the National Health Service. In addition the Bank of England was nationalised along with the coal, electricity, gas and railway industries. In 1951 the Conservative Party won the general election; but by this time the Conservatives were largely committed to the welfare state. There followed a period known as the 'Butskellite consensus' (named after the respective Conservative and Labour leaders, Butler and Gaitskell), in which both Conservative and Labour governments, with a commitment to the welfare state, apparently shared a belief that society should collectively provide for vulnerable groups.

During the 1950s and into the 1960s it was widely assumed that, through the combined effects of economic growth, Keynesian fiscal policies to ensure high and stable levels of employment and the welfare state, poverty had all but been abolished. Indeed, a Labour Cabinet Minister felt able to write that the 'Fabian blueprints for social welfare, redistributive taxation, nationalisation and national minima' now formed 'part of the law of the land' (Crossman, 1952, pp. x, 1–2). The remaining task for Fabians was to defend the gains that had been made and solve any technical or administrative problems. However, further empirical evidence gathered during the 1950s and 1960s demonstrated that poverty and inequity persisted after the inception of the welfare state. This rediscovery of poverty was primarily undertaken by those associated with or sympathetic to the Fabian Society; see, for example, Titmuss (1962), Coates and Silburn (1970), Townsend (1979), Black Report (1980), Goldthorpe (1980), Halsey (1980), Field (1981) and Le Grand (1982).

Many Fabians realised that the post-war Labour government had not achieved nearly as much as had been hoped and the belief that a narrow conceptualisation of the welfare state was sufficient was criticised. The importance of other agencies in determining economic advantages and disbenefits became crucial to the Fabian analysis of the failure of welfare. Thus, for example, Titmuss (1958) identified two additional forms of welfare: occupational welfare, which referred to benefits provided to those in certain types of work, and fiscal welfare, which referred to tax advantages. Both of these systems benefited the better off more than the less well off. Bosanquet and Townsend (1972) later widened the notion of welfare to include not only health, education, housing and social security but also benefits from employment, unearned income, ownership of wealth and benefits from fiscal policies. Frank Field (1981) argued that the redistributive effects of post-war government activities were reversed by other forms of state action and inaction. Field identified five different 'welfare' states: the 'traditional benefit welfare state', the 'tax allowance welfare state', the 'company' and 'private market' welfare states and 'the welfare state resulting from unearned income'. Taken overall, the cumulative redistributive effects of the welfare state were outdone by these other systems, confounding attempts to move towards greater equality.

After 1979, the so-called post-war welfare consensus was over. The Conservative government was characterised by a belief that inequality was inevitable and in certain circumstances desirable, since it might act as a device for encouraging individuals to better themselves. The welfare state was regarded as too extensive, costly and bureaucratic. The answer was to 'roll back' the welfare state and encourage more private provision (see chapter 9). The Fabian Society was active in defence of state-provided welfare as well as in continuing to influence Labour's welfare and fiscal policies.

The Fabian tradition has been criticised, especially by Marxists, Feminists and those on the Right. Marx and Engels criticised 'bourgeois socialism', of whom the Fabians might be said to form a part. Such socialists failed to challenge structural inequalities and merely sought to provide a nostrum to capitalism through limited social reform. Marxists argue that such piecemeal changes could never fundamentally alter the balance of power and inequality in society. In fact, social reform might actually have the effect of 'prolonging the life of the capitalist social order and blunting the edge of the revolutionary propensities of the working class' (Mishra, 1975, pp. 293–5). The belief in enlightened and neutral administrators working to accomplish the policies of the government is regarded as rather naive and idealist. The bureaucracy of government is often regarded as obstructive and self-interested. More fundamentally, a faith in the possibility that government policies might be translated into real positive changes for the least well off has been seriously questioned. For feminists, the Fabian obsession with incremental change in discrete areas tended to obscure any analysis of power and the ability of the powerful to thwart attempts by a government inclined towards greater equality or redistribution. In particular, the early Fabians failed to question the patriarchal nature of society and gender inequality persisted in the assumptions about the work and caring roles that men and women had, and this was seen as an important omission.

CONCLUSION

These three theoretical strands – Liberalism, Marxism and Fabian theories – are key approaches to the analysis of society and the way individuals should interact. The approaches are summed up in table 8.1.

Table 8.1 Comparison of liberalism, Marxism and Fabian theories

	Nature of human interaction	Society should be characterised by
Liberalism	individualism	markets and competition
Marxism	class conflict	central planning and direction
Fabianism	co-operation/reluctant collectivism	an acceptance of the market and competition but also a recognition that state planning should be utilised to move towards a fairer society.

These theories' approach to the analysis of welfare which have been discussed over a considerable time period, in comparison with those discussed in the next chapter. Each of these three approaches has been developed over time, particularly in response to changing social and economic structures, and new imperatives. Liberal philosophy, for example, has been developed by some feminist writers in a strand of right-wing feminist theory which shares much of the original thinking of classic liberalism (Williams, 1989). Similarly, Marxist theory has developed, as discussed here, to incorporate ideas about welfare and the welfare state, whilst Marxist feminism and socialist feminism developed in the attempt to produce an analysis which could explain women's specific position in the labour market and in the home. Chapter 9 will explore some of the more recent directions in social policy analysis.

REFERENCES

Barnett, C. (1986) *The Audit of War: The illusion and reality of Britain as a great nation*, London: Macmillan.

Beveridge, W. (1942) 'Social Insurance and Allied Services', Cmnd 6550, London: HMSO.

Bosanquet, N. and Townsend, P. (1972) *Labour and Inequality: Sixteen Fabian essays*, London: Fabian Society.

Coates, K. and Silburn, R. (1970) *Poverty: The forgotten Englishman*, Harmondsworth: Penguin.

Crossman, R. H. S. (ed.) (1952) *New Fabian Essays*, London: Turnstile Press.

Field, F. (1981) *Inequalities in Britain: Freedom and the welfare state*, London: Fontana.

Forder, A., Caslin, T., Ponton, G. and Walklate, S. (1984) *Theories of Welfare*, London: Routledge & Kegan Paul.

Friedman, M. and Friedman, R. (1980) *Free to Choose*, London: Secker & Warburg.

George, V. and Wilding, P. (1985) *Ideology and Social Welfare*, London: Routledge & Kegan Paul.

Giddens, A. (1971) *Capitalism and Modern Social Theory: An analysis of the writings of Marx, Durkheim and Max Weber*, Cambridge: Cambridge University Press.

Goldthorpe, J. (1980) *Social Mobility and the Class Structure in Modern Britain*, Oxford: Clarendon Press.

Gough, I. (1979) *The Political Economy of the Welfare State*, London: Macmillan.

Halsey, A. H. (1981) *Change in British Society*, Oxford, Oxford University Press.

Harris, J. (1977) *William Beveridge: A biography*, Oxford: Clarendon Press.

Hayek, F. A. (1960) *The Constitution of Liberty*, London: Routledge & Kegan Paul.

Hennessy, P. (1992) *Never Again*, London: Jonathan Cape.

Le Grand, J. (1982) *The Strategy of Equality: Redistribution and the Social Services*, London: Allen & Unwin.

Malthus, T. (1983) *An Essay on the Principle of Population*, London: Penguin.

McLellan, D. (1986) *Marx*, London: Fontana Press.

Mill, J. S. (1910) *On Liberty*, London: Everyman. (Reprinted (1996) as a single volume also containing the texts *Utilitarianism and Considerations on Representative Government*.)

Mishra, R. (1985) 'Marx and Welfare', *Sociological Review*, 23(2): 287–313.

Muller, J. Z. (1993) *Adam Smith in His Time and Ours*, New York: Free Press.

Novak, M. (1991) *The Spirit of Democratic Capitalism*, London: IEA Health and Welfare Unit.

Rousseau, J. J. (ed.) (1993) *The Social Contract and the Discourses*, Trans. G. D. H. Cole, London: Everyman's Library.

Smith, A. (1991) *An Inquiry into the Causes of the Wealth of Nations*, London: Everyman's Library.

Titmuss, R. (1958) *Essays on the Welfare State*, London: Allen & Unwin.

Titmuss, R. M. (1962) *Income Distribution and Social Change: A study in criticism*, London: Allen & Unwin.

Townsend, P. (1979) *Poverty in the United Kingdom*, Harmondsworth: Penguin.

Townsend, P. and Davidson, N. (1992) *Inequalities in Health: the Black Report and the Health Divide*, London: Penguin.

Webb, S. and Webb, B. (1920) *Constitution for the Socialist Commonwealth of Great Britain*, London: Longman Green.

Williams, F. (1989) *Social Policy: A critical introduction*, Cambridge: Polity Press.

Working Group on Inequalities in Health (1980) *Inequalities in Health: Report of the Research Working Group on Inequalities in Health: Chairman Sir Douglas Black*, London: Department for Health and Social Security. (The Black Report.)

Wright, A. (1996) *Socialisms: Old and new*, London: Routledge.

ANNOTATED READINGS

Lengthier and comparative discussions of the three theoretical positions outlined in this chapter may be found in George and Wilding's *Ideology and Social Welfare* and more recently in Lavalette and Pratt's *Social Policy: A Conceptual and Theoretical Introduction*, both of which also discuss the positions discussed in chapter 9. A more detailed exposition of classical liberal ideas can be found in the writings of John Stuart Mill and Adam Smith, while further discussion of Marxist approaches to the welfare state may be found in Ian Gough's *Political Economy of the Welfare State* and a very readable discussion in Wright's *Socialisms: Old and New*. Fabian expositions of the welfare state are perhaps less easily found today but readers can refer back to Richard Crossman's *New Fabian Essays*.

9 Contemporary theoretical perspectives

by Judith Carlson

OBJECTIVES

■ To consider the radical (or neo-liberal) critique of the classical welfare state, its political success in the 1980s and 1990s and its impact on British social policy.

■ To explore the radical critiques of welfare presented by feminist, anti-racist and post-modern writers and the variety of strands of thought within each of these radical critiques.

INTRODUCTION

The preceding chapter focused on a series of well-established theoretical strands in social policy. This next chapter concentrates on more recent theoretical interventions, some of which build upon established bodies of theory. For example, the New Right draws heavily on classical liberalism. Other perspectives, including feminism, anti-racism and postmodernism, are more innovative and might be better characterised as offering a series of radical critiques of existing theory and practice.

This chapter uses broadly the same approach to analysing theory as that encountered in chapter 8. Each theory is introduced in relation to its historical context. This is followed by a review of the key theoretical claims made in relation to the welfare state. Then we proceed to an analysis and evaluation of the prescriptions put forward for social policy. The chapter begins with the New Right and moves on to consider feminist, anti-racist and postmodern interventions in welfare theory.

'NEW RIGHT' THEORIES

Theoretical perspectives identified with the New Right have a long heritage in liberal and conservative traditions of political theory. Some of this material was reviewed in chapter 8. What is new about the New Right is its association with the critique of the post-war welfare state, through the work of Hayek, Friedman and a variety of right-wing think-tanks. Much of the New Right critique of the welfare state emphasised the values of monetarism over Keynesianism. But the debate was rather abstract and failed to capture the public imagination until the crisis years of the 1970s. New Right perspectives are largely normative and prescriptive: there is little interest in the question of how welfare states arise and whose interests they serve, instead the emphasis is on an analysis of the damage which it is claimed welfare states do to the individual and to the economy and on providing a vision of an alternative utopia. Typologies of the New Right usually identify two theoretical strands: neo-liberalism and neo-conservatism.

Neo-liberals see the redistributive welfare state as mainly an economic problem which has a negative impact both at the micro-level of individual economic incentives and at the macro-level in the effect on the economy as a whole.

At the micro-level, the high levels of personal and corporate taxation associated with redistributive approaches to welfare are said to reduce individual incentives to work and invest, because the gains to be made from hard work and risk-taking are diminished. Wealth creation is thus stifled leading to economic stagnation. In contrast, if the wealth creators are set free, wider advantages in the form of 'trickle down' will benefit the population at large. At the other end of the social scale, redistribution damages incentives by taking the edge off poverty, because the welfare state uses need instead of desert (what people deserve to get) as the primary criteria for allocating benefits.

At the macro-level, Keynesian demand management is seen as inflationary. Keynesians seek to manipulate demand in order to secure full employment. Demand can be injected into the economy by running budget deficits to fund an expansion of public expenditure and through the relaxation of interest rates and consumer credit controls to promote more spending by individual consumers. Keynes assumed that the inflationary pressures created by this could be kept under control through surplus budgeting in good years. Neo-liberals see this as naive because it means cutting back government programmes during boom years and would be electorally unpopular (Mishra, 1984). They further argue that electoral politics is an unsuitable arena for making decisions about distributive justice because politicians subject to electoral pressures are likely to spend public money in irresponsible ways. This means that the interests of the powerful and articulate are more likely to be served than those of the needy and explains why the middle classes have done so well out of the welfare state. In contrast, markets are seen as impartial, not subject to 'conscious social control' or capture by particular interest groups, and as the best way of co-ordinating human activity and reconciling individual interests without resort to coercion (Hayek, 1944). Market provision is also seen as directly accountable to its clients and more responsive to their needs and preferences, so it is superior in quality to public sector services.

Neo-conservatives argue that the welfare problem is not primarily economic but moral. They complain that individuals never have to deal with the consequences of their actions: they are cushioned by the idea that their problems derive from social causes rather than from inappropriate behaviour on their own part; and the state always steps in to pick up the pieces when things do go wrong. The welfare state is dubbed the 'nanny' state because it infantilises its clients and encourages irresponsibility. Welfare is said to create 'perverse incentives': instead of compensating misfortune as it was designed to do, it actually produces needs which could otherwise have been avoided. This is termed 'avoidable dependency' (Harris, 1988).

These theories have various implications for welfare provision. The neo-liberal utopia is arrived at by allowing material incentives full play, and by the application of free market principles in social policy. The emphasis is upon privatisation, deregulation and the introduction of quasi-markets in the public sector. Consumerism is increased by reducing taxes, which enables people to finance their own welfare provision, and by the introduction of vouchers which enable individuals to buy goods and services from the provider of their choice instead of being forced to use state services (Friedman, 1962; Friedman and Friedman, 1980). This is designed to create consumer sovereignty, forcing providers to offer good quality services which respond to customer choice.

Neo-conservatives treat poverty and unemployment as moral problems and propose a system of conditional benefits which specifically exclude the relief of 'avoidable dependency' by applying only to needs considered to be outside of personal control. For example, unmarried mothers and those producing large families when they cannot support them financially would be forced to suffer the economic consequences of their actions (Minford, 1991). Neo-conservatives have been preoccupied with the impact of the welfare state on the family. Their solution is to reinforce the breadwinner role of the father (Morgan, 1986). Within marriage this is achieved by undermining sources of women's financial independence such as child benefit, maternal employment and equal pay legislation. Outside marriage the emphasis is on enforcing parental responsibility, as in the 1991 Child Support Act.

Neo-conservatives have also called for a return to the local and judgmental forms of relief which had their zenith in the Victorian Poor Law. Neo-conservatives seek the remoralisation of society through social policy. A locally based or parochial approach to poor relief is considered superior to the crude and inaccurate rules which centralised state systems adopt in giving help to their clients. The parochial system offers a personalised approach in which the poor become accountable to local taxpayers and philanthropists and subject to close scrutiny. Benefits in kind are viewed favourably because they are stigmatising and unpopular and hence 'less-eligible'. Preferred providers are family, neighbourhood, community, private self-provision and charitable agencies, all of which are populated by active citizens.

CRITIQUE OF NEW RIGHT THEORY

If we evaluate the New Right policy prescriptions on the basis of their own value parameters and expectations, we would have to say that the practical results of following New Right policies have been disappointing. The deregulation of bus services is a case in point: while there has been duplication of services on profitable routes, many non-profitable routes have lost their bus services altogether. Where are the benefits to consumers here? Moreover, while there has indeed been an increase in inequality in Britain during the 1980s, trickle-down effects have not materialised. Instead the poor were poorer at the end of the decade in absolute as well as in relative terms (Townsend, 1993a). The degree of polarisation which has been seen in Britain and America in recent years has attracted much critical scrutiny. It has been seen as a direct and harmful consequence of following neo-liberal policies. The end result is an abandoned and increasingly disaffected underclass, an insecure middle class which can no longer rely upon the welfare safety net in times of need and a new overclass which has quite literally opted out of society by buying full portfolios of private insurance provision and electing to live in gated communities which may have their own tax-raising and law-making powers. Hutton (1996) coined the term 'thirty, thirty, forty society' to describe the emerging social divisions between the 30 per cent disadvantaged, the 30 per cent marginalised and insecure and the 40 per cent who are privileged.

Clearly the New Right have underestimated the problems of integration in a market society and failed to recognise the cohesive and supportive functions of welfarism. This has not escaped the attention of right-wing social theorists and political activists and has led to the emergence of communal liberalism. Communal liberals (e.g. Davies, 1991; Gray, 1992; Willetts, 1992; Green, 1993) insist upon a mixed economy of welfare based on a combination of civic virtue, the social market and the enabling welfare state. While the preference is for volun-tarism and the market there is no blind faith in their ability to deliver welfare in the absence of state intervention. Thus voluntary action may be supported by state funding and markets must be embedded in broader social and political institutions in order to ensure that they are never permitted to operate in anti-social ways. In addition the welfare state would itself have a role to play – but only where the resources of civil society proved inadequate to the task. This communitarian approach has much in common with New Labour's approach to social policy.

The individualist methodology adopted in New Right perspectives entails a blank refusal to consider the impact of structural factors upon the actions of human subjects. Indeed, New Right policy prescriptions are inherently racist and sexist because they eschew redistribution and act instead to reproduce existing inequalities and increase polarisation between social groups. In addition to this, the gendered implications of New Right policies have become increasingly apparent in expectations that women are willing and able to provide care in families and in the voluntary sector. Yet the active citizen of the New Right appears to be gender neutral.

Anti-democratic tendencies are apparent in both neo-liberal and neo-conservative strands of the New Right. These tendencies stem from a critique of the idea that the state is a neutral arbiter of competing interests. For the New Right, the state is partial and corrupt while the market, with its 'hidden hand', impartially adjudicates and distributes on the basis of desert (what people deserve to get). For neo-liberals in particular, the market therefore epitomises the democratic process.

FEMINIST THEORIES OF WELFARE

This section focuses on five contemporary strands of feminism. While there are clear differences between them, what unites them and makes them feminist is that they all draw attention to gender as a key social division. All seek to describe and account for women's current position as an oppressed social group and prescribe strategies for change. There are two key themes in feminist debates on the welfare state. First, the welfare state is something of a paradox for feminists: it can provide women with opportunities and help to redress existing inequalities but it can also act to control women, reinforcing their existing social roles and status either by design or by default. So welfare states can be seen as systems of stratification which can act to reinforce or undermine gender hierarchies (Orloff, 1993). Secondly, there has been a major tension in feminist theory and practice over equality and difference – both of which are now widely seen as problematic.

Liberal feminists have not really engaged in an analysis of the organisation of welfare and hence have not produced an account of how welfare states come about and whose interests they serve. However, these themes are implicit in Liberal feminist attitudes towards the state. These are based on the liberal pluralist model which, in its classical form, holds that the state is a neutral arbiter of competing interests. Liberal feminists may in fact concede that historically the state has tended to represent male interests but believe that it is open to infiltration by women and that once women have achieved an adequate level of representation within the state, then prevailing prejudices will change.

Liberal feminists argue that women and men are fundamentally similar, and that biological differences have no significant implications for ability and can be easily mitigated via enlightened approaches to childcare policy. Strategies rest upon women's incorporation into existing frameworks for civil, political and social rights of citizenship. Since these are based on public participation the emphasis is upon encouraging women to engage in paid employment and other forms of public participation. There have been two key approaches to achieving this. First, there have been attempts to alter the statutory framework to secure formal equality for women under the law such as the 1970 Equal Pay Act and 1975 Sex Discrimination Act. These are rights-based strategies which make use of the law to correct gender inequalities and facilitate social justice based upon desert (what people deserve to get). Secondly, because of the belief

Exhibit 9.1

> ### 'Radical' and 'radical'
> Readers should note that where the first letter of the word 'radical' is capitalised this is a
> reference to a specific strand of feminism and should not be confused with the wider usage of
> the word as the antithesis of conservative.

that negative attitudes towards women are based upon irrational prejudices, there have been attempts to change social attitudes through equal opportunities awareness training.

Radical feminism diverges from liberal feminism in several important respects. First, men and women are effectively identified as separate classes whose interests conflict. Power is distributed along patriarchal lines with men acting as the oppressors of women. The welfare state is a bastion of male power which reflects the patriarchal nature of society and functions to control women. Secondly, claims about women's unique qualities explicitly underpin much Radical feminist thought. Radical feminists have challenged the desirability of equality, arguing that this rests upon women's assimilation to an aggressive and competitive male culture. Radical feminists insist upon an essentialist politics of difference which accords a positive value to the feminine. Women's reproductive biology is seen as the source of unique feminine qualities of nurturance, non-violence and connectedness summed up by Ruddick (1980) as a capacity for 'maternal thinking'. Thirdly, Radical feminism has been identified with the assertion that 'the personal is political' – one of the most distinctive contributions which feminism has made to political and social theory. This slogan seeks to capture the links between interpersonal relations in the domestic sphere (for example, the division of labour in relation to parenting, housework and the provision of informal care) and the positions of men and women in relation to employment and formal political participation. It challenges orthodox assumptions in political theory that there is a strict dichotomy between public and private spheres, with only the former being recognised as an authentic political domain. Radical feminists insist upon a politics of everyday life in which even the most intimate personal interactions are recognised as political.

Exhibit 9.2

> ### Attitudes towards gender difference and social policy
>
> | Significance of gender | Strategy for gender and social policy | |
> | --- | --- | --- |
> | Liberal feminism | minimal significance | redress/compensate |
> | Radical feminism | biological and irreducible | source of feminine ethics for separatism |
> | Socialist feminism | socially constructed | redress/compensate |
> | Postmodern feminism | socially constructed | deconstruction |

Radical feminists have been especially interested in the private sphere and the ways in which the state intervenes to control women's sexuality and reproductive biology. The first of these themes is addressed by the concept of 'compulsory heterosexuality' (Rich, 1980), which claims that women's sexuality and bodily autonomy are effectively restricted by the state. Heterosexuality and monogamy are made compulsory through the use of sanctions like refusing or revoking maternal custody in cases involving lesbian mothers or where the wife has committed adultery (Smart, 1984; Rights of Women Lesbian Custody Group, 1986). The state's failure to intervene in the private sphere in cases of sexual and physical violence, which leaves women with no alternative to staying in a violent relationship, also bolsters male power within the family (MacKinnon, 1983; Stanko, 1985).

The second theme focuses on the medicalisation of childbirth and the development of reproductive technologies which are viewed as manifestations of 'womb envy' leading men to try and take control of reproduction out of the hands of women (Kittay, 1984; Corea, 1988). The Feminist International Network Against Reproductive and Genetic Engineering (FINNRAGE) which was set up in 1984 has drawn attention to the harmful implications of reproductive technology, and has opposed the expropriation of the female body as raw material for the technological production of human beings (Corea, 1988).

Because they see the welfare state as patriarchal, Radical feminists believe that it lacks any potential for undermining existing gender hierarchies and are emphatically anti-statist. In place of state intervention, they stress the importance of self-directed, non-hierarchical provision: Radical feminists were pivotal in the emergence of the refuge movement in the early 1970s and have been instrumental in the setting up of well-woman clinics, women's health centres and rape crisis counselling services. There has been much stress upon women's reproductive health and the importance of women acquiring information and knowledge about their own bodies (for example, Boston Women's Health Collective 1971/8).

Socialist feminism has been informed by, and has in turn informed, Marxist theories of the state. Socialist feminists have put forward a dual systems theory in which women's position in society is believed to be jointly determined by the twin systems of production and reproduction, or capitalism and patriarchy (Mitchell, 1971; Eisenstein, 1979; Hartmann, 1979). Within this dual system there is a tension between women's role as workers and their role as carers. It is the competing pull of capitalism and patriarchy upon the state which accounts for such contradictions. This theoretical approach emphasises the macro-social factors shaping welfare policies.

Although the welfare state has been seen as contradictory in the sense of, in that it embodies the interests of the working class, gained through struggle (O'Connor, 1973; Gough, 1979; Offe, 1984), it also has different effects on men and on women. Clearly the welfare state sometimes does support patriarchal power relations, when it withholds opportunities for women to live outside the nuclear family through its arrangements for the distribution of social housing and social security (Orloff, 1993; O'Connor, 1993). However, the welfare state also at times makes it possible for women to live outside traditional families. Indeed, Scandinavian feminists have not tended to think of welfare states as a constraint upon women but have concentrated on exploring their 'woman friendly' dimensions.

Socialist feminists emphasise the role of the welfare state in structuring the reproductive sphere and in promoting a particular family form based on the assumption of a male breadwinner with a dependent wife. This empowers men within the family because the welfare of other family members rests upon men's benevolence. Socialist feminists have highlighted the potential consequences for women and children where resources are not shared fairly within the household (Pahl, 1989). So, like Radical feminism, this strand points to the political nature of inter-personal relations in the private sphere. But it diverges significantly from Radical feminism in its insistence that it is social arrangements, not biology, which gives rise to gender differences. This is not to deny that there are any biological differences between men and women, but to insist that the significance given to those differences is socially constructed and undesirable, creating inequality.

Socialist feminist strategies look simultaneously to the spheres of production and reproduction although, like liberal feminists, they tend to emphasise the public or productive sphere and equality. However, socialist feminists try to resolve the problem of material differences between men and women by stressing the importance of the socialisation of domestic labour and childcare as preconditions for women's entry into the public sphere. Greater attention has also been paid to inequalities in interpersonal relations and the importance of restructuring welfare in ways which no longer underpin female dependency and a traditional sexual division of labour (MacIntosh, 1981). To be 'woman friendly', welfare states must offer women alternatives to dependence upon men within the family. This would include a right to paid employment and a right to form autonomous households, adequately supported by state benefits. The state must also stop expecting women to undertake unpaid care work on behalf of other family members and encourage men to take equal responsibility for unpaid work done in the domestic sphere. Without this women's financial independence can only be bought at the cost of increasing time poverty (Orloff, 1993).

The identification of *black feminism* as a coherent theoretical strand (e.g. Williams, 1989; Mama, 1992) rests upon a shared critique advanced within the work of black feminists in respect of the arguments and strategies adopted by mainstream white-dominated feminism. Black feminists point out that black women's experiences of the welfare state are structured by 'race' as well as gender and frequently differ in important ways from white women's experiences. A key manifestation of this can be seen in the arena of reproductive rights. Second wave feminists campaigned vigorously for the extension and protection of abortion rights. But their campaign was largely irrelevant to black and third world women who were more likely to find their reproductive freedom compromised by anti-natalist sanctions such as coerced abortion and sterilisation. Black and third world feminist insights on reproductive freedom have been significant in redirecting feminist campaigns from abortion to reproductive rights and have served to put the issue of anti-natalism and sterilisation abuse firmly on the international human rights agenda.

White feminists have also concentrated critical attention on the family as a source of women's oppression requiring redress through state intervention. Black feminists have not rejected these claims but point to the significance of the family as a site of resistance in struggles against racism – struggles in which the state is often the perpetrator. It has thus become apparent that it is important to maintain a sphere of life in which the state's authority is limited. However this sphere must incorporate guarantees of justice and equality and must ensure that vulnerable members are fully protected from abuse (see Okin, 1989).

A third area of criticism has involved white feminist campaigns against sexual violence which have sometimes included calls for increased policing in areas which coincide with high levels of black residence. Given black communities' negative experiences of policing, this can clearly be seen as an insensitive strategy. There is even evidence that police responses to domestic violence within black communities have been used as opportunities to carry out immigration inquiries (Mama, 1989a, b). This is a common experience faced by black people coming into contact with welfare services and it increases reluctance to use them. It is especially harmful in the case of domestic violence as any victim fearing deportation may be discouraged from seeking assistance.

Since black women are more likely than white women to experience the welfare state as repressive rather than enabling, many black feminist strategies rest upon protest, resistance and the creation of autonomous provision. For example, the 'No Pass Laws to Health Campaign' opposed NHS practice of handing injured black patients on to the police, while autonomous refuge provision has been set up to assist Asian women escaping domestic violence. While to date there has been a tendency towards anti-statism, future developments in the direction of anti-racist feminist prescriptions for the welfare state are anticipated (Tang Nain, 1991; Mama, 1992).

The critical interventions of black and third world feminists have been an important impetus behind the development of *postmodernist feminism*. Not all black and third world feminists are postmodernists, but postmodernism has provided a helpful framework for raising questions about the inclusiveness of existing approaches and has supplied many feminists with a channel to express their dissatisfaction with the theoretical and strategic frameworks offered by existing feminist theories. Criticisms have been directed at feminist tendencies to use a universal category 'Woman' and insist that all women have shared interests. This approach obscures important differences between women, making feminism a movement of white middle-class women, falsely claiming to represent the interests of their black and third world 'sisters' when they had little knowledge of their experiences.

For postmodern feminists 'the state' has a very particular meaning. Postmodern feminists adopt an ascending analysis of power, claiming that power always comes from the bottom up and that 'the state' lacks sovereign power. This means that 'the state' is not a separate entity which sits at the top of the social hierarchy imposing its power on civil society from the top down, rather it is an effect or by-product of the power relations and political struggles which pervade civil society. The particular set of policies which constitute 'the state' will depend upon which of those struggles is dominant at any particular historical moment (Allen, 1990; Pringle and Watson, 1992). This means that it is quite possible for 'the state' to operate as if it were capitalist or patriarchal but that it is also open to challenge by feminists. Postmodern feminists claim that 'the state' can be changed for the better if we engage in a project of radical democracy (Laclau and Mouffe, 1985) which builds an alliance between various groups of women and recognises a plurality of interests rather than a singular set of 'women's interests'. In this way difference is no longer seen in binary terms as masculine or feminine but is pluralised as differences. These differences are seen as socially constructed rather than biologically determined and, while existing constructions of differences may mean that they are allied with inequality, they can be deconstructed and remade in ways which promote equity without undermining diversity. Welfare states have a major part to play in this process of reconstruction.

CRITIQUES AND ASSESSMENT

Liberal feminism has been challenged on normative, methodological and empirical grounds. Its emphasis on desert (what people deserve to get) as the criteria for social justice is insufficiently radical, and empirical evidence shows that it has done little to challenge the substantive material inequalities between men and women. Indeed it may have exacerbated them. The Equal Pay Act did produce a once and for all narrowing of the gap between men and women's pay, but women's average weekly earnings are still less than three quarters of those received by men (*Social Trends* 24, table 5.5). It has also become apparent that women's increased participation in the public sphere has not been matched by changing roles for men in the private sphere, and women are now faced with a double burden of productive and reproductive labour. So the liberal feminist strategy, far from liberating women, actually brings them additional burdens and has led to a significant increase in time-poverty amongst women. The liberal feminist commitment to individualism also seriously underestimates the differences in power between men and women and between different groups of women, which means that it tends to be white middle-class women who benefit most. In other words liberal feminist strategies give some women the opportunity to compete on a more level playing field with some men. A related criticism focuses on liberal feminism's politics of representation: liberal feminists argue that by increasing the number of women in the public sphere, women's interests will automatically be served. This assumes a common set of 'women's interests' and overlooks the impact of other social divisions, particularly 'race' and social class. There is in fact no guarantee that a female MP would represent 'women's interests'. There is also a tendency to assume that women have special insights to bring to the public sphere which will help redress its competitive masculine orientation. Clearly some form of essentialism based on innate biological differences is slipping back in here and this contradicts liberal feminists' insistence that men and women are fundamentally similar (Phillips, 1991).

Radical feminism has been challenged for its functionalist view of the patriarchal state and its biological reductionism. Because Radical feminists perceive difference as immutable their strategies are highly utopian and problematic: reform of patriarchal society is perceived as impossible and undesirable, leaving political and personal separatism as the only solutions. But are these solutions sustainable or, indeed, desirable? *Socialist feminism* has also been described as functionalist (the state is patriarchal capitalist) but recent developments within this strand have sought to redress this problem by recognising the potential for 'woman friendly' policies. There are parallels here with both liberal and postmodern feminists' recognition that the state is open to challenge by feminists. *Black, third world and postmodern feminists* have helped to pull feminism out of the equality versus difference impasse and provide it with a new strategic model based on a recognition of multiple differences and the importance of equity.

ANTI-RACIST CRITIQUES

In Britain, anti-racist critiques have largely arisen from a recognition of the inferior social citizenship rights awarded to immigrant groups – particularly those coming from new Commonwealth countries during the post-war period – and subsequent struggles for equal rights of social citizenship. However, it is important not to reduce the study of 'race' and racism to a discussion of post-war immigrants: in some countries this can obscure the experiences of earlier migrant groups (for example, Irish people in Britain) as well as the indigenous minority (for example, Aborigines and Native Americans) or majority groups (for example, Black South Africans).

In order to devise appropriate strategies to combat racism it is useful to distinguish some of its key manifestations. Ginsburg (1992a) identifies three modes of racism: subjective, institutional and structural. Subjective racism is explained in terms of individual prejudice, although this may be influenced by structural factors, particularly competition for scarce employment and other resources. Institutional racism can refer to explicit and intentional modes of exclusion, or to *de facto* outcomes of institutional procedures based upon the stereotyping of minority groups and a failure to recognise particular needs. Institutional racism is not adequately explained by the individual prejudice of those responsible for service delivery, although where a significant degree of discretion is built into institutional procedures, subjective racism can be a compounding factor. Structural racism refers to the indirect consequences of national and international policies and processes, such as immigration policy and housing policy and socio-structural factors, for example, the national and international division of labour. The residualisation of local authority housing can be seen as an example of structural racism because it has caused disproportionate disadvantage to some minority groups in Britain and has reinforced the inequalities created by 30 years of institutionally racist allocation policies (Ginsburg, 1992b). Racism is a complex process: all three modes are present throughout the policy-making process and all three must therefore be targeted by anti-racist strategies. This requires intervention at a variety of levels so perspectives which emphasise any one type of racism at the expense of the other two are likely to be flawed.

Anti-racist theoretical perspectives on the welfare state in Britain developed in close alignment with sociological theories on 'race' and racism, often drawing on the sociology of race relations which originated in the United States in the work of the Chicago School (1920s–1950s). Much of this work assumed that race relations were types of social relations which prevailed between persons with different physical and cultural characteristics. The Chicago School argued that a process occurred in which race relations could be expected to shift over time from contact and conflict to accommodation and assimilation (Solomos, 1989). The promotion of good race relations was thought to rest on mediating conflict in the early stages and encouraging assimilation in the longer term. In Britain this strand has been associated with the work of John Rex who has focused on the exclusion of post-war immigrants from social citizenship. However, Rex argued that it was material inequalities rather than physical characteristics which gave rise to conflict: immigrants were positioned as a racialised underclass and seen by the indigenous working class as competitors for scarce resources, such as jobs and housing. Gate-keepers to the welfare state shared this outlook with the rest of the indigenous working class and acted in ways which perpetuated immigrants' exclusion from social citizenship. Rex saw their practices as examples of subjective racism, rooted in personal attitudes and behaviours rather than institutional procedures.

Race relations strategies rest upon the same set of assumptions as those under-pinning liberal feminism (see above). Both perceive the state as a neutral vehicle for the reform of attitudes. As with feminism, this has been the dominant policy paradigm in race relations. At the national level this has given rise to three

Race Relations Acts (1965, 1968 and 1976) and, at the local level, to the adoption of equal opportunities policies by local authorities. Indeed, the 1980s have been described as the decade of municipal anti-racism (Lloyd, 1994). Ethnic monitoring procedures were adopted by personnel departments and local authority housing departments to evaluate selection and allocation procedures. Local authorities also introduced racism awareness (RAT) and equal opportunities training into staff development programmes (particularly for personnel involved in recruitment and service delivery), and increased local democracy by enhancing community consultation procedures. In education an emphasis on multiculturalism was designed to bring about cultural pluralism by encouraging tolerance of minority cultures. In social services, specialist sections staffed by 'ethnic minorities' were developed in an effort to develop culturally sensitive forms of assistance (Denney, 1995).

Some commentators have pointed out that the 'race' riots of 1958 and 1981 seem to have acted as a catalyst in the inauguration and extension of liberal strategies (Solomos, 1989; Gilroy, 1992). Before the 1960s the state had done nothing to assist the integration and settlement of black immigrants, their resulting concentration in areas of housing stress was defined in retrospect as problematic largely on grounds of concentration rather than social justice (Jacobs, 1985). As a result many commentators have been sceptical about the motivations behind these interventions. Nevertheless, a number of the strategies have helped challenge institutional as well as subjective forms of racism: ethnic monitoring, for example, has been crucial to policy evaluation and revision; and the 1976 Race Relations Act has facilitated successful challenges to indirect discrimination including institutional discrimination by local authority housing departments. However, the strategies do tend to oversimplify the problem of racism (Gilroy, 1987) and have been implemented within the context of a national and international economic climate and a central policy framework which has not always been 'friendly' (Williams, 1989).

In contrast with the subjective emphasis of the race relations approach, several theoretical perspectives have emphasised the problems of structural and institutional racism. Orthodox Marxists seek to understand racism as an important component in the development and reproduction of capitalism (Sivanandan, 1974, 1976). Jacobs (1985) uses a case study of the role of local authority housing departments to argue that the welfare state plays a direct role in the reproduction of racism within the indigenous working class. His account is centred on claims of institutional racism within the welfare state: rationing procedures and managerial strategies, rather than personal attitudes and behaviours, which lead to exclusion or unequal access. In housing this process reinforces residential segregation which creates ghettos of severe deprivation. This fosters racial conflict and distrust in two ways. First, those unfamiliar with the processes which give rise to ghetto-isation often believe that it is the black presence in the area which is the primary problem. Secondly, the existence of deprived ghetto estates creates competition within the working class for access to more desirable parts of the stock and militates against greater solidarity between black and white. Since immigrants and their families are never properly integrated into the working class, subsequent generations can continue to function as a low-paid reserve army of labour.

This theoretical approach has been criticised for its economic determinism: racism is viewed as a capitalist strategy of divide and rule which is reproduced by the welfare state and absorbed by the white working class as a form of false consciousness. The implication is that if capitalism were overturned, racism would disappear alongside it. Neo-Marxist writers have developed a more sophisticated approach which emphasises the 'relative autonomy' of racism from capitalism. This perspective is evidenced in the work of the Birmingham Centre for Contemporary Cultural Studies. These accounts recognise that racism pre-dates capitalism but claim that since the advent of capitalism there has frequently been a relationship between the two (Hall, 1980).

The importance of gender is also recognised in this work. Thus, 'race', class and gender might all articulate in complex ways to make black women a reserve army par excellence: Afro-Caribbean women, for example, are located in some of the lowest paid, most menial jobs (Carby, 1982). Neo-Marxists agree with orthodox Marxists that the welfare state plays a key role in reproducing race, class and gender divisions and, in turn, relies upon such divisions to help contain the costs of welfare provision by using black women and men to staff key services like the NHS. Ultimately, whilst avoiding the crude determinism of orthodox Marxism, the relative autonomy approach still suffers from a residual determinism. This led some neo-Marxists to adopt a postmodern analytic framework.

For postmodernists (Bauman, 1989, 1993; Gilroy, 1993; Hall, 1988b; Miles, 1994; Rattansi, 1994; Williams, 1992) racism is a far more complex phenomenon than is suggested by either the subjectivist accounts of race relations or the functionalist accounts given by many Marxists. In relation to subjective racism, postmodernists claim that racism articulates with other aspects of identity, some of which may reinforce whilst others may challenge racist identities. For example, Billig (1978) describes a member of the National Front who felt committed in his role as a trades union official to fight equally for black and white members alike and who also had black friends (cited Rattansi, 1992, 1994). This indicates that racism cannot be simply a unified form of 'false consciousness' as Marxists are prone to suggest and is better characterised as complex ambivalence than straightforward antipathy. Similarly, institutional racism cannot be seen 'as a smooth, reproductive machine, but as an internally contradictory set of processes' (Rattansi, 1994) located within a network of racialised power relations.

Postmodernists prefer to emphasise autonomous black community-based initiatives as an alternative to state-centred anti-racist strategies: the latter create dependency and do not promote democratic solutions (Gilroy, 1992). Minority and ethnic community-based organisations have been a strong element both in challenges to mainstream social policy provision and in the provision of alternative and supplementary services. Such contributions have been documented in relation to education (Tomlinson, 1985; Farrer, 1988, 1992), housing (Harrison, 1993) and responses to racial harassment (Desai, 1987). In certain cases during the 1980s there has been a coincidence between this emphasis on self-help and the context of an enabling welfare state which has helped to empower autonomous community groups.

A further approach to theorising racism has recently developed within European studies and international social policy. The claim is that we have seen a shift from ethnocentric to Eurocentric racism (Williams, 1995). Racism is linked with structural changes including the globalisation of the economic order, the technological revolution, the international division of labour and the development of economic imperialism with the rise of multinationals. The focus is upon the impact of economic imperialism, international monetarism and restrictive immigration policies. These themes have significant implications for questions of social justice (Townsend, 1993b). The focus on Europe comes about because of the position of the European union as a response to these developments. The single European market attempts to construct a protected trading bloc for member states (Paul, 1991). While this has led to the dismantling of internal frontiers it has also led to the reinforcement of external boundaries prompting talk of 'fortress Europe'. Both import and immigration controls have been tightened with negative implications for 'third world' countries. Many ex-colonies have developed export-oriented economies which are highly dependent on long-standing trade arrangements with their 'mother' countries. EC restrictions on imports from non-EC countries could spell disaster for such countries (Paul, 1991; Townsend, 1993b).

Restrictive policies towards immigration are seen in part as an international conspiracy to increase the exploitation of 'third world' labour and have displaced the emphasis on social citizenship within the national context in favour of a broader approach focused on black and third world peoples' citizenship in the international arena (Paul, 1991). Sivanandan (1989a) speaks of the development of an international underclass of refugees, immigrants and asylum seekers squeezed between those international processes which have displaced them from their countries of origin and those which increasingly refuse them legal entry into developed countries. There appears to have been a significant increase in the number of illegal immigrants and these persons are subject to super exploitation (Pierson, 1991; Ginsburg, 1992b). Sivanandan (1989a) claims that post-industrial society could not run without this cheap, illegal and rightless labour force.

Structural racism is the most difficult mode to successfully challenge. Sivanandan argues for socialist strategies which emphasise the need for solidarity and a recognition that other people's battles are in fact everybody's business. For

Townsend it involves challenging the power of international monetarism and curbing the impact of economic imperialism or exploitation by multinational corporations. He calls for the development of an international welfare state with international rights of social citizenship and policies for redistribution.

CRITIQUES

Some commentators have complained that equal opportunities policies and the emphasis on cultural sensitivity have been used to facilitate a process of incorporation (Gilroy, 1987). For example, black professionals, such as police officers, social workers and youth workers, may be actively recruited by the state to act as more effective agents of social control. However, Farrer (1988) concludes that although the intention of policy makers is to use them as agents of social control, the 'independent political motivations' of the workers means that they often resist their prescribed role.

Nevertheless, the liberal race relations model can be criticised on methodological grounds because it over-simplifies the problem of racism and advocates strategies which are less than effective. Cultural pluralism is based on an assumption that racism is an irrational prejudice based upon ignorance and that a dose of rationalism in the form of multiculturalism is the answer (Rattansi, 1992). RAT similarly emphasises subjective racism leaving institutional racism untouched (Gurnah, 1984; Sivanandan, 1985). In the case of equal opportunities, Sivanandan (1989b) talks of a 'numbers game' which deals only with the arithmetic of discrimination and refuses to engage with its politics. It thus rearranges the distribution of inequality but leaves the structures themselves intact. Indeed, it is possible that the promotion of equal opportunities for a given group of persons may serve to increase inequalities of opportunity between members of the affected group: that a 'reduction in inter-group inequality leads to an increase in intra-group inequality' (Edwards, 1994). This outcome has been observed in the American context whereby 'the race-specific policies emanating from the civil rights revolution, although beneficial to advantaged black people ... do little for those who are truly disadvantaged' (Wilson, 1977, cited Ginsburg, 1992b). This underlines the problems associated with liberal-rights-based approaches and prompts Wilson to argue that discrimination and social exclusion can only be redressed via the implementation of universal social welfare programmes – in other words via a strategy for social justice based on the criteria of need rather than desert.

POST-MODERNISM AND THE WELFARE STATE

Postmodernism argues that class is of declining political significance in post-industrial society, emphasising instead the importance of 'new social movements'. Postmodernism has its roots in the French students' and workers' rebellion of 1968, which signalled that existing political institutions were no longer able to deal with the dissatisfaction of the masses and that class-based politics were of decreasing political relevance. In France and elsewhere, the women's liberation, civil rights, ecology and gay and lesbian movements indicated that more sophisticated, democratic and inclusive forms of political struggle were called for in order to challenge the multiple sources of power and oppression which permeated society.

Recently, there have been attempts to distinguish two forms of postmodern theory. 'Strong postmodernism' has been rejected in social policy on two counts. First, it insists upon moral relativism which implies that all normative positions are equally valid including those which are racist and sexist. Secondly, it proposes the death of the human subject and undermines any possibility of human agency in shaping society, and this has been seen as politically debilitating. Instead it is the 'weak' or 'soft sceptical' (Benhabib, 1992) form of postmodernism which has been widely adopted in the discipline of social policy.

Some of the most important insights derived from postmodernism centre upon a new understanding of power and a shift of focus away from the perspective of the state. Social policy evolved as a state-centred discipline initially focused on thinking in practical terms about how need ought to be administered via the welfare state (Taylor-Gooby, 1981) and later on thinking critically about the arrangements made by the state for meeting social needs. Much of the latter material emphasised the social control function of the welfare state and left little room for the role of service users in the policy process. Postmodernism has both a descriptive and a normative part to play here. In other words it has been concerned both to make visible the contribution already made by service users in the policy process (e.g. Gordon, 1989) and to advocate new approaches to defining and meeting social needs which extend opportunities for recipients to voice their own needs and preferences (e.g. Percy-Smith and Sanderson, 1992; Hawtin et al., 1994).

Postmodernists have challenged the sovereign view of power put forward in Marxist and liberal pluralist models of the state, arguing instead for a micro-theoretical approach which sees 'the state' as an effect of a dispersed network of power relations. In this model power does not come from the top down but ascends from the bottom up. Since 'the state' is an effect of wider power relations its content at any historical moment will be significantly influenced by the most dominant power struggles within the network. As a result 'the state' may appear to reflect capitalist interests yet its shape is not economically determined as in Marxist theory. Many social policies in fact came about through the pragmatic responses of human subjects to their circumstances. It was only later on that these strategies became attached to 'the state'. For example, working-class self-help in Victorian Britain was subsequently linked to 'the state' through the 1911 National Insurance Act. This was implemented in the face of opposition from many sections of the working class and shows the complexity of the policy-making process.

Postmodern theories of power and the state have also challenged Marxist claims about the social control functions of social policy. Power is not theorised primarily in terms of repression, direct prohibition and constraint from the top down. The principal focus lies instead with the ways in which power functions to produce citizens who are capable of self-discipline (Rose and Miller, 1992). Knowledge is central to this process and, so, intimately tied up with the exercise of power. Foucault used the term 'power/knowledge' to describe this link. The link is visible in what Foucault terms 'biopower'. This is a form of social rationalisation which works by *disciplining* individuals and *regulating* populations. Regulation entails interventions to manipulate natality, mortality, morbidity and longevity and is made possible by the study of demography and epidemiology. Disciplinary power targets everyday life and seeks to render the individual human body more productive, docile and useful through the application of knowledge. This is a process of normalisation in which the body is disciplined not by repressive means but by constructing a series of norms which individuals are encouraged to aspire to. For example, healthy eating, safe sex and responsible parenthood are normative forms of behaviour which individuals might adopt. But they choose to do so because they are themselves empowered by this. The point is that these norms are available for negotiation by individuals. Other norms, such as heterosexuality, may be more likely to meet with resistance thus producing differences in the form of deviations from the norm. Disciplinary power seeks to suppress such difference by creating a hierarchy of choice which always privileges the norm. Postmodernists see this as a dangerous process because misfits may find themselves faced with social exclusion incarceration, institutionalisation or even systematic extermination (Bauman, 1989; Hewitt, 1994, p. 41). This point is supported by growing evidence of the influence of eugenics on social policy in the early twentieth century.

Another key area of postmodern insight in social policy relates to the definition and administration of need and the emphasis placed on consensus and universality in Fabian and social democratic approaches. Postmodernists have described universalism as a 'terroristic' attempt to forge unity in the face of enduring diversity (Lyotard, 1984). This can be illustrated by the equality versus difference debate: feminists complain that 'equality' is defined in male terms and that consequently it can only be realised by suppressing the differences that distinguish women from men (Thompson and Hoggett, 1996, p. 25).

Postmodernists have offered a series of recommendations which might help social policy to avoid some of the pitfalls of universalism and move towards a more inclusive conceptual and theoretical approach. This approach would be underpinned by a politics of difference which instead of seeking to reconcile (and thereby suppress) differences into a single consensus, would use difference

141

as a resource for multiplying sources of resistance to existing normative categories and classifications. The principle of universalism is not rejected outright because the need to redress inequities remains. But difference could be protected if diversity and equity (based on need and empowerment) were to replace sameness and equality as the principles underlying universalism (see Mouffe, 1993, p. 83). This would entail a bottom-up approach in which needs would no longer be defined by experts but would be negotiated from below and delivered in a manner which would empower users of social policy, and be accountable to them (Percy-Smith and Sanderson, 1992).

CRITIQUE

Postmodernist emphasis on micro-analysis and local struggles has been seen as disabling, particularly in the context of post-industrialism and the globalisation of capital. The problem is that some postmodernists, in their concern to avoid the determinism or reductionism of grand theories like Marxism, have gone to the other extreme and are unable to offer a politically relevant analysis. Baudrillard, for example, sees social reality as 'hyperfragmented', indeterminate and unmappable (Best and Kellner, 1991, p. 258). Clearly, this is politically debilitating, for one cannot devise strategies if one has no cognitive maps to provide orientation.

Williams (1992) argues instead for a 'structured diversity' approach which brings social structures including social class back into the analysis. Soft sceptical postmodernists thus continue to engage with theory on a macro-level but insist upon a non-reductionist, multi-causal approach. Some have argued for a multi-perspective approach which combines macro- and micro-analyses and refuses moral relativism in favour of adopting principled theoretical positions (Best and Kellner, 1991; Soper, 1993; Squires, 1993). Others have continued to emphasise a political economy approach in the form of post-Fordist perspectives which demonstrate how recent structural processes have compromised the capacity of nation states to act autonomously (Jessop, 1994). These contributions provide a useful corrective to postmodern tendencies to over-emphasise micro-social processes or change from below.

CONCLUSION

This chapter has reviewed a series of exciting developments in contemporary welfare theory: feminism, anti-racism and soft-postmodernism share a radical emphasis and lean decisively toward a need-oriented conception of social justice. This radicalism, however, frequently tends towards anti-statism. Thus, in each of these three perspectives there is some emphasis on the importance of grassroots political activity. In addition, both feminism and soft-postmodernism suggest a politics of everyday life on the basis of their shared interest in inter-personal relations and recognition that power is everywhere and that every relationship is a power relationship. However, these three perspectives more often than not adopt an ambivalent stance to the role of the state as a crucial tool for the administration of need and implementation of redistributive policies. In the case of postmodernism the perception of continuity between the state and civil society means that emphasis on grassroots organisation does not in fact amount to anti-statism.

In direct contrast, the New Right have few radical insights to offer. Their version of anti-statism insists upon an irreducible division between the state and civil society and would impose strict limits on the former while giving the latter free rein through the market, the family and voluntary action. Each of these arrangements for meeting social need would impose its own respective disciplinary regime on individuals; collectively they are designed to bring about the remoralisation of society. The New Right's view of morality does not of course incorporate a needs-based view of social justice, and empirical evaluation of New Right policies suggests that they produce social polarisation and social insecurity for perhaps a majority of people.

REFERENCES

Allen, J. (1990) 'Does Feminism Need a Theory of the State', in Watson, S. (ed.), *Playing the State: Australian feminist interventions,* London: Verso.

Baudrillard, J. (1983) 'The Ecstasy of Communication', in Foster, H. (ed.), *Postmodern Culture,* London: Pluto Press.

Bauman, Z. (1989) *Modernity and the Holocaust,* Oxford: Polity Press.

Bauman, Z. (1993) 'Racism, Anti-racism and Moral Progress', *Arena,* 1: 9–21.

Benhabib, S. (1992) *Situating the Self: Gender, community and postmodernism in contemporary ethics,* Cambridge: Polity Press.

Best, S. and Kellner, D. (1991) *Postmodern Theory: Critical interrogations,* London: Macmillan.

Billig, M. (1978) *Fascists: A Social Psychological View of the National Front,* London: Harcourt Brace Jovanovich.

Boston Women's Health Collective (1971/8) *Our Bodies Ourselves,* British edn., Phillips, A. and Rakusen, J. (eds), Harmondsworth: Penguin.

Carby, H. (1982) 'White Women Listen: Black feminism and the boundaries of sisterhood', in CCCS, *The Empire Strikes Back,* London: Hutchinson.

Central Statistical Office (1994) *Social Trends,* 24, London: HMSO.

Centre for Contemporary Cultural Studies (1982) *The Empire Strikes Back: Race and racism in 70s Britain,* London: Hutchinson.

Corea, G. (1988) *The Mother Machine: Reproductive technologies from artificial insemination to artificial wombs,* London: The Women's Press.

Davies, S. (1991) 'Towards the Remoralisation of Society', in Loney *et al.* (eds), *The State or the Market: Politics and welfare in contemporary Britain,* London: Sage.

Denney, D. (1995) 'Hall', in George, V. and Page, R. (eds), *Modern Thinkers on Welfare,* Hemel Hempstead: Harvester Wheatsheaf.

Desai, U. (1987) 'Racial Harassment, Housing and Community Action', *Race and Class,* 29(2): 69–76.

Edwards, J. (1994) 'Group Rights versus Individual Rights: The case of race-conscious policies', *Journal of Social Policy*, 23(1): 55–70.

Eisenstein, Z. (ed.) (1979) *Capitalist Patriarchy and the Case for Socialist Feminism*, New York: Monthly Review Press.

Esping-Andersen (1990) *The Three Worlds of Welfare Capitalism*, Oxford: Polity Press.

Farrer, M. (1988) 'The Politics of Black Youth Workers in Leeds', *Critical Social Policy*, 23: 94–117.

Farrer, M. (1992) 'Racism, Education and Black Self-organisation', *Critical Social Policy*, 36: 53–72.

Foucault, M. (1978) *The History of Sexuality: An introduction*, London: Penguin.

Foucault, M. (1979) 'Governmentality', *Ideology and Consciousness*, 6: 5–29.

Fraser, N. (1989) *Unruly Practices: Power, discourse and gender in contemporary social theory*, Oxford: Polity Press.

Friedman, M. (1962) *Capitalism and Freedom*, Chicago: University of Chicago Press.

Friedman, M. and Friedman, R. (1980) *Free to Choose*, London: Secker & Warburg.

Gilder, G. (1982) *Wealth and Poverty*, London: Buchanan & Enright.

Gilroy, P. (1987) *There Ain't No Black in the Union Jack*, London: Hutchinson.

Gilroy, P. (1992) 'The End of Anti-racism', in Donald, J. and Rattansi, A. (eds), *'Race', Culture and Difference*, London: Sage. Also in Ball, W. and Solomos, J. (1990) *Race and Local Politics*, London: Macmillan.

Gilroy, P. (1993) *The Black Atlantic, Modernity and Double Consciousness*, London: Verso.

Ginsburg, N. (1992a) 'Racism and Housing: Concepts and reality', in Braham, P., Rattansi, A. and Skellington, R. (eds), *Racism and Antiracism: Inequalities, opportunities and policies*, London: Sage.

Ginsburg, N. (1992b) *Divisions of Welfare: A critical introduction to comparative social policy*, London: Sage.

Gordon, L. (1989) *Heroes of Their Own Lives: The politics and history of family violence*, London: Virago.

Gough, I. (1979) *The Political Economy of the Welfare State*, London: Macmillan.

Gray, J. (1992) *The Moral Foundations of Market Institutions*, London: Institute of Economic Affairs.

Green, D. (1990) 'Foreword', in Murray, C., *The Emerging British Underclass*, London: Institute of Economic Affairs.

Green, D. (1993) *Reinventing Civil Society: The rediscovery of welfare without politics*, London: Institute of Economic Affairs.

Gurnah, A. (1984) 'The politics of racism awareness training', *Critical Social Policy*, 11: 6–20.

Hall, S. (1980) 'Race, articulation and societies structured in dominance', *Sociological Theories, Race and Colonisation*, Paris: UNESCO.

Hall, S. (1988a) 'Thatcher's Lessons', *Marxism Today* (March).

Hall, S. (1988b) 'Brave New World', *Marxism Today* (Special Issue, October).

Harris, R. (1988) *Beyond the Welfare State: An economic, political and moral critique of indiscriminate state welfare, and a review of alternatives to dependency*, London: Institute of Economic Affairs.

Harrison, M. (1993) 'The Black Voluntary Housing Movement: Pioneering pluralistic social policy in a difficult climate', *Critical Social Policy*, 13(3): 21–35.

Hartmann, H. (1979) 'The Unhappy Marriage of Marxism and Feminism: Towards a more progressive union', *Capital and Class* no. 8; revised in Sargent, L. (ed.) (1981) *Women and Revolution: A discussion of the unhappy marriage of Marxism and feminism*, London: Pluto Press.

Hawtin, M., Hughes, G., Percy-Smith, J. and Foreman, A. (1994) *Community Profiling: Auditing social needs*, Buckingham: Open University Press.

Hayek, F. A. (1944) *The Road to Serfdom*, London: Routledge.

Hewitt, M. (1983) 'Bio-politics and Social Policy: Foucault's account of welfare in theory, *Culture and Society*, 2(3): 67–84.

Hewitt, M. (1994) 'Social Policy and the Question of Postmodernism', *Social Policy Review*, 6.

Hutton, W. (1996) *The State We're In*, London: Vintage.

Jacobs, S. (1985) 'Race, Empire and the Welfare State: Council housing and racism', *Critical Social Policy*, 13: 6–28.

Jessop, B. (1994) 'The Transition to Post-Fordism and The Schumpeterian Workfare State', in Burrows, R. and Loader, B. (eds), *Towards a Post-Fordist Welfare State?* London: Routledge.

Kittay, E. F. (1984) 'Womb Envy: An explanatory concept', in Trebilcot (ed.), *Mothering: Essays in feminist theory*, Totowa, New Jersey: Rowman & Allanheld.

Laclau, E. and Mouffe, C. (1985) *Hegemony and Socialist Strategy: Towards a radical democratic politics*, London: Verso.

Law, I. (1996) *Racism, Ethnicity and Social Policy*, Hemel Hempstead: Harvester Wheatsheaf.

Lloyd, C. (1994) 'Universalism and Difference: The crisis of anti-racism in the UK and France', in Rattansi, A. and Westwood, S. (eds), *Racism, Modernity and Identity: On the western front*, Oxford: Polity Press.

Lyotard, J. F. (1984) *The Postmodern Condition: A report on knowledge*, Manchester: Manchester University Press.

MacIntosh, M. (1978) 'The State and the Oppression of Women', in Kuhn, A. and Wolpe, A. M. (eds), *Feminism and Materialism: Women and modes of production*, London: Routledge & Kegan Paul.

MacIntosh, M. (1981) 'Feminism and Social Policy', *Critical Social Policy*, 1(1): 32–42.

MacKinnon, C. A. (1983) 'Feminism, Marxism, Method and The State: Toward a feminist jurisprudence', *Signs*, 8(3): 635–58.

Mama, A. (1989a) 'Violence Against Black Women: Gender, race and state responses', *Feminist Review*, 32: 30–48.

Mama, A. (1989b) *The Hidden Struggle: Statutory and voluntary sector responses to violence against black women in the home*, London: London Race and Housing Research Report.

Mama, A. (1992) 'Black Women and the British State: Race, class and gender analysis for the 1990s', in Braham, P., Rattansi, A. and Skellington, R. (eds), *Racism and Antiracism: Inequalities, opportunities and policies*, London: Sage.

Miles, R. (1989) *Racism*, London: Routledge.

Miles, R. (1994) 'Explaining Racism in Contemporary Europe', in Rattansi, A. and Westwood, S. (eds), *Racism, Modernity and Identity: On the western front*, Oxford: Polity Press.

Minford, P. (1991) 'The Role of the Social Services: A view from the New Right', in Loney *et al.* (eds), *The State or the Market: Politics and welfare in contemporary Britain*, London: Sage.

Mishra, R. (1984) *The Welfare State in Crisis: Social thought and social change*, Hemel Hempstead: Harvester Wheatsheaf.

Mitchell, J. (1971) *Woman's Estate*, New York: Pantheon Books.

Morgan, P. (1986) 'Feminist Attempts to Sack Father – A case of unfair dismissal?', in Anderson, D. and Dawson, G. (eds), *Family Portraits*, London: Social Affairs Unit.

Morgan, P. (1995) *Farewell to the Family? Public policy and family breakdown in Britain and the USA*, London: Institute of Economic Affairs.

Mouffe, C. (1993) 'Liberal Socialism and Pluralism: Which citizenship?', in Squires, J. (ed.), *Principled Positions: Postmodernism and the rediscovery of value*, London: Lawrence & Wishart.

Murray, C. (1984) *Losing Ground: American social policy, 1950–1980*, New York: Basic Books.

Murray, C. (1990) *The Emerging British Underclass*, London: Institute of Economic Affairs.

Murray, C. (1994) *Underclass: The crisis deepens*, London: Institute of Economic Affairs.

O'Connor, J. (1973) *The Fiscal Crisis of the Welfare State*, New York: St James Press.

O'Connor, J. S. (1993) 'Gender, Class and Citizenship in the Comparative Analysis of Welfare State Regimes: Theoretical and methodological issues', *British Journal of Sociology*, 44(3): 501–18.

Offe, C. (1984) *Contradictions of the Welfare State*, London: Hutchinson.

Okin, S. M. (1989) *Justice, Gender and the Family USA*, Basic Books.

Orloff, A. S. (1993) 'Gender and the Social Rights of Citizenship: The comparative analysis of gender relations and welfare states', *American Sociological Review*, 58: 303–28.

Pahl, J. (1989) *Money and Marriage*, Basingstoke: Macmillan.

Pateman, C. (1989) 'The Patriarchal Welfare State', in Pateman, C., *The Disorder of Women*, Cambridge: Polity Press.

Paul, R . (1991) 'Black and Third World Peoples' Citizenship and 1992', *Critical Social Policy*, 32: 52–64.

Percy-Smith, J. and Sanderson, I. (1992) *Understanding Local Needs*, London: Institute for Public Policy Research.

Phillips, A. (1991) *Engendering Democracy*, Cambridge: Polity Press.

Pierson, C. (1991) *Beyond the Welfare State? The New Political Economy of Welfare*, Cambridge: Polity Press.

Pringle, R. and Watson, S. (1992) ' "Women's Interests" and the Post-structuralist State', in Barrett, M. and Phillips, A. (eds), *Destabilising Theory: Contemporary feminist debates*, Cambridge: Polity Press.

Rattansi, A. (1992) 'Changing the Subject? Racism, Culture and Education', in Donald, J. and Rattansi, A. (eds), *'Race', Culture and Difference*, London: Sage.

Rattansi, A. (1994) ' "Western" Racism, Ethnicities and Identities in a "Postmodern" Frame', in Rattansi, A. and Westwood, S. (eds), *Racism, Modernity and Identity: On the western front*, Cambridge: Polity Press.

Rattansi, A. and Westwood, S. (eds) (1994) *Racism, Modernity and Identity: On the western front*, Cambridge: Polity Press.

Rich, A. (1980) 'Compulsory Heterosexuality and Lesbian Existence', *Signs*, 5(4): 631–60.

Rights of Women Lesbian Custody Group (1986) *Lesbian Mothers' Legal Handbook*, London: The Women's Press.

Rose, N. and Miller, P. (1992) 'Political Power Beyond the State: Problematics of government', *British Journal of Sociology*, 43(2, June): 173–205.

Ruddick, S. (1980) 'Maternal Thinking', *Feminist Studies*, 6.

Ruddick, S. (1984) 'Preservative Love and Military Destruction: Some reflections on mothering and peace', in Trebilcot (ed.), *Mothering: Essays in feminist theory*, Totowa, New Jersey: Rowman & Allanheld.

Sainsbury, D. (1993) 'Dual Welfare and Sex Segregation of Access to Social Benefits: Income maintenance policies in the UK, the US, the Netherlands and Sweden', *Journal of Social Policy*, 22(1): 69–98.

Sawicki, J. (1991) *Disciplining Foucault: Feminism, power and the body*, London: Routledge.

Sivanandan, A. (1974) *Race, Class and the State*, London: Institute of Race Relations.

Sivanandan, A. (1976) 'Race, Class and the State: The black experience in Britain', *Race and Class*, 17(4).

Sivanandan, A. (1985) 'Race Awareness Training and the Degradation of Black Struggle', *Race and Class*, 26.

Sivanandan, A. (1989a) 'New Circuits of Imperialism', *Race and Class*, 30(4): 1–19.

Sivanandan, A. (1989b) 'All that Melts into Air is Solid: the hokum of new times', *Race and Class*, 31(3): 1–30.

Smart, C. (1984) *The Ties That Bind: Law, marriage and the reproduction of patriarchal relations*, London: Routledge & Kegan Paul.

Solomos, J. (1989) *Race and Racism in Contemporary Britain*, London: Macmillan.

Soper, K. (1993) 'Postmodernism, Subjectivity and the Question of Value', in Squires, J. (ed.), *Principled Positions: Postmodernism and the rediscovery of value*, London: Lawrence & Wishart.

Spallone, P. (1989) *Beyond Conception: The new politics of reproduction*, Basingstoke: Macmillan Education.

Squires, J. (ed.) (1993) *Principled Positions: Postmodernism and the rediscovery of value*, London: Lawrence & Wishart.

Stanko, E. A. (1985) *Intimate Intrusions: Women's experience of male violence*, London: Routledge & Kegan Paul.

Tang Nain, G. (1991) 'Black Women Sexism and Racism: Black or anti-racist feminism?', *Feminist Review*, 37: 1–22.

Taylor-Gooby, P. (1981) 'The Empiricist Tradition in Social Administration', *Critical Social Policy*, 1(2): 6–21.

Thompson, S. and Hoggett, P. (1996) 'Universalism, Selectivism and Particularism: Towards a postmodern social policy', *Critical Social Policy*, 16(1) (issue 46, February): 21–43.

Tomlinson, P. (1985) 'The "Black Education" Movement', in Arnot, M. (ed.), *Race and Gender: Equal opportunities policies in education*, Oxford: Pergamon Press.

Townsend, P. with Donkor, K. (1996) *Global Restructuring and Social Policy: The need to establish an international welfare state*, Bristol: Policy Press.

Townsend, P. (1993a) 'The International Welfare State', *Fabian Review*, 105(2): 3–6.

Townsend, P. (1993b) *The International Analysis of Poverty*, Hemel Hempstead: Harvester Wheatsheaf.

Townsend, P. (1995) *The Rise of International Social Policy*, Bristol: Policy Press.

Townsend, P. and Davidson, N. (1988) *Inequalities in Health*, London: Penguin.

Willetts, D. (1992) *Modern Conservatism*, London: Penguin.

Williams, F. (1989) *Social Policy: A critical introduction*, Cambridge: Polity Press.

Williams, F. (1992) 'Somewhere Over The Rainbow: Universality and diversity in social policy', *Social Policy Review*, 4: 200–19.

Williams, F. (1995) 'Race/Ethnicity, Gender and Class in Welfare States: A framework for comparative analysis', *Social Politics*, 2(2): 127–59.

Wilson, E. (1977) *Women and the Welfare State*, London: Tavistock.

Yeatman, A. (1994) *Postmodern Revisionings of the Political*, London: Routledge.

ANNOTATED READINGS

Three recent attempts to cover contemporary political perspectives are Fiona Williams (1989) *Social Policy: A critical introduction* (Cambridge: Polity Press, second edition forthcoming), Christopher Pierson (1991) *Beyond the Welfare State? The New Political Economy of Welfare* (Cambridge: Polity Press) and Michael Lavalette and Alan Pratt (1997) *Social Policy: A conceptual and theoretical introduction* (London: Sage).

A recent text which presents useful empirical material on racism and social policy with an introduction on theory is I. Law (1996) *Racism, Ethnicity and Social Policy* (Hemel Hempstead:

Harvester Wheatsheaf). Vic George and Paul Wilding (1994) *Welfare and Ideology* (Hemel Hempstead: Harvester Wheatsheaf) covers the New Right, feminist and green perspectives on welfare alongside the Fabian and Marxist perspectives which were reviewed here in chapter 8. A more advanced text which includes an exploration of New Right and post-modern approaches, again alongside the Fabian and Marxist perspectives, is Martin Hewitt (1992) *Welfare Ideology and Need: Developing perspectives on the welfare state* (Hemel Hempstead: Harvester Wheatsheaf).

Concluding comment to Part III

This part has introduced the reader to the nature and range of ideologies and theoretical perspectives used to analyse welfare provision and direct its practice. These ideologies are used to justify state intervention in welfare policy and moreover are used to prescribe the level and extent of that intervention. What each of the different theoretical positions outlined allows us to do is to evaluate, against different criteria, the relative success or failure of (particularly government) social policy.

We have suggested, following the examples of other writers, that ideologies explaining social policy may usefully be divided into two distinct camps: the first a more traditional set of explanations and theories falling into liberal, Fabian or Marxist schools of thought. Secondly, we discuss more recent and radical theoretical departures and newer strands of welfare theory falling into the New Right, feminist or post-modern.

Although this is often difficult material to absorb, looking at social policy and welfare developments through such different theoretical lenses allows us to perceive social policy as a whole as well as partially and allows us to develop our critical analysis and explanation of social policy.

Part IV

POLICY AREAS

Introduction to Part IV

Part IV explores in more detail the key social policy areas in Britain. We will consider the so-called 'Big Five' areas of income maintenance, education, health, housing and the personal social services but will consider also wider policy areas such as employment, family, criminal justice and the impact of Europe and the international dimension. These final areas are often not considered to be part of social policy but are dealt with in texts more normally associated with economics, law or political science, but which we consider to be central to the making and understanding of social policy.

Each chapter will take as its starting point the Beveridge Report, examining major policy developments since Beveridge and the legacy of the post-war settlement. Subsequent Acts of Parliament and their effects will be examined and placed within their contemporary political, socio-economic and policy-making contexts which face contemporary social policy makers, service providers and service users. Each chapter will conclude with an explanation and analysis of current developments and thinking and with a discussion of the key issues faced by that particular service sector or policy area.

10 Poverty and social security

OBJECTIVES

- To examine the development of the state role in income maintenance.
- To examine the 'rediscovery of poverty' during the 1960s.
- To consider the role of the state in alleviating poverty.
- To consider the changing landscape of poverty and poverty relief at the end of the twentieth century.
- To explore different strategies adopted for the distribution of cash benefits.

INTRODUCTION

This chapter focuses on state income maintenance, and the role of social security in the British welfare state. The idea that central and local government has a role to play in the relief of poverty has a long history in Britain, although the nature of that relief has changed over time as the welfare state has developed. The study of income maintenance systems requires a consideration of the method the state uses to provide an income to the population in need, and also a consideration of the implications of whatever system is adopted. State income maintenance can be minimal or generous, it can be given in cash or in resources and goods, and it can be conditional – for example requiring the recipient to seek paid employment – or non-conditional, where the individual is given help without any such requirements. Payment can be made to individuals in their own right or to individuals on behalf of others, as in benefits to the head of household for collective consumption. The ways in which these issues are resolved by different governments is indicative of the objectives underpinning the benefit system. Thus, as discussed later, in the chapter on family policy, the payment of state benefits may support some family types but not others. Similarly, the level at which benefits are paid to different groups reflects assumptions about needs and about 'desert'.

This chapter begins with a brief discussion of the development of a system of poverty relief in Britain, and the role of income maintenance in the welfare state which emerged after the Second World War. Subsequent sections describe the different benefit systems in Britain in the late 1990s and then look at some of the issues which arise out of the benefit system and which are important to an understanding of poverty in Britain at the end of the twentieth century.

THE HISTORY OF STATE INCOME MAINTENANCE

The involvement of central and local government in the relief of poverty is relatively recent. Those in poverty in earlier times were mainly assisted by charity, in the form of both the informal help which is provided by family and friends, and often on a reciprocal basis, and the more formal efforts of philanthropic organisations. The Victorian Poor Law of 1834 marks a significant development in the provision of public assistance. The Act replaced the previous systems of relief established by the Elizabethan Poor Law, which had created a system of locally organised relief for the indigent, based on their attachment to the locality. By the early 1800s this system was becoming increasingly unable to cope with the move towards an industrialised and urban-based society, in which one tenth of the population were classed as 'paupers' (Midwinter, 1994). The Victorian Poor Law attempted to create a system which matched these changes whilst maintaining the principles of the earlier Elizabethan Act, in particular the notion of local systems of relief and the minimum level at which relief should be provided (Hill, 1996).

The Act introduced a system of poverty relief managed by local Boards of Guardians and based on the principle of 'indoor relief', through the institution of the workhouse and the principle of 'less eligibility', which required that assistance to those in need should represent less than a worker might obtain by their own efforts. Similar ideas – that benefits should be less attractive than earnings, in order to deter those who might prefer claiming social security to paid employment – remain implicit, to a greater or lesser extent, in income maintenance systems today. The fear of 'welfare scroungers' can be found in both the ideology of the last Conservative government, with its talk of the 'something-for-nothing' society, and the Labour government's principle of 'welfare-to-work' benefits (see later).

Earlier chapters have discussed this period of development in the welfare system in more detail and it is not intended to go over this again here. However, in brief, the Victorian Poor Law remained largely unchanged until developments during the first half of the twentieth century removed more and more of its role in the relief of poverty. The introduction of national insurance for some groups of workers, in the 1911 Act, reduced the reliance of these workers on poverty relief during short periods of unemployment and ill-health. However, with the economic depression of the inter-war period both the national insurance system and the Poor Law came under increasing pressure, with the huge growth in the number of people out of paid work for long periods. The Unemployment Act of 1934 removed many of the functions of the old Victorian Poor Law, and by the introduction of means-tested payments for those unemployed and not covered by the 1911 Act created an important precedent for the arrangements in the later legislation (Hill, 1996).

'SOCIAL INSURANCE AND ALLIED SERVICES': THE 1942 BEVERIDGE REPORT

The Beveridge Report, 'Social Insurance and Allied Services', published in 1942, was the blueprint of an integrated system of social security to be put in place after the Second World War as a major aspect of post-war reconstruction. Beveridge argued that 'Social insurance fully developed may provide income security; it is an attack upon Want' (p. 6). But the Report went on, 'Want is only one of five giants on the road of reconstruction and in some ways the easiest to attack. The others are Disease, Ignorance, Squalor and Idleness' (p. 6). This is important, for the report was based on two assumptions – that government policies would seek to maintain full employment and that there would be a comprehensive and universal health care system – which were seen as integral to the success of the new system (Beveridge, 1942, p. 8). Beveridge proposed a dual-system of benefits, centred on the employed. The need for income maintenance was seen to arise when the employed person was temporarily absent from the labour market – whilst unemployed and between jobs, for example, or whilst sick. Thus people would pay into an insurance-based system whilst in work and claim during short-term periods of need. Policies to create full employment, together with a universal health care system, would in turn reduce numbers of claimants. The contributory system would also meet the needs of others – children and wives would be provided for through benefits paid to the male earner. And for those, relatively few, cases where there were insufficient contributions, means-tested assistance benefits would provide. This was the theory, at least. The system of contributory benefits was described as an insurance scheme – but it was based on actuarial principles. That is, the system, described as 'pay-as-you-go', was intended to fund benefits paid in one year out of the contributions collected that same year. The alternative, that an individual's contributions are intended to fund their own collection of benefits over time, including after retirement, was not adopted. The implications of this are that the system must collect each year sufficient to pay the needs of claimants – in a year with large numbers of claimants, such as in a period of widespread unemployment, the demands on the system may be greater than can be met without some other form of funding – such as through general taxation. Similarly, there are long-term implications for the system arising from an ageing society, in which the number of pension claimants is increasing. These implications have turned out to be significant over the years since the system was first introduced.

The assumption of full employment in particular was central to the critique of this new benefits system and central to the reason why it failed to deliver as promised. Feminists have been critical of a system based on a male pattern of earnings which sees women as financial dependants and which allowed married women in paid employment to pay reduced contributions. As paying full contributions would in most cases fail to deliver improved benefits, most married women exercised this right to pay less, and as a result enjoyed only restricted access to contributory benefits in their own right – for example, when the marriage broke down. This assumption of women's financial dependence, and Beveridge's vision of marriage as a 'team' of equals, exposes women to the risk of poverty both when they are in households with men, but dependent on their generosity, and when they are not 'attached' to a man.

In addition, a significant factor in the failure of Beveridge's ideas was the way in which society changed. As a result of demographic trends – the increasing numbers of single parents, for example, and increasing numbers of divorces – together with economic trends, and the rise in unemployment – means-tested benefits have become central rather than marginal. Fewer people can rely on insurance benefit, as an increasing number of people are excluded from the labour market for a variety of reasons – responsibility for children, old age, youth, disability and sickness – without having sufficient contributions to claim contributory benefits (Cochrane and Clarke, 1993). The contributory nature of the new system also reproduced, in the payment of benefits, the structural inequalities of a labour market in which certain groups were advantaged and others were not.

Beveridge's proposals also failed to find a solution to the difficulty of differences in the cost of housing. Whilst the means-tested national assistance system did allow for the full payment of rent, the system as a whole failed to appreciate the variation in housing costs across the country and the different needs which this would create. A further problem of the new system was that the levels of contributory benefits which were introduced were set, against Beveridge's wishes, too close to the means-tested benefits, and in some cases claimants were better off relying on the means-tested system because of the additional payments allowed under this scheme – the payment of rent, for example.

Beveridge envisioned a time when means-tested benefits would wither away as more and more people were covered by their contributions from earnings, or by their attachment to someone who was so covered (Cochrane and Clarke, 1993). However, this has not happened, and in 1995–6 means-tested benefits represented 50 per cent of the total amount paid out by central government in social security.

But how much was paid to beneficiaries under the new scheme? In calculating the level at which means-tested benefits were paid under the new system, the Beveridge Report (1942) followed a 'subsistence' definition, along the lines of the poverty research of Seebohm Rowntree, which incorporated the cost of basic necessities but nothing beyond (see exhibit 10.1).

Exhibit 10.1

> ### Primary poverty – Seebohm Rowntree: Poverty: a study of town life
>
> A family living upon the scale allowed for in this estimate must never spend a penny on railway fare or omnibus. They must never go into the country unless they walk. They must never purchase a halfpenny newspaper or spend a penny to buy a ticket for a popular concert. They must write no letters to absent children, for they cannot afford to pay the postage. They must never contribute anything to their church or chapel, or give any help to a neighbour which costs them money. They cannot save, nor can they join a sick club or Trade Union, because they cannot pay the necessary subscriptions. The children must have no pocket money for dolls, marbles or sweets. The father must smoke no tobacco, and must drink no beer. The mother must never buy any pretty clothes for herself or for her children, the character of the family wardrobe as for the family diet being governed by the regulation 'Nothing must be bought but that which is absolutely necessary for the maintenance of physical health and what is bought must be of the plainest and most economical description'. Should a child fall ill, it must be attended by the parish doctor; should it die, it must be buried by the parish. Finally, the wage earner must never be absent from his work for a single day. (Rowntree, 1901, pp. 167–8)

The definition of primary poverty which Rowntree devised was, as he himself acknowledged, an extreme measure which did not include expenses which people have because they are members of a society in which they have certain social responsibilities and expectations. However, even after the new system of social security was introduced, poverty remained in parts of British society.

THE 'REDISCOVERY' OF POVERTY

Beveridge's proposals were enacted in the National Insurance Act 1946 and the National Assistance Act 1948. For ten years, little changed in terms of the structure and administration of the new system. However, towards the end of the 1950s and in the early years of the 1960s a number of critiques of the existing social security system began to emerge, in particular from academics working at the London School of Economics, then headed by Richard Titmuss. The so-called 'rediscovery' of poverty in this period stems from research which demonstrated that a sizeable number of people were living at levels below the level of means-tested benefits (see, for example, Abel-Smith and Townsend, 1965; Townsend, 1957). Some of these were people beyond retirement age, others were in paid employment earning less than the level at which National Assistance was paid. Many were people who were unwilling to claim benefit or people who did not know of their entitlement to benefit (Hill, 1996). A later piece of research by Townsend estimated that up to 9 per cent of the population at the end of the 1960s was in poverty, and up to 28 per cent of the population could be described as in or on the margins of poverty (Townsend, 1979). These findings led to the development of public lobbying and the formation of pressure groups, in particular the Child Poverty Action Group, seeking reforms in the social security system, increases in the level at which benefits were paid, and also to broaden both take-up and the population covered. Subsequent sections explore the extent to which the changes that were introduced had any effect. First, however, it is important to explore the question of benefit levels and poverty, and also the debates over how benefits should be paid – through means testing or universal systems; based on contributions or not.

DEFINING AND MEASURING POVERTY

If social security systems exist to relieve poverty, it seems difficult to accept that a country which has a highly developed system of social security – such as Britain – might also still suffer from poverty. This was precisely why the 'rediscovery' of poverty at this time was so highly publicised, and remains hotly debated. What was important then, and still is, is the way in which poverty can be defined in developed countries.

The term *absolute poverty* refers to those without the basic necessities to sustain human life. Those who are in absolute poverty do not have their fundamental needs met – for food, water, shelter and warmth. Whilst there may be large numbers of the population in developing countries who are living in absolute poverty, there are few such people in the developed world. However, in recent years, with the growth of the homeless population, it is possible to see how even in Britain there are people living in absolute poverty. In addition to those living in such total destitution, there are groups of people who suffer from what has become known as *relative poverty*, those who, in relation to other people, have a very poor standard of living. Peter Townsend's definition of such relative poverty has become widely used:

> people are relatively deprived if they cannot obtain, at all or sufficiently, the conditions of life – that is, the diets, amenities, standards and services – which allow them to play the roles, participate in the relationships and follow the customary behaviour which is expected of them by virtue of their membership of society. If they lack or are denied resources to obtain access to these conditions of life and so fulfil membership of society they may be said to be in poverty. (Townsend, 1993, p. 36)

This definition uses the standard of living enjoyed by, or taken for granted by, the majority of people as the base line from which poverty can be measured. Poverty is generally taken to mean the level of income at which deprivation is inevitable.

The difficulty with these definitions has long been the issue of how deprivation and an acceptable standard of living might be defined. Townsend's major study of poverty in Britain in the 1960s (Townsend, 1979) used a list of necessities devised by academics. This research was significant in determining the level of income necessary to buy these necessities – Townsend calculated that in order to avoid relative poverty an income was needed which was between 140 and 150 per cent of the social security level. However, the research was criticised by some (see Piachaud, 1987, for example) on the basis that the list of necessities for a minimum standard of living was based on the individual perception of academics, not the ideas of poor people themselves. In addition, the research asked people if they lacked certain goods and services, but not why they did not have these things. David Piachaud argued that some people might choose to go without certain goods because they do not want them, not because they cannot afford them. This question of 'choice' is particularly difficult. It could be argued that in replying to a researcher, as well as in everyday thinking, people may prefer to say that they choose not to have certain goods and services which they cannot afford. 'Choice' is related to the likelihood that choice can be effective. This could be true throughout society, not just amongst those who are poor. For example, I may choose not to have certain luxuries because I know that I am unlikely ever to be able to afford them – in effect I am choosing not to want these goods, and thus be dissatisfied and disappointed.

One solution to this question of choice has been found in the Breadline Britain surveys carried out in the early 1980s and again in the early 1990s, in which a sample were asked a number of questions about goods and services. Respondents were asked, first, whether they thought most people in society should be able to afford these goods and services, and then asked whether they had these items, and, if not, whether this was because they did not want them or because they could not afford them. The issue over 'effective' choice remains, but the survey at least allowed for the possibility that people choose not to have such basic items as a warm winter coat or three meals a day. In addition, this kind of 'consensus' measure of deprivation – based on items seen as necessities by a majority of a large sample – does at least remove the criticism that the list of necessities is based on the ideas of a few academics rather than a more representative group.

Exhibit 10.2

Poverty in Britain in the 1990s: The Breadline Britain survey

The 1990 Breadline Britain survey found that:

- Approximately 11 million people – 20 per cent of the population – were living in poverty in Britain in 1990.
- The number of people who could be described as living in poverty increased by almost 50 per cent between 1983 and 1990.
- Approximately 5 million people were unable to afford an acceptable diet.
- Approximately 7 million people were unable to afford key items of clothing, such as a winter coat.

Source: Gordon and Pantazis (eds) (1997).

Exhibit 10.2 shows the findings of the most recent Breadline Britain survey on the numbers and characteristics of people in poverty in Britain in the 1990s. As this shows, such a study suggests that poverty remains a central problem in British society.

UNIVERSAL VERSUS SELECTIVE BENEFITS

One way of exploring the range of benefits a country offers its population in times of financial need is through the division between what are called *universal* and *selective benefits.*

Universal benefits are those which are paid to a given population, without a requirement that the beneficiary proves a need. Thus a benefit which is paid to claimants without means testing is a universal benefit. Universal benefits can be restricted in other ways – for example, the benefit is paid only to certain categories of people. There are in fact few universal benefits in Britain. The best known is the benefit paid to those who are responsible for bringing up children: child benefit. This is, at present universal, in that the claimant is not obliged to prove need and there is no means test.

The main advantage of universal benefits is that they are almost entirely free of the stigma that attaches to claiming means-tested benefits, and that as a result take-up is very high, ensuring that those who are eligible will gain in the way the benefit intends. The argument against universal benefits is that they are not targeted at those in greatest need, and that this means that the benefit is inevitably paid to some people who do not need the additional resources the benefit represents. With child benefit one argument in favour of maintaining this as a universal benefit has been that, whilst the payment may go to some households who are not in great need, it is a payment which goes in most cases directly to women caring for children. For some women, who do not receive equal or adequate money from their partner, this sum of money which they receive independently is very important indeed – even though the level at which the benefit is set is very low. For this reason pressure groups such as the Child Poverty Action Group (CPAG) and feminist groups have campaigned against any proposals to make this a selective benefit (Hill, 1996).

Selective benefits are those which are paid on the basis of means testing to those who fall below a pre-set level of income and are defined as in need. The claimant is required to give detailed information to the benefits officer about their income and about any assets they may have, and information about regular outgoings and responsibilities. As a result, claiming selective benefits is both a complex process, compared with universal benefits, and one which requires claimants to divulge what they may consider to be private information – about earnings and savings, for example – to an outsider. For both reasons – the complexity and the need to share private information – and because the actual amount gained in benefit may be small, selective benefits have a much lower take-up rate than universal benefits. An estimated £3 billion (1995 figure) goes unclaimed each year by people who would be eligible for payment if they were to claim. Selective benefits are also seen as carrying a stigma, as they are paid only to those in need. Thus the act of claiming such a benefit is the equivalent of telling others that you are in need. Many people, and in particular older people who remember earlier stigmatised systems of relief, prefer not to claim all that they are entitled to as a result.

The terms 'universal' and 'selective' are useful in highlighting the issues which are important in the ways in which benefits are organised and claims are assessed. For example, a universal child benefit could be seen as more than a benefit to meet need or relieve poverty. A society can choose to pay child benefit in recognition of the costs of raising a child and to acknowledge that there is a collective benefit to society from children, particularly where they have grown up out of the reach of poverty. Equally, a society could choose to pay a pension to all older people, in recognition of the value of their contribution to society.

However, most social security systems are seen as an expensive demand on the public purse, and are therefore structured so as to minimise the cost. In such systems, benefits are paid more to relieve poverty, particularly of groups seen as vulnerable – children, older people and people who are sick or who have a disability – than to recognise the value of different groups in society. The objective of such systems is to reduce reliance on the system.

The terms universal and selective, then, may help to focus ideas on the debate between 'desert' and 'necessity', but increasingly do not help describe the benefits which are actually paid. One way of dividing benefits in terms of their eligibility criteria which does reflect the actual benefits system is that devised by Hill (1993). Hill divides benefits in terms of their contributory nature, the extent to which benefits are contingent or dependent on certain conditions, and the extent to which benefits are means tested. *Contributory benefits* are those benefits which individuals and their employers have paid towards whilst in paid employment, through national insurance contributions which are deducted from earnings. People who are self-employed are also required to make contributions to national insurance. Payment of contributory benefits is, therefore, dependent on the individual having made sufficient contributions in the relevant period to qualify. Not surprisingly, certain groups are unlikely to qualify for these benefits: people who are in part-time employment, people who work in the 'informal' economy, where national insurance is not collected, and people whose work records are too short. Contributory benefits are more often collected by those who have been in full-time regular employment – hence the criticism that inequalities in pay and conditions in the labour market are replicated in contributory systems. Statutory maternity pay, statutory sickness pay and jobseeker's allowance are examples of contributory benefits, although the jobseeker's allowance is also means tested to an extent (see exhibits 10.3–10.6).

Exhibit 10.3

Benefits for children

The major benefits available for families with children in 1997:

- **Child benefit**: universal benefit paid to those responsible for bringing up a child. Tax-free, not based on national insurance contributions. Paid for each child under 16, and for young people aged 16–18 whilst in full-time education.
- **One parent benefit**: additional sum universal, to people bringing up a child alone. Paid only for oldest child.
- **Income support**: a means-tested benefit to people on low incomes who work less than 16 hours/week: includes allowance for each dependent child/young person, up to age 16. Income support is not dependent on contributions.
- **Family credit**: paid to people in paid work, who are also responsible for one or more child under 16 (19 if in full-time education). Not contributory, but it is means tested. Amount received linked to income, number of dependants, savings and hours worked. Childcare costs may be taken into account.

Benefits for pregnant women:

- **Statutory maternity pay**: paid to women in paid employment for more than 26 weeks by the 25th week of their pregnancy, payment linked to earnings. Taxable.
- **Maternity allowance**: paid to women who do not qualify for SMA. Contributory.

Exhibit 10.4

Benefits for people with a disability/illness

The major benefits available for people with a disability or illness in 1997 were:

- **Disability living allowance**: tax-free benefit, not contributory, mostly not means tested. For people under retirement age, who need help with personal care and/or help with mobility.
- **Disability working allowance**: tax-free benefit for people who have an illness or disability which limits their ability to work but who work more than 16 hours/week. Not contributory but is means tested, linked to earnings and number of dependants. Only available to those already receiving another benefit related to disability or incapacity for paid work.
- **Invalid care allowance: for those *caring* for someone with a disability**: taxable, not contributory. Paid to those of working age caring for someone with a severe disability, who is receiving a benefit themselves, such as the disability living allowance.
- **Statutory sick pay (SSP)**: paid to people in employment who are absent from work for four or more consecutive days. Paid by employers.
- **Incapacity benefit**: paid to people of working age who are not in paid work due to illness/disability. Contributory. Two modes: short-term and long-term, and two rates: lower and higher. Based on assessment to do own job, in first 28 weeks of claiming, then assessment to do a range of work-related activities. Not means tested but may be taxable.
- **Severe disablement allowance**: tax-free, non-contributory.
- **Attendance allowance**: tax-free, non-contributory, not means tested, paid to those needing help with personal care due to illness or disability.

Exhibit 10.5

Benefits for older people

The major benefits available for people over retirement age in 1997:

- **Retirement pensions**: taxable, contributory. Not means tested. Married women who do not qualify with their own contributions may be entitled on basis of husband's contributions.
- **State Earnings related Pension**: additional contribution paid to 'top up' the basic state pension.
- **Income support**: Means tested, non-contributory, taxable. Additional payments for older people.
- **Free NHS prescriptions**: all people over 60.

Contingent benefits are those which are dependent on certain conditions. Thus payments which are paid to someone with a disability are contingent on an assessment – most often by a medical professional – that the individual has a sufficient level of disability to merit the benefit. The disability living allowance is such a contingent benefit. As might be imagined pressure groups associated with disability (such as the Disability Alliance) have been critical of the way in which many contingent benefits depend on the assessment by an external authority, usually medical, of severity of disability; a mechanism which is both stigmatising and often degrading for the individual, as well as reliant on a medicalised notion of ability and disability.

As already noted, *means-tested benefits* are those which are related to income and savings. The principal means-tested benefit is income support, paid to those with insufficient income for their needs. The major benefits in 1997 are shown in exhibits 10.3–10.6. One caveat should be added here. Benefits tend to change over time, both in terms of the amount paid, as might be expected, but also in terms of the actual benefits themselves and how they are applied. The arrival of the Labour government in 1997 brought changes to the existing system of benefits which is not surprising after 18 years of Conservative rule. However, benefits in Britain are also influenced by European Law and

Exhibit 10.6

Benefits for the unemployed

The major benefit available for people who are unemployed in 1997:

- **Jobseeker's allowance**: taxable. Either contributory, or if insufficient contributions paid, means tested. Paid to those who are capable of work and actively seeking work.
- Under the **welfare-to-work** scheme, introduced by the Labour government, young people who refuse training or a job will lose at least 60 per cent of their benefit. Long-term unemployed and lone parents to be helped back into paid employment, with subsidies for employers.

rulings made by the European Union. For this reason, this chapter is to offer details on the level at which benefits are paid: one of the best finding out which benefits are on offer at any one time, how much i claimants of a particular benefit and the current eligibility criteria is to one of the Department of Social Security leaflets, available at any major post office.

SOCIAL SECURITY IN THE POST-WAR PERIOD

In this section we look at some of the issues and themes of social security in the first years of the welfare state. Initially, public expenditure on welfare took an increasing percentage of the gross national product (GNP), and social security's share of welfare expenditure in particular grew (Cochrane and Clarke, 1993). The 'rediscovery' of poverty referred to earlier, during the late 1950s and early 1960s, had produced pressure for change, and in particular increases in the level of benefits paid (Cochrane and Clarke, 1993). But this increase in the level of benefits occurred against a backdrop of rising costs of welfare in real terms, population changes which also led to increasing expenditure on social security benefits, and increasing demands from other welfare services. Changes introduced by the Labour Party during their periods in office included the replacement of the National Assistance Board by the Supplementary Benefits Commission in 1966 and the associated renaming of the national assistance benefit as supplementary benefit. This was followed by an amalgamation of the Department of Health with the Department of Social Security, to create a 'super-ministry' in the Department of Health and Social Security (DHSS) in 1968 and the eventual introduction in 1978 (after the 1975 State Pensions Act) of the State Earnings Related Pension (SERPS) to provide an enhanced, or 'superannuated' pension scheme for workers other than those already in a private scheme who were allowed to opt out (see Alcock, 1987; Glennerster, 1995; Hill, 1996).

The approach to family poverty during the 1970s was varied. The 'rediscovery' of poverty amongst families with children led to a search for ways in which family poverty might be relieved. In 1976 the system of family allowances – universal benefits paid to families with children – was replaced by child benefit. Child benefit was not taxable, unlike family allowance, but it was financed by the removal of tax allowances for children, and this meant that in effect the government was taking money from men's pay packets to give to women in child benefit. As a result, the benefit was introduced in stages to avoid, in particular, action from the male-dominated trades union movement (Deacon, 1995). Ideas about a negative income tax which would create a system of payments to low-income families were discussed but not implemented, but a system to help those bringing up children who were in low-paid employment was introduced in 1971: family income supplement (FIS). This means-tested benefit was thus targeted at the working poor, to reduce one of the major causes of poverty – low pay combined with the responsibilities of raising a family. Being means tested, it had a low take-up rate and also created for many a 'poverty trap', where improvements in pay did not increase the income going into the home, because any increase was offset by a reduction in the FIS benefit. Despite this, FIS remained in place until it was replaced in the late 1980s by another, means-tested benefit for families in low-paid employment, Family Credit.

By the time the Labour Party lost power at the end of the 1970s the Labour government had presided over an increasingly austere and cost-cutting set of welfare policies. At the same time, there is an increasing public perception that the welfare state had failed, and of a move towards centre stage of an image of 'welfare scroungers' – benefit claimants who have no intention of seeking employment (see Golding and Middleton, 1983).

SOCIAL SECURITY DURING THE 1980s – 'TARGETING' BENEFITS

We turn now to consider a significant period during the history of social security – that of the 18 years of Conservative government from 1979 to 1997. The incoming Conservative government in 1979 promised a decreasing role for the welfare state and an increasing role for individual provision and the free market. Throughout the 1980s and early 1990s the Conservative government sought to reduce public expenditure on state income maintenance systems, at a time when demographic change and labour market factors led to an increase in the numbers of claimants and in the cost of social security. In part this attempt to cut the cost of the social security bill was related to the commitment to reduce the Public Sector Borrowing Requirement (PSBR) and in part it was related to the ideological background of the Conservative Party. Margaret Thatcher's government utilised growing public disillusionment with existing welfare policy, which was seen as intrusive and a disincentive to individual action, and also as demoralising, to reduce the role of the state in welfare provision. Whilst this 'rolling back' of the welfare state overall proceeded slowly, the social security system was one of the first to be targeted for change (Cochrane and Clarke, 1993). Change was initially brought about through two means. First, the value of benefits was reduced over time. One way this was achieved was by the removal of earnings-related additions to contributory benefits, so that whilst contributions still acted to determine eligibility, the benefit was paid at a lower flat rate. The value of benefits was also reduced through the failure to increase rates in line with inflation. Some benefits – such as child benefit – were frozen, whilst increases in others, such as pensions, were realigned with the more slowly moving price index than with the faster rising wage index. Secondly, the numbers eligible for benefits were reduced by changes in eligibility criteria – removing those seen as 'voluntarily unemployed', for example, from unemployment benefit (Loney, 1987; Cochrane and Clarke, 1993). Young people in particular suffered from the changes introduced in this period, finding themselves no longer eligible for means-tested state assistance or housing benefit unless registered with Youth Training Schemes (YTS). Many of these changes were piecemeal, yet collectively this 'chiselling' away at the benefit system (Loney, 1987) added up to a major shift towards means-tested systems of relief and a shift in ideology, reflecting the view that benefits should be a 'safety net' (and one close to the ground) rather than a 'sofa'.

In 1985 more radical changes were promised when the Conservative government announced a major review of the benefits system, known as the Fowler review after Norman Fowler, then Conservative Minister for Social Security. The 1986 Social Security Act which followed created a new system of state assistance – income support – which was to be more streamlined, with fewer different categories and complications. The Act introduced payment on the basis of premiums added to a basic sum, on the basis of different categories of need – for older people, children, people with a disability and so on. The Act also withdrew the payment of one-off lump sums which had been paid to claimants to meet particular occasional needs – such as for new furniture or clothing. Instead, claimants with such needs became eligible for a loan from the Social Fund. Loans were discretionary rather than automatic, even if the need was proven, and also were, as the name tells us, to be paid back – out of income support benefits. The effect was to further reduce the level of benefits for those who were 'successful' in being awarded a loan, and to further increase the claimant's poverty.

The second major change introduced in the 1986 Act was the replacement of family income supplement by family credit which was to be assessed in the same way as income support and which was designed to enable families to get back to paid employment and out of the poverty trap. Family credit, however, has a very low take-up rate; partly because of the complexity of claiming the benefit, partly because of a lack of information about it, and partly because there is a long delay – up to six months in some cases – before it is paid.

The third element of state assistance tackled in the 1986 Act – though this was largely a case of rewriting earlier 'botched' (Hill, 1996) legislation – related to housing benefit, benefits paid to those on low incomes to help meet the costs of housing. As in the earlier Beveridge Report, housing need presents questions of how best to meet the variable costs of housing for different claimants and issues of equity relating to whether a claimant is buying their own home, renting privately or from the local authority. The 1986 Act sought to bring the rules for housing benefit in line with those for income support and family credit, although there was also a desire to end the practice whereby claimants would use the money paid directly to them to meet their housing costs to meet other needs, leaving their housing payments in arrears.

One of the last changes made to the social security system by the Conservative government before the 1997 Labour election victory was the introduction of the 'jobseeker's allowance' in the autumn of 1996. Unemployed people – now called 'jobseekers' – receive an allowance whilst looking for work, and receive help in finding employment with jobsearch seminars and job plan workshops. However, 'jobseekers' have to be ready and available for full-time paid work (up to 40 hours a week) and prove that they are seeking work. Unemployed people who do not take work which is offered, or who do not follow directions given to them by the employment officer, can suffer sanctions including the loss of benefit. The unemployed person also is prevented from specifying too high a wage as the minimum they would accept, and they can only limit their availability to their usual occupation for a restricted period, after which the 'jobseeker' must accept any reasonable employment or face sanctions.

The trend during the 1980s and early 1990s was therefore towards an increasing emphasis on selective benefits, the idea that benefits should be targeted on those most in need, and the desire to decrease reliance on these benefits. There is a clear undercurrent of 'less eligibility' in the move towards decreasing the value of benefits and increasing the role of the more stigmatised means-tested benefits rather than welfare as a right.

Underpinning this shift towards a marginalised state system based on minimum needs was the ideology of a number of writers, and in particular von Hayek and Friedman (see chapter 9). However, there was also an increasing interest in the idea of an intractable underclass, and the thinking of the New Right and far right in Britain drew also on the work of people like Charles Murray (see exhibit 10.7).

Murray's thesis was an updated, 1990s version of what was called a 'culture of poverty' by Oscar Lewis in the 1960s, and by Keith Joseph as a 'cycle of disadvantage', when he was Conservative Minister for Social Services, in the 1970s. Although the research Joseph instigated into this transmitted deprivation found

Exhibit 10.7

The concept of the underclass: Charles Murray

The 'underclass' does not refer to degree of poverty, but to a type of poverty. It is not a new concept. I grew up knowing what the underclass was; we just didn't call it that in those days. In the small Iowa town where I lived, I was taught by my middle-class parents that there were two kinds of poor people. One class of poor people was never even called 'poor'. I came to understand that they simply lived with low incomes, as my own parents had done when they were young. Then there was another set of poor people, just a handful of them. These poor people didn't lack just money. They were defined by their behaviour. Their homes were littered and unkempt. The men in the family were unable to hold a job for more than a few weeks at a time. Drunkenness was common. The children grew up ill-schooled and ill-behaved and contributed a disproportionate share of local juvenile delinquents. (Murray, 1990, p. 1) little evidence of such a culture of poverty over generations, the debate was resurrected in the 1980s and 1990s as an explanation of continuing poverty. At the heart of these theories is the argument that there are some groups for whom poverty is a way of life, rather than a temporary misfortune. Such groups – recognisable by their tendency towards deviant behaviour in every respect – are held to form an underclass that reproduces itself over time. The values and norms of the group are passed on to subsequent generations in a never-ending cycle.

Welfare systems, it was argued, fuelled such a cycle:

> Welfare benefits, distributed with little or no consideration of their effects on behaviour, encouraged illegitimacy, facilitated the breakdown of families, and replaced incentives favouring work and self-reliance with perverse encouragements for idleness and cheating. (Thatcher, 1993, p. 8)

Murray's ideas were seized upon by those on both the right and left who saw an over-generous welfare state as the cause of people's willingness to abdicate their own responsibility and increasingly expect the state to provide. Certain groups, however, emerged within this approach as the major villains – and key amongst these was the lone mother on benefit. Lone parents were particularly targeted for their long-term reliance on welfare benefits, but are also seen as the source of a major problem in itself: juvenile delinquency (Murray, 1990). However, the notion of an underclass was not restricted to the ideology of the Conservative Party: the 1997 Labour Party manifesto also included the idea of a growing underclass.

SOCIAL SECURITY SYSTEMS DURING THE LATE 1990s – 'WELFARE TO WORK'

The Labour government which was elected in 1997 announced a new approach to benefits, which aims to link benefits with work in a new way. The Labour Party campaign in the run up to the 1997 election, which they won by a large majority, claimed 'we will get the unemployed from welfare to work', and that they would 'stop the growth of an underclass' (Labour Party Manifesto, 1997, p. 10). The major drive of the welfare budget, coming two months after the 1997 election, was a 'welfare to work' strategy which focused on initiatives to return benefit claimants to the labour market. Lone parents, for example, are to be encouraged back into the labour market once the youngest child was in full-time school, with help in the search for jobs, training and after school care. Lone parents will be given advice and help from an individual 'caseworker' in drawing up an action plan to develop their job search skills and to find childcare. Lone parents who participate in the plan will receive family credit on a 'fast track' basis to avoid the typically long delays before benefits are paid, and also faster treatment from the Child Support Agency. The Labour government also increased the amount lone mothers could offset against family credit for the costs of childcare, which reduces the poverty trap they can encounter when going back to work.

The second major aspect of the Labour strategy to decrease the number of claimants focused on reducing the number of long-term unemployed, with tax rebates to employers who employed long-term claimants. These tax rebates would only last for the first six months of the new employment, however, giving rise to some concern that this would merely subsidise employers over a short period but offer no incentive for employers to retain staff over a longer period, and is insufficient time for an unemployed person to gain new skills and qualifications to help them in the job market.

The third part of the welfare-to-work plan is the development of an employ-ment and training scheme for young unemployed people – who lose a substantial part of their benefit (at least 60 per cent) if they refuse a place on a training scheme or refuse a job which is offered them. Young unemployed people are offered the choice of work in the private sector, with the employer again offered a subsidy to take them on, work in the voluntary sector, including an environmental task force, or further training. Again, the scheme, which lasts for six months, has been criticised as giving employers subsidised labour but offering too little to young people in terms of training.

However the Labour government has also introduced the national minimum wage, and this may lead to a reduction in the poverty of some workers, especially women, who make up the majority of those employed on very low wages. Alter-natively, some have argued that a minimum wage would create a pressure on the labour market which may increase unemployment. This aspect of the minimum wage is discussed in more detail in chapter 15.

ISSUES IN SOCIAL SECURITY

This is necessarily a brief review of some of the major issues arising in the study of poverty and social security systems.

Gender, poverty and state income maintenance systems

In recent years there has been increasing focus on the extent to which the risk of poverty is 'gendered' – that is, that women may be more at risk of poverty than men. Studies of lone parents (Millar, 1989), older women (Finch, 1992; Groves, 1992; Walker, 1992) and women in two-parent households (Graham, 1994) have all highlighted women's risk of poverty, due to a combination of women's reduced involvement in paid labour, which is in turn related to their caring responsibilities, and women's poorer prospects when in paid work, with lower rates of pay and poorer pensions in particular.

Whilst some writers have suggested that there has been a 'feminisation of poverty', with increasing numbers of women in poverty over the years (Scott, 1984), it is more likely that women's poverty has become more visible over time. This is particularly due to increasing numbers of women who are lone parents and women's poverty in old age. Feminists have also highlighted the failure of the social security system to prevent women's poverty – partly because of the low rate at which benefits are paid, and partly because the system assumes women's dependence on men and therefore fails to recognise the ways in which women are at risk. The Beveridge Report explicitly stated that married women would be dependent for income support on their spouse, and that the male head of household would be the major claimant. As a result, the system which is responsible for relieving poverty can only see women in the context of economic dependency – and women are penalised if they are seen as 'co-habiting' whilst on benefit. This is discussed in more detail in chapter 16.

Rural poverty

One relatively underresearched aspect of poverty is the experience of rural areas. Most studies of poverty have been based in urban areas, and there is now a large body of literature which describes and analyses poverty and deprivation in urban areas. There is far less which attempts to tackle the same question for those living in rural areas. However, there are important differences in the way in which poverty and deprivation are experienced in rural areas, which many studies fail to highlight because of an over-reliance on 'indicators' – such as the level of home ownership, car ownership, unemployment and over-crowding – which are less accurate measures of poverty in rural areas. In particular, whilst non-car-ownership is a fairly robust indicator of deprivation in urban areas, poor people in rural areas are more likely to put money into car ownership because of the inadequacy of public transport. Thus, whilst this indicator would suggest less poverty in rural areas, there may in fact be more. Where people on low incomes decide to own a car, not only is the car likely to be older and in poor condition but they also then have less money available for other necessities. Similarly, a telephone and a television may be greater necessities in an isolated area than in urban areas. In addition, the cost of living in rural areas is often higher – where local village shops, for example, have higher prices than larger supermarkets found in urban areas. These difficulties will also impact differently on different groups of the rural population – women at home during the day, for example, will suffer greater isolation where the family car is used for travel to work by their partner, and there is little or no public transport.

CONCLUSION

The social security system in Britain went through considerable change during the 18 years of Conservative rule, and, whilst much of that change was piecemeal, the overall effect of what Loney (1986) called 'chiselling' was to increase the role of means-tested selective benefits, rather than universal benefits. The theme of the 1980s was the importance of 'targeting' benefits and the need to combat fraud and an over-reliance on state handouts. With the arrival of the 1997 Labour government, we see a shift towards enabling people to get off benefit and back into the labour market. The underlying link with the labour market, then, is unchanged, and whilst these policies are aimed at improving the quality of life for people currently living on appallingly poor levels of benefit, it remains to be seen how well these policies will work in practice.

REFERENCES

Abel-Smith, B. and Townsend, P. (1965) *The Poor and the Poorest*, London: Bell.

Alcock, P. (1987) *Poverty and State Support*, London: Macmillan.

Beveridge, Sir W. (1942) 'Social Insurance and Allied Services', Cmnd 6404, London, HMSO.

Cochrane, A. and Clarke, J. (eds) (1993) *Comparing Welfare States*, London: Sage.

Deacon, A. (1995) 'Spending more to achieve less? Social Security since 1945', in Finch, J. (1993) and Mason, J., *Negociating Family Responsibilities*, London: Tavistock/Routledge.

Glennerster, H. (1995) *British Social Policy Since 1945*, Oxford: Blackwell.

Golding, P. and Middleton, S. (1983) *Images of Welfare*, Oxford: Martin Robertson.

Graham, H. (1994) *Hardship and Health in Women's Lives*, Hemel Hempstead: Harvester Wheatsheaf.

Groves, D. (1992) 'Women and Financial Provision in Old Age', in Maclean, M. and Groves, D., *Women's Issues in Social Policy*, London: Routledge.

Hill, M. (1993) *Understanding Social Policy*, 4th edition, London: Blackwell.

Hill, M. (1996) *Social Policy: A comparative analysis*, London: Prentice Hall/Harvester Wheatsheaf.

Labour Party Manifesto (1997)

Loney, M. (1986) *The Politics of Greed: The new right and the welfare state*, London: Pluto Press.

Midwinter, E. (1994) *The Development of Social Welfare in Britain*, Buckingham: Open University Press.

Millar, J. (1989) *Poverty and the Lone Parent: The challenge to social policy*, Aldershot, Avebury.

Murray, C. (1990) *The Emerging British Underclass*, London: IEA.

Piachaud, D. (1987) 'Problems in the definition and measurement of poverty', *Journal of Social Policy*, 16(2): 147–64.

Scott, H. (1984) *Working Your Way to the Bottom: The feminisation of poverty*, London: Pandora.

Thatcher, M. (1993) *The Downing Street Years*, London: HarperCollins.

Townsend, P. (1957) *The Family Life of Old People: An enquiry in East London*, London: Routledge & Kegan Paul.

Townsend, P. (1979) *Poverty in the United Kingdom*, Harmondsworth: Penguin Books.

Townsend, P. (1993) *The International Analysis of Poverty*, Hemel Hempstead: Harvester Wheatsheaf.

Walker, A. (1992) 'The Poor Relation: Poverty among older women', in Glendinning, C. and Millar, J. *Women and Poverty in Britain: the 1990s*, Hemel Hempstead: Harvester Wheatsheaf.

ANNOTATED READINGS

Michael Hill's *Social Security in Britain* provides an overview of the social security system and social security policy in Britain up to the early 1990s. Townsend's work provides a thorough and useful analysis of poverty both within Britain and in an international and comparative context, while Pete Alcock's *Poverty and State Support* attempts to synthesise an analysis of both the issues of poverty and of the adequacy of the social security system.

The work of Hilary Graham, Jane Millar and Sarah Payne all present informative and detailed analysis of poverty faced by women, older women and lone parents, whereas a more individualised view of the causes of poverty may be found in the writings of Charles Murray and his exposition of an emerging British underclass.

11 Education and training

OBJECTIVES

- To explore the development of compulsory state-run education services in Britain.
- To examine the reasons for the expansion of further and higher education.
- To consider recent attempts to raise educational standards and to link education policy with employment policy and the needs of the economy.

Education services in Britain, as we have already seen in chapter 2, were a comparatively late development in the British welfare state. Continued debate over the proper role for the state in the delivery and development of a national system of education meant that the first significant intervention did not come until the final quarter of the nineteenth century. However, the legacy of vested and sectional interests remained, and right through the early decades of the twentieth century the best that most children could hope for was an elementary education. Despite the raising of the school leaving age to 14 at the end of the First World War and the abolition of fees for elementary schooling, what we know today as secondary schooling remained largely fee paying and therefore exclusive.

Elementary education remained simply basic instruction in the so-called 'three Rs' of reading, writing and arithmetic and took place within 'all-age' schools which did not separate junior and senior children (Glennerster, 1995). Proposals after the First World War to widen educational provisions to 14–16 year olds were to fall following the widespread cuts in public spending introduced by the 'Geddes Axe' in 1922 (Timmins, 1995). Continued economic recession and the crash of the 1930s ensured that austerity marked much government policy throughout the inter-war years. It was not, therefore, until the appointment as Minister for Education of R. A. (Rab) Butler in 1941 that the government signalled its intention, as in much else, to review the whole structure and direction of British education.

When Butler came into office most children in Britain, especially those from working-class families, would leave school at the age of 14, although a small proportion of those might be lucky enough to earn scholarships to go to secondary schools. The vast majority of those children would leave school with no formal

qualifications, with only 19,000 nationally staying in s
(Timmins, 1995, p. 73). For most children the education
severe disappointment, and the possibility of entering
non-existent. The pressure for the reform of what had l
outdated education system, based upon ideas of privilege
which served the nation poorly, was great.

Butler sought to address the nation's education system .
three fronts: first, to introduce technical education and train
directly into the employment needs of the nation. Secondly,
of compromise with the religious lobby over Church school   _ worny
issue of religious instruction inside state schools and, finally, to address how
the country should handle the issue of public schools. The religious question in
education, as we have already suggested, was the cause of long-standing and
bitter disputes between various elements of Christianity which Butler hoped to
win over with the introduction of 'controlled' or 'aided' schools. Simply put, a
controlled school would be run by its local authority who would implement an
agreed religious syllabus whereas an aided school would be run by a board of
governors and Church appointees in which the Local Education Authority
(LEA) would meet the running costs. In aided schools, the religious content of
the syllabus and the nature of religious instruction would be agreed by the
school's governing body and it was hoped that the various Churches involved
would be satisfied that the right 'brand' of religion would be delivered. The question of public schools, which, it was felt, were as fraught with dangers as that of
religion, was rather side-stepped as Butler announced that an independent
enquiry would report on the public schools issue.

Butler's proposal for the wider education system, embodied in the Education
Act of 1944, was his now famous, or infamous, tripartite settlement. Schools themselves were to be distinguished by the nature of the education they would provide. Grammar schools would cater for the academic 'high-flyer', those children
who might be expected to enter professional careers, business or management.
Technical schools would be established for those children who could be described
as having an 'applied' nature and who might go on to work in engineering or
crafts. Finally, secondary modern schools would cater for those children who
might be described neither as academically nor technically minded. The
method by which children would be distinguished for entry to one of these
three schools would be by a commonly taken examination, the eleven-plus.
This tripartite structure would cater for children from the age of 11 to the
newly raised school leaving age of 15 and the Act proposed to raise this to 16
as soon as was practicable, though this was not until 1972.

The new system of educational provision was to be administered by a similar
tripartite relationship between the government in Whitehall at the newly created
Education Ministry and the Treasury who would be responsible for the financial

en to local authorities. Local Education Authorities, which were in number from 315 to 146 in an attempt to simplify their responsibilities, meanwhile would have the function of managing the schools themselves and taking a role in the strategic planning of education in their area. This strategic role would extend across the three sectors in primary and secondary schools and the provision of colleges of further education, and later still into the higher education arena when polytechnics were founded. Finally teachers would have a role in providing and delivering the curriculum and therefore for the standards of educational provision within the schools in which they worked (McVicar, 1996). Finally the Butler Act also laid down a three-way division within education. By its focus on the provision of secondary schooling, between the ages of 11 and 16, the Butler Act reinforced a distinction between the primary education sector (pre-11) and the tertiary sector (post-16 education) and the university sectors. Given that education was also to have a tripartite administrative structure, the system overall allowed local authorities to invest in different priorities with some choosing to stress the foundations laid in the primary sector with others preferring greater investment in secondary schooling.

What the Act would do, finally, was to provide education for all children at no cost though we may of course argue that this was still an elementary education. The system went further by providing the opportunity for bright working-class children to attend grammar schools, on the basis of merit rather than ability to pay, since fees for local grammar schools would be abolished. The Act also, Butler hoped, would address the old and thorny issue of technical education and the fear, frequently vocalised, that Britain was beginning to lag behind her economic competitors. In addition to the newly created technical schools, local authorities would now have the duty to provide technical- and craft-based courses in the further education sector, which was later extended by Wilson's 'white heat' in the creation of polytechnics and the expansion of vocational education in the 1960s.

Despite the wholesale structural, administrative and educational changes introduced by the Butler Act, however, it has been criticised for what it failed to achieve, and for the issues that it failed to tackle. As we note above, the question of public schooling was side stepped and we may even argue that the ethos of privilege ingrained in the public school system was to be institutionalised through the state grammar schools. The Act also institutionalised, within state education, a role for religion and the Church which has continued to be a focus of conflict and has raised new concerns as Britain has developed its modern multi-faith identity. The Act further, it may be said, failed to address the vexed question of technical education. Where it appeared to offer the prospect of wholesale expansion in technical subjects, it in fact tended to marginalise technical education and Britain's education system became one offering bipartisan schooling, through the 'academic' grammar schools and the more 'practical' secondary moderns. Indeed many local authorities appeared to regard the question of technical education as a question not for themselves but for employers and their system of apprenticeships (Lowe, 1993; Timmins, 1995).

The two decades following the passage of the Butler Act is a time that we might well characterise as a period of consolidation. Vestiges of the system established in the nineteenth century withered (mostly) and new directions in education were sought, such as the creation of new universities in the late 1950s, signalling the beginning of the higher education expansion of the following decade. Yet the new system was not without criticism most vehement of which was directed towards the eleven-plus examination. Rather than be regarded as an examination designed to match each pupil with the secondary school most suited to their ability the eleven-plus became a mark of success or failure. This was particularly so given the failure of many local authorities to develop technical schools, as the eleven-plus came to distinguish those who 'passed' and went on to the grammar and those who 'failed' and were consigned to the secondary modern. For many parents and politicians, to attend a secondary modern became a badge of failure, a failure reinforced by the underfunding of such schools when compared to the grammar schools. Such concerns helped in part to confirm the direction of the education debate through the 1960s and into the 1970s and brought society's attention to bear on the subject of equality.

For many parents and politicians the combined effect of selection at the age of 11 together with the preserved elitism of the grammar schools system could mean only one thing, that working-class children would continue to be short-changed by British state education. Furthermore the perception of success of failure inherent in the national policy of 'selection at 11' led to the accusation that teachers were simply labelling children, at an early age, as gifted or as failures. Advocates of the system argued that grammar schools gave bright working-class children the opportunity to succeed on their merits rather than their parent's ability to pay and that it was right to allocate more resources to the higher achievers to allow them to develop their full potential. To its critics, however, the tripartite system, which favoured the grammar school child, meant that large numbers of children still received inferior quality education, little better than the elementary schooling which Butler had sought to reform.

This was an argument that was to continue running for many decades to come, but in the 1950s the protagonists divided over the issue of whether or not to move to a comprehensive schooling system and to bring an end to the tripartite divide. Increasingly the Labour Party favoured a comprehensive solution, which some local authorities had already adopted, and so it was that when returned to government Labour sought to bring about a comprehensive revolution in education. From 1965 the Secretary of State for Education, Tony Crosland, required all local authorities to submit proposals to construct local secondary schooling on a comprehensive basis. It was at this stage, however, a request to local authorities rather than a requirement sanctioned by Act of Parliament. The arguments between the pro-grammar and pro-comprehensive factions rumbled on for the rest of that decade but the goal was not to be realised until the Education Act of 1976 which required a wholesale switch from the by now bipartisan system to a comprehensive one. The Labour government continued to stress its goal to end the inequity in an education system which provided a privileged system of education for an elite group of pupils, and the 1976 Act attacked this system directly by restricting the ability of local authorities to continue funding grammar school places. What that government, nor its predecessor between 1964 and 1970 did not do, however, was to address the wholly elitist private education system which it left largely untouched. But for the mass of Britain's children, secondary education was in future to be comprehensive and not selective.

The Labour government of the 1960s did, however, plan to address educational elitism on an entirely different front, that of higher education. Access to university education remained, even for many grammar school children, an elusive dream. The Conservative governments of the 1950s had already signalled their intention to look afresh at the question of higher education, with the creation of new universities towards the end of the decade (some were newly created and others upgraded from University College to full University status). The Conservatives had also established the Robbins Committee on Higher Education which reported in 1963 and which recommended a doubling in student numbers. The cause of the higher education sector was given a further much needed boost by Harold Wilson, greatly concerned with Britain's apparent failure in industry and innovation to keep up with the rest of the world, who promised to launch a technological revolution. This revolution was intended to invest in a new type of higher education, vocational in its nature and which heavily emphasised engineering and the development of new technologies, such as computing and telecommunications. This new type of higher education was to be delivered at a new type of higher education institution, the Polytechnic, which would provide degree-level education in practical and technical subjects, and so, it was hoped, also end the age-old arts bias of British university education. The Polytechnics, as with state schools and further education colleges, were to be under the control of the Local Education Authority who were in this way to have a strategic overview of the whole educational system from nursery and primary school through to degree-level education within their locality.

One final area of innovation in higher education in the 1960s, and very much the feather in Wilson's cap, was the foundation of an altogether different type of university, the Open University. This was to be an institution, which began teaching from 1967, with the aim of providing graduate-level education for committed adults who had missed the opportunity in earlier life. The education offered was also to be of a qualitatively different type to that offered in other higher education institutions. Little of the teaching would take place in the conventional classroom and much education would be delivered using distance learning techniques supported by well-resourced teaching materials and supplemented by television and radio programmes and the development of the 'summer school'.

STANDARDS AND EDUCATION REFORM

As we have seen above, the reorganisation and in many cases creation of a new education system in the post-1945 era, had as one of its central goals the provision of schooling for the mass of the population. A great step forward was taken in the creation of a system capable of providing schooling, beyond the elementary level and at no cost, to working-class children. Later in this period arguments over equity and elitism in education prevailed and Britain's system of education moved into a period in which it attempted to deliver greater social equality via its schools and expanding university sector. However, the skeleton hiding in this particular cupboard, which was to come into the open towards the end of the 1970s, was the issue of educational standards. Prime Minister James Callaghan highlighted the issue in 1976 when he launched the great education debate. Once again Britain appeared to be lagging behind its economic competitors, the expansion of technical education in the 1960s had had apparently little effect. But of most concern was the evidence of growing illiteracy and innumeracy amongst Britain's school leavers, which critics blamed on the move towards comprehensive schooling and the adoption of fashionable teaching methods by some local education authorities. They felt that the bias against grammar school education exhibited by successive Labour governments in the 1960s and 1970s had driven down the quality and standard of education for all schoolchildren.

Exhibit 11.1

- to support economic growth and improve the nation's competitiveness and quality of life by raising standards of educational achievement and skills;

- to promote an efficient and flexible labour market by enhancing choice, diversity and excellence in education and training, and by encouraging lifelong learning.

Such fears found resonance in the Conservative Party, and its new leader, who saw the hand of collectivism wielded by socialist local government and which denied the wishes and desires of parents who they felt to be the best judges of the needs of their children. The Thatcher governments of the 1980s approached education with the same reforming zeal as they did other areas of the public sector. They placed part of the blame for Britain's economic ills at the doors of 'trendy' educationalists whom they charged with conducting educational experiments on the nation's children instead of equipping those children for their own future and neglecting the needs of the most able children (Hill, 1997). Instead of providing children with a solid foundation at school and seeking to build upon academic excellence and potential, as they saw the grammar schools had done, they charged that educators were too preoccupied with issues such as equality. The government saw its task as one which would liberate both schools and parents from the deadening hand of local authority socialism and return decisions about education to the nation's parents.

They resolved that academic standards would be raised and that the power of the market place could be brought to bear in education. Parents would be able to 'shop-around' for the best type of school for their child, and the large numbers of parents seeking to send their children to better performing schools would force other schools to improve their standards in order to compete. They began, with the Education Act of 1980, by removing from Local Education Authorities the requirement to plan for comprehensive education and re-established the scheme to allow bright children, whose parents were of limited means, to attend fee-paying schools, the Assisted Places Scheme. Major change in the control and structure of Britain's education system was not to come, however, until the end of the decade, 'until the Education Reform Act 1988, Conservative education policy could be described as incrementalist' (McVicar, 1996, p. 222).

Before that Act, however, the government had sought to pave the way for its more radical agenda. As we have noted above, the Conservatives expressed their support for the selective, and competitive, education of the grammar school but they also began to introduce other measures they felt would enhance 'parent power' and weaken the position of the LEA. The government signalled its intention to remove from local authorities the power to determine, by means of catchment areas, which school a child should attend and tried to introduce the right for parents to choose. In a similar vein the number of LEA appointed representatives on school governing bodies, usually party political appointments, would be restricted. The LEA, however, did retain the duty to make strategic decisions about the number of school places required and to make sure that schools were not too heavily over-subscribed, and realising these two apparently conflicting goals, would often prove difficult. The difficulties were further compounded as schools would remain, for the time being, under the managerial control of the LEA.

The Education Reform Act, however, provided the sea change in education policy that the more radical conservatives had been seeking. That Act introduced a five-fold assault against Britain's stagnant education system by proposing the introduction of grant maintained schools (GMS), locally managed schools (LMS), school league tables, a national curriculum and standardised testing. The Act also addressed the wider education system and proposed the freeing of both polytechnics and further education colleges from LEA control, thereby also creating a *de facto* market in both post-16 and post-18 education.

Grant maintained schools, it was intended, would permit greater decentralisation in school management away from the local authority and into the school itself. The process would allow schools to opt out of LEA control and allow them to determine their own policies on, for example, entry and selection. Such schools would be funded directly by the Department of Education (DES, now DfEE) and would later have restrictions on raising their own (private) investment relaxed. Management of such a school would pass to the school's own management team: the head teacher and deputy head teachers, along with the school's governing body.

For those schools who did not opt out of local authority control, they too would become decentralised in their management by the introduction of the concept of locally managed schools. Such schools would themselves control around 85 per cent of their total expenditure with the local authority retaining control largely over capital costs and the provision of other educational services, such as educational welfare or the careers service. By these two measures, GMS and LMS, the government hoped to create an 'internal market' in education with schools forced to compete for pupil numbers. Since the system would allocate resources on the basis of the numbers of children enrolled with a school, the school would have an incentive to provide high educational standards or risk losing income and face possible closure. Successful schools, measured by their increased intake, would, on the other hand, prosper and grow. The government hoped by this 'carrot and stick' approach that schools, having been freed from the bureaucratic control of their local authority, could improve educational standards.

The other side to the market coin, however, is that of demand. The government had to find a mechanism by which parents could make informed choices about the best school for the needs of their children. Simply relaxing the restrictions imposed by a local authority on the numbers a school was allowed to enrol was not enough, parents also needed some way in which to measure the educational performance of individual schools and be able to compare them. The government therefore sought to introduce school league tables, rather like football league tables, which would rank schools in order of their success and allow parents to compare the performance of schools within their area. However, it must be remembered that such league tables were introduced at a time of continued criticism of falling standards of achievement and of teaching. How then would parents know what the league tables meant?

The government's answer to the standards debate was to move 'back to basics' in education. Criticisms had long been made, back to the Black Papers of the 1960s, that standards of basic literacy and numeracy, the three Rs, were falling, that despite much investment in new teaching methods children were still leaving school unable to read, write or do simple mathematics. The government sought to emphasise the teaching of basic educational skills in such a way that would improve standards across the country by the introduction of a national curriculum.

This would provide schools with a standard syllabus, which had to be delivered, and would prescribe targets to be met at different levels within a child's school career. The Secretary of State had the power to decide how much time in each week would be spent in particular subjects, such as maths, English, science or languages, and had ultimate power over the content of the curriculum, though this has largely been devolved to the National Curriculum Council. Critics of a national curriculum pointed to the denial of opportunities to pursue interests, such as music or drama, since so much time would be spent studying the core subjects, or to the possible effects on children's health of a reduction in sports and games education. Others were particularly concerned at the concept of a 'national' curriculum to be taught to a multi-cultural society with a wide range of backgrounds and educational abilities or expectations. Inner-city schools, with large numbers of children who lacked English as a first language, it was felt might be marginalised by this new system and labelled as failing schools, whereas compared to other schools they were starting from different points in the education race.

To measure the increase in educational standards that the national curriculum would bring, and to further measure the performance of schools themselves, the Act also introduced standardised testing of children in the form of the standardised attainment tests or SATs. The proposal was that schools should administer a set of standard tests across a range of subjects covered in the national curriculum and at different points in the lifetime of a school child. So the government proposed that each child should take the tests at the age of seven, 11, 14 and 16 in order to gauge the progress of each child. The final proposed test at age 16 was eventually dropped since this is also of course the age at which GCSEs are taken and thus a system of testing at three points was introduced. To critics the proposal appeared to be a return to the days of selection and the eleven-plus examination by another name and the fear that children might find themselves labelled as failures at a very early age. To the government's supporters the national curriculum and SATs together would provide an essential return to traditional educational values and would provide fuel for the developing education market by giving parents a much greater range of information on which to base their decisions about school choice.

The final area of major change introduced by the 1988 Act was in the reform of the higher and further education sectors. Both polytechnics and local colleges of further education were under the control of LEAs but the changes that were taking place in the role of local authorities and LEAs meant that this was no longer to be the case. Polytechnics in particular had long been pressing for an end to the 'binary divide' between themselves and the more traditional universities. In some ways we might say that the structure of higher education mirrored the divisions between grammar and secondary modern schools that had ended two decades earlier. The university sector was felt to be offering perhaps more cerebral and traditional academic courses of study, whilst the polytechnics offered more practical or vocational courses. Yet the distinction was, and always had been, an artificial one, both types of institutions offered degree and post-graduate education, and the distinction between the so-called vocational polytechnics and academic universities was becoming increasingly blurred. Polytechnics had always offered the more traditional academic courses of study and universities offered the vocational.

Fundamental differences existed, however, in the way in which each type of institution was run and managed. Universities operated rather like quasi-independent contractors to the Department of Education and Science; they had their own power to confer degrees and other awards and they had considerable freedom in the way in which they were managed. Universities also held relatively greater freedoms in controlling their finances and in their ability to generate their own income outside of their contract with the DES. Polytechnics, on the other hand, were controlled and managed from within the LEA and its education committee who often might pursue different priorities in the statutory sector but also found themselves subject to government controls over public sector borrowing. Polytechnics were also unable to confer their own awards, but instead polytechnic degrees were overseen by the Council for National Academic Awards (CNAA).

The Act also sought therefore to end the binary divide and release polytechnics from the control of local authorities. So from 1989 to 1990 polytechnics and colleges of higher education achieved what was called 'incorporated status' – they became public corporations funded, as the universities were, directly from central government funds. Later the two funding councils were themselves merged into a single Higher Education Funding Council and the binary divide ended completely as polytechnics won the right to change their status and become universities. From 1992 further education colleges went through the same process of incorporation as they too were removed from the control of their local authority and placed on an independent managerial and financial basis. We may argue that much of the changes made to the system of education at the end of the 1980s were as much to do with reducing the power of local authorities as they were with improving educational standards. We can also say that the introduction of an education market place in both the pre- and post-16 sectors was done for strong ideological rather than educational reasons. What the government sought to do, as with many other areas of public life and in our social services, was to develop a cult of the consumer, and welfare services that were responsive to their customers rather than alternative political or bureaucratic agendas. But, we must remember, the motivation for change also remained an economic one. A central issue in education policy both today and throughout the recent history of the development of state education is the need to compete in world markets. We have seen that part of the motivation behind Butler's tripartite structure was to match children to the most appropriate form of education for the type of employment they would find themselves in as adults. Similarly the motivations behind Wilson's white heat of technology and the expansion of vocational higher education was the feeling that Britain was falling behind the rest of the world in technological advances. Once again behind Callaghan's education debate was the fear that underlying the 1970s recession in Britain was a failure of the education system to equip our children with the skills they needed to compete in the labour market and for Britain to compete in the world economy. Similarly the education reforms, as well as being motivated by ideological concerns, possess an economic imperative and the fear that Britain is facing a 'skills shortage', that is that its work-force is not sufficiently educated in the skills demanded by a modern economy. It is in this context that we now turn our attention to the role of training and technical education.

British education has over many years faced the charge that its schools and universities provide too much of a generalised, arts-based education and do not do enough to motivate children's interest in science, technology and engineering. More damningly, perhaps, Britain is commended for producing skilled inventors and entrepreneurs who can find little support in Britain and consequently take their skills and ideas overseas where they are said to be better valued and rewarded. The arts-based culture was said to be so deeply ingrained in British society that the most highly valued civil servants were those with private education and Oxbridge degrees in classics who were able to complete *The Times* crossword before their day's work started (Fulton Report, 1968; Wright, 1987). Whilst we can recognise that the government has at various times attempted to address the question of technical and vocational education, the charge of lack of political will remains a strong one.

We have already suggested that the plan for technical schooling embodied within the Butler Act was left to wither. Most local authorities concentrated their efforts in creating the grammar and secondary modern schools, or later comprehensives, and as a consequence few technical schools were built. Indeed since the mark of educational success was a place at grammar school, with the apparent failures condemned to what were clearly regarded as second-class secondary modern schools, there was little incentive to develop the technical schools envisaged by Butler. Instead education authorities attempted to strengthen the provision of technical subjects within the existing school structure (Lowe, 1993). Technical education received a small, and perhaps token, shot in the arm in the 1960s in Wilson's plans for technological revolution in the creation of polytechnics and the Industrial Training Board in 1965.

Perhaps, however, the greatest motivation to address the question of technical and vocational education was that provided by successive economic crises in the 1970s and 1980s. The Manpower Services Commission (MSC) which operated from 1974 was given a specific role in the overview of training and vocational education and co-ordination of the activities of the Industrial Training Boards (its duties were taken over by the Training Commission in 1987 after the MSC was wound up). The MSC developed or was responsible for the operation of a range of initiatives in the training or reskilling of industrial workers. Schemes such as the Youth Opportunities Programme (YOP), which later became the Youth Training Scheme (YTS), was designed to provide training and work experience for school leavers who employers suggested lacked even the basic skills to obtain employment. This was later extended into schools themselves in the form of the Technical and Vocational Education Initiative (TVEI) and in the greater, and now routine, provision of periods of work experience or placements whilst pupils were still at school. The aim of such schemes was that young people should leave school to enter further education, full-time training or employment and should not only be able to look forward to unemployment. Such aims were reinforced by changes in benefit regulations that effectively removed the right to claim social security benefits from all school leavers between the ages of 16–18, and reduced the amount payable for all young people up to the age of 25. This position has been reinforced by the new Labour government's New Deal programme, which intends that unemployment will simply not be an option.

In addition to the identification of youth unemployment as a particular area of concern, retraining or reskilling of unemployed older workers has been high on the government's agenda since the mid 1970s. The advent of mass redundancies and the virtual elimination of some industries in Britain, coal-mining, steel production, shipbuilding and much of the motor industry, has created amongst the ranks of the unemployed a mass of older workers ill suited to alternative employment. The effect of a lifetime's employment in a single industry, often with a single employer, and the decimation of Britain's industrial base, has left the older unemployed (often male) worker nowhere to go. Government policy has therefore sought to concentrate efforts in the provision of training to allow workers to switch to other industries; however, the geographical concentrations of such industries has often made such retraining appear fruitless. Additionally, training policy has attempted to introduce new groups of workers, in particular women, to the labour force. Thus training in new industries, information technology and data processing for instance and often with assistance from the European Social Fund, has provided a further expansion in the training budget. This has led to an apparent paradox in an ever-growing workforce alongside persistently high unemployment (see chapter 15 regarding employment policy).

EDUCATION, EDUCATION, EDUCATION

The election of a Labour government in 1997 promised a wholesale and wide-ranging rethink of education policy, as much else, since they promised that education would be the cornerstone of their new Britain. Education and training, in the form of an Employment Action Plan, would be central to the New Deal which aims to provide every adult with the opportunity (or duty) to find employment. Employment policy and education were to work hand in hand and would focus on the multiple aims of increasing employability, combating social exclusion and equipping young people with workplace skills (DfEE, 1998a). A new Skills Task Force would establish an education policy which promised to emphasise the provision of basic skills and to raise the standards of basic literacy and numeracy, whilst an Investing in Young People Strategy promised to introduce a statutory right to time out of employment for training. The Action Plan also promised to develop a system of 'lifelong learning', which seeks to end the idea that education is confined to our years of schooling. Instead, and in order to create a skilled and flexible workforce, lifelong learning stresses the imperative of continued upgrading of skills for the information age (see Exhibit 11.2).

The government made its detailed proposals in the year following the election which were to include: Education Action Zones, Education Development Plans, the creation of the so-called 'super teachers' or Advanced Skills Teachers and the development of partnerships between schools, teachers and parents (DfEE, 1997, 1998b). The proposals include a statutory requirement for Local Education Authorities to prepare three-year Education Development Plans from April 1999 which set targets within schools for the raising of standards of literacy and numeracy. Such plans, the government hopes, will raise not only standards in children but also the quality of teaching and management in schools, and will be monitored through the system of educational inspections carried out by the Office for Standards in Education (OFSTED). Furthermore, the government proposed to create a series of Education Action Zones, 25 in the first instance, to again raise educational standards and to tackle disadvantage and social exclusion. Within the Action Zones schools would be able to make use of the Advanced Skills Teachers but the government also envisage the establishment of Out of Hours

Exhibit 11.2

By age 19, 85 per cent of all people should have five GCSE passes	By age 21, 60 per cent of all people should have two A-level passes
60 per cent of the workforce to have achieved NVQ level 2	30 per cent of the workforce to have achieved NVQ level 4
70 per cent of organisations employing over 200 people to achieve Investors in People status	35 per cent of organisations employing more than 50 people to achieve Investors in People status
	15 per cent of organisations employing less than 50 people to achieve Investors in People status

Exhibit 11.3

> **Ten Point Plan in training**
> 1 All schools to have targets to raise attainment at age 16
> 2 Wider vocational options for 14–16 year olds
> 3 Standardised school leaving date in June of each year
> 4 New National Record of Achievement
> 5 Learning Card to encourage post-16 education
> 6 Targeting of Career Service support
> 7 New Start scheme for disaffected 14–16 year olds
> 8 Statutory right to training up to GNVQ level 2
> 9 System of National Traineeships to achieve GNVQ level 2
> 10 Improving quality of post-16 education

Learning, Literacy Summer Schools and Family Literacy Schemes. With such initiatives the government hopes to change the culture of education 'at school' to one of lifelong learning. This message is again reinforced in the government's plans to strengthen the system of training education in Britain which intends to set National Training Targets and to promote a University for Industry whilst promising to increase the numbers taking the Modern Apprenticeship by 60,000 annually.

REFERENCES

Working Group on Inequalities in Health (1980) *Inequalities in Health: Report of the Research Working Group on Inequalities in Health: Chairman Sir Douglas Black*, London: Department for Health and Social Security. (The Black Report.)

Department for Education and Employment (1997) *Excellence in Schools*, London: HMSO.

Department for Education and Employment (1998a) *Employment Action Plan*, London: HMSO.

Department for Education and Employment (1998b) *Education Action Zones*, London: HMSO.

Fulton, Lord (1968) 'The Civil Service: Report of the Committee', Cmnd 3638, London: HMSO.

Glennerster, H. (1995) *British Social Policy Since 1945*, London: Blackwell.

Hill, M. (1997) *Understanding Social Policy*, 5th edition, London: Blackwell.

Lowe, R. (1993) *The Welfare State in Britain Since 1945*, London: Macmillan.

McVicar, M. (1996) 'Education', in Farnham, D. and Horton, S. (eds), *Managing the New Public Services*, 2nd edition, London: Macmillan.

Timmins, N. (1995) *The Five Giants: A biography of the welfare state*, London: Fontana.

Wright, P. (1987) *Spycatcher*, London: Penguin.

ANNOTATED READINGS

For an historical overview of the development of education policy it is perhaps useful to examine some of the general social policy texts, for instance, Rodney Lowe's *Welfare State in Britain Since 1945*, Timmins' *Five Giants: A Biography of the Welfare State* or Glennerster's *British Social Policy*

Since 1945. Most recent policy proposals are described in the various publications by the Department for Education and Employment. A very useful and wide ranging overview of the development of British education policy is to be found in A. H. Halsey *et al.* (1997) *Education: Culture, Economy and Society*, Oxford: Oxford University Press.

12 Health policy

OBJECTIVES

- To consider what is meant by the term 'health policy' in Britain.

- To examine the development and structure of the NHS as a mechanism for delivering health policy and alternative policies to the medical treatment of illness.

- To consider the role and power of professional groups within the NHS.

- To evaluate the relative success of post-war British health policy and the prevalence of inequalities in health.

- To describe and analyse the introduction of the NHS internal market as a possible solution to the dilemma of resource allocation.

INTRODUCTION

The focus of this chapter is health policy in Britain during the post-war period, and issues affecting the distribution of health in Britain in the 1980s and 1990s. Health care in Britain is dominated by one major institution, the National Health Service (NHS), which came into being in July 1948 as part of the post-war welfare state and which remains central to British health care, despite changes in its organisation over the years. However, whilst the NHS provides the greatest part of health care in the formal sector, this takes place within a wide context, in which there are also private suppliers of health care, in the chronic sector, in support services and in the acute sector. The work of the NHS also overlaps with the social services, particularly in the context of community care for vulnerable groups. Other sources of health care include occupational provisions – particularly in the field of preventive care – and the voluntary sector. Finally, health care is also provided, informally, in the home.

In addition, other policy areas contribute to the promotion or otherwise of health, and the study of 'health policy' might legitimately include a range of other issues which affect health. If we look at transport policy, for example, we might focus on subsidies to encourage or discourage different forms of transport, or taxes on those fuels which are a greater threat to the environment or to health. We might consider how far housing policy includes a commitment to a certain standard of housing, and the extent to which such standards are actively pursued.

In a short introductory chapter to health policy all of these issues cannot be explored. However, it is important to bear in mind such ideas when studying policies relating to the planning and delivery of the formal health care system for a number of reasons. First, and perhaps most importantly, the exclusion from most discussions of health policy of these other issues reflects the ways in which both policy makers and the public generally have come to accept that

Exhibit 12.1

Measuring health and illness

There are two major ways in which health can be measured: mortality and morbidity.

Mortality: Mortality data comes from figures for deaths. In Britain mortality statistics come from death certificates, which collect information on the age of the deceased, their last known occupation, their country of birth, their sex and the major or primary cause of death. This data is collected by the Registrar-General and can then be used to calculate a range of mortality statistics, including:

- **Life expectancy:** life expectancy figures, for example, show average life span, and are usually quoted as 'life expectancy at birth'.
- **Crude death rates:** crude death rates are usually expressed as the number of deaths per 1,000 population, or per 100,000 population.
- **Death rates for babies and young children:** these are the most commonly used crude death rates. Perinatal mortality rates, for example, are the number of stillbirths together with deaths in the first week of life, expressed as a proportion of live births.
- **Standardised Mortality Ratio:** this frequently used measure of mortality compares deaths in a given group with national death rates, and controls for differences between groups on the basis of age and sex. An SMR of 100 is the average, an SMR of below 100 is a better than average chance of survival while SMRs above 100 show that a group has a higher than average risk of mortality.

The problem with mortality data is that it does not measure health, but death. Cause of death often will not reflect the kind of health someone experienced during their lifetime, so while measures based on death tell us something about the distribution of life chances in a society, they do not tell us much about the distribution of health during a lifetime.

Morbidity: Morbidity data is a measure of illness experienced. There are a range of different measures, but the most commonly used ones include:

- **Consultation with health professionals:** this measure is based on frequency of visits to GPs and other medical professionals.
- **Self-reported measures:** this is widely used in government and other surveys and relies on the individual's report of illness or disability in a given time period.
- **Work absence data:** some measures of morbidity use absence from paid employment, although this is limited in value for whole populations, as those not in paid employment are not included, and also decisions to take time off paid work due to ill-health are related to other issues, particularly pay.

health policy means treatment of illness within a medical setting. That is, our discussions about health policy are dominated by concerns over the provision of medical treatment, in which the medical profession play a central role. The, discussion tends to focus on questions relating to funding, the distribution of medical resources, the organisation of the medical services and so on. Questions such as whether, as a society, we might be better spending more of our health resources on improving nutrition, removing poverty and deprivation, and increasing opportunities for health-promoting activities, are rarely asked.

A second related theme is the power of the medical profession in the formulation of health policy – for example, in decisions about the distribution of health resources across different specialty groups and different kinds of services or treatments – and how far this power has been curtailed in the 1990s (Day and Klein, 1991; Allsop, 1995).

A third theme is that of assessing the success of British health policy. On what basis could we say that health policy since the Second World War has worked? If we measure outcome we are largely restricted to data on morbidity and mortality.

In the post-war years mortality has decreased and life expectancy has improved (Abel-Smith, 1978; Ham, 1992) – is this due to the introduction of a universal health care system or other influences, such as improved standards of nutrition and housing (Doyal, 1979; McKeown, 1979; Hart, 1985)? Equally, we could measure improvements in the delivery of care itself – looking at access to health care, waiting times or measures of patient satisfaction. In making international comparisons, statistical indicators, which are often used, suggest we can measure the success of a country's health policy by per capita expenditure (Wanuk-Lipinski and Illsley, 1990; Rublee and Schneider, 1991). These are, however, rather crude measures which tell us little about the value of such services or treatment, and which measure clinical activity, rather than health care need, which will vary between countries.

THE DEVELOPMENT OF THE NATIONAL HEALTH SERVICE

State involvement in health care has a long history, although this involvement grew slowly. Under the provisions of the 1834 Poor Law local boards of guardians were required to provide health care for paupers unable to work due to ill health (Fraser, 1984; Allsop, 1995; Thane, 1996). By the late nineteenth century the emerging medical professions were to some extent regulated with the passing of the 1858 Medical Act and, later, the 1902 Midwives Act (Fraser, 1984). There was also increasing central and local government involvement in public health measures, with a series of public health acts which substantially increased local authority involvement in areas such as sanitation and water supply, food inspection and burial (Fraser, 1984; Midwinter, 1994).

The 1911 National Insurance Act, under which a number of occupational groups were to be insured against ill-health, with contributions paid by employee, employer and the government, increased central government's role in health care (Fraser, 1984; Moon and Gillespie, 1995). Insured workers received health care through a system of 'panel' doctors – General Practitioners registered with an insurance panel. Cover did not at first extend to hospital treatment, and also only covered the person in paid employment and not their dependants (Allsop, 1995). Thus, whilst the 1911 Act introduced a system of health care for certain groups of people, many remained outside this system and continued to rely on a range of solutions – the more affluent bought treatment from the general practitioner and private hospitals, some people paid a weekly subscription to clubs and received payment when ill, and others depended on the health care offered by the voluntary hospitals and Poor Law infirmaries, run as public general hospitals by local authorities after 1929 (Abel-Smith, 1978; Allsop, 1995).

By the 1920s and 1930s the system was under increasing strain. The categories of employees who could benefit under the 1911 National Insurance Act had been extended to include more occupations, and over 40 per cent of the population was covered (Allsop, 1995), but, at the same time, increasing unemployment meant that there were large numbers of people who were outside the system, and without enough funds to pay for treatment or to pay to subscription clubs. Hospitals were facing increasing costs, with improved methods of treatment, whilst the value of donations received and fees charged to private patients was decreasing. When the Second World War broke out in 1939 the voluntary hospitals were virtually bankrupt, and the years leading up to the war saw the publication of a number of reports on the future of health care: including the Dawson Report (1920) on medical services, a Royal Commission on National Health Insurance (1926) and a report from an independent research institute, Political and Economic Planning (PEP, 1937). Whilst the reports differed to some extent in their analysis of the solution, they largely agreed over the problems – the overlap between differently funded services, the lack of co-operation and collaboration between services, and the lack of a rational planning mechanism which meant that some areas of the country were under-provided, whilst there was a concentration of, and competition between, services in other areas. Existing health services were seen as inequitable, inefficient and poorly managed (Ham, 1992).

The service that was eventually created was the outcome of deliberations between the civil servants, the political parties and, in particular, Aneurin Bevan, the Labour Minister for Health who was responsible for the final stages in the development of the NHS, and the powerful medical profession, represented by the BMA and the Royal Colleges. There was no direct representation for those who would become the users of the new service. The effect of the power of the medical profession in these discussions was, argues Ranade (1994):

to medicalise large areas of policy and define them as off-limits to lay influence. It also led to the creation of a lopsided system in line with the structure of medical priorities and values. Curative, hospital based medicine dominated at the expense of prevention, health promotion and community services, and high priority was given to the treatment of short-term episodes of acute illness to the detriment of the care and rehabilitation of the chronically ill. (p. 9)

There are a number of detailed accounts of the struggle over the shape of the National Health Service and in particular the difficulties which arose with the medical profession over issues of control and autonomy (Abel-Smith, 1964; Webster, 1991; Allsop, 1995). In essence, Bevan had to negotiate two different agreements with the hospital doctors and the general practitioners. Hospital doctors were less concerned with their status as state employees, but wanted to retain control over their work, their conditions of employment and their right to run fee-paying beds and to offer private medicine within the new NHS hospitals. Hospital doctors further acquired the right to determine some part of their remuneration through merit awards – causing Bevan's bitter comment that he had 'stuffed their mouths with gold' (cited in Allsop, 1995). General practitioners, however, wished to retain their independent status as self-employed contractors, as in the 1911 National Insurance Act. In the end, Bevan secured the co-operation of the general practitioners with an agreement over payment, largely by capitation, on the basis of the number of patients they had on their list. The existing separation between hospital consultants and general practitioners was retained, as were the rights of doctors to treat patients privately on a fee-paying basis (Allsop, 1995).

The National Health Service was created by the 1946 National Health Service Act, and came into being two years later, in July 1948. The provision of a universal and fully comprehensive health care system was a critical aspect of the new welfare state and was seen as a major factor in its hopes for success (Ranade, 1994). The National Health Service was created as a universal service – covering all members of the British population, regardless of income or status. The National Health Service was also to be fully comprehensive, covering all kinds of health needs, was to be equitable, with equal access to the services, and, finally, the new NHS was to be free at the point of delivery. This meant that the patient would not be expected to pay directly for services or treatment, unlike the insurance-based systems found in other countries, where patients are often required to pay for some or all of the treatment and then reclaim some or all of the cost from either the government or the insurance system (Moon and Gillespie, 1995).

How far have these principles been eroded or lost since 1948? Universality remains, although some groups have had difficulties – having to prove nationality, for example. The idea of a fully comprehensive service has been eroded by decisions taken by health authorities in the face of underfunding – for example, some health authorities have refused to carry out certain kinds of treatment which they have defined as cosmetic or unnecessary (Ham, 1992). It should be

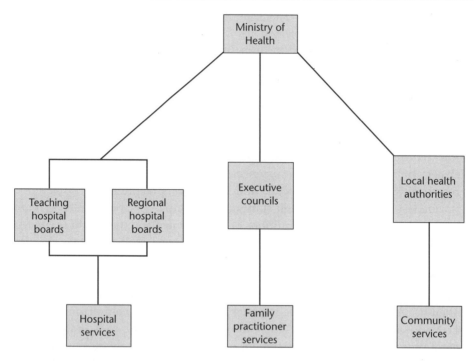

Fig. 12.1 Structure of the NHS in 1948

noted, however, that in many respects the services never were fully comprehensive. Contraceptive services, for example, were not provided under the NHS until the 1960s.

Equity of access has never been resolved. Attempts were made during the 1970s and 1980s, under the recommendations of the Resource Allocation Working Party (RAWP, 1978), to redistribute resources in favour of poorer health authorities with greater need. However, such attempts largely failed to achieve their targets. Similarly research into the utilisation of health services has suggested that the middle classes make more use of, and benefit more from, services, particularly preventive services (Tudor-Hart, 1971; Cartwright and O'Brien, 1976; Ham, 1992).

Finally, the NHS was designed to be free at the point of delivery. This lasted until the introduction of charges for some services – charges for prescriptions, spectacles and false teeth – in 1951 – which Bevan considered such a fundamental betrayal of the principles of his NHS that he (together with Harold Wilson) resigned from the Cabinet.

The service was designed on a tripartite structure, with three separate branches: the hospital services, which included both acute and chronic hospitals; the primary health care system, including GPs, dentists (for the first time ever, free dental treatment was universally available), pharmacists and ophthalmists; and the public health responsibilities of local authorities, which they were to retain.

Exhibit 12.2

Key events in the history of the NHS – some of the key papers, consultative documents and legislation

1948–79

1956 The Guillebaud Report: Report of the Committee of Enquiry into the cost of the National Health Service

1959 The Mental Health Act

1962 A Hospital Plan for England & Wales

1968 The Seebohm Report: Report of the Committee on Local Authority and Allied Personal Social Services (Cmnd 3703)

1968 Department of Health and Social Security (DHSS) formed

1971 DHSS Better Services for the Mentally Handicapped

1975 DHSS Better Services for the Mentally Ill

1972 National Health Service Reorganisation in England (Cmnd 5055) and Wales (Cmnd 5057) – followed by 1973 NHS Reorganisation Act

1973 Creation of Joint Consultative Committees, for joint planning of community care

1974 The creation of Community Health Councils

1976 Joint Finance established for community care

1976 Resources Allocation Working Party (RAWP) report: 'Sharing Resources for Health in England'

1976 DHSS Prevention and Health: Everybody's Business: A Reassessment of Public and Personal Health

1976 DHSS Priorities for Health and Social Services in England

1977 DHSS Priorities for Health and Social Services: The Way Forward

1979 The Royal Commission on the Health Service

1979–97

1979 'Patients First' consultative paper (Cmnd 9663) – response to the Royal Commission

1981 DHSS Care in Action: A Handbook of Policies and Priorities for the Health and Personal Social Services in England

1981 Care in the Community: A Consultative Document for Care in England

1982 'Rayner' scrutinies of expenditure in the NHS to search for cost savings

1983 NHS Management Inquiry, chaired by Roy Griffiths

1983 Publication of Performance Indicators, devised in 1982

1983 DHSS Circular HC (80) 8 – Health Services Management: Competitive Tendering in the Provision of Domestic, Catering and Laundry Services

1985 Parliamentary Select Committee on Social Services Report on Community Care

1986 Audit Commission report: Making a Reality of Community Care

1987 Ministerial Review of the NHS

1988 Community Care: An Agenda for Action – report prepared by Roy Griffiths

1989 White Paper: Caring for People: Community Care in the Next Decade and Beyond

1990 National Health Service and Community Care Act 1990

Funding for the new National Health Service was to come, initially, from two sources. The largest proportion came from the Consolidated Fund raised through national taxation. There is not, therefore, a specified proportion of taxes which goes directly to the health care system; instead funding is allocated annually by the Treasury, in competition with other claims. A small proportion came from the National Insurance fund, reflecting the contributory principle of the 1911 Act. From 1951 onwards funding also came from charges levied on prescriptions and other services, and, whilst the proportion of total funding raised from this source has remained minor in comparison to the proportion coming from general taxes, it has grown, particularly during the 1980s and 1990s. These three remain the major sources of funding.

The early years of the NHS identify the dominant themes in the history of the NHS: the central question of costs, the ever-increasing demands made on the NHS, and issues of control over both expenditure and the division of resources within the service. Early assumptions that expenditure would stabilise, after initially high costs to meet the needs of those who had been unable to afford treatment before the NHS, proved wrong: the amount spent each year continued to rise. Debate focused on the organisational structure, questions of priority setting and the allocation of resources inside the NHS in the 'search for control' (Allsop, 1995). However, whilst the same themes remain central to health policy in the 1990s, the solutions may be seen as quite different.

THE 1980s – THE MARKET SOLUTION?

In 1979 the report of the Royal Commission on the NHS (chaired by Sir Alec Merrison), and the subsequent White Paper, 'Patients First', recommended the abolition of one tier of NHS administration, the Area Health Authorities, in order to reduce the complexity of the existing structure and to decentralise decision making, and in 1982 the re-organisation went ahead. However, there was an increasing desire to control existing clinical freedom over the expenditure of health resources, a theme that was to develop further over the decade that followed (Ham, 1992; Allsop, 1995).

The Rayner scrutinies of public expenditure which took place in the same year set the tone for the rest of the decade, with the focus on scope for 'efficiency savings' in the health services, which aimed to improve performance without increased levels of funding (Petchey, 1986). In 1982 Performance Indicators were introduced, which allowed the performance of different districts, measured in efficiency, to be compared; whilst 1983 saw the introduction of competitive tendering, which required authorities to seek bids for essential services, such as cleaning and catering from outside contractors (Ham, 1992; Ranade, 1994).

The NHS Management Inquiry and the first Griffiths report followed in 1983 (Petchey, 1986). The major conclusion of this report was that the NHS suffered from poor management; the solution was seen to lie in a shift away from 'consensus' style management with the introduction of general managers with greater responsibility for decision making. The NHS was to be overseen by a new Health Services Supervisory Board, responsible for policy and set apart from the Department of Health.* The 'essential tension' (Ranade, 1994) between central government's desire to control and the need for local autonomy in the NHS was to be achieved by layers of general management responsible for tight control over expenditure.

Whilst the government minimised the extent to which the report meant further re-organisation of the NHS, so soon after the 1982 re-organisation, the changes were significant in what was implied. Throughout the 1980s there was a growing emphasis on the efficient management of resources, using techniques brought in from the private sector and the market place. In fact, the Griffiths changes did not see a great increase in the number of managers brought in from outside – on the whole the NHS paid too little and offered too little job security and too few 'perks' to attract high-ranking management from the private sector (Petchey, 1986).

Funding remained the central issue in the 1980s. In a system where resources are determined largely by the amount of funds awarded each year by the government, when there are other demands on public expenditure, there is no way of anticipating the right level of resources. Funding requirements do not only depend on how well funds are spent – an issue increasingly the focus of the Conservative government's attention during the 1980s – but also on demand, treatment methods and demographic change. In 1986 the House of Commons Social Services Select Committee concluded that the NHS needed a minimum 2 per cent funding increment annually to maintain existing services, partly because of changes in the population structure, with more people living to old age which increased demands on the health care system, and more people with disability surviving to an older age than in the past, and partly because of new, more expensive, treatment methods (Social Services Select Committee, 1986). Funding had failed to rise by the required amount – the 1986 Social Services Committee estimated that the 'under-funding' of the health services was almost £1.3 billion (Allsop, 1995) – and discontent amongst those working in the services grew. In 1987, amidst rising public concern, with more people turning to private medicine, increasing bed and ward closures and growing waiting lists, the crisis in NHS funding led to a statement from the Royal Colleges highlighting the lack of resources.

In 1988 a Prime Ministerial review was set up in response to the crisis and the desire from within the Conservative party and right-wing advisers to alter the basic structure of the tax-funded NHS towards something more like the American system of health care (Allsop, 1995; Mohan, 1995). The White Paper that followed, 'Working for Patients' (1989), and the subsequent 1990 NHS and Community Care Act were in many ways less dramatic than had been expected. Nonetheless they provoked a major debate and resistance, particularly from the health professions (Ham, 1992).

---

* In fact shortly after the introduction of the HSSB the position of chair was taken by the Minister of Health, thus ending the concept of separation from Health Ministry influence (Allsop, 1995).

THE 1990 NHS AND COMMUNITY CARE ACT

The National Health Service will continue to be available to all, regardless of income, and to be financed largely out of taxation. (Working for Patients)

The 1990 NHS and Community Care Act introduced major changes to the structure of the NHS, in particular through the creation of an internal market which would be based on managed competition. This was to be achieved by a division of responsibility between the purchasers of health care and the providers of health care. Purchasers would primarily be the district health authorities, who would purchase health care on behalf of their local populations, together with those general practitioners (GPs) who took on fund-holding status. Providers would largely be NHS hospitals who took on the status of a Trust, and were able to contract to provide health treatment. Trusts, which are required to operate as a financially viable concern, took over the buildings and assets of the hospital, and can set their own rates of pay for their staff, thereby reducing the national negotiating power of health unions. Fund-holding general practitioners are both purchasers and providers, giving primary health care to patients on their list, but also being able to buy specialist treatment when necessary. In addition, providers can also be from the private sector – thus private fee-paying hospitals are also able to contract with health authorities to provide services. After the changes were introduced there have been some amendments, for example the minimum list size required for a GP practice to seek fund-holding status had been halved by 1996, to encourage take-up. In addition, the term purchasing has been replaced by 'commissioning' to reflect the process whereby health care is contracted for. District Health Authorities have also changed names, becoming Health Authorities whilst their number has reduced through mergers (Allsop, 1995; Mohan, 1995). Health authorities are now required, under these changes, to take account of the health needs of the local population in purchasing health care – that is, in drawing up contracts with Trusts or other providers. In addition, contracts have had to include commitments to 'quality' (Allsop, 1995).

One of the most confusing aspects of the changes in the NHS has been the different ways in which they have been taken up in different areas. Although the majority of NHS hospitals have taken on Trust status, a smaller proportion of general practitioners have become fund-holders, with one in four patients registered with a fund-holding GP by 1993 (Ranade, 1995). Until the mid 1990s those GP practices which were not fund-holding were governed by the Family Health Services Authorities, which were responsible to the old Regional Health Authorities. However, by the mid 1990s the number of regions had been reduced and most health authorities had merged with the Family Health Services Authorities to create a larger agency commissioning health care to meet the needs of the local population (Allsop, 1995). In addition, some areas have introduced 'locality planning' with a consortia of GPs who do not want to become fund-holders

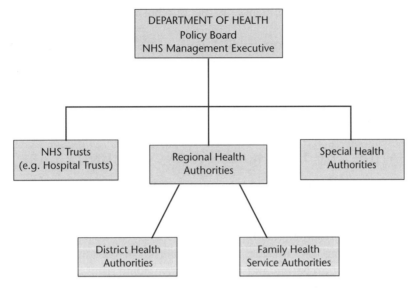

Fig. 12.2 Structure of the NHS after the 1990 NHS and Community Care Act

Exhibit 12.3

Health targets in the 1990s

The key targets of the **1992 Health of the Nation** programme were to achieve by the year 2000:

- Heart disease and stroke: to reduce deaths by 40 per cent among under-65s and by 30 per cent among those aged 64–75
- Cancer: to reduce deaths from the following causes:
  - breast cancer by 25 per cent
  - cervical cancer by 20 per cent
  - lung cancer in under-75s by 30 per cent in men and 15 per cent in women
- Mental health: to reduce suicides by 15 per cent and suicides among severely mentally ill by 33 per cent
- Sexual health: to reduce gonorrhoea by 20 per cent (by 1995) and conception among under-16s by 50 per cent
- Accidents: to reduce deaths among under-15s by 33 per cent, deaths among 15–24 year-olds by 25 per cent, and deaths among over-65s by 33 per cent

The key targets identified in the **1998 Our Healthier Nation Green Paper** were to achieve by the year 2010:

- Heart disease and stroke: to reduce the death rate from heart disease and stroke and related illnesses among people aged 65 years and under by at least a further third
- Cancer: to reduce the death rate from cancer among people aged under 65 years by at least a further fifth
- Mental health: to reduce the death rate from suicide and undetermined injury by at least a further sixth
- Accidents: to reduce accidents by at least one-fifth

but who want to acquire influence in the purchasing decisions of the health authority.

The reforms were introduced without small area testing, as is more often the case with other large-scale changes in public services (Allsop, 1995). Concerns were expressed initially over whether the reforms represented slow privatisation, the introduction of a two-tiered service and queue jumping for fund-holding patients. What, then, have been the results of the changes?

EVALUATING THE 1990 HEALTH AND COMMUNITY CARE ACT

Initially, changes were minimised to some extent by controls set by the government. Health Authorities were required to maintain a 'steady state' in their operations, which meant that they were limited in how far they could move contracts between different providers (Ham, 1992; Allsop, 1995).

Arguments against the introduction of the internal market and the division of functions between purchasers and providers have come from different sources. The medical profession were opposed to what they perceived as a restraint on their clinical freedom (Mohan, 1995). Outside the NHS, commentators have argued that competition is an inappropriate way of managing health care provision. Not only is the split seen as wasteful of resources, with higher administration costs, but also as creating instability and uncertainty which prevents long-term planning and rewards short termism (Mohan, 1995). One of the basic premises of the internal market is that competition, if working well, should drive down costs, but this may be with the hidden cost of reduced quality (Ranade, 1994), despite provisions to include quality as part of the contracting process. In addition, although purchasers are required to consult with local populations when planning their expenditures, evidence suggests this does not always convert into purchasing decisions which meet local needs and, as Allsop (1995) has pointed out, purchasers are not ultimately responsible to local populations but to their management board.

In addition, the internal market cannot deliver competition in areas where there are few purchasers or few providers, with virtual monopolies. Further, the contracting process does not encourage health authorities to count so-called 'hidden' costs (Mohan, 1995). For example, there is an incentive for hospitals to seek early discharge for patients, as costs of care after discharge are carried by others, whether family or friends, the voluntary sector, the social services or the health authority through community health services. Similarly, there may be an incentive for fund-holding GPs to treat more patients themselves rather than referring to specialist services which they would have to fund (Allsop, 1995) – an interesting reversal of the criticism of the impact of the 1911 National Insurance Act which encouraged panel doctors to refer patients to hospitals in order to reduce their own costs, particularly of prescriptions (Abel-Smith, 1964).

It seems at present that the current divide between purchasers and providers will remain. Supporters of the market argue that it is better to separate responsibility for health care planning from responsibility for health service delivery, as this in theory divorces planning from the powerful vested interests of, for example, hospital doctors. In addition, the increased information on the costs of different procedures means that resource decisions can be taken more openly, in the light of this information rather than because of pressure different professional groups are able to apply to the system. Whilst it is acknowledged that the contract system might encourage early discharge, if discharge is medically appropriate then it is better for the patient to be cared for outside the hospital – thus, what is needed is better support in the community rather than longer periods of hospital care.

HEALTH CARE UNDER THE LABOUR GOVERNMENT

The Labour government which was elected in 1997 committed itself to remaining within the public spending limits set by the former Conservative government for the first year of office, and this affected early decision making on health care. In the first few months the government both promised additional funding for the health services, and also that money would be transferred from bureaucracy to patient care – a focus which reflects in many ways the earlier Conservative concern over efficiency.

Early in the administration the Health Minister introduced changes which would reduce the role of the internal market in the delivery of health services, and this move towards a reformed system was reinforced by the White Paper on the health services which was published late in 1997. This White Paper, 'The New NHS – Modern, Dependable', laid out a series of proposals for change which some commentators described as moving the British system closer to the Health Maintenance Organisations (HMOs) found in the USA. The key points of the paper were the abolition of the internal market which had been introduced by the Conservative government in the 1990 Act, and an increased role for primary health care via GPs and community nurses. 'Locality planning' would replace GP fundholding by allowing GPs in primary care groups, of around 50 GPs covering approximately 100,000 patients, to control budgets for their area. There are to be fewer health authorities (HAs), and hospital trusts are to lose their status as independent contractors, falling under the control of HAs. The division between purchaser and provider, however, is to remain, but, whilst primary care groups are to negotiate contracts with the trusts as providers, this is meant to operate in a spirit of commitment to provision and quality rather than the profit motive in mind.

It is too early to judge the impact of these changes. Some of the major criticisms of the earlier system – that it created a two-tier system and that health should not be delivered by a market oriented system – have been met by these proposals. There is to be greater openness, with more public meetings, and quality is to be maintained through a system of committees and the role of the HA in overseeing the system. However, it remains a system with little input from patients themselves and in some ways returns power to the clinicians, whereas the 1990 reforms increased the power of administrators.

ISSUES IN HEALTH POLICY

We turn now to look, briefly, at some of the issues which are relevant to a study of health policy.

Health promotion policy

As we saw earlier, the original structure of the NHS and the position of the medical profession within the health services encouraged a focus on curative medicine and the treatment of acute illness. Health promotion policy in Britain also focuses on individual patterns of ill-health and health damaging behaviour, and largely seeks individualistic solutions. In 1992 the Conservative government published the 'Health of the Nation', a strategy document outlining a set of targets for improvements in the population's health by the year 2000, as part of the World Health Organisation's strategy of 'Health for All 2000' (Ranade, 1994).

Prior to the Health of the Nation (HON) strategy, health promotion activities had largely focused on different health hazards, such as smoking, the abuse of alcohol and accidents in the home, with health education programmes designed to change individual patterns of behaviour. Slogans from these early campaigns highlighted this individualistic approach (Rodmell and Watt, 1986). In addition, earlier health promotion activities were criticised as either ethnocentric or racist. The Rickets Campaign in the 1970s, for example, arising out of concern at increasing rates of rickets amongst young people of Asian background, proposed solutions which focused on behavioural change for the Asian community, including a change in the traditional diet and clothing of Asian people (Pearson, 1986). The Asian Mothers and Babies campaign similarly implicitly blamed Asian culture for low birth-weight babies and higher rates of infant mortality amongst women of Asian origin, whilst ignoring questions of poverty and policy solutions, such as the introduction of linkworkers, which seems to have greater impact on maternal and child health (Pearson, 1986; Torkington, 1991).

The Health of the Nation approach likewise focuses on individual change. The strategy document followed an analysis of the major causes of ill-health and premature death (Smith and Jacobson, 1988) and included targets based on measurable health data – a reduction in deaths from coronary heart disease,

Exhibit 12.4

Inequalities in health: Examples of the data

Table 1 Standardised Mortality Ratios by social class – Men, 1991–3

Social class		SMR
I	Professional	66
II	Managerial and technical	72
III NM	Skilled non-manual	100
III M	Skilled manual	117
IV	Partly skilled	116
V	Unskilled	189
England and Wales		**100**

Table 2 Age-standardised death rates per 1,000 people, by housing tenure 1981–92

	Men (45–64)	Women (45–59)
Owner occupiers	7.3	3.2
Private renters	10.6	4.8
Local authority tenants	12.3	5.1

Table 3 Morbidity: Percentage of people reporting limiting long standing illness, by socio-economic group and sex

Socio-economic group	Men	Women
Professional	15	17
Employers and managers	16	17
Intermediate non-manual	19	20
Junior non-manual	19	27
Skilled manual	24	23
Semi-skilled manual	23	26
Unskilled manual	29	34

Sources: Tables 1 and 2: Adapted from Drever, F. and Whitehead, M. (1997) *Health Inequalities* (London: ONS); Table 3: General Household Survey (1997) *GHS 1996 Living in Britain* (London: ONS).

lung cancer and suicide, for example – together with targets on identifiable risk factors, such as smoking, alcohol consumption and levels of obesity. Dietary targets, such as a reduction in consumption of saturated fats, focus on education about the levels of fat a healthy diet should contain. However, research shows that people in all social classes know about healthy diets (Ranade, 1994) – the difficulty in adopting a healthy diet is partly the result of current food policy – for example, the lack of a clear labelling policy – and partly because healthy diets are largely more expensive and therefore harder for low-income groups to afford (Lang and Cole-Hamilton, 1986; Ranade, 1994).

Often the debate is expressed in terms of 'personal choice' over healthy behaviour, combined with ignorance. Thus the task of health promotion may be seen as decreasing ignorance, which in turn should increase the number of times the 'right' choice is made. The problem with this approach is that choice needs to be set within the context of the individual's circumstances. Hilary Graham's work on women and smoking illustrates this – women on low incomes may take poor health decisions when they smoke but in the wider context of the family's health, this decision may reflect a form of 'health compromise'. Smoking may allow the woman a break from the pressures of parenting when other alternative 'treats' are less available, and may help to decrease tension (Graham, 1990). Although there are health costs attached to this behaviour, attempts to change behaviour which are taken out of the context in which such compromises are worked out are unlikely to succeed.

MENTAL HEALTH SERVICES

The majority of people (around 90 per cent) with mental health problems in Britain are treated by their GP. Psychiatric treatment is also provided in the community by Community Mental Health Teams (CMHTs) which are likely to include both medical workers (psychiatrists, psychiatric nurses) and social service staff (psychiatric social workers). In addition, some people may attend day centres and out-patient psychiatric appointments at the general hospital. A minority of people are admitted for in-patient treatment, mostly remaining in hospital for a relatively short period.

Recent trends in psychiatric treatment in Britain mean that there has been an increasing drive towards community care, with a reduction in the number of psychiatric in-patient beds and the closure of large psychiatric hospitals. People who do require in-patient treatment are now likely to be treated in a psychiatric unit within a general hospital.

However, although there are fewer in-patient beds, the number of psychiatric admissions each year has gradually increased. The majority of admissions are people who have been treated as an in-patient before, that is, they are being re-admitted to hospital. This has given rise to the phrase 'revolving door', to reflect the fact that many patients experience an on-going cycle of admission, discharge and re-admission. Care in the community has been criticised for the apparent inability of services to meet the needs of patients, particularly those with severe and enduring mental health problems. In the early 1990s, a series of incidents involving people with severe mental health problems increased public concern over the weaknesses of community care, and the Conservative government introduced the idea of supervised discharge for psychiatric in-patients, which would in theory improve access to support services in the community. The Conservative government also introduced some additional funding for psychiatric care but this was widely seen as insufficient to meet the demands placed on the system.

Others have criticised the mental health services for their focus on medicalised solutions and the failure to give mental health patients alternatives to pharmaceutical treatment and to in-patient treatment. Pressure groups such as MIND also highlighted the very serious problems stemming from the policy of mixed wards which left women in-patients vulnerable to sexual violence.

In the late 1990s mental health care continues to be largely based in the community with a mixture of providers, GPs, CMHTs and specialist psychiatric staff, and the issue of funding also continues to be problematic.

INEQUALITIES IN HEALTH

In 1980 the government published the Black Report, the outcome of a working party on inequalities in health, which sought to establish the extent to which different groups had a different experience of health and different mortality risks. The report concluded that people in lower occupational groups had greater risks of ill health and suffered higher mortality rates at all ages. In addition, whilst mortality rates in the higher occupational groups had decreased in the past 20 years, mortality rates for those in classes IV and V had scarcely changed and, for some conditions, had actually deteriorated. A later report, The Health Divide (1987), suggested that this inverse ratio between health experience and occupational class had not disappeared, as do data published during the 1990s (Townsend, Davidson and Whitehead, 1992).

The Black report discussed a number of explanations for this difference. The 'artefactual' explanation suggests that the apparent differences in health between lower occupational groups and those in higher occupational groups are the result of statistical inaccuracies, and, in particular, the different size of the occupational groups, and the fact the calculations are based on people of working age in paid employment (excluding the unemployed, the permanently sick and students for example) means that we are assessing health inequalities on the basis of a very small proportion of the population (Illsley, 1987). This is particularly problematic with differences in mortality rates, as there are far fewer deaths before retirement age than there are after, when some other means of judging resources and social class needs to be used (Townsend, Davidson and Whitehead, 1992).

However, although it is true that the occupational groups are small and have changed size over the years – which means that it is difficult to talk of trends in inequality over time – a comparison is still possible between occupational groups I and II combined, and occupational groups IV and V combined. Such a comparison means that the groups are a reasonable size and have remained

Exhibit 12.5

Community care

Community care refers to the care needs of vulnerable people in society, where those needs are met outside institutional care. It is a term capable of a broad range of definitions, and the meaning of community care changes both over time and in different settings. Community care is relevant to the study of health policy because of the overlap – in terms of responsibility for care and funding care – between the health authorities and the local social services. In earlier years, much of the care needs of vulnerable groups – people with learning difficulties, mental health problems, physical disabilities and older people with particular needs for care – were met through the provision of institutional care. However, the concept of caring for such people outside the institution has been an objective of health policy for some time – community care was seen as an aim in the early years of the NHS and in subsequent legislation – such as the 1959 Mental Health Act, and in papers such as the 1971 DHSS paper, Better Services for the Mentally Handicapped.

One of the major problems in providing good effective care in the community has been the difficulty of funding the services – should staff, equipment and accommodation such as day centres be paid for by the nationally funded health authorities or by the locally funded social service departments? How can money best be transferred from one part of the public sector to another – and who should fund the valuable work of the voluntary sector? Similarly, the division of professional responsibility has proved complex and community care has often been criticised for failing to meet the complex needs of individuals. Thus a person who needs a range of different kinds of help – help with dressing, cooking, cleaning, transport, and also help with some health problems – may find not all their needs are met due to the range of professionals who might potentially be involved in their care.

The 1990 NHS and Community Care Act introduced 'care managers' in the attempt to overcome this difficulty. Care managers, who are mainly social service staff, assess the needs of individuals, together with the user themselves, and co-ordinate the overall delivery of care packages to those people in need of support in the community.

However, funding and the related issue of rationing, where services are not available, remain controversial. Linked in with this is the recent development in the health care system to charge some long-stay patients with chronic rather than acute health problems – on the basis that such people are being provided with personal care rather than health care. The dividing line between health care and personal care is usually far from straightforward, however.

As we move into the next century, there is increasing concern over an ageing population. The proportion of the population over retirement age has grown substantially in the last decade and policy solutions to the potential need for care of this group have yet to be developed, both in Britain and in other developed countries.

---

relatively unchanged over time (Hart, 1987). The comparison also reveals that inequality persists between the higher and lower groups, and for some conditions and in some age groups, the gap has indeed widened (Townsend, Davidson and Whitehead, 1992). Also, focusing on people under retirement age gives a powerful indication of the relative disadvantage in terms of 'years lost' by some groups in comparison with others (Hart, 1987).

The second explanation – that of social selection – argues that inequalities in health between occupational groups result from upward mobility experienced by those with good health and downward mobility experienced by those who have poor health. Thus, we should expect to find inequalities in health, but it is the health that causes the class position, rather than the other way round.

Studies used in support of this position show that health in childhood affects later occupational class, and there is reason to suppose that poor health might affect the individual's ability to gain good employment – particularly where health problems have interrupted schooling. However, some of the major diseases accounting for early mortality have a relatively short period between onset and death, rather than reflecting difficulties dating back to childhood, and do not lead to particularly marked downward mobility (Whitehead, 1987). Whilst there is evidence that health selection does have some effect, it appears likely that this effect occurs largely in the first half of life and accounts for 'only a small proportion of the overall differential between the social classes' (Whitehead, 1987).

The third explanation focuses on the behaviour of people in lower occupational groups, and asks whether it is likely to be more or less health damaging than the behaviour of those in higher occupational groups. People in lower groups smoke more than those in higher occupational groups and people in higher occupational groups are more likely to take part in some form of exercise, which may be a protective factor in a range of illnesses, including coronary heart disease and breast cancer (GHS, 1996). However, alcohol consumption varies less by socio-economic status, particularly for men, and studies show that, for both men and women, there are more heavy drinkers in the higher occupational groups (GHS, 1996).

There is also evidence to suggest that the health damage of some activities, such as smoking, is exacerbated by living and working in a poor environment (Phillimore, 1989; Blaxter, 1990) and the individual's ability to withstand disease is affected by factors such as nutrition. Studies of survival of people with cancer show that those in lower occupational groups are not only more likely to contract cancer, but are also more likely to die of this illness (OPCS, 1990).

The fourth explanation – the 'structural' or 'materialist' position – argues that people in lower occupational groups are more exposed to poverty and deprivation, and these are major causes of ill-health and early death. Studies show that the groups who experience poor nutrition, poor quality housing, higher levels of unemployment and environmental pollution also suffer higher rates of particular illnesses, both physical and mental (Payne, 1991; Townsend, Davidson and Whitehead, 1992; Graham, 1993).

It is often difficult to prove a causal association, that is, that poverty causes poor health. Areas with high rates of ill-health and early death are also largely areas with high rates of unemployment, poverty and bad housing (Townsend, Phillimore and Beattie, 1988), but we cannot assume that it is the same people who suffer this deprivation who also suffer poorer health. Studies such as these are using aggregate data for an area, rather than tracing individual lives. However, research in the 1980s demonstrated the causal association between poor housing and particular respiratory conditions, and studies have also shown an increased risk of early death amongst those suffering from poor nutrition and deprivation in childhood (Byrne *et al.*, 1986; Joffe, 1989; Lovett *et al.*, 1990).

In the debate over inequalities in health it is likely that we must take account of both material and behavioural factors, whilst recognising the ways in which healthy choices are limited by an impoverished life. Health policy remains largely framed around the delivery of services when ill-health has shown up, and the delivery of information to change individual behaviour. Studies which have attempted to suggest ways in which health policy might tackle inequalities in health have largely focused on the need to engage with local communities in the formulation of appropriate health care for that community (Benzeval, Judge and Whitehead, 1995). However, in 1997 the new Labour government announced the appointment of a new Minister for Public Health who was to develop strategies to reduce inequalities in health. This meant an increased focus on factors such as poverty, unemployment and poor housing alongside individual risk factors.

WOMEN, HEALTH CARE AND THE FEMINIST CRITIQUE

Women's experience of the health care system – both as users and as providers of health care, in the formal labour market and informally in the home – has been a central focus of feminist research. Women's health experience reveals an interesting paradox – women have a greater life expectancy in comparison with men, but are more likely to suffer illness during their lives. In 1996 female life expectancy at birth was 79.7, whilst male life expectancy at birth was 74.4 (*Social Trends*, 1996). However, women also report more morbidity (GHS, 1996). Women's higher rates of illness are in part due to women's greater longevity, as increasing age brings increasing risks of particular illnesses which do not threaten life but which do affect mobility and often require medical attention. In part, women's greater morbidity is a result of women's reproductive system, although many of women's health consultations are not related to ill-health but the medical profession's control over contraception, ante-natal care and delivery – normal healthy processes (Miles, 1991). Some of women's greater morbidity is explained by women's higher risk of being diagnosed as mentally ill (Ussher, 1991).

The feminist critique has highlighted a number of areas of women's health as of particular concern. Issues relating to women's reproductive health show the ways in which women's fertility has become subject to the control of the medical profession (Kitzinger, 1992; Oakley, 1992). With contraception there has been a shift from male methods of contraception, available over the counter, to female methods which are controlled by the medical profession – the coil, the diaphragm, and, from the 1960s onwards, the contraceptive pill. There has also been a shift in the management of childbirth, with more women giving birth inside hospital (Miles, 1991). Feminist research challenged the notion that this was healthier and safer for the mother and baby, and argued that the medicalisation of childbirth pathologises what is a natural process. As the routine management of labour increased, so too did intervention, with increases in the rate of induction, episeotomy and caesarean sections. Many of the interventions that became standard during the 1970s – shaving and the use of enemas, for example – were not justified by medical evidence (Oakley, 1984) and women complained about the depersonalised process in which they felt powerless over choices of how to have their baby (Kitzinger, 1992). Many of these practices have now been changed, partly in response to demands from women, and whilst childbirth remains largely hospitalised, women are now encouraged to have a greater say over how they would like to have their baby. However, the greater use of obstetric technology, such as monitors during labour, may reduce choice by increasing anxieties and the pressure to move to a swifter conclusion of the labour.

Abortion has also been an issue. Termination of pregnancy was illegal until the 1967 Act which legitimated abortion under certain conditions. However, this did not give women the 'right to choose', as the consent of two doctors is needed. Consent is not determined primarily by the medical safety of the procedure, but by the doctors' judgement of the woman's state of health or mind. Abortion is also not equally available to all women – access depends on a number of factors, including not only where a woman lives, but also how the woman presents herself to the doctor. And, as black feminists have pointed out, black women are less likely to be refused abortion, but more often find that abortion is conditional on sterilisation or long-lasting contraceptive methods such as Depo-Provera (Bryan, Dadzie and Scafe, 1985; Torkington, 1991).

In the area of mental health, feminist analysis has highlighted the over-representation of women amongst those treated for mental illness – both inside the hospital and in the primary health care system – and the greater proportion of women prescribed psychotropic drugs – in particular tranquillisers and anti-depressants (Miles, 1988; Ussher, 1991). However, again, there are differences between different groups of women in terms of their risks of being treated for psychiatric illness – working-class women and black and minority ethnic women are more often diagnosed as mentally ill and are more likely to receive Electro-Convulsive Treatment (ECT) in comparison with middle-class and white women (Miles, 1988; Ussher, 1991). Black women are also more likely to be admitted to psychiatric hospital as involuntary patients under the 1983 Mental Health Act (Bryan, Dadzie and Scafe, 1985).

The majority of workers in the health care system are women: over 70 per cent of the workforce (Doyal, 1994, 1995). However, women are under-represented in the higher levels of the occupational hierarchy, both in administration and management and in the medical professions (Doyal, 1994, 1995). Where women are consultants, it is more often in less well-paid, lower status 'female' specialisms, such as child psychiatry and paediatrics (although, perhaps surprisingly, obstetrics is a male specialty). This over-representation of men in the top positions may change, as men and women are admitted to medical school in equal numbers, but this remains to be seen. Again, black women have a different experience, being concentrated in the low-paid and insecure jobs within the health care system (Doyal, 1983).

In addition, women carry out much of what might be seen as health care work outside the formal health care sector, on an informal basis (Graham, 1985). Attention has been given in recent years, in particular, to the unpaid work of carers in their support of older people and vulnerable members of society. There is also the care of household members suffering from short-term or acute illness – nursing a child with flu, for example. In addition, there is also the health maintenance work carried out in the privatised home, partly in domestic labour – the work involved in maintaining a clean and safe home environment, and the preparation of food, for example – and also the work of encouraging a healthy lifestyle, and teaching younger members of the household about health (Graham, 1984). To a large extent this work is carried out by women – often replicating the role of women in the hierarchy of labour in the formal health care system as nurses and ward cleaners, for example tending to the sick and helping to maintain a safe hospital environment (Doyal, 1995).

MINORITY ETHNIC GROUPS AND HEALTH

Evidence from a variety of sources has shown that people from minority ethnic groups tend to suffer poorer health than the population as a whole (Donovan, 1984; Balarajan and Raleigh, 1990; Townsend, Davidson and Whitehead, 1992). This is an over-simplification, as there are some diseases and conditions which are experienced less often by people from some minority ethnic groups. It is also important to remember that the term 'minority ethnic groups' covers a number of different groups of people who have different cultures, practices and experiences (Smaje, 1995). One of the difficulties with an analysis of ethnicity and health is that figures on the health experience of people from minority ethnic groups are difficult to find. Mortality data, for example, only shows deaths among people who were born outside Britain (see Balarajan and Raleigh, 1990), yet an increasing proportion of the ethnic minority population were born in Britain.

However, data do reveal a range of inequalities in health. For example, people of Pakistani origin have lower rates of cancer and mental illness, but suffer high levels of infant mortality, whilst people of Afro-Caribbean origin have higher rates of stroke (Balarajan and Raleigh, 1990; Townsend, Davidson and Whitehead, 1992; Andrews and Jewson, 1993; Smaje, 1995). GP consultation is higher amongst both men and women from minority ethnic groups (OPCS, 1995). People from minority ethnic groups – in particular, people of Afro-Caribbean origin and Irish origin – are more likely to be diagnosed as mentally ill than the population as a whole. People from minority ethnic groups are also more likely to be compulsorily admitted to hospital under the 1983 Mental Health Act (Knowles, 1991; Moodley and Perkins, 1991) and to receive treatment against their wishes.

One possible explanation of inequalities in health experienced by minority ethnic groups is poverty, and the greater risk of deprivation for people from minority ethnic groups, combined with the impact of racism and discrimination on health (Donovan, 1984; Andrews and Jewson, 1993). An important factor is the delivery and organisation of the health services: studies have found that people from minority ethnic groups are less likely to be satisfied with their health care and are less likely to be referred for specialist treatment (Fenton, 1985; Larbie, 1985; McNaught, 1988; Knowles, 1991; Smaje, 1995). People from minority ethnic groups may be hospitalised for psychiatric illness as a result of racism and the failure of the services to understand the needs of some groups (Knowles, 1991).

It is important, however, that health policy does not portray people from minority ethnic groups as helpless victims, particularly in terms of their health care. Campaigns against the rickets education programme, for example, and groups such as OSCAR (Organisation for Sickle Cell Anaemia Research) have done much to increase awareness within the NHS of the conditions themselves and of the failure of the NHS to respond adequately (Bryan *et al.*, 1985). In many areas initiatives around specific health needs and often in response to local consultation have improved the delivery of services for some populations (Smaje, 1995). Since the mid 1990s the NHS has introduced ethnic monitoring in some services, which will add to what is known about inequalities in health within different ethnic groups and to how policy might best tackle these differences. In addition, the Labour government committed itself to a review of inequalities in health suffered by minority ethnic groups in 1997.

Exhibit 12.6

Health policy: Developments from 1997 onwards

1997 New role of Minister of State for Public Health created, with Tessa Jowell as first incumbent
1997 New Advisory Committee on Resource Allocation to consider funding across the NHS
1997 'A Modern and Dependable NHS for the Next Century' (NHS White Paper)
1998 First wave of health action zones announced
1998 'Our Healthier Nation' (Green Paper on Public Health)

CONCLUSION

> The field in which the claims of individual commercialism come into most immediate
> conflict with reputable notions of social values is that of health ... no society can legiti-
> mately call itself civilised if a sick person is denied medical aid because of lack of means.
> (Bevan, 1961, cited in Ranade, 1994, p. 11)

In the late 1990s we have a health service which has retained the central characteristics of the service designed in the 1940s for a post-war Britain. The NHS is still
the major provider of health care in this country, and is still funded largely by
central government finance. It still spends the larger part of its money on hospital
and acute care, and criticisms levelled against the services over a number of years
– concerning the underfunding of chronic care, the over-powerful medical
profession and the lack of holistic approach – are still largely true. In the early
part of this decade, major changes were introduced which some felt threatened
the basic principles of the NHS. However, as we move towards the end of the
century the greatest problem in health policy remains funding, whilst realisation
of fears over the 'creeping' privatisation of the service have yet to materialise.

REFERENCES

Abel-Smith, B. (1964) *The Hospitals, 1800-1948: A study in social administration in England and Wales*,
London: Heinemann.

Abel-Smith, B. (1978) *The National Health Service: The first thirty years*, London: HMSO.

Allsop, J. (1995) 'Health: From seamless service to patchwork quilt', in Gladstone, D. (ed.), *British
Social Welfare: Past, present and future*, London: UCL Press.

Andrews, A. and Jewson, N. (1993) 'Ethnicity and Infant Deaths: The implications of
recent statistical evidence for materialist explanations', *Sociology of Health and Illness*, 15(2):
137–56.

Balarajan, R. and Raleigh, V. S. (1990) 'Variations in Perinatal, Neonatal, Postneonatal and Infant
Mortality by Mother's Country of Birth', in Britton, M. (ed.), *Mortality and Geography: A review
in the mid 1980s*, London: HMSO.

Benzeval, M., Judge, K. and Whitehead, M. (eds) (1995) *Tackling Inequalities in Health: An agenda
for action*, London: King's Fund.

Blaxter, M. (1990) *Health and Lifestyles*, London: Tavistock/Routledge.

Bryan, B., Dadzie, S. and Scafe, S. (1985) *The Heart of the Race: Black women's lives in Britain*,
London: Virago.

Byrne, D., Harrison, S. P., Keithley, J. and MacCarthy, P. (1986) *Housing and Health: The relationship
between housing conditions and the health of council tenants*, Aldershot: Gower.

Cartwright, A. and O'Brien, M. (1976) 'Social Class Variations in Health Care', in Stacey, M. (ed.),
The Sociology of the NHS, Sociological Review Monograph, Keele University.

Day, P. and Klein, R. (1991) 'Britain's Health Care Experiment', *Health Affairs*, 1: 39–59.

Department of Health (1989) 'Working for Patients', Cmnd 55, London: HMSO.

Department of Health and Social Security (1976) 'Resource Allocation Working Party: Sharing
resources for health in England', Report of the Resource Allocation Working Party, London:
HMSO.

Department of Health and Social Security (1979) *Patients First*, London: HMSO.

Donovan, J. (1984) 'Ethnicity and Health: A Research Review', *Social Science and Medicine*, Vol. 19(7), pp. 663–70.

Donovan, J. (1986) *We don't Buy Sickness: It just comes*, Aldershot: Gower.

Doyal, L. (1979) *The Political Economy of Health*, with Imogen Pennell, London: Pluto Press.

Doyal, L. (1983) *The Political Economy of Health*, London: Pluto Press.

Doyal, L. (1995) *What Makes Women Sick: Gender and the political economy of health*, Basingstoke: Macmillan.

Doyal, L. (1996) 'Changing Medicine: Gender and the politics of health care', in Gabe, J., Kelleher, D. and Williams, G. (eds), *Challenging Medicine*, London: Routledge.

Elston, M. A. and Doyal, L. *Unit 14: Health and medicine*, Milton Keynes: Open University Press.

Fenton, S. (1985) *Race, Health and Welfare: Afro-Caribbean and South Asian people in Central Bristol: Health and social services*, Bristol: University of Bristol, Department of Sociology.

Fraser, D. (1984) *The Evolution of the British Welfare State: A history of social policy since the Industrial Revolution*, London: Macmillan.

General household survey (1996), London: HMSO.

Graham, H. (1985) *Health and Welfare*, Basingstoke: Macmillan.

Graham, H. (1990) 'Behaving Well: Women's health behaviour in context', in Roberts, H. (ed.), *Women's Health Counts*, London: Routledge.

Graham, H. (1993) *Hardship and Health in Women's Lives*, New York: Harvester Wheatsheaf.

Ham, C. (1992) *Health Policy in Britain: The politics and organisation of the National Health Service*, Basingstoke: Macmillan.

Hart, N. (1985) *The Sociology of Health and Medicine*, Ormskirk: Causeway.

Hart, N. (1987) 'Social Class Still Reigns', *Poverty*, 67: 17–19.

Illsley, R. (1987) 'The Health Divide: Bad welfare or bad statistics?', *Poverty*, 67: 16–17.

Joffe, M. (1989) 'Social Inequalities in Birth Weight: Timing of effects and selective mobility', *Social Science and Medicine*, 28: 613–19.

Kitzinger, S. (1992) 'Birth and Violence against Women: Generating hypotheses from women's accounts of unhappiness after childbirth', in Roberts, H. (ed.), *Women's Health Matters*, London: Routledge.

Knowles, C. (1991) 'Afro-Caribbeans and Schizophrenia: How does psychiatry deal with issues race, culture and ethnicity?', *Journal of Social Policy*, 20(2): 173–90.

Lang, T. and Cole-Hamilton, I. (1986) *Tightening Belts: A report on the impact of poverty on food*, London: London Food Commission.

Larbie, J. (1985) *Black Women and the Maternity Services: A survey of thirty young Afro-Caribbean women's experiences and perceptions of pregnancy and childbirth*, London: Training in Health and Race.

Lovett, A. A., Gatrell, A. C., Bound, J. P., Harvey, P. W. and Whelan, A. R. (1990) 'Congenital malformations in the Fylde Region of Lancashire, 1957–73', *Social Science and Medicine*, 30: 103–9.

McKeown, T. (1979) *The Role of Medicine: Dream, mirage or nemesis?* Oxford: Basil Blackwell.

McNaught, A. (1988) *Race and Health Policy: A study of the National Health Service in England and Wales*, London: Croom Helm.

Midwinter, E. C. (1994) *The Development of Social Welfare in Britain*, Buckingham: Open University Press.

Miles, A. (1991) *Women, Health and Medicine*, Milton Keynes: Open University Press.

Mohan, J. (1995) *A National Health Service?: The restructuring of health care in Britain since 1979*, Basingstoke: Macmillan.

Moodley, P. and Perkins, R. E. (1991) 'Routes to Psychiatric In-Patient Care in an Inner London Borough', *Social Psychiatry and Psychiatric Epidemiology*, 26: 47–51.

Moon, G. and Gillespie, R. (eds) (1995) *Society and Health: An introduction to social science for health professionals*, London: Routledge.

Oakley, Ann (1984) *The Captured Womb: A history of the medical care of pregnant women*, Oxford: Blackwell.

Oakley, A. (1992) 'Getting at the Oyster: One of many lessons from the social support and pregnancy outcome study', in Roberts, H. (ed.), *Women's Health Matters*, London: Routledge.

OPCS (1990) *Longitudinal Study: Mortality and social organisation, England & Wales 1971–1981*, London: HMSO.

OPCS (1995) *Morbidity Statistics from General Practice: Fourth national study 1991–1992*, London: HMSO.

Payne, S. (1991) *Women, Health and Poverty: An introduction*, Hemel Hempstead: Harvester Wheatsheaf.

Pearson, M. (1986) 'Racist Notions of Ethnicity and Culture in Health Education', in Rodmell, S. and Watt, A. (eds), *The Politics of Health Education: Raising the issues*, London: Routledge & Kegan Paul.

Petchey, R. (1986) 'The Griffiths Reorganisation: Fowlerism by stealth?', *Critical Social Policy*, 7(17): 87–100.

Phillimore, P. (1989) 'Shortened Lives: Premature death in North Tyneside', Bristol: School of Applied Social Studies, University of Bristol: Bristol Papers in Applied Social Studies, No. 12.

Ranade, W. (1994) *A Future for the NHS?: Health care in the 1990s*, London: Longman.

Rodmell, S. and Watt, A. (eds) (1986) *The Politics of Health Education: Raising the issues*, London: Routledge & Kegan Paul.

Rublee, D. A. and Schneider, M. (1991) 'International Health Spending: Comparisons with the OECD, *Health Affairs*, 10(3): 187–98.

Smaje, C. (1995) *Health, 'Race' and Ethnicity: Making sense of the evidence*, London: King's Fund Institute.

Smith, A. and Jacobson, B. (eds) (1988) 'The Nation's Health: A strategy for the 1990s', A Report from an Independent Multidisciplinary Committee, London: King Edward's Hospital Fund for London.

Social Trends (1996), London: HMSO.

Thane, P. (1996) *Foundations of the Welfare State*, London: Longman

Torkington, P. (1991) *Black Health – A Political Issue: The health and race project*, Liverpool: Catholic Association for Racial Justice and Liverpool Institute of Higher Education.

Townsend, P., Davidson, N. and Whitehead, M. (1992) *Inequalities in Health: The Black Report and the health divide*, London: Penguin.

Townsend, P., Phillimore, P. and Beattie, A. (1988) *Health and Deprivation: Inequality and the north*, London: Croom Helm.

Tudor-Hart, J. (1971) 'The Inverse Care Law', *The Lancet*, 27 February 1971, pp. 405–12.

Ussher, J. M. (1991) *Women's Madness: Misogyny or mental illness?*, New York: Harvester Wheatsheaf.

Wanuk-Lipinski, E. and Illsley, R. (1990) 'International Comparative Analysis: Main findings and conclusions', *Social Science and Medicine*, 31(8): 879–89.

Webster, C. (ed.) (1991) *Caring for Health: History and diversity*, Buckingham: Open University Press in association with the Open University.

Whitehead, M. (1987) *The Health Divide: Inequalities in health in the 1980s*, London: Health Education Authority.

ANNOTATED READINGS

There are a number of very good texts on health policy in Britain. Wendy Ranade's text, *A Future for the NHS: Health care in the 1990s* (1994, Longman) is a valuable review of the more recent changes in the NHS and provides discussion of important issues such as health promotion, inequalities and ways of analysing health and health policy. The text by Townsend, Davidson and Whitehead (1992, Penguin) includes both the original Black Report on inequalities in health and more recent material, while the more recent Benzeval, Judge and Whitehead (1995, King's Fund Institute) is an interesting analysis of how policy might tackle inequalities in health. Chris Smaje's book, *Health, 'Race' and Ethnicity: Making sense of the evidence* (1995, King's Fund Institute), is a good review both of material on ethnicity and health and of the role of policy makers in redressing inequality. Finally, Lesley Doyal's book, *What Makes Women Sick: Gender and the political economy of health* (1995, Macmillan), is a good introduction to women's health on a global basis.

13 Housing policy in Britain

OBJECTIVES

- To outline the development of state involvement in the subsidy of housing provision and the construction of public rented accommodation.

- To examine the development of different housing sectors – private rental, public rental and owner occupation.

- To examine the housing boom of the 1950s and 1960s.

- To outline the policy of slum clearance and the subsequent change to environmental and housing improvements.

- To consider the development and operation of the private housing market – the creation of a 'property owning democracy'.

- To consider policies designed to assist the homeless.

HISTORICAL BACKGROUND

Historically the question of housing policy was one of the last areas of social provision to attract the attention of a nascent and developing welfare state. It was not until the years of the First World War that the question of housing for the working classes received serious attention on the British political agenda when the protests of workers against the profiteering of their landlords, in sensitive industrial areas, such as munitions and shipbuilding in and around Glasgow, forced the Lloyd-George government to act. Initially their response was to subsidise rents in order to buy industrial peace and it was not until the years following the war that the state's interest in the construction and management of public housing projects began in earnest. Even then the response was short lived as public expenditure restrictions in the early years of the 1920s restricted the ability of local municipal authorities to finance house building.

As Malpass and Murie (1990) indicate, before 1914 'there was barely a recognisable housing policy' but the years of the First World War, during which housing production fell, meant that by 1918 there existed a severe housing shortage that the private building sector was unable to address. During the inter-war years housing policy developed on two fronts: the control of rents in the private rented sector and the subsidy of local authority building, partly prompted by

216

the various programmes of slum clearance, particularly after 1930. Emphasis, however, remained with the private building sector which alone constructed 100,000 dwellings every year from 1925 to over 250,000 annually between 1934 and 1938, with local authorities averaging only 25,000 completions annually during the same period (Malpass and Murie, pp. 42–5). Thus housing policy as a part of the formative welfare state remained hardly recognisable, but there was nonetheless a shift in the pattern of tenure as private ownership began to take over from private rentals as the preferred option – herein lies the roots of Britain's 'property owning democracy'.

Public housing was then, at this time, very much a minority undertaking with many authorities reluctant to enter the property development market. But those that did, especially those controlled by Labour councillors, sought to show that workers' housing needed no longer to be slums, and in so doing mirrored works undertaken by the co-operative and trades union movements. They sought instead to install the range and type of facilities that they considered were the best that could be bought, and the space available in many early public housing projects was generous. They were keen to show that a future Labour government could construct and successfully manage quality homes for their working-class constituents at affordable rents. However, the building costs of those early projects were high as authorities sought to maintain high quality and at the same time were forced to pay high labour costs to attract skilled building workers away from the private sector (Malpass and Murie, 1990, p. 52).

This general picture remained largely unaltered during the inter-war years as the majority of newly built houses were, as we have seen, in the privately owned sector. Government interest in housing instead focused on the question of inner-city congestion and slum clearance. It was only really as a result of the Second World War, and the effects of civilian bombing together with the desire to fulfil the promises of the 'khaki election' to build homes for heroes, that housing policy was placed more centrally on the policy stage. The programmes of slum clearance continued, although priorities began to change as building standards were gradually lowered in an attempt to accelerate the building programme. Urban planning, as a result, became chaotic as towns began to spread as new suburbs sprang up and the back-to-back terraces of the town centres disappeared. Local authorities were, as Malpass and Murie (1990) indicate, fulfilling a residual role at this time, as they sought to rehouse those people displaced by slum clearance, whilst for those who had the resources and opportunity a privately owned suburban semi-detached became a realisable dream.

The early years of the 1940s were witness to a radical shift in housing priorities for the policy makers of the post-war years. Some 3.5 million dwellings were either wholly destroyed or substantially damaged by air raids by 1945 and the slum clearance programmes, which had temporarily halted, could renew apace. The housing crisis facing this generation's set of returning war heroes was thus far more severe than that seen in 1918–19 and the incoming government was required to act quickly and moreover to build quickly. Both major parties promised rapid completion rates in house building to replace those properties damaged or destroyed and to allow slum clearance to resume, and visionary urban architects were able to find ready employment within local authorities and to give life to their creations in towns like Portsmouth and Coventry. However, there was a difference in emphasis, with Labour favouring public building projects and municipal management of new estates and with the Conservatives retaining their traditional loyalty to the private building industry and adopting the new slogan that promised the creation of a 'property-owning democracy'. We are thus, from these rather different ideological stances, able to identify clear periods in the development of post-war housing policy and priorities. The years up to 1953 were characterised by rapid growth in municipal housing projects, in part attributable to the creation of new towns. The emphasis was very much one of rapid construction to meet short-term need in the face of shortages of both materials and labour. From the mid 1950s for a decade, the rapid pace of building continued but the responsibility for that building was laid squarely at the feet of the private building industry.

Through the 1960s perspectives appeared to change yet again and it was belatedly realised that the war against slum clearance could never be won as social standards in housing continued to grow, thus always leaving a proportion of housing in the category of 'unfit'. Emphasis once again shifted as the principle of 'renewability' was adopted and government monies made available for, initially, the renovation of poor quality housing stock and latterly of inner-city environments, as governments defined both General Improvement Areas and later Housing Action Areas.

By this time Britain had established a firmly polarised housing sector dominated by powerful lobbies for both municipally controlled rented stock and private ownership. The tale of affordable and flexible privately controlled rented stock within the housing sector is one which is well rehearsed elsewhere and need not be repeated in detail here. Suffice it to say that the private rented sector had undergone a seemingly permanent and terminal decline squeezed out by successive governments' preferences for alternately public and private housing and, depending upon your perspective, either serious neglect or over-regulation of the private rented sector.

Housing then, at least as an identifiable area of government policy, is almost exclusively confined to the post-1945 era and may be characterised by an air of euphoria, at least on the part of the housing bureaucracy, as they reached successive construction targets. However, dramatic failure, particularly in municipal projects, was always just around the corner and in the 1980s the ground was laid bare for a revolution in property ownership and the large-scale disposal of council-owned property. Perceptions of the public at large and especially of many tenants were that their municipal landlord embodied much of the bad private practice that they professed to abhor. Public authorities were frequently as inflexible as any private landlord in their regulation of tenants and they were charged, not unfairly, with replacing the inner-city slums with suburban or high-rise slums: poorly built, poorly maintained and inefficiently managed or used as dumping grounds for the authorities most troublesome tenants. And, although after 1975, authorities may justifiably point to increased central control over their finances which restricted their ability to act, for instance in controlling how capital from council house sales may be utilised, this was indeed the rock upon which the dream of quality workers' housing foundered.

The picture for the 1980s promised to change radically the landscape of British housing policy. The 1979 election returned a government which promised to withdraw from the lives of ordinary people and to make a reality their ideal of a property and share-owning democracy. In their eyes this meant tight control of the profligate fiefdoms populated by Labour councillors. The sale of council houses was one of the central planks of the 1979 victory for the 'housewife Prime Minister', whose self-reliance philosophy found much favour with discontented tenants.

The 1980s, as we have seen elsewhere, was a decade in which the large-scale provision of state-funded welfare was increasingly questioned and challenged and in the field of housing we witness possibly the most successful attempt to alter radically the pattern of welfare provision. Public dissatisfaction with council housing was well publicised and local authorities were often regarded as landlords of the most poorly built and inadequately maintained stock which they managed in a regime as harsh as any of the Poor Law guardians. Local authorities too were accused of over-bureaucracy and unresponsiveness to the needs of their tenants when they adopted practices which ghettoised ethnic-minority households and lone-parent headed households within the most inadequate housing, the least well maintained and most unsuitable. It was in the 1980s too that the problems stored up by rapid construction in the post-war years came home as many authorities began to find it untenable to maintain and renovate deteriorating stock any longer. Many began to turn instead to the wholesale demolition of housing and whole estates, which were often little more than 30 years old and ironically enough built to house families moved out in slum clearance programmes.

HOUSING POLICY – CURRENT TRENDS

It is often tempting to begin a review of current housing policy trends with the 1979 election and the manifesto promises of the first Thatcher administration. But we can detect the beginnings of policy change within the final years of the previous Labour government. Labour's traditional and ideological support for state-owned and subsidised rented accommodation was fundamentally questioned when it was unable to maintain commitments to expanding public expenditures in the middle of the decade and 'in its 1977 Green Paper, its endorsement of the balance between tenures was weighted towards home ownership' (Doling, 1993). Although from the mid 1950s Labour had implicitly conceded the electoral popularity of home ownership, such consensus was not openly acknowledged until this point.

However, the 1979 election victory for Margaret Thatcher heralded something of a revolution. The next decade would be one in which home ownership was promoted as the preferred form of tenure, alongside the 'dismantling of the public rented sector' and the 'deregulation of private renting', by which process housing ceased to be regarded as a public or merit good and the provision of a decent home was no longer considered part of government's basic responsibility, and came instead to be regarded as a private good and the government's role one of market regulation (Malpass, 1996, p. 459 and Linneman and Megbolugbe, 1994, p. 641). The decade began almost triumphantly as the 1980 Housing Act introduced the right of council tenants to purchase their homes at substantial discounts made easier by the subsequent deregulation of financial markets which made the obtaining of a mortgage far easier. Local authorities would then be left to provide what was frequently referred to as residual housing, for the poorest of tenants, and specialist housing for particular needy groups, such as the elderly (although this too changed with the 1991 deregulation of the community care industry – see chapter 14).

The right to buy was substantially buoyed by the economic boom of the mid 1980s and the general availability of low-cost credit. However, the picture changed rapidly and dramatically at the end of the 1980s as the economic boom turned to recession and the economy, controlled largely by interest rates, seriously undermined the efficacy of the burgeoning housing market. Mortgage default, negative equity and even repossession became the norm for millions of homeowners in the 1990s. In the private rented sector, the government sought to revitalise the market by deregulating and creating incentives for private landlords, whilst at the same time attempting to force the transfer of local authority lets into the hands of alternative landlords in the form of 'tenants' choice'. Perhaps most fundamentally, the 1980s heralded a shift in housing finance away from the subsidy of house building toward one built more around the means-testing of individuals in both the public and private housing spheres.

PUBLIC HOUSING IN THE 1980s

The privatisation of public rented housing has been viewed by some as an attack on the welfare state at its weakest link which was portrayed as the dismantling of a relatively unpopular service. It was therefore here, where the market had already proved itself a popular success as people 'invested in bricks and mortar' that the New Right experiment may be said to have begun. 'Council housing was the perfect symbol for the failings of the public sector; unpopular, socially stigmatising, incompetently managed and oblivious to consumer preferences' (Cole and Furbey, 1994, pp. 183–8). The consensus that accepted that there was a significant role for the local authority (or more generally the state) sector to play in the provision of low-cost rented accommodation had dissolved. Home ownership was accepted by both sides of the political divide as desired by the electorate and therefore politically supportable. The Conservative Party was able to exploit this by offering the prospect of the right to buy council houses.

So it was in 1980 that the Housing Act of that year introduced the right for council tenants, of at least three years, the option to own their own council home, by purchasing it at a substantial discount and so to benefit from rising prices in the housing market, which appeared set to continue ad infinitum (Malpass, 1996). The revolution in home ownership was supported by an equally dynamic revolution in the British financial sector which itself was to undergo the 'throes of deregulation' (Doling, 1993). The government felt that the privatisation of housing provision would serve a number of related purposes. First, and politically, it would break the political monopoly enjoyed by Labour councillors on Britain's inner-city housing estates – the logic of the times somewhat dictated that a home-owner was a Conservative voter. Secondly, the desperate condition of some of those same housing estates would be remedied by an injection of funds from new home-owners and the removal of the local authorities' bureaucratic stranglehold, which in turn would raise standards on those estates. Thirdly, many economic questions could be addressed as public expenditure would be more easily controlled by the Treasury and may even fall as revenues from council house sales began to accumulate. Finally, the overall economic picture could only continue to improve as a booming housing market stimulated other, related sectors of the economy at large.

This scenario obtained throughout much of the 1980s as between 1983 and 1989 both the economy and in turn the housing market enjoyed an unprecedented boom, during which time over 1 million council houses were transferred from state to private ownership, tenants encouraged by continually rising rents over the same period. Government opted to use the mechanism of council house sales, first to individual tenants who were to be encouraged by a discounted price compared to the market value of the property and determined by the length of their tenancy (the maximum would be a 70 per cent discount) and by the right to obtain a mortgage. Secondly, and later in the decade, sales to other landlords were encouraged either at the instigation of the local authority itself or at the initiative of the tenants.

Table 13.1 illustrates the scale of the privatisation of public sector housing and indicates that between 1984 and 1994, the ownership of almost 1.5 million public

Table 13.1 Sale and Transfer of Dwellings, 1984–94

Year	Local Authority sales	New town sales	Housing Association sales	Total sales	Cumulative total
1984	116,020	6,275	15,284	137,579	137,579
1985	103,901	4,687	12,106	120,694	258,273
1986	99,049	4,020	12,916	115,985	374,258
1987	119,328	5,284	11,061	135,673	509,931
1988	170,617	7,293	15,142	193,052	702,983
1989	190,460	8,894	13,210	212,564	915,547
1990	140,915	4,424	9,425	154,764	1,070,311
1991	78,874	2,952	8,059	89,885	1,160,196
1992	72,881	1,749	6,865	81,495	1,241,691
1993	69,863	1,696	9,074	80,633	1,322,324
1994	68,506	1,965	8,763	79,234	1,401,558
Totals	1,230,414	49,239	121,905	1,401,558	

Source: Department of the Environment.

sector dwellings was transferred. The transfers were almost all to owner occupation, and to sitting tenants, but these figures do not show the number of properties transferred from local authorities to housing associations, which may therefore rightly be considered a transfer within the public sector (but a nonetheless transformed public sector as private financing within the housing association movement). Despite this, however, local authorities continue to provide some 70 per cent of rental sector housing and council house sales appear to have reached something of an impasse (Whitehead, 1993; Linneman and Megbolugbe, 1994).

The development of this policy of council house sales in the 1980s showed a number of things. First, numbers of sales remained small and the new owner occupiers were largely drawn from the financially more secure tenants, in particular those in secure employment. That group of tenants were encouraged in purchasing their council houses by rapidly increasing rent levels (see figure 13.1) and restrictions to housing benefit regulations. Secondly, the transfer of housing stock was of a particular type, and most typically of suburban houses with gardens rather than flats or homes located within the inner city (Doling, 1993; Malpass, 1996). The stock therefore that remained in the control of local authorities was often the least popular, least well maintained, the tenants of which were in less-secure employment or the long-term unemployed. The policy of council house sales had in effect created a residualised public rented housing sector which has in turn effectively put an end to the sale of council houses, as the remaining tenants have neither the financial resources nor the inclination to purchase.

Government policy, at least in the latter part of the 1980s and early 1990s, has thus changed course with the establishment, in many fields of welfare provision,

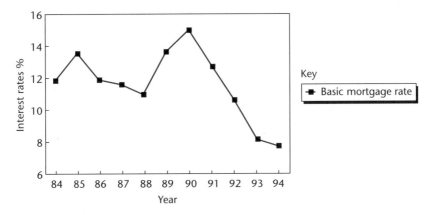

Fig. 13.1 UK interest rates, 1984–94

Source: Housing Statistics.

of the 'enabling' local authority. What this has meant for local government is a change of role away from direct provision of services towards one in which the authority oversees and regulates services provided by a range of different organisations, private, voluntary and charity (see, for example, chapters on education and community care policies). In terms of housing, the role of Councils is developing into a role involving the maintenance of standards and regulation of rents in the private rented sector, the administration of the housing benefits system, the enforcement of environmental health standards and the temporary accommodation of the statutory homeless.

However, the story of council housing in the 1980s only explains part of the picture of public rental housing in Britain. A significant, though proportionately small, number of dwellings are available to rent within housing association control, which although non-profit organisations remain, largely at least, publically funded. Indeed the statistics provided above, of council house transfers, fail to show that, over the same period, some 155,000 council houses in England were transferred to the control of housing associations, and therefore remain within the public rental sector.

Over the decade of the 1980s and into the early 1990s the government has sought to significantly expand the role of housing associations within the housing sector. This included encouragement and legislative recognition of those schemes which, usually at the initiative of local councils, effected the transfer of housing to association control. But, as part of this change of role, associations have seen their revenue support from public funds fall as they have been encouraged to seek private sources of finance to supplement public funds. As a result, and to encourage private investment, housing association rents have risen to a market level in order to offer better rates of return to private investors.

223

However, housing associations remain relatively small providers within the overall housing sector; there exist a small number of large associations (of more than 10,000 units), whereas there has been a proliferation of small, locally (community) based and managed associations (often managing less than 100 units). Therefore the ability of most associations to attract private finance remains negligible, and many feel that to do so would fundamentally alter their role of providing affordable rental accommodation. Where they have raised private finance, rents too have risen, and thus higher-income groups have been attracted to such accommodation, not the poorer groups within society. Also, as properties have been renovated and improved, this has made them more attractive to tenants under the right-to-buy legislation, although restricted to non-charitable associations (Malpass, 1993), and this also reduces the stock of housing for rent (Kleinman, 1990).

HOME OWNERSHIP

The availability of cheap credit and loans secured against homes ensured that the house market expanded rapidly and house prices continued a rapid ascent by which owners' investment was amply rewarded. The housing market itself reached a peak during 1988/9 as the credit boom coincided with new government restrictions to mortgage interest tax relief and house sales reached a frenzy before the August deadline.

The furore of the 1980s housing boom was, however, to end swiftly and dramatically. The end of the 1980s brought with it economic recession and as inflation began to rise the government's solution was to raise interest rates in order to slow down the economy. This recession brought with it numerous problems for the newly created 'mass' housing market. First, was the question of unemployment which rose rapidly in the early months and years of this recession and in precisely those areas which had experienced the greatest housing market activity such that 'growing numbers of people who had gained access could not afford to remain home owners' (Malpass, 1996). Secondly, the recession introduced negative equity to the housing market on a massive scale and left many millions of home owners unable to sell their homes as house prices fell, and saddled with mortgage debt which now outstripped the market value of their homes (Malpass, 1996).

As the recession continued mortgage lendors increasingly resorted to litigation and began to repossess homes, a trend which reached an all-time high of over 75,000 repossessions in 1991. Although the number of repossessions has since fallen, they remain at an unprecedented level, and the numbers of mortgages in arrears has remained stubbornly high. The green shoots of recovery in the housing market continue to be difficult to discover despite continued attempts to 'talk up the market' and only at the end of the 1990s does more long-term

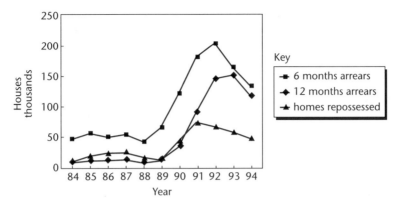

Fig. 13.2 Mortgages outstanding and repossessions, 1984–94

Source: Housing Statistics.

stability appear to have returned. The problems of the housing recession have perhaps been further compounded by restrictions in government support for home owners with cuts in the rate of mortgage interest tax relief and reductions or restrictions in the level of assistance available through income support.

The decade of the 1980s established, ideologically and politically, home ownership as the most desirable form of housing tenure (Doling, 1993), which, as we have already witnessed, was encouraged by government policies which enforced the sale of public-owned and rented properties and forced rapid rent increases across the public rental sector. Allied to these policies, deregulation in British financial markets made mortgages, and loans secured against property, increasingly attractive. As the 1990s approached the 1980s dream of the property- and share-owning democracy seemed to have become a nightmare and the British housing market entered what has been termed an 'affordability crisis' (Linneman and Megbolugbe, 1994).

As figures 13.1 and 13.2 indicate the number of mortgages in arrears (of six months) and serious arrears (12 months) together with the numbers of homes repossessed (the figures include voluntary surrender) followed closely the rapid rise in interest rates towards the end of the decade. To use the economic jargon, the economy had, after the deregulation of financial markets, overheated and had to be calmed by rapid and high rises in interest rates. Initially the government's market ideology prevented intervention in the form of support for those who had suffered in the housing market and economic recession. But later pragmatism, at least electoral pragmatism, forced the government to initiate rescue packages. Repossessions, particularly in the affluent south-east of the country, were a highly sensitive political issue and homelessness was becoming increasingly visible.

The main form of policy response came to be known as the rent to mortgage scheme whereby housing associations along with building societies were encouraged to acquire properties, and their occupants would become either tenants or shared owners. Housing Benefit may then become payable and the government undertook to pay mortgage payments direct to mortgage lenders (Bramley, 1994). The market for house purchase has remained depressed throughout the decade of the 1990s and only in the spring of 1997 did the Council of Mortgage Lenders report significant increases in the numbers of new mortgage offers made, rises in average house prices for the first time in a decade and increased house sales. The new government has promised to try to ameliorate the worst of the economic fluctuations affecting the housing market and reduce the boom bust housing cycle, but the Chancellor, Gordon Brown, has suggested further reductions in the rate of mortgage tax relief under the MIRAS scheme, continuing a policy introduced by the previous administration.

THE PRIVATE RENTAL SECTOR

As we have seen above the private rental sector has, over the course of the twentieth century, apparently been in a state of terminal decline. Governments over the years, particularly in the years after 1945, have promoted alternately public rented council housing or the private construction of the property-owning democracy, which became in the 1980s firmly rooted in the popular imagination. Governments have variously sought to revitalise the private rented sector, whether to fill gaps in housing policy which were not met by other sectors or to promote private entrepreneurship and landlordship, or sought to regulate what they perceived to be a firmly established relationship of exploitation, especially where the sector provided low-income tenancies. The sector continues to suffer high levels of housing disrepair and deprivation in comparison to other sectors as many landlords find themselves either unable or unwilling to provide more than basic housing amenities.

Responses to the private rented sector of British housing often depends upon political or ideological presuppositions; whether you view the landlord as the evil exploiter of frequently poor tenants, or as a hard-working entrepreneur attempting to provide a much needed service in an over-regulated housing market. Additionally, housing renovation grants from the government, a policy paradoxically aimed at supporting private landlords, has reduced the availability of rental accommodation as some landlords have taken advantage of the relatively quick profits to be made from house sales.

Successive governments in the 1980s recognised that in addition to a decline in the overall numbers of low-rent council accommodation available, although as we have noted rents in that sector rose rapidly, there would still be a demand for rented accommodation by people perhaps more mobile in their employment. Government therefore sought to develop strategies which would revive the private rental sector by making the development of rental accommodation a more attractive investment. This would involve, in line with those governments' market ideology, attempts to deregulate control of the sector, allowing rents to rise in line with 'market' levels rather than the notion of a 'fair rent' which had been introduced in the 1972 Housing Finance Act. Secondly, this process would involve changes in the security of tenure offered to tenants, by allowing greater access of landlords to their property by the introduction of the assured shorthold tenancy. Additionally new landlords would be encouraged to enter the sector with the introduction of the Business Expansion Scheme, which also aimed to address the increasing visibility of homelessness by converting empty flats, for instance those above shops, into habitable accommodation. This ethos was embodied in what the 1987 Conservative manifesto termed a 'Right to Rent' which aimed to encourage building societies and housing associations into the rental sector in addition to the small landlord (Malpass and Murie, 1990, p. 52).

It is perhaps significant to note that this area of housing policy was largely neglected by government in the early years of the decade as it sought to promote home ownership and the sale of council owned accommodation. It is also significant to note, although coincidentally, that the new focus of attention coincided with the sharp decline in the private housing market and homelessness began to increase alongside much publicised repossessions (Crook, 1990). It is also important to note that the policy made little impact in terms of increasing available rented stock, as table 13.2 illustrates, whereas the number of rental units available in the private sector changed little over the ten years between 1984 and 1993. As a percentage of available stock the sector has continued to decline and whilst housing association lets have increased, this has not been enough to replace those units lost in the process of council house sales and the overall quantity of rented accommodation has declined. Indeed, with the

Table 13.2 Number of rental units available (in thousands)

	Private rentals	Per cent	Housing Association rentals	Per cent	Local Authority rentals	Per cent	Total rentals
1984	2,318	10.5	530	2.4	6,107	27.6	8,955
1985	2,283	10.2	553	2.5	6,002	26.8	8,838
1986	2,224	9.8	571	2.5	5,903	26.1	8,698
1987	2,157	9.5	593	2.6	5,776	25.3	8,526
1988	2,095	9.1	622	2.7	5,587	24.2	8,304
1989	2,087	9.0	660	2.8	5,361	23.0	8,108
1990	2,135	9.1	715	3.0	5,182	22.1	8,032
1991	2,240	9.4	746	3.1	5,079	21.4	8,065
1992	2,292	9.6	812	3.4	4,971	20.8	8,075
1993	2,310	9.6	882	3.7	4,868	20.2	8,060

Source: Housing Statistics, DoE.

incoming Labour government's priorities stressing education, health, the economy and constitutional change, housing policy comes low on their list; the first sentence in the manifesto relating to housing policy states 'most families want to own their own homes', again recognising the shift in popularity of home ownership. But the manifesto does suggest that the government will attempt to establish a partnership in the rental sector, which seeks to do away with the strict divides between local authority, housing association and private rents. They propose the release of capital receipts from council house sales to allow new council building and stock rehabilitation and measures to improve the rights of tenants, especially in houses in multiple occupation (HMOs), together with local authority licensing of landlords (Britain will be better with New Labour, Labour Party, 1997). However, attempts to specifically arrest the further decline of this sector of housing appear low down on the incoming government's list.

HOMELESSNESS

The 1990s and much of the 1980s has been characterised by what has been termed an affordability crisis in British housing (Bramley, 1994). Policies aimed at widening the base of home ownership, both council house sales and financial deregulation, have been largely successful, but at a price. The stock of affordable rented accommodation has continued to decline, and the low rent sector has developed as low-quality housing for the poorest of tenants. Councils are left with stock which has proved the most difficult to maintain successfully in a climate of continued financial restrictions and housing associations have been unable to fill the gap left in the provision of social housing. Similarly, as we have seen above, the private landlord has not significantly expanded provision as the government hoped in the early part of the 1990s. Against this background we must now turn to what has been one of the hallmarks of the housing scene, the rise in homelessness, and most visibly youth homelessness.

The rise in the homeless can be identified in a number of related areas. The economic downturn of the 1980s, as we have noted, severely curtailed the revolution in home ownership of the early years of that decade and unemployment led to a rapid rise in mortgage arrears and ultimately repossessions. Dwindling stocks of low rent accommodation, paralleled by rising rents in that sector, have taken rented accommodation beyond the reach of many poorer families (as housing benefits are restricted) but at the same time have caused a massive increase in spending on rent subsidies via housing benefits. Most importantly, perhaps, changes in benefit regulations for young people have almost ended the possibility of young people obtaining rented accommodation until they reach their mid twenties. The situation is exacerbated because single people are not regarded as a priority by local authorities when accepting claims for help under the Housing Act.

These individuals also represent a demographic change in Britain as we enter a period in which more young people are entering the housing market and the desire for living singly continues to increase as people choose to marry later in life. Unemployment together with lack of access to cheap, low-quality accommodation and benefit reductions continues therefore to contribute to increasing numbers of homeless individuals (Bramley, 1994). The government has offered a partial response, though not directly to increasing homelessness, in the form of its mortgage rescue scheme which more specifically addresses the problems of home ownership and repossession as a result of the economic crisis. Successive ministers and back-benchers have also suggested that there is no need for any individual to remain homeless and that many do so from choice – why then should government act to remedy a self-inflicted crisis?

The new Labour government promised, in its manifesto, to address the question of homelessness by allowing local authorities to release capital funds gained by the sale of council housing and thereby increasing available rental stock. More specifically addressing the question of youth homelessness, they stress their 'welfare to work' policy which they hope will decrease the incidence of homelessness by increasing access to stable and secure employment and thus increasing access to the housing sector. This is clearly a long-term question, given the Blair government's promise to stick to current public spending targets over the two years from 1997 to 1999 and it perhaps falls to future texts to address the success of the new government in this respect.

REFERENCES

Bramley, G. (1994) 'An Affordability Crisis in British Housing: Dimensions, causes and policy impact', *Housing Studies*, 9(1).

Cole, I. and Furbey, R. (1994) *The Eclipse of Council Housing*, London: Routledge.

Crook, A. D. H. (1990) 'Deregulation of Private Rented Housing in Britain: Investors' responses to government housing policy', in van Vliet, W. and van Weesep, J., *Government Housing: Developments in seven countries. Volume 36, Urban Affairs Annual Reviews*, London: Sage.

Doling, J. (1993) 'British Housing Policy: 1984–1993', *Regional Studies*, 27(6): 583–8.

Kleinman, M. (1990) 'The Future Provision of Social Housing in Britain', in van Vliet, W. and van Weesep, J., *Government Housing: Developments in seven countries. Volume 36, Urban Affairs Annual Reviews*, London: Sage.

Labour Party (1997) *Britain will be Better with New Labour*, London: Labour Party.

Linneman, P. D. and Megbolugbe, I. F. (1994) 'Privatisation and Housing Policy', *Urban Studies*, 31(4/5): 635–51.

Malpass, P. and Murie, A. (1990) *Housing Policy and Practice*, 3rd edition, London: Macmillan.

Malpass, P. (1993) 'Housing policy and the housing system since 1979', in Malpass, P. and Means, R., *Implementing Housing Policy*, Buckingham: Open University Press.

Malpass, P. (1996) 'The Unravelling of Housing Policy in Britain', *Housing Studies*, 11(3): pp. 459–70.

Whitehead, C. M. E. (1993) 'Privatising Housing: An assessment of UK experience', *Housing Policy Debate*, 4(1): 101–39.

ANNOTATED READINGS

Perhaps the most useful and enduring overview of British housing policy is the volume by Malpass and Murie, *Housing Policy and Practice*, now in its fourth edition. Also useful is the text by Malpass and Means, *Implementing Housing Policy*. For an account of the decline of (municipal) public sector housing see Cole and Furbey's *Eclipse of Council Housing*. Another book providing a general overview is that by Brian Lund (1996), *Housing Problems and Housing Policy*, London: Longman.

14 Personal social services

OBJECTIVES

- To examine the development of the personal social services from their charitable roots to the era of state intervention.
- To examine the reasons behind the reorganisation of personal social services and the development of state social work services.
- To elaborate the critiques of social work services advanced by neo-liberals, feminist writers and Marxist critics.
- To describe and assess the implementation of the internal market in personal social services.

Here we look at policy changes in the personal social services since the Second World War and attempt to make connections between those changes and deeper ideological and empirical changes in state theory and state activity.

INTRODUCTION

Before getting into the meat of the chapter, it is useful to consider the roots of post-war state intervention in the personal social services (PSS). This is so because some recent critics of Conservative social policy have characterised it as heralding a return to the social and political values that nourished pre-war non-interventionism in welfare.

Most welfare historians trace the origins of modern PSS back to the middle of the nineteenth century. Some appear to see a positive and unilinear progression from the tradition of Victorian philanthropy through to co-ordinated state provision in the twentieth century (Woodroofe, 1971). The ideology of the Poor Law (itself of much earlier origin) which marked the provision of help in the nineteenth century – dividing the poor into deserving, and therefore worthy of philanthropic action, and undeserving, to be punished for their feckless behaviour – is seen by some as also permeating the attitudes and activities of twentieth-century state welfare agencies (George, 1973).

Others have argued that twentieth-century PSS grew out of the failure of philanthropy. Philanthropic action, often administered by the same people who administered the Poor Law, had failed to eradicate social needs, and this failure was seen in the late nineteenth century as a blow to national prestige (Seed, 1973, p. 9).

Some recent commentators have seen the growth of private charity organisations like the Charity Organisation Society in a different light. Parry (1979) identifies the evangelical Christian revival of the mid nineteenth century as the seed bed from which social work grew and flourished (Parry, Rustin and Satyamurti, 1979). Evangelical Christianity, with its emphasis on personal salvation, is seen as having led to philanthropic work with an emphasis on rescuing the immoral or preventing immorality. The first sign of modern personal social services appeared during the 1850s with the introduction of paid welfare workers associated with the Church and directed mainly at the moral welfare of women and girls (Walton, 1975, p. 41).

Others see the origins of state PSS as rooted in quite a different morality. For Steadman Jones (1971) the ancestry of nineteenth-century philanthropic and social welfare action are better seen in the need for a well-socialised proletariat in order to integrate all sections of the population into the structure, culture, norms and values of capitalist society and prevent social revolution. He reminds his readers of the philanthropist Samuel Smith's caution that

> I am deeply convinced that the time is approaching when this seething mass of human misery will shake the social fabric, unless we grapple more earnestly with it than we have done ... The proletariat may strangle us unless we teach it the same virtues which have elevated the other classes of society (Smith, cited in Steadman Jones, 1971, p. 291).

No doubt the ideologies of nationalism, evangelical Christianity, capitalist self-interest and secular philanthropy overlapped and interacted in the early development of PSS.

Out of this hotchpotch of nineteenth-century social welfare activity developed, in the twentieth century, a series of systems of social welfare which were to exist until the late 1940s. PSS activities which focused particularly, though not exclusively, on the poor were undertaken by a strong charity sector and a variety of central and local government departments (Woodroofe, 1971, pp. 193–8). Coverage of need was patchy and the activities of different agencies were largely unco-ordinated. It was not until the late 1940s that the state started to develop comprehensive social welfare services as part of a wider welfare state package.

THE INCEPTION OF STATE SOCIAL WORK

Following the Second World War, three state PSS agencies were created. These agencies, located at the level of the local state, replaced in large part the multiplicity of independent and government agencies which had previously carried out personal social service functions. These agencies, which existed until the early

1970s and were primarily concerned with services to children, the physically and mentally sick and disabled and the elderly, carried out a range of mostly statutory responsibilities. These were especially concerned with the provision of residential or substitute care for clients in situations where home-based care was regarded as inappropriate, inadequate or damaging (see Sainsbury, 1977, for a fuller description of the services).

THE REORGANISATION OF STATE SOCIAL WORK

In the early 1970s, following the report of the Seebohm Committee (Seebohm, 1968) in 1968 and the passing of the Local Authority Social Services Act in 1970, PSS was reorganised into unified local authority departments charged with the provision of statutory and non-statutory services to those in need. Further developments in PSS have occurred through the 1980s and early 1990s. In the early 1980s, the Barclay Report (1982), recommended the introduction of community social work strategies. Local authority social services departments and other PSS agencies were encouraged to develop alternative practices to meet social need. Community social work presumed a movement away from the one-to-one focus of traditional social work towards the encouragement and facilitation of self-help by individuals, social networks and communities. Barclay also recommended that the social work role, for many post-war years that of therapist, should be transformed. An important element of that transformation would be a move to the role of enabler. Social workers would support and enable informal carers rather than provide all the care themselves (Hadley and Cooper, 1984; Hadley, Dale and Sills, 1984; Hadley, Cooper, Dale and Stacey, 1987).

The most recent organisational change in PSS has followed the enactment of the National Health Service and Community Care Act (1990). From 1993, local authority social services departments have become the co-ordinating agency for community care. This has significant ramifications. First, these departments are key players in the assessment of social need, as long-stay hospitals and institutions are closed, and are replaced by care in the community. This immense change has come at a time when form has been given to the social services departments as strategic enablers. In this new world, local authority departments have become the assessors of need and the purchasers of services rather than the monopoly providers of PSS. The objective of this chapter is to understand these changes in modern social policy.

PERSONAL SOCIAL SERVICES IN THE POST-WAR PERIOD

How then do we explain the development and objectives of PSS in the post-war, pre-Thatcher period?

It appears clear that, for two post-war decades at least, PSS policy was driven by a social democratic engine. That dynamic was based on essentially Fabian notions of human nature, professional action and the appropriate role of the state.

Some social democratic writers see services as having developed out of a developing collective conscience in modern British society. In other words, thinking about policy and its enactment were coloured by a belief in the perfectibility of humankind. Sometimes such views are made explicit.

Slack, commenting on the introduction of state social work with children, says of the Curtis Report, '[it] was based on a new and more sympathetic approach to human need. Emphasis was laid on the differences of each child and his value as an individual' (Slack, 1966, p. 111).

Post-war PSS reflected, in large part, a commitment to meet need through the activities of government and state: 'whenever or wherever a social service is introduced it is to meet a need that has, whether soon or late, been recognised as real or unmet' (Slack, 1966, p. 93). Or, as Titmuss suggests: 'As the accepted area of social obligation widened, as injustice became less tolerable, new services were separately organised around individual need' (Titmuss, 1968, p. 21).

The development of services for children and young people illustrates the social democratic social policy project well. A common theme in the literature is that social legislation, in the period we are considering developed out of 'a widening and deepening knowledge of need' (Barker, 1979, p. 178) and was part of a continuous and cumulative process evolving 'constantly . . . in the direction of greater generosity and wider range' (Barker, 1979, p. 178).

So that the Children and Young Persons Act (1963) which sanctioned preventive social work to combat the need to receive troubled or troublesome children into local authority care, and the 1969 Act of the same name, which laid down a framework intended to minimise the number of child and young adult offenders appearing before courts – and saw a treatment or welfare model as more appropriate than a justice model in such cases – are both seen as prime examples of social democratic social policy. They appeared, at least at the time, as manifestations of the informed reactions of a benevolent state.

Social workers and others had become increasingly convinced, in the post-war years, that the causes of many problems associated with childhood were of a social or familial nature rather than located within some sort of individual pathology. Consequently, it was argued that problems of children's relationships with their parents or siblings were best dealt with within the family setting. Similarly, problems of juvenile criminality, associated with causative factors wider than the individual, were more justifiably dealt with by welfare intervention than by punishment.

Such legislation might therefore reasonably be seen as humane responses, by the state, to greater knowledge about the causes of social difficulties. Evidence had been produced of a wider network of factors associated with such problems than had previously been accepted. That evidence had prompted a number of further investigations by the state and by political parties (Home Office, 1965, 1968; Longford, 1966) and had culminated in rational and moral responses in the form of social legislation to cater for a minority of people experiencing difficulties.

The reorganisation of local authority social services in the early 1970s also owes its shape to social democratic ideas. In the 20 years following the inception of a state-controlled social service system, knowledge of two kinds was amassed by practitioners and administrators in the services. First, it became accepted that the tripartite organisation of state services led to duplication of tasks and uneven coverage of need (Seebohm, 1968). Secondly, as we have already noted, 'knowledge' was being generated that the causes of need for a minority of the population were wider and more complicated than had previously been thought (Abel-Smith and Townsend, 1965; Longford, 1966). As a consequence, practitioners, academics and sympathetic Labour politicians called for a unified service which would understand and meet the needs of the individual in relation to family, community and society (Marshall, 1975, pp. 143–64). These calls, supplemented by the reports of various government committees, and particularly the Seebohm Report, led to the reorganisation of state social work.

Post-war PSS development was, then, in some senses at least, the result of collective commitment to meet the needs of disadvantaged individuals or groups. That commitment was itself, in large part, the result of increases in knowledge and understanding. Or so it seemed to social democrats.

For supporters of social democracy, PSS had limited but important objectives. Only a minority of disadvantaged people, it was believed, still fell outside the advantages conferred by a transformed and welfare-oriented post-capitalist society. Certainly, by the 1950s the aims of PSS were conceived as the 'relief of residual distress' (Crosland, 1956, pp. 85–94). Though primary poverty was believed to have been eradicated by the welfare state, residual secondary poverty continued to exist alongside the problems of physical and mental illness and disability present in any society. The primary function of PSS was therefore to be the amelioration of such conditions.

Some 1950s commentators make this more explicit. Penelope Hall (1952), arguing that all major social problems had been successfully tackled by welfare state policies, proposed that the personal social services should tackle more sophisticated problems.

> The most urgent problems ... today are such symptoms of a sick society as the increasing number of marriage breakdowns, the spread of juvenile delinquency and the sense of frustration of the worker in spite of improved pay and conditions ... that is, problems of maladjustment rather than material need. (Hall, 1952, p. 8)

If this conviction that primary need had been outlawed was shattered by the 'rediscovery of poverty' in the 1960s (Abel-Smith and Townsend, 1965), the basic approach to policy remained substantially unchanged. The aims of PSS came to include helping government more fully to understand how pockets of deprivation and need remained in a post-war society characterised by rising living standards and relative affluence (Jenkins, 1972; Joseph, 1972). Poverty and need along with a catalogue of other problems were increasingly regarded as being outside the control of the individual. However, following Crosland's view that capitalism had been transformed, problems of deprivation and need were assumed as having roots in institutions intermediate to the individual and society. Thus the aims of Seebohm departments were to include the articulation and treatment of individual problems in the context of family and community (Seebohm, 1968). These aims were also to be met by state-sponsored community development projects (in the early 1970s) seemingly established to research and then change communities and thus ameliorate or eradicate need amongst marginal populations (Loney, 1983).

PSS policy in the post-war period was, then, clearly part of the social democratisation of the state and its direction was supported by both the major political parties. It assumed the existence of a moral/rational consensus on need and need satisfaction. More than this it was based on a particular view of the perfectibility of humankind and the superiority of welfare over punishment. Though dominant throughout this period, this approach had its detractors, as did the wider approach to social policy in general. Those detractors, from the left and right, mounted a searing attack on the aims of PSS in this period.

THE LEFT CRITIQUE

As we would expect, views from the Marxist left during this period suggested that PSS policy under social democratic stewardship acted not to increase welfare but as a handmaiden to capitalism.

The capitalist state, according to this perspective, always safeguards the interests and development of capitalism. The post-war British welfare state therefore functioned to promote capital accumulation (O'Connor, 1973), economic efficiency and social stability (Saville, 1957) and ideological conformity (Barratt-Brown, 1972).

The place of PSS in this scheme is that of a state institution operating primarily, though not exclusively, to promote social stability and the conformity of working-class people to ruling-class ideology. During the period under consideration, this function had been carried out in a number of ways including the use of social case work techniques: 'a pseudo-science – that blames individual inadequacies for poverty and so mystifies and diverts attention from the real causes' (Case Con, 1970). Capitalism was also protected by other, and seemingly more progressive, forms of social work activity, such as group work and community work. Such activities served simply to pathologise the group or the community rather than the individual. Social work, then, whether practised in the form of case work, group work or community work, acted socially to integrate, or socially to control, working-class people. In Corrigan's words, 'throughout the western world, states are characterised by one of the two major symbols of control in capitalist society; the tank or the community worker' (Corrigan, 1975, p. 25). Social case work, one of the major tools in the armoury of the post-war PSS, was a coercive activity which defined socially caused problems as family or individual crises (see Wilson, 1977). Community work and group work are seen as 'means by which society induces individuals and groups to modify their behaviour in the direction of certain cultural norms' (Gulbenkian Foundation, 1968, p. 84).

However, some Marxist writing, though critical of social democracy as theory and practice, suggests that the picture is a little more grey. For these writers, the state exhibited, during the post-war period, a limited autonomy from the British ruling class.

For many writers from this perspective (Corrigan and Leonard, 1978; Bolger et al., 1981; Jones, 1983), PSS in post-war Britain operated within a dialectic of welfare (Leonard, in Bean and MacPherson, 1983).

To some of these writers, social democratic theory is at least half right: post-war capitalism was qualitatively different to its inter-war forebear. Co-ordinated services were established and operated for most of the period in a changed political atmosphere and structure. The spirit of 1945 (Jones, 1983) was sustained throughout much of the period. PSS legislation and social work practice during that period reflected the clear influence of the social democratisation of state structures and social values. State policies and social work practices, while stopping far short of the provision of total welfare, demonstrated a tendency for state social provision progressively to meet some of the social needs of ordinary people as well as being concerned with containment and control (Gough, 1979; Leonard, in Bean and MacPherson, 1983). From this perspective, then, co-ordinated state services managed at one and the same time to effect the contradictory aims of meeting some of the social needs of its clients while meeting the economic and political 'needs' of a dominant class in capitalist society. Welfare state social work moved from punishment to rehabilitation. Post-war social democratic politics had provided 'the ideological climate for [the] more liberal and humane welfare theories and practices to be extended to the unorganised and impoverished dependent poor' (Jones, 1983, p. 39). However, for these Marxists at least, such changes in practice and aims represented little more, at times, than a replacement of biological determinist theories of social problem causation by a set of family pathology explanations. Nonetheless, such a shift, though limited and still ideologically useful to powerful social interests, is seen as having effected a move towards understanding social problems within a wider social context than hitherto.

Policies and practices related to youthful delinquency and family problems were seen, from this perspective, as reflecting the social democratisation of welfare. The Children and Young Persons' Act (1969) was therefore conceptualised as part of a process which tended both to liberate and control.

Here, the argument is that the 1969 Act and the reorganisation of personal social services, with which it was associated temporally and philosophically, point up both the progressive and conservative nature of PSS under social democracy. The Act and the reorganisation are seen as products of the contradictions inherent in the capitalist system. For both sought to establish the primacy of a welfare model in the theory and practice of social welfare: the Act by elevating the welfare needs of young offenders above abstract considerations of justice in sentencing, the reorganisation by promoting the idea that the new social service departments would provide for the welfare needs of all in a non-stigmatising way. At the same time, however, both social policy developments were rooted in an ideology of family pathology which saw residual problems in social democratic Britain as the result of malfunctioning family units. Such an ideology reinforced a new form of social control in social work. Individuals, previously held responsible for their own difficulties were, in late-twentieth-century British social democracy, to be subject to social control through treatment rather than punishment. They were to be controlled through the identification and policing of families – often seen as the root of problems of deviance and poverty (see Donzelot, 1980).

For all Marxists, the crucial weakness in social democratic welfare theory and practice was this. In one form or another, citizens were regarded as responsible for socially induced problems. For social democracy in theoretical form and social democratic welfare practice operated an ideology of pathology. If the individual was liberated from responsibility for social problems, then the family or the community took the individual's place (Clarke, 1980). If social democratic PSS policy had any virtue then it was, for Marxists, in the practical implications of the move from an ideology of punishment to an ideology of treatment.

FEMINIST ASSAULTS

Post-war PSS policy was not, however, simply the target of the Marxist left. Increasingly, social work services were intellectually and politically assailed by the women's movement.

Feminist commentators on the development of co-ordinated state social work services make a particular contribution to the understanding of PSS development. Put simply, these commentators underline the importance of women in the development of social work from its nineteenth-century roots through to the dawning of the welfare state. The conditions associated with the early development of social work – philanthropic concern, fear of social revolution, dented national pride, etc. – led to the provision of voluntary services staffed largely by women. That social work activity was the activity of an elite is undisputed

(Brook and Davis, 1985) but for much of the pre-welfare state period that elite was female. Middle- and upper-class women, often unmarried but sometimes the wives of the rich, were recruited into the ranks of a social work preoccupied with the rescue of widows, orphans, prostitutes and the poor in general. As a result a paradoxical situation often arose in which, according to Wilson,

> middle class women with no direct experience of marriage and motherhood themselves took on the social task of teaching marriage and motherhood to working class women who were widely believed to be ignorant and lacking when it came to their domestic tasks. (Wilson, 1977, p. 46)

This notwithstanding, social work in the late nineteenth and early twentieth centuries became largely the province of middle- and upper-class women (a process well documented by Timms, 1967, and Walton, 1975). Feminist writers (including Wilson, 1977; Brook and Davis, 1985) have also been instrumental in excavating from a largely male-oriented history the reminder that, although such social work activity was predominantly the province of women, the management committees of the voluntary organisations which administered the activity were predominantly men. In this task they have been ably assisted by some male commentators (notably, Walton, 1975).

Feminist analysis of social democracy's aims for PSS draws attention to the relationship between the state and the family in capitalist (and other 'advanced') societies. For Gieve, the welfare state in general and PSS activities in particular 'highlights the link between the state and the family and the way in which the state systematically bolsters the dependent-woman family' (Gieve, in Allen, 1974). For Loney and collaborators, 'the welfare system as it stands (or totters) is utterly dependent upon a specific construction of gender' (Loney, Boswell and Clarke, 1984).

For most feminist writers, post-war welfare state social work, and particularly its family interventionist activities, reinforced women's unequal and oppressed position in capitalist society as well as reinforcing other dominant ideas. Pascall, echoing many other feminist writers, sees the modern family as a deeply ambiguous social formation (Pascall, 1983). Although the family may be seen as an arena where the values of caring and sharing are upheld, it is also the arena where women's dependency is nurtured. It therefore constitutes the focal point for exploitative relationships between men and women. According to many feminist writers, the theory and practice of post-war social work entrenched, reinforced and reproduced women's dependency on and exploitation in the family and perpetuated fundamental inequalities between the sexes.

To appreciate the key concepts in a feminist understanding of the aims of post-war social work it is useful to reconstruct here the important steps in feminist arguments about welfare. One of the most influential of contemporary feminist writers on welfare has argued that the welfare state constituted 'a set of ideas about the family and about women as the linch-pin of the family' (Wilson, 1977, p. 9). As such it was also a mechanism by which women's traditional roles as wife and mother were controlled (Wilson, 1977, p. 40). Post-war social work performed functions which both protected the interests of a dominant social class and oppressed or exploited women. It did so by constructing an ideal type of family and by monitoring or policing families which failed to conform to this ideal type.

In contemporary capitalist society such family formations also imply the creation and sustenance of economic dependency for most women. Social work, it is argued, operated as one amongst many state institutions which played an important ideological role in perpetuating women's dependency and exploitation.

How then, exactly, did social work carry out these functions? Feminist writers may point to a large number of developments in state social work to support a view that the aims of social work were deeply discriminatory or oppressive to women. Below we outline but a few examples from the theory and practice of social work:

1. It has been argued, for instance, that the report of the Curtis Committee on Child Care (though chaired by a woman and having women as half its membership) reinforced an increasingly popular view, shared by Bowlby (1953), that the care of children was best carried out in families with non-working, dependent mothers (Brook and Davis, 1985, p. 15).

2. It is further argued that the dependant–breadwinner form of family organisation was reinforced by the subcommittee of the women's group on Public Welfare in 1948 which argued 'Frequently a family can survive in spite of a weak or vicious father but it is rare that it can survive with an incapable mother' (Women's Group, 1948, quoted in Brook and Davis, 1985).

3. Social work, it is argued, has imbibed an ideology of maternal care (see Ehrenreich and English, 1979) which, in practice, has restricted women's capacity to find approval in any other role than that of dependent wife and mother. To this end, social work's concern in the 1950s and 1960s with latch-key children placed working-class women especially in an impossible double bind. If such women did not work their families were often driven into poverty. If they did, they ran the risk of being labelled by social work agencies as neglectful mothers (Brook and Davis, 1985, p. 16). Competent parenting, it is contended from this perspective, is interpreted in social work theory and practice as competent mothering. Competent mothering implies the absence of paid work outside the home and thus economic dependency on a man, preferably in a state sanctioned dependant–breadwinner family.

4. Similarly, it is argued, problems of delinquency and maladjustment are often, implicitly or explicitly, conceptualised in social work as problems of malfunctioning families and often as problems arising from absent, working, mothers (Comer, 1971), or as a result of child-rearing occurring outside the safe confines

of the dependant–breadwinner nuclear family. Specifically, it is argued by some feminists, social work constructs a model of successful child development which implies the necessity of a 'normal' family context. Moreover, the creation of such a context is seen as depending on the competence (and perhaps full-time presence) of the mother (McIntosh, in McLennan, Held and Hall, 1984, pp. 228–9).

5. Finally, it is argued, state policies encourage, whilst underfinancing, community care of the old or sick, and social work practices rooted in the concept of partnership with carers further reinforce traditional family patterns and, in consequence, women's oppression/exploitation as carers (see Finch and Groves, 1983; McIntosh, in McLennan, Held and Hall, 1984; Brook and Davis, 1985).

What emerges then from this rather thematic reconstruction of feminist arguments about social work is a view that the aims and functions of post-war social work included the crucial aims of:

1. reinforcing through theory and practice an ideology of the family rooted in a dependant–breadwinner form of family structure;
2. policing families (see Donzelot, 1980; Meyer, 1983), especially those who fail to conform to such patterns;
3. entrenching, reinforcing and reproducing the discrimination, exploitation and oppression of women in contemporary society.

A rather more complex set of issues is implied by the recent work of the feminist social scientist, Fiona Williams (1990). She draws attention not only to the ways in which social policies have systematically reinforced the exploitation or oppression of women but to the inter-relationship between the major forms of structural oppression. As a consequence PSS policy, viewed from Williams' perspective, acts most potently to reinforce the tendency of the patriarchal capitalist western state to discriminate against women who are black, working class or both. This sort of study, while pointing to the impact of social policies on women as a category, allows more sophisticated analyses of the differential effect of social policies on different groups of women.

THE ATTACK FROM THE RIGHT

As we have seen in chapter 3, radical right formulations see social welfare as having developed as the result of the creation of a bogus consensus on the need for state provision. Many, if not all, of the arguments adduced by proponents of anti-collectivism in relation to welfare in general were adduced in the specific cases of social work provision and PSS policy.

For the ultra-right, state provision of PSS, like other state social services, led post-war Britain towards state coercion (Hayek, 1944, p. 52; Friedman, 1962,

p. 13). PSS, by according citizen rights to all sections of the population, contributed to social discord (Friedman, 1962, chapter 10) and, because of its increasing call on the public purse, to reducing economic growth and prosperity. State social work was seen as having diminished individual responsibility because it 'reduces the breadwinner's individual responsibility for his family's well being, and for the pursuit of independence it substitutes permanent mutual dependence as the much more fragile basis of mutual respect' (Bremner, 1968, pp. 52–3). PSS provision, by superseding 'the voluntary co-operation of individuals' (Friedman, 1962, p. 13) also reduced freedom: it reduced democracy, choice, respect, the role of the family and contributed to social disorganisation.

The new right apologists of the post-war years not only attacked PSS social democratic style. In its place, they prescribed a much reduced role for state social work in contemporary British society. Instead of offering a more or less universal service, social welfare services were best undertaken in the main by the family and the community. Thatcher, echoing Friedman, argued that 'if we are to sustain, let alone extend, the level and standard of care in the community, we must first try to put responsibility back where it belongs, with the family and with the people themselves' (Thatcher, 1977, p. 83).

PERSONAL SOCIAL SERVICES AND THE NEW CONSERVATISM

As we have seen above, the election of Conservative governments throughout the 1980s and into the 1990s has effected changes to PSS policy. Hints of this, if they were necessary, came early in Mrs Thatcher's first administration. Often citing the work of the radical right, ministers, or the Premier herself, signalled a restructuring of PSS that would involve voluntarism and residualising the state.

Such a pre-eminent role for voluntary, family or community services, and a consequential residual role for state social work, is clear in the advice of Patrick Jenkin, then Secretary of State for Social Services, that 'The Social Services departments should seek to meet directly only those needs which others cannot or will not meet ... Their task is to act as a safety net ... for people for whom there is no other, not a first port of call' (*Guardian*, 21 January 1981).

Thatcher herself told the 1981 annual conference of the Women's Voluntary Service that the main burden of social welfare provision should fall on the voluntary sector of welfare, with statutory social services functioning simply as residual gap fillers, underpinning the work of the voluntary sector.

The scene was set, then, for the transformation of statutory PSS agencies into enabling organisations. Those organisations would enable informal carers or the neighbourhood (the Barclay Report) to act as commissioners of service, in a situation where much provision was offered by voluntary or private welfare bodies.

At one level at least, the new Conservatism of the 1980s and 1990s has encouraged a return to pre-welfare state approaches in PSS. While carers get on with caring and the independent and private sectors carry out state-financed philanthropy, the state is being slowly removed from centre stage in the provision of PSS. In so doing, of course, an attempt to bury the trails of social democratic welfare, perhaps ultimately doomed to success, is being made. For this marginalisation of state PSS activity also marginalises the totems of social democracy itself.

First, the idea that the state has a responsibility to meet all welfare needs has been superseded by the idea that the state's responsibility is to enable informal carers, or kin, or the community to care. Secondly, the professionalisation of welfare, seen by Thatcher's new Conservatives and the radical right as largely responsible for the growth of welfare monopolies, is being swept aside by the elevation of informal and untrained care. Finally, the social democratic idea that individual needs are best met by collective state provision is severely dented.

Another dent to social democratic PSS policy directions can be discerned in current government statements on law and order (see *Guardian*, 21 October 1993). The clear re-emergence of a hard line on law and order – criminals should be punished not rehabilitated, prisons are punitive institutions not resocialisation centres – has carried with it attacks on social work. A criminal justice system predicated, as it has been for the last decade, on diversion from custody is in large part the creation of the social work lobby. That system is to be restructured and social work and probation activities within the criminal justice system are to be made more consistent with a punitive justice model.

At the time of writing, we appear to stand on the cusp of removal of the state from large-scale provision of PSS. Whether services will be further rationalised must remain, for now, a matter of conjecture. However, the journey so far has taken us some considerable distance from the social democratic starting-point of this and other welfare state services.

REFERENCES

Abel-Smith, B. and Townsend, P. (1965) *The Poor and the Poorest*, London: Bell.

Barclay, P. (1982) *Social Workers: Their role and tasks*, London: Bedford Square Press.

Barker, J. (1979) 'Social conscience and social policy', *Journal of Social Policy*, 8(2): 177–206.

Barratt-Brown, M. (1972) *From Labourism to Socialism*, Leeds: Spokesman Books.

Bolger, S., Corrigan, P., Docking, J. and Frost, N. (1981) *Towards Socialist Welfare Work*, London: Macmillan.

Bowlby, J. (1953) *Childcare and the Growth of Love*, Harmondsworth: Penguin Books.

Bremner, M. (1968) *Dependency and the Family*, London: IEA.

Brook, E. and Davis, A. (1985) *Women, the Family and Social Work*, London: Tavistock.

Case Con Collective (1970) 'Case-Con Manifesto', in *Case-Con*, 1, London: Case Con Collective.

Clarke, J. (1980) 'Social Democratic Delinquents and Fabian Families', in Fitzgerald, M. *et al.* (eds), *Permissiveness and Control*, London: Macmillan.

Comer, L. (1971) *The Myth of Motherhood*, Leeds: Spokesman Pamphlets.

Corrigan, P. (1975) 'Community Work and Political Struggle', in Leonard, P. (ed.), *The Sociology of Community Action*, Keele: University of Keele.

Corrigan, P. and Leonard, P. (1978) *Social Work Practice Under Capitalism*, London: Macmillan.

Cowley, J., Kaye, A., Mayo, M. and Thompson, M. (1977) *Community or Class Struggle*, London: Stage One Publications.

Crosland, C. A. R. (1956) *The Future of Socialism*, London: Johnathon Cape.

Department of Health (1990) *National Health Service and Community Care Act*, London: HMSO.

Donzelot, J. (1980) *The Policing of Families*, London: Hutchinson.

Ehrenreich, B. and English, D. (1979) *For Her Own Good*, London: Pluto Press.

Finch, J. and Groves, D. (1983) *A Labour of Love: Women, work and caring*, London: Routledge.

Friedman, M. (1962) *Capitalism and Freedom*, Chicago: University of Chicago Press.

George, V. (1973) *Social Security and Society*, London: Routledge & Kegan Paul.

Gieve, K. (1974) 'The Independence Demand', in Allen, S. (ed.), *Conditions of Illusion*, London: Feminist Books.

Gough, I. (1979) *The Political Economy of the Welfare State*, London: Macmillan.

Gulbenkian Foundation (1968) *Community Work and Social Change*, London: Longman.

Hadley, R. and Cooper, M. (1984) *Patch-based Social Services Teams*, Lancaster: Department of Social Administration, Lancaster University.

Hadley, R., Dale, P. and Sills, P. (1984) *Decentralising Social Services: A model for change*, London: Bedford Square Press.

Hadley, R., Cooper, M., Dale, P. and Stacey, G. (1987) *A Community Social Worker's Handbook*, London: Tavistock.

Hall, P. (1952) *The Social Services of Modern England*, London, Routledge & Kegan Paul.

Hayek, F. A. (1944) *The Road to Serfdom*,

Home Office (1965) 'The Child, the Family and the Young Offender', Cmnd 2742, London: HMSO.

Home Office (1968) 'Children in Trouble', Cmnd 3601, London: HMSO.

Jenkins, R. (1972) *What Matters Now*, London: Fontana.

Jones, C. (1983) *State Social Work and the Working Class*, London: Macmillan.

Joseph, Sir K. (1972) 'The Cycle of Deprivation', speech delivered to a Conference of the Pre-School Play Group Association.

Leonard, P. (1983) 'Marxism, the Individual and the Welfare State', in Bean, P. and MacPherson, S. *Approaches to Welfare*, London: Routledge & Kegan Paul.

Loney, M. (1983) *Community Against Government*, London: Heinemann.

Loney, M., Boswell, D. and Clarke, J. (1984) *Social Policy and Social Welfare*, Milton Keynes: Open University Press.

Longford, 1966 *Crime: a challenge to us all*, London: Labour Party.

Marshall, T. H. (1975) *Social Policy*, revised edition, London: Hutchinson.

Meyer, P. (1983) *The Child and the State*, Cambridge: Cambridge University Press.

O'Connor, J. (1973) *The Fiscal Crisis of the State*, New York: St Martin's Press.

Parry, N., Rustin, M. and Satyamurti, C. (eds) (1979) *Social Work, Welfare and the State*, London: Edward Arnold.

Pascall, G. (1983) 'Women and Social Welfare', in Bean, P. and MacPherson, S. *Approaches to Welfare*, London: Routledge & Kegan Paul.

Sainsbury, E. (1977) *The Personal Social Services*, London: Pitman.

Saville, J. (1957) 'The welfare state: an historical approach', *New Reasoner*, 3.

Seebohm, Sir F. (1968) 'Report of the Committee on Local Authority and Allied Personal Social Services', Cmnd 3703, London: HMSO.

Seed, P. (1973) *The Expansion of Social Work in Britain*, London: Routledge & Kegan Paul.

Slack, K. (1966) *Social Administration and the Citizen*, London: Michael Joseph.

Steadman Jones, G. (1971) *Outcast London*, Oxford: Oxford University Press.

Thatcher, M. (1977) *Let Our Children Grow Tall*, London: Centre for Policy Studies.

Timms, N. (1967) *Psychiatric Social Work in Great Britain*, London: Routledge & Kegan Paul.

Titmuss, R. (1968) *Commitment to Welfare*, London: Allen & Unwin.

Walton, R. (1975) *Women in Social Work*, London: Routledge & Kegan Paul.

Walton, T. (1984) 'Justifying the Welfare State', in G. McLennon, D. Held and S. Hall eds, *The Idea of the Modern State*, Milton Keynes: Open University Press.

Williams, F. (1990) *Social Policy: A critical introduction*, Cambridge: Polity Press.

Wilson, E. (1977) *Women and the Welfare State*, London: Tavistock.

Woodroofe, K. (1971) *From Charity to Social Work*, London: Routledge & Kegan Paul.

ANNOTED READINGS

For an historical overview of the development of Britain's personal social services and social work see Robert Adams (1996), *The Personal Social Services*, London: Longman. The Finch and Groves volume, *A Labour of Love*, is an informative exploration of caring and the role of women as carers. For a view on the most recently implemented changes to Britain's social services, see J. Lewis and H. Glennerster (1996), *Implementing the New Community Care*, Buckingham: Open University Press.

15   Employment policy

OBJECTIVES

- To consider the role of employment policy in the foundation and development of the British welfare state and the pursuit of 'full employment'.

- To examine the reasons for rapidly rising unemployment in the 1970s and the subsequent end of full employment as an objective of government policy.

- To explore reasons for the subordination of employment policy to monetary policy in the 1980s.

- To explore reasons for government regulation in the workplace.

- To consider the importance of training policy in the achievement of employment objectives and the issue of the 'skills shortage'.

BACKGROUND: EMPLOYMENT POLICY AFTER KEYNES AND BEVERIDGE

> The maintenance of a high and stable level of employment was one of the fundamental assumptions of the Beveridge Report and an objective to which all governments were positively committed after 1944. (Lowe, 1993, p. 99)

Employment policies have, over time, occupied an ambiguous position in the consideration of social policy. Texts may omit or give only cursory consideration to the area of employment, save for the issue of unemployment and resulting issues of income maintenance, as employment is often regarded as more properly the realm of economic rather than social policy; indeed employment is perhaps the area of social policy with the strongest links to wider economic and public policy. Yet at the same time employment policy occupies a crucial position in the post-war development of social policy in Britain, as it provided the second arm of post-war reconstruction, and without which the welfare state could not exist. Full employment would both finance the development of the welfare state, and government welfare policy would help to maintain economic growth, and thus full employment. The two were to be symbiotic; without the economy and full employment the welfare state could not survive.

Full employment thus became symbolic of welfare state policy throughout the years from the late 1940s to the end of the 1970s, and governments on both sides of the political divide sought to ensure steady growth, increasing prosperity and full employment along with low inflation. Employment levels remained high throughout the period 1945–75 and in the six years prior to this Britain experienced continued labour shortages. The 1944 white paper Employment Policy, born out of the 1930s decade of massive economic depression and mass unemployment, set governments' commitment to the maintenance of high and stable levels of employment by the manipulation of the economy and levels of demand. The Conservative party and governments of the post-war period, however, continued to stress traditional economic maxims of a balanced budget and free trade but conditions remained favourable enough not to challenge the idea of a full employment economy. The Conservatives in power were not themselves averse to government intervention when necessary and this illustrates one of the downsides of the Keynesian orthodoxy of demand management and economic intervention as governments showed themselves all too willing to use measures to provide short-term boosts to the economy and to their electoral fortunes (Whiteside, 1995, pp. 56–9).

Over the 30 years following the end of the Second World War the maxim of full employment and welfare expansion seemed to hold true as the economy grew steadily and the numbers in employment continued to expand; levels of inflation and unemployment remained low. In Britain, and elsewhere in Europe, the number of people in employment grew as opportunities for women and migrant labour presented themselves. Keynesian policies of demand management appeared to have succeeded and put an end to the cycle of boom and slump in the British economy, and it was possible to guarantee economic prosperity and growth.

The onset of the 1970s however, as we have seen elsewhere, marked a decisive shift in the post-war economic settlement as what appeared to be a terminal crisis beset western economies. Unemployment began to rise, steadily at first, more

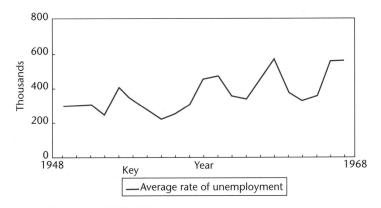

Fig. 15.1 Unemployment, 1948–68

Source: HMSO (1971) *British Labour Statistics, Historical Abstracts, 1886–1968*.

rapidly later and inflation also began to rise and what signalled change in employment policy was that the unemployed no longer appeared to be the transitional few of the previous 30 years, but were long term, indeed almost a permanent 'reserve army'. What also marked the end of Keynesian economics was the inability of government to control inflation and the failure of economic manipulation which saw public finances invested into companies such as British Leyland on a large scale, but apparently to little effect (Middlemass, 1979). Those companies continued to lose money and were unable to modernise; they had become uncompetitive in the world economy and government intervention no longer seemed to work.

Additionally, Britain seemed to be continually lagging behind in the sunrise industries of the 1970s and 1980s. Technology and communications were at that time rapidly developing and despite its reputation for innovation and development Britain seemed sadly unable to develop commercially in the new industries. Existing plant and machinery was not being replaced, for instance with computer technology in motor manufacture which other countries were rapidly adopting, and new technology generally seemed to be viewed with a near luddite suspicion in British industry compared to its counterparts in Europe and the Far East. This picture was set against a background of a promise made by the Labour Prime Minister, Wilson, in the 1960s to lead the world's technological revolution and a classically Keynesian investment of public funds in a massive expansion of Polytechnic-based technical and vocational education.

EMPLOYMENT POLICY IN THE 1980s

The triumph of Margaret Thatcher as Conservative leader in 1975, however, marked the beginning of the end of Keynesian policies. The developing Thatcherite hegemony stressed the virtues of inequality, self-help and individuality over what it viewed as the dangerous corporate political management that had developed. The party began to define its role as one of dismantling the post-war settlement and in particular the power of organised labour, which they felt had come to dominate the political process and which they said was at the root of the economy's ills (Coates, 1989).

So it was that, with the election of a new government in May 1979, a new economic orthodoxy was introduced to Britain and a new hegemony in industrial relations enforced. Monetarism, that set of economic policies enacted by the successive Thatcher and Major governments, emphasised the control of inflation by the manipulation of the money supply, rather than the maintenance of full employment as the prime economic objective. It was argued that labour was a commodity like any other in a market economy and that therefore the levels of supply of and demand for labour should be left to the market; the price of that labour would be determined by the market and not the demands of organised trades unions, whose demands for wage increases alongside protective labour legislation, would price British labour out of the world market. The evidence for such an analysis was to be found in the so-called 'Tiger-economies' of the Far East which exhibited characteristics of high demand, high productivity, low labour costs and low levels of government 'interference'.

The task for government in 1980s Britain was to distance itself, as far as possible, from the activities of the labour market and to deregulate that market so that employment, and unemployment, could reach their 'natural' market levels and most importantly the government could concentrate its efforts on the control of inflation. In effect then, unemployment was to be used both to discipline the labour market and to help control inflation which would also be attacked using controls on the money supply and interest rates. The long-term goal was to achieve permanently low inflation from which new (real and permanent) jobs would be created. Additionally the government's role would be to help in creating a workforce for the future; highly flexible, highly skilled and above all low cost in order to increase British industrial competitiveness (see chapter 11 for a discussion on education and training policy). Similarly government defined its role in terms of one which did not make non-employment a more attractive option than employment, in other words benefits policy would make a clear move back towards the principle of less-eligibility established in the nineteenth-century Poor Law, a punitive policy which would not be seen to reward idleness. The change of government then also marked a change in the principles upon which employment policy was to be based, one which viewed unemployment behaviourally as the responsibility of the individual, rather than structurally as something intrinsic to the economic situation and out of the hands of individual control.

Government in the 1980s also committed itself to the modernisation of Britain's industrial base which it held to be hampered by lack of investment and the inability of management to manage their enterprises. Here blame was placed firmly at the door of the trades unions. The unions had been able, during the years of consensus politics, to demand their place in the planning of the country's economy and in negotiations with management (the years of beer and sandwiches in Downing Street). This in turn had restricted the ability of management to act decisively in time of economic crisis. Government's role was then to free the hand of management by re-establishing the free market in labour relations and removing the ball and chain of protective labour legislation and restrictive practices which dominated British industrial relations.

The rhetoric of taming the unions struck a familiar chord with electors whose despair over the 'winter of discontent' was manifest. The social contract drawn up between the then Labour government and the TUC proved impossible to enforce as increasing inflation led to higher wage demands backed up by the threat of imminent strike action. The government appeared unable to control its friends (and paymasters) in the unions and the incoming government promised to control matters with a firm hand; in the words of Andrew Gamble, Britain was to have a free economy but a strong state. The 'major obstacles to a free economy were identified as the spreading network of corporatist institutions which were encroaching on the functioning of the free market' (Gamble, 1994, pp. 100–1). The role of the state was to be that traditionally defined as the protection of external borders and the maintenance of law and order and not the routine roles of economic and welfare management that the state had assumed.

The new regime of industrial relations during the 1980s began with the introduction of restrictions on picketing and the closed shop, but were, at best, modest measures. But in significant areas of industry, those nationalised industries controlled by government, the government began to appoint managers with private sector backgrounds, what Gamble refers to as 'a new breed of managers . . . to put the industries into competitive shape' (Gamble, 1994, p. 113). In adopting this strategy the government began to ready itself for a conflict with organised trades unions which it felt was necessary if British industry was to recover. These plans were being laid at a time of severe economic recession during which unemployment rates rose rapidly in the wake of the second oil price rise in 1979; the number of unemployed in Britain rose from 1.25 million in 1979 and had doubled within 18 months of the new Conservative government achieving office, by 1985 it had reached 3 million (a figure previously assumed to be unsustainable in the Keynesian model of economic management). As a short-term response the government reacted by boosting those short-term retraining schemes, such as the Youth Training Scheme and the Community Programme, and by changing the counting base for unemployment figures, for instance by removing the unemployed who were near to retirement (1981) and school leavers (1983). Such moves attracted vehement criticism as their effect was to artificially reduce the number of officially unemployed and to disguise the rate of dependency on state benefits. (Figure 15.2 compares official unemployment figures with those produced by the Labour Research Department which calculates rates on their 1980 basis.) But whereas previous governments had feared such a level of unemployment and the levels of social unrest that it may engender, the Conservatives adopted a bullish 'no pain no gain' attitude buoyed by Margaret Thatcher's stance of 'there is no alternative'.

The early years of the 1980s appeared to some to spell a rise in industrial conflict as the government prepared itself to challenge some of the 'sacred cows' of trades union tradition and practice. Long and often bitter conflicts were witnessed in industries such as steel, Britain's docks, the newspaper publishing industry (a 12 month strike at *The Times* and fights with the new press barons) and most dramatically a year long dispute with the miners. But whereas previous governments had buckled and fallen at the hands of trades unions in what came to be regarded as battles for the control of the soul of the nation, the Thatcher governments refused to back down and stood firm by new regulations introduced

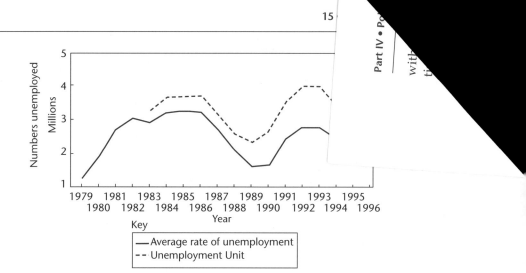

Fig. 15.2 Unemployment data, 1979–89

Source: N. Johnson (1990) *Reconstructing the Welfare State*, Labour Research Department.

through parliament for the control of strikes, such as the limit of six pickets at a workplace and the ban on secondary and 'flying' pickets. The effect of regulatory change has been dramatic and Britain now has one of the lowest levels of industrial dispute and days lost through industrial action amongst modern capitalist economies or in its own history.

EMPLOYMENT POLICY

Aside from the regulation of the employment market and industrial relations within that market, what is the purpose of employment policy? The effect of early legislation, such as the National Insurance Act (1911), was to define government employment policy as that which aided the unemployed to find employment and later sought to provide training opportunities to allow the unemployed to reskill. This early policy stance has by and large remained unchanged as government today still seeks to help the unemployed back to work both by finding suitable vacancies or suitable training opportunities, see for example the 1997 Labour government's 'Welfare to Work' programme which reiterates both the employment matching function of government and the training/retraining function. (See chapter 11 of this volume for discussion regarding training policy and education.)

In addition to what we may conveniently term primary employment policy we may also identify secondary objectives, for example the pursuit of equal treatment within the employment market and legislation for equal pay or regulations against sexual harassment. Furthermore we may identify a number of factors, which, whilst not necessarily objectives of employment policy, are important factors in the pursuit of both primary and secondary objectives. Important variables in the employment policy field include the balance between full- and part-time employment within the economy, the rise of women's employment over the whole of the post-war period and crucially alongside increasing female employment the seemingly inexorable rise of low-paid and temporary employment. Further factors to consider in contemporary employment policy are the nature of skills; as the nature of employment has changed over the period of the 1980s new hallmarks have been developed; thus a re-skilled and crucially multi-skilled and flexible labour force willing to accept new work patterns has become the standard of any progressive economy.

Employment policy in the post-war period has, however, been of a fundamentally different nature. The Beveridge Report based the foundation of the welfare state after 1944 upon the premise of full employment at levels that would be both high and stable, an aim of government policy which exhibited a high degree of consensus in the post-war world (see Lowe, 1993). Beveridge was, rightly, criticised for promoting a notion of peculiarly male full employment and this notion of full employment has developed into one also of maximum employment (Esping-Andersen, 1997), so much so that many who do not seek employment, for whatever reason – for example, family raising – risk the approbation of their peers. The extension of the ideal of full to maximum employment has, however, important implications for the direction of employment policy. That is, that employment policy has further widened its remit to include elements of childcare for working parents and the financial subsidy of childcare arrangements.

As we have already indicated, employment policy also has intrinsic links with the education and training of a workforce. It has in part been the high and persistent levels of youth unemployment which has caused government to readdress its education strategy in order to meet the needs of employers in a world of rapid change in the use of high technology. At the other end of the age scale, government has favoured the promotion of early retirement above the retraining of the older unemployed, a feature which is especially noticeable in areas of decline in traditional industries, such as engineering, where responsibility has, usually, been transferred out of the orbit of the employment service to, for example, regional policy. Responsibility for employment policy has been lodged with the Department of Employment, now merged into the Department for Education and Employment, however, direct government provision has been rare. Employment and training has, since 1974, been largely the responsibility of government sponsored quangos, first the Manpower Services Commission and latterly the Training and Enterprise Councils. An important distinction between these two organisations is the state-led nature of the first compared to the quasi-independent and market-dominated characteristics of the second. What this widespread pattern of responsibility for the implementation of employment policy tells us is, as Moon concludes, that it is multi-dimensional (Moon, 1983, p. 304).

The field of play in which employment policy resides in the 1990s has been largely determined by the change in the political agenda which took place in the 1980s. Employment, perhaps more than any other element of the welfare state, has become seen as the responsibility of the individual with government's role one which set out to discourage unemployment as a socially expensive and morally indefensible luxury. The Conservative governments of that decade have been less willing to pander to electoral demands that something must be done, dismissing previous policies as short-term, quick fixes. Secretaries of State for Employment instead have stressed the creation of 'real' jobs built on the economic successes of government economic policy; whether we may wish to dismiss such claims as political rhetoric is to some degree irrelevant since the same language now permeates the manifesto of 'new' Labour, signalling something of a new consensus in employment policy.

Political rhetoric aside, what are the issues that employment policy is attempting to address? Perhaps highest on the policy agenda is the scrutiny currently afforded to both youth and long-term unemployment, and clearly the implications that this has for both education and training. In the pro-individualist 1980s, employment policy has become less concerned with the provision of direct employment opportunities or employment subsidy and has approached policy from an economically determined stance which suggests that it is both the responsibility of the individual to find and retain work in a market which is able to provide the necessary opportunities. Government employment policy has, in contrast to the Beveridgean consensus of full employment, become indirect.

However, other employment issues have, directly, preoccupied government, perhaps most notably the question of the role of the European Union in shaping national employment policies and the thorny issue of the social provisions of the European treaties. European directives aimed at the control of social dumping, or the attempt to create a 'level European playing field' by preventing countries gaining a competitive advantage by reducing their own employment protection measures, have been regarded by British governments and employers as Brussels' attempts to impose a new corporate consensus. British governments have felt that their efforts to enforce the primacy of the market over institutionalised vested interests were threatened by a backdoor European socialism.

Additionally, as the pursuit of full employment, as a government responsibility, has given way to full and maximum employment, at least as long as the economy is strong enough to support such goals, so the treatment of women workers and the interplay of work and family responsibilities, for men and women, has come to the fore. Debate surrounding the employment of women versus their role in the home, and its neglect, is no longer sufficient and is too simplistic; modern industrial nations invest greatly in an essentially universal education system which provides women with the skills that employers require, to seek to confine women to the home as a solution to male unemployment is both insulting and a waste of considerable skill and talent. Policy must therefore address, seriously, the questions of equality of reward, treatment in the workplace and pension provision in a system based upon the out-dated notion of full male employment. In addition the increasingly complex relationship between work and family where both parents (assuming a two parent family) are in work, continually raises new questions and dilemmas.

YOUTH AND THE LONG-TERM UNEMPLOYED

Both youth and long-term unemployment have been recognised as serious policy problems since the advent of mass unemployment in the mid 1970s and have been addressed by a proliferating number of schemes through the 1980s. Government has introduced a range of measures over the past two decades intended to tackle them; the first of note is the Youth Opportunities Programme (YOP) replaced by the Youth Training Scheme (YTS) both of which addressed specifically the question of unemployed school-leavers and which were bolstered by severe benefit restrictions for 16–18 year olds and later further restrictions for 18–24 year olds who sought to claim benefits. But, in addition to schemes aimed at the unemployed person, the government has also adopted policies aimed at encouraging employers to take on unemployed workers; for instance the New Workers' Scheme paid employers an allowance for each unemployed worker they took on at a rate under a given wage ceiling, thus offering employers a direct wage subsidy.

Unemployed youngsters aged between 18 and 24 were offered the job training scheme which gave an allowance of £10 above benefit levels if the unemployed person participated in recognised training. Alongside reduced levels of benefit payments for the under 25s, these benefits brought the principles of workfare into British employment policies. A further direct subsidy scheme, the jobstart allowance, offered the unemployed person an allowance, for six months only, for 18 year olds who accepted work below a given wages ceiling. Such schemes are essentially interim in their nature, seeking to fill a perceived gap between the skills and training provided by compulsory education and those required by employers. Older, and long-term unemployed workers (perhaps those made redundant from traditional industrial sectors) were offered programmes of training and retraining in the forms of schemes such as Employment Training (ET) and Restart, or in the case of workers approaching retirement offered nothing save for the recognition that they would be unlikely to work again and so paid long-term rates of benefit.

Alongside these specific schemes the government designed more general programmes to help workers navigate their way around the employment market. Jobclubs provide support in making job applications, writing CVs for

Exhibit 15.1

Employment measures outlined in Chancellor's Budget – 1997

In place of welfare there should be work. So today this Budget is taking the first steps to create the new welfare state for the twenty-first century.

But for millions out of work or suffering poverty in work, the welfare state today denies rather than provides opportunity. It is time for the welfare state to put opportunity again in people's hands.

First, everyone in need of work should have the opportunity to work. Second, we must ensure work pays. Third, everyone who seeks to advance through employment and education must be given the means to advance. So we will create a new ladder of opportunity that will allow the many, by their own efforts, to benefit from opportunities once open only to a few.

Starting from next year, every young person aged 18–25 who is unemployed for more than six months will be offered a first step on the employment ladder. Tomorrow the Secretary for Education and Employment will detail the four options, all involving training leading to qualifications:

- a job with an employer;
- work with a voluntary organisation;
- work on the environmental task force;
- and, for those without basic qualifications, full time education or training.

With these new opportunities for young people come new responsibilities. There will be no fifth option – to stay at home on full benefit. So when they sign on for benefit they will be signing up for work. Benefits will be cut if young people refuse to take up the opportunities. This new deal for the young – is comprehensive, rich in opportunity, linked to the development of skills and has already attracted the support of some of Britain's leading companies.

I urge every business to play its part in this national crusade to equip this country for the future by taking on young unemployed men and women.

I appeal to every voluntary organisation to make a further contribution to their community by taking on a young person. And I will make it possible for every member of this House to act as an ambassador for this venture, encouraging young people in their constituencies, consulting, talking to local businesses and bringing them together to play their part in this new deal for young people.

There are 350,000 adult men and women who have been out of work for two years or longer. The second component of our Welfare to Work programme will offer employers a £75 a week subsidy to employ long-term unemployed men and women. Yet many of them who lack skills are debarred by the 16 hour rule from obtaining them. For this group – the unskilled – the 16 hour rule will be relaxed. So that when the long-term unemployed sign on for benefit they will now sign up for work or training.

---

instance, and facilities such as telephones to pursue possible employment, while Restart aims to adjust workers' expectations of the job market. Government perceived there to be a problem with workers made redundant seeking jobs which would maintain their standards of living, rather than accepting other more suitable vacancies. Further to such measures aimed at direct employment, government, in the enterprise fervour of the 1980s, sought to encourage self-employment, subsidising the start-up of new businesses through the Enterprise Allowance Scheme. Such schemes as those described briefly above, have as their underlying goal, the reappraisal of workforce expectations: high wages and job security were to be consigned to the past and Britain was to develop a flexible, mobile and above all competitive (low-wage) economy in order to address the threat posed by the eastern Tiger economies. And such underlying themes are not confined to the policies of the 1980s Conservative governments, the new Labour Chancellor, Gordon Brown, has maintained these lines of thought in his employment policies outlined in his July 1997 Budget (see exhibit 15.1). The new Labour Chancellor, it seems, now recognises and acknowledges the deep and fundamental changes that have taken place in British employment and promises the end of welfare dependency.

WOMEN AND EMPLOYMENT

As we have suggested one of the most fundamental changes to the post-war world of employment policy has been the increasingly important role occupied by women. What has often been written of in terms of women's refusal to return contentedly to the home at the end of the Second World War but to demand recognition of the contribution they had made, in peace time has become a demand for equality of access to the labour market and equality of treatment within the workplace. As the role of women has developed both the state and employers have had to address new issues and concerns, thus the question of childcare, both for women themselves and as the number of families with both parents working has increased, has become of crucial concern.

Britain has in the past tended to congratulate itself for its early foray into equal opportunities, passing the Equal Pay Act (1970) and Sex Discrimination Act (1976). But women's employment in that time seems to have attracted seemingly cursory attention from government in the years since the passing of such legislation. Perhaps we should not be surprised given that the government of the day rejected interventionist measures and stressed that women workers should rely on the equalising effects of the market which would recognise and reward their skills and talents. One significant development of employment policy in the 1990s has been the expansion of nursery provision for those workers with young children. The response to this issue has, however, largely been from within the private sector.

State funded nursery provision has declined markedly as central government restrictions on local authority funding have caused the closure of many nurseries, whilst the reprioritisation of education around the demands of the national curriculum led schools away from the provision of nursery places. Instead the private sector has responded with both an increase in the number of private nurseries and of work-based nursery facilities. Such moves were, somewhat belatedly, recognised by government with its introduction of nursery vouchers in 1996, which gave parents some help in meeting nursery costs which they could then choose to 'top-up'. Although this scheme was short-lived, being abolished by Labour's new Education Secretary in 1997, it did at least begin to officially recognise this sea-change in the nature of employment. Similarly, one of the last acts of the Conservative governments was to extend social security benefits (Income Support and Family Credit) to allow parents with low incomes greater access to nursery provision.

The 1997 Budget took these developments further declaring the advent of a National Childcare Strategy, which would place the provision of child care for working parents at the centre of employment policy in the future. Linked closely to Gordon Brown's welfare to work policies, the Strategy aims to train up to 50,000 young people as childcare assistants and to further extend the disregard of child-care costs in the calculation of welfare benefits (in addition parents claiming housing benefit and council tax benefit would be able to claim childcare costs). Brown further promises to extend the provision of after school clubs (though many also operate as before school clubs) and homework clubs as the Labour government seeks to extend nursery provision to every four year old and to address a longer-term objective of employment policy, that which aims to improve educational standards.

On the wider front, some commentators are beginning to question an employment policy which emphasises the pursuit of mass employment. Families with two working parents, who may typically leave their children with a nursery or pre-school club at an early hour, only to retrieve them in time to return their children to their beds, are said to be developing a culture of 'time poverty', in which contact with each other and their children is lost to the pressures of the workplace. Those parents are being joined increasingly by lone-parents who it now seems will be denied what the government apparently regards as an escape route from employment. Lone-parents will be provided with 'opportunities' to take up employment or training, and it seems that they too will be denied the 'fifth option – to stay at home on full benefit'. Parents who argue for recognition of their parenting role are it seems to be silenced by an employment policy which seeks to replace welfare dependency with work. Dressed in the language of an anti-poverty strategy, lone-parents will be invited to job search interviews when their youngest child reaches the second term of full-time schooling and one can only suspect, at this early stage, that compulsion will not be far behind.

Whilst not seeking to deny the clear link between lone-parenthood and poverty, the government it seems is all too prepared to accept the primacy of the economy in determining priorities in employment policy. We appear to continue on a road which regards widespread mass employment as its holy grail, in an era which pursues ever-longer working hours and greater productivity from an increasingly temporary and low paid workforce. To continue along this road is to continue to deny the wider role of employment in the face of an economic imperative.

LOW PAY

One final issue to consider within the realm of employment policy is the question of low pay. As the 1980s and 1990s have progressed and the employment market has been disciplined the question of low pay has received increasing attention and publicity. Alongside the question of low pay has been the development of homeworking which has received sadly scant attention. Whereas homeworking has been portrayed as the breakthrough of the computer age, allowing workers to increase their productivity via the telecommunications network without the costs and stresses of commuting, the bulk of homeworking is that supplied by low pay industries seeking to further reduce their costs.

The Labour government when elected promised to introduce legislation that would establish a minimum wage right across Britain – minimum wages had previously existed in certain sectors but had been abolished along with the Wages Councils in the 1980s. To this end the government established a Low Pay Commission in 1997 which was to hear evidence and report. In June 1998 the Low Pay Commission report was issued and it concluded that a national minimum wage of £3.70 per hour should be introduced by June 2000 but that an initial rate of £3.60 per hour be introduced from April 1999. The Commission also recommended that a development rate be introduced of £3.20 per hour, rising to £3.30 per hour in June 2000. The development rate would be paid to people engaged in training and would form the national minimum for people aged between 18 and 20. Young people between 16 and 17, the Commission recommended, should not be regarded as full participants in the labour market but engaged in education, training or apprenticeship, and therefore should be exempted from the provisions of the national minimum wage.

Employers and their representatives argued that the minimum wage would distort the labour market and consequently have adverse effects on employment, indeed that its adoption would generate unemployment. Similarly it was argued that the minimum wage is an inefficient method of addressing poverty. The low paid may themselves be members of relatively affluent households and not therefore poor, whereas the genuine poor may find themselves unable to find work at all because of the existence of a minimum wage. They also cited surveys, both recent and historical, which confirm the thesis that a minimum wage raises unemployment, especially in certain labour market sectors, such as agriculture (Oi, 1997; Robinson, 1997).

Exhibit 15.2

> ### Low pay in Britain
>
> The Low Pay Commission Report of 1998 indicated that low pay was most prevalent among women in part-time employment without formal qualifications. Further indicators of likely low pay were the younger workers, those in manual employment, lone parents in work and homeworkers. The highest sectors of low-paid employment were to be found in private and voluntary employment and in the category of employment termed 'hospitality' and in particular the catering and retail trade.
>
> Women, they said, still earned on average 20 per cent less than men, after almost 30 years of equal pay legislation.
>
> The Commission also reported that average rates of pay for the highest decile of earners had risen by 41 per cent in the period 1983–97, whereas the lowest decile showed an increase over the same period of only 19 per cent with the average rise being 28 per cent. Thus although average earnings have continued to rise in Britain the differential between those at the upper and lower ends of the earnings scale have continued to widen. To reinforce this the Commission also reported DSS figures indicating that the numbers of families claiming family credit in the period 1988–97 had more than doubled.

Representatives of workers, on the other hand, suggest that there is a clear-cut case for the introduction of a minimum wage which would both benefit and protect millions of low-paid workers. They argue that effects on employment levels, and in particular the fear of rising unemployment, are unfounded and that many employers would regard the minimum wage as beneficial to themselves, since it would level the economic playing field (Labour Research Department, May 1997). Trades unions, however, were disappointed to hear the recommended level of £3.60 in the first instance, having based their own campaign on a rate of at least £4 per hour. The low rate they felt was one which played up to the employers who the government did not wish to antagonise early in their term of office and which would be of little benefit to the low paid, since many workers were already paid at, or above, that rate. We may instead surmise that a rate set below or close to the *de facto* minimum wage level will in fact depress wage levels as employers allow wages to fall to the national minimum over time.

CONCLUSIONS

The function of employment policy, as we can see, is essentially one which manipulates and supports labour markets. Historically politicians have favoured manipulation as they attempted to maintain 'full employment' as part of the post-war settlement. In more recent times, times of recession and the end of the ideal of full employment, policy has switched its attentions more to the support of the labour market, by attempting to provide programmes of training and reskilling for workers dislocated by redundancy or for the young unemployed.

Employment policy at the end of the 1990s has a role defined as central to government policy. The New Deal represents something far more than another employment programme as the government attempts to address wider questions of social exclusion, education and skills, and the regeneration of family and community networks. Central to this vision is the thought that government's role is to provide opportunity to individuals and the principal opportunity it seeks to provide is the opportunity to participate in work. We may even say that their ethos goes beyond the provision of opportunity but instead stresses the social duty of work and duties to support family, participate in local communities and to shy away from criminal activity. And, whilst the government seeks to promote its New Deal through a wide range of activities, employment policy and the ability to engage in the labour market is placed at the centre of their strategy.

REFERENCES

Coates, D. (1989) *The Crisis of Labour: Industrial relations and the state in contemporary Britain*, Oxford: Philip Allan.

Esping-Andersen, G. (1997) 'Hybrid or Unique? The Japanese welfare state between Europe and America', *Journal of European Social Policy*, 7(3): 179–90.

Gamble, A. (1994) *The Free Economy and the Strong State: The politics of Thatcherism*, 2nd edition, London: Macmillan.

Johnson, N. (1990) *Reconstructing the Welfare State: A decade of change 1980–1990*, London: Harvester Wheatsheaf.

Labour Research Department (1997) 'Minimum Wage: A clear cut case', Labour Research, May.

Lowe, R. (1993) *The Welfare State in Britain since 1945*, London: Macmillan.

Marsh, D. (1991) 'British Industrial Relations Policy Transformed: The Thatcher legacy', *Journal of Public Policy*, 11(3): 291–313.

Mayhew, K. (1991) 'The Assessment: The UK labour market in the 1980s', *Oxford Review of Economic Policy*, 7(1): 1–17.

Middlemass, K. (1979) *Politics in Industrial Society: The experience of the British system since 1911*, London: Deutsch.

Moon, J. (1983) 'Policy Change in Direct Government Responses to UK Unemployment', *Journal of Public Policy*, 3(3): 301–30.

Oi, W. (1997) 'The Consequences of Minimum Wage Legislation', *Economic Affairs*, June.

Robinson, C. (1997) 'The Minimum Wage Debate', *Economic Affairs*, June.

Whiteside, N. (1995) 'Employment Policy: A chronicle of decline?', in Gladstone, D. (ed.), *British Social Welfare: Past, present and future*, London: UCL Press.

ANNOTATED READINGS

To an extent readings for this chapter overlap with those in chapter 11, particularly when considering training policy, so it is useful to refer back to that chapter. Useful texts more directly focused on employment matters include J. Phillpott

(1997) ed., *Working for Full Employment*, London: Routledge, whilst the work of Lawrence Mean (1997) *From Welfare to Work*, London: IEA, gives a very useful perspective on workfare in the United States and on current thinking in Britain behind welfare to work and the New Deal. An interesting, if narrowly focused, debate on the National Minimum Wage may be found in the articles by Oi and Robinson in the journal *Economic Affairs*.

16 Family policy

OBJECTIVES

■ To consider what is meant by the term 'family policy' within the framework of British social policy.

■ To outline the role of state intervention in the family.

■ To explore the interaction of different policy areas in the development of family policy.

■ To consider the potential for the development of specific family policies in the areas of domestic violence and child protection and the development of family law.

INTRODUCTION

> The family is the most basic unit . . . 'The family', however, is not and never has been, one of uniform type or structure . . . Moreover, the family changes both its function and composition over the life cycle. Thus any arbitrary definition of 'the family' is unhelpful and misleading in that it defines out of existence many family forms that are a reality and which social policy and social arrangements must take into account. (Australian Institute of Families, cited in Weeks, 1991, p. 225)

In Britain we do not have a Ministry for the Family with an associated budget and agenda for action. Families and family life are affected by many different policy decisions, as well as the ways in which policy is delivered, and it is across a range of policies that 'family policy' can be identified. So, whilst other chapters in this section have explored specific policy areas, such as education or health, here we explore policies which might be argued to represent 'family policy' in Britain in the 1990s, asking what the impact is on family life as a result of these policies, and what kinds of families do best and what kinds of families do least well out of social policy in Britain. We also consider contradictions in family policy, where some policies might act to support particular family forms whilst others might not.

The family is also a major provider of welfare in Britain, and this too is relevant (Muncie *et al.*, 1995). Some of our family policy is designed to reinforce this family welfare system and the role of families in caring for dependents (Van Every, 1991;

Muncie *et al.*, 1995) and some is designed to avoid conflicting with that family system of welfare and family responsibilities.

At present, the family occupies central stage with British politicians. It is also of central concern for a range of other commentators. To many feminists, for example, 'the family' is a means of explaining women's position both in the private household and in the public world of paid employment and the labour market (Firestone, 1972). For others, the family is seen variously as a 'haven in a heartless world' (Lasch, 1977; Elshtain, 1981), the source of all of our problems or as something which should be left in peace. All of us have some connection with a family – whether we grew up in a conventional family household or not, whether we now live in a family or expect to in the future – and our ideas about 'the family' affect the ways in which we judge family policy.

DEFINING 'THE FAMILY'

One of the first tasks must be to define what we mean by the family. One of the difficulties in doing this is the way in which there is a tendency, in the media and in politics, for example, to talk of 'the family' as though there is only one, natural, way of ordering society, in terms of reproduction, the raising and educating of children, and the expression of sexuality (Weeks, 1991; Muncie *et al.*, 1995; see, for example, Parsons, 1959; Murdock, 1968; Mount, 1982). However, there is no universal family form and if we look at families in other cultures and at changes in family life over time, we see that there are a number of different ways in which these responsibilities and needs are organised (Gittins, 1993; Muncie *et al.*, 1995).

In Britain today there are many different kinds of families, including the stereotypical nuclear family made up of a heterosexual married couple, with one or more children living in the same household. Whilst only a small proportion of households in Britain today reflect this family, it remains dominant as a model of family life. However, in the past 15 years there has been a growth in the number of unmarried couples who live together with one or more children. Increasing numbers of households might be described as reconstituted families where either or both adults have children from an earlier relationship. In addition, a major change in the 1980s and 1990s has been the great rise in numbers of lone parents, with one adult living with one or more children.

There are, however, other family types – for example, a family of two adults of the same sex living together with the children of one or both partners would share many characteristics with the conventional married family, in terms of living and sleeping arrangements, cooking and childcare arrangements and so on. Some people may live in larger family households which include extended family – grandparents, aunts, uncles and others. Even with extended families, however,

Exhibit 16.1

Households in Britain, 1979 and 1994

	1979	1994
Households which are:		
One person only	23%	28%
Married/cohabiting couple without dependent children	34%	33%
Married/cohabiting couple with dependent children	31%	24%
Lone parent with dependent children	4%	7%
Other	8%	8%
Percentage of people living in each type of household:		
One person only	9%	11%
Married/cohabiting couple without dependent children	29%	31%
Married/cohabiting couple with dependent children	49%	41%
Lone parent with dependent children	5%	8%
Other	7%	9%

Source: General Household Survey, 1996.

Notes: In 1994, the family of two adults of the opposite sex living together with one or more dependent children made up only a quarter of all households in Britain. The traditional nuclear family – even when this definition is extended to include non-married couples, represents only a small proportion of household types in the country, and this has been a relatively consistent pattern over time. The majority of households do not have dependent children – in 1994 well over half of all households had no dependent children, again a fairly consistent pattern over time.

However when we look at people, instead of households, we find that about half the population are living in a 'family' situation – if we include people living in married/cohabiting households with dependent children, who in 1994 made up over 40 per cent of the total population, and lone parent households with dependent children, which in 1994 represented 8 per cent of households.

The statistics also reveal assumptions about what is seen as a family – for example, married and cohabiting couples are grouped together in the 1996 GHS, with the table listing these simply as 'married couples' – cohabitation has become, in the eyes of government statisticians at least, the same as couples who are legally married. Similarly, the table tells us about childhood and dependency – households with 'dependent' children are distinguished from households with 'non-dependent' children.

there may be differences: some extended families, for example, may be formed when an older person in need of care moves into the family home of a son or daughter, whilst in others one generation will bring new family members into an existing household, when they marry.

It is therefore quite complex to decide what is, and what is not, a family. Any definition needs to be able to encompass a range of types of family household and not marginalise those who do not fit the dominant model. Within family policy we are able to trace both the conventional and the unconventional family – the one more often favoured by policy, whilst the other may be penalised or even prohibited in some sense. What, then, is family policy?

Exhibit 16.2

Recent trends in household size, births, marriage and divorce in Britain in the 1990s

Household size: Average household size has decreased from being 2.7 persons per household in 1971 to 2.44 persons per household in 1994. The rate of decrease was faster in the 1970s and 1980s, and has tended to slow down in the early 1990s.

Average size of household is higher among ethnic minority groups – with on average 3.22 persons per household. Households where the head is of Pakistani or Bangladeshi origin have the highest average size – 4.76 persons per household, whilst households where the head is black (these are all GHS definitions of ethnicity) are similar in size to white population, having an average of 2.59 persons per household.

Lone parent households: As a proportion of *families with dependent children*, lone parent households have increased over time:

Families with dependent children

	1971	1979	1994
Married/cohabiting couples	92%	88%	77%
All lone parents	8%	12%	23%
Made up of:			
Lone mothers	7%	10%	21%
single/never married	1%	2%	8%
once married	6%	8%	13%
Lone fathers	1%	2%	2%

Source: General Household Survey, 1996.

Marriage and cohabitation

Since the early 1980s there has been an increasing trend in the proportion of both women and men who are cohabiting, particularly amongst the younger age groups. By 1995, over a third of both men and women aged 25–29 were cohabiting.

The popularity of marriage has decreased since the 1960s: in 1993 the *rate* of both first marriage and remarriage was half the rate of 1961. In 1961 there were nearly 350,000 first marriages, compared with 210,000 in 1994. The average age of first marriage has been increasing – in 1993 the average age for women on first marriage was 26, and for men it was 28.

Divorce, however, has increased since the early 1960s, particularly in the years after the *Divorce Reform Act 1969* came into force, in 1971.

Birth and children

The number of children women have – the fertility rate – has decreased over the latter half of the century, and in particular during the late 1960s and early 1970s, with an overall fall from 90 births per 1,000 women in 1961 to around 62 births per 1,000 women in 1994. The average age of women at the time of giving birth to their first child has increased during this period – women in 1994 are more likely to be over the age of 30 at the time of having their first child. In addition, there has been an increase in the number of women who remain childless.

▶

Exhibit 16.2 *continued*

> The proportion of children born to mothers who are not married has also increased considerably in recent years – in 1960 the figure was 5 per cent, by 1994 nearly one third of all live births were to women who were not married. However, an increasing proportion of these births outside marriage have been registered, on the birth certificate, with both the mother's and the father's name.

DEFINING FAMILY POLICY

Because in Britain we do not have (as yet) a Ministry for the Family or a clear set of policies which together are presented as family policy, there is a certain amount of flexibility over what might be regarded as 'family policy' (Van Every, 1991; Fox Harding, 1996). A broad view might legitimately argue that policy which affects family life could be seen as representing family policy. Alternatively we could simply focus on those policies where the impact of the policy on families is made explicit and is presented, by those making the policy, as being 'family policy'. For example, in the early 1990s the Conservative Party focused on one particular family – lone parents – as a policy problem. The introduction of the Child Support Act in 1991 as a result of the debate over lone parents represents a family policy with the explicit aim of reducing the incentive to become a lone parent and increasing the incentive for parents to stay together.

If we take the broad view, that policy which affects families might be seen as family policy, this could include education policy, health policy, housing and so on. We may also go beyond conventional welfare analysis to consider other areas of public policy which can affect some families: immigration policy in the 1990s, for example, affects those families trying to unite or reunite when one member or more was not born inside Britain (Van Every, 1991).

In this chapter we will largely focus on those areas of policy which have some implicit or explicit concept of 'the family' and the needs of this family. We will be interested in the shape of this implicit family – what do these policies tell us about ideal family life – which families are supported, rewarded or encouraged by state intervention, and which are ignored, penalised or discouraged by such intervention? In taking this focus, the chapter will consider areas of policy which also are studied elsewhere in this text. Here, however, we look through a different lens, to ask the question, what about 'the family'?

THE DEVELOPMENT OF STATE INTERVENTION IN FAMILY LIFE

The family is seen in Britain, and in most Western countries, as essentially a private affair (Muncie *et al.*, 1995). The family is also seen as being better when it remains private, and welfare is often presented as directed at individuals rather than families to maintain this idea of the private family (Muncie *et al.*, 1995). The public face of intervention by the state is when a family is failing, at which point families lose the right to privacy. Thus, for example, a suspicion of child abuse or neglect can lead to state intervention, via the social services, although the public outcry surrounding the removal of children from their homes in cases of suspected sexual abuse (as in Cleveland in the late 1980s) suggests that even in such cases the family's implied right to privacy may be privileged.

Despite this essential notion of the family as a private affair, there has been a long history of intervention by the state. Whilst it is difficult to find one date as the definitive point where such intervention started, we could begin with the Victorian Poor Law Amendment Act, 1834, under which pauper families faced separation from one another in the workhouse. Although the implementation of the Poor Law was variable across the country, with some parishes more inclined to continue to grant outdoor relief and allow families to remain together (Thane, 1996), separation was seen as one means of encouraging the poor to find a way out of their situation in order to be reunited as a family.

Over time the distinction in policy between the 'deserving' and the 'undeserving' poor helped to create the additional notion of the deserving family, so that the family that was sober, industrious, and prudent was more likely to receive charitable help (Gittins, 1993). Within this model family, however, men and women were viewed differently, with the father expected to be in full-time paid employment and the mother expected to take responsibility both for the clean house and for the moral welfare of the household. The deserving family was also to be legally married, and to exercise restraint in sexual matters, in order to limit the size of the family.

With the development and increasing role of central government policy we see an associated impact on family life. The introduction of compulsory education for children may have been a response to 'the havoc caused by children who had neither work nor school to attend' (Midwinter, 1994, p. 82) as a result of the prohibition of child labour under the Factory Acts, but the change also affected the household economy and the scope and nature of women's work. Married women's participation in the labour market has always been associated with the ways in which children might be cared for, and the ways in which the state has offered or required education for children. The introduction of compulsory schooling, however, reduced the availability of older children to care for younger ones while women worked in paid employment and increased women's participation in poorly paid 'homeworking' which could be combined with childcare. Similarly, legislation to restrict the paid employment of women, however rhetorical,* implied an increasing protectiveness of women in Victorian society, and an increasing emphasis on women's domestic duties (Oakley, 1974).

---

* In many areas the 1842 Mines Act was ignored, whilst the Factories Acts of the time did not apply to many numbers of female occupations, including domestic service and various outwork or 'sweated' trades.

Thus policy developments during this period, together with the growth of Victorian ideals about 'family life', and the increasing strength of the demand by organised male labour for a 'family' or 'breadwinner's wage', collectively exerted a pressure on families and how they might operate.

During the early part of the twentieth century, state involvement in the private world of families increased. For example, housing policy after the end of the First World War expanded the role of public or 'social' housing, for the respectable working classes, and was designed around particular notions of 'family life', whilst the 1918 Maternity and Child Welfare Act created ante-natal clinics which would monitor women, and in particular working-class women, in raising their children. And with this increasing intervention we see a development from the policing of family behaviour, and intervention when families failed or broke down, to include policies which by their nature help to construct the ideal family type. By 1942 we see, in the Beveridge plan, a model of 'the family' in the new welfare state, with separate roles for men and women:

> the great majority of married women must be regarded as occupied on work which is vital though unpaid, without which their husbands could not do paid work and without which the nation could not continue. In accord with the facts the Plan for Social Security treats . . . man and wife as a team. (Beveridge, 1942, p. 50)

ISSUES IN FAMILY POLICY

In this section we look in more detail at specific examples of policies which affect families today. What kinds of choices do such policies offer, and to which kinds of families? Is the diversity of living arrangements in Britain today recognised in such policies, or are some families marginalised and not catered for in these policies? Is there an ideal type of family underlying family policy? We look first at those policies which, whilst appearing neutral, contain implicit assumptions about families and what they need, and help to construct this ideal family type. The second part of this discussion then focuses on what the state does when families 'go wrong' – in particular looking at policy around domestic violence and child abuse.

HOUSING POLICY AND THE FAMILY

As we have seen in chapter 13, housing in Britain can be divided into three major sectors – owner occupied, privately rented and public housing – each to a greater or lesser extent affected by national housing policy. There has been a shift over the past 20 years towards an increasing proportion of households living in privately owned housing, with a decrease in housing rented from the local authorities (Murie, 1995). This shift has occurred largely as a result of government support for private home ownership and a desire to reduce the role of the public sector in private renting, such that during the 1980s a large number of properties were transferred from the public rented sector to the private owned sector when local authorities were required to offer council housing to tenants for purchase (Malpass and Murie, 1994). Housing policy affects the housing choices available for different kinds of family, and as a result is a major influence on the lives of families inside the private home.

With the active encouragement of home ownership through Mortgage Interest Tax Relief (MITR), government policy not only favours those who can afford to buy their own homes but also favours those who 'fit' the conventional family type (Woods, 1996). Eligibility for a mortgage is assessed on a number of characteristics, but primarily on the buyer's perceived ability to repay the money lent. As this is calculated as a multiple of earnings, households with at least one high earner are privileged (Fox Harding, 1996). Men, on average, earn more than women – Equal Opportunities legislation having failed to eradicate the gap between male and female earnings (Glennerster, 1995). Men are also more likely to work full time, whilst women with children are more likely to be in part-time employment, if at all. This means that female-headed households are less often eligible for mortgage borrowing, and more likely to be reliant on rented accommodation, particularly when they have children (Austerberry and Watson, 1986). The difficulties women face in trying to find alternative housing when trying to leave a relationship can also serve to 'imprison' women, and their children, in violent and abusive relationships (Pringle, 1995).

The housing market, then, rewards people living in two-adult households, particularly where there are two earners. Until 1993 there was encouragement for non-conventional households, in that two single people buying a house together would qualify for twice the tax relief that would be given to a married couple. This, however, was removed in the late 1980s, as a means of saving treasury money as much as a desire to regulate non-conventional house purchasers (Fox Harding, 1996).

Those families unable to afford home ownership are likely to find themselves either in private rented accommodation or in the dwindling public sector. In local authority housing there is again an implicit message about what constitutes a family, both in terms of who is eligible for such housing and in the design of the housing itself. Public housing provision in Britain is directed towards the housing need of children (Watson, 1986, 1987): to qualify for local authority housing, a family means one or more adults together with one or more children, whilst in most areas households without children will be ineligible. Lone parents are eligible for housing, although they are more frequently offered poor quality accommodation, and may be required to share a bedroom with the children (Watson, 1986; Murie, 1995).

Similarly, although housing for large families was built during earlier years, more recently the design of local authority housing has been based on a model of the family as two adults, two children. This excludes larger extended families from most local authority accommodation and implicitly discriminates against families which do not fit this model – some minority ethnic groups, for example, have a larger average household size as a result of a greater tradition of multi-generation households (Austerberry and Watson, 1986; Fox Harding, 1996).

However, the local authority has an obligation to house families which contain children and which have been made homeless, which is part of the general requirement of local authorities to protect vulnerable people, including children. In many areas, homeless families are likely to be housed in temporary accommodation, often 'bed and breakfast' hostels, until suitable public sector housing becomes available (Young, 1995). The right-to-buy policy, combined with the inability of local authorities to replace lost housing stock, means that such families will often have a long wait whilst the impact of living in such accommodation can lead to health problems, family breakdown, educational difficulties and behavioural problems in children (Conway, 1988).

The private rented sector makes up a minor proportion of accommodation in Britain. Nonetheless, it represents an important source of housing for some of the most vulnerable groups in society. As we have seen in chapter 13, in the 1980s under the Conservative government deregulation in this sector gave less security of tenure and fewer rights to tenants (Murie, 1995). Families experience greater difficulty than individuals in finding suitable accommodation in this sector as owners often discriminate against families, whilst the cost of renting in many areas is prohibitive, and less rented accommodation is family sized (Fox Harding, 1996). As a result, families in the private rented sector are more likely to be paying high rents for relatively low standard accommodation.

SOCIAL SECURITY, INCOME MAINTENANCE AND THE FAMILY

Social security in many ways constructs notions of what is to be seen as a legitimate family. Whilst benefits are paid to individuals, they are also paid on behalf of dependents. The 'conventional' family with a male wage earner and economically dependent wife and children was an explicit part of Beveridge's original plans, in which men, with their greater attachment to the labour market, would be the focus of the new contributory benefits and the main claimant. This conceptualisation of the different roles of women and men within families remains in the system today.

As we have seen in chapter 10, there are a range of different benefits for people in financial need. Benefits for families on income support – the major means-tested, non-contributory benefit in Britain – include additional payments for child and adult dependants. Since the mid 1980s it has been possible for either adult in a couple to be the named claimant for income support. However, in the overwhelming majority of cases it remains the man who is named as the head of household and who receives the benefit (Pascall, 1997).

Income support also restricts the independence of young people. A young person cannot claim income support whilst still at school, and those who have left school up to the age of 19 can only claim income support in certain circumstances: if they are caring for their own child, seriously disabled, or separated from their parents and not in touch with them. Up to this age, young people are to remain the financial responsibility of their parents. Assumptions that children should remain within their families until 19, and that they have lower economic needs in their early 20s, have been criticised for increasing the strain upon families and increasing rates of homelessness amongst young people, as they seek to avoid family conflict and – at times, abusive situations – by running away (Pringle, 1995).

Other 'family' benefits include family credit, claimed by people in employment on low wages, with responsibility for children, and child benefit, a universal non-means-tested benefit. Child benefit is payable to either the father or mother, although in the majority of cases it is the mother who claims. Whilst child benefit is aimed at supporting families with children, it has been frozen at various points in the last ten years and during this period there have been debates over whether it should be replaced by a means-tested benefit (Deacon, 1995).

Perhaps the most famous of benefit restrictions in terms of 'family life' is the 'cohabitation rule', which prevents people claiming a single person's benefits when they are cohabiting. The definition of cohabitation reveals the model of 'the family' inherent in the social security system. Cohabitation is deemed to occur when the adult members of the household share a sexual relationship and/or common housekeeping (Pascall, 1997). Thus a claimant who takes in a lodger who shares the cooking may well be denied benefit on the grounds of cohabitation. If the claimant is living with someone who is in paid employment, it is argued, that person should support them as a spouse would. Whilst ostensibly the cohabitation rule is gender-blind and applies equally to women and men, it is women claimants who have most often been denied benefit under this rule, particularly under the income support system, and the original criteria make clear the presumed 'family' in this rule:

> It would be unjustifiable for the State to provide an income for the woman who has the support of a man to whom she is not actually married when it is not provided for the married woman. (Supplementary Benefits Commission, 1976, cited in Pascall, 1986, p. 215)

The cohabitation rules uphold the marital relationship whilst seeking to place cohabiting on the same level, which in some ways would appear to be contrary to the model of the family found elsewhere – particularly in the tax laws. The rule, like tax laws, also fails to acknowledge the existence of cohabitation between two people of the same sex, as lesbian and gay claimants are not affected (Hill, 1993).

The cohabitation rule has been criticised by the women's movement, in that it seeks to make women dependent for their own upkeep and that of their children on a man, whilst the rule puts additional pressure on any new relationships they may make (Pascall, 1986) – ironically, this may serve to make the cohabitation rule 'anti-family', in that women are reluctant to begin new relationships if this would mean loss of benefit. The ruling also presumes a sharing of resources within the household, whilst studies have shown that women are often denied equal access to household resources (see Millar and Glendinning, 1993). As a result, many would argue that women should be assessed for benefit in the light of their own needs and those of their children, rather than be seen as the economic dependants of a man.

The 1991 Child Support Act now requires absent parents to contribute towards the upkeep of their children. Again, the wording of the legislation is gender neutral but it has largely been men who have been pursued as the absent parent. Mothers in paid employment might gain from this support, but those on benefit do not gain, as the father's payments are deducted from their benefit. The Child Support Agency, given the task of assessing the support payments of absent fathers, focused initially on men in paid employment, who were easy to trace and whose support payments, if taken off the benefits paid to the mothers, might help reduce the social security budget.

The Child Support Act reflects and attempts to reinforce notions of the 'good family', with two parents and a sense of responsibility not only towards the children but also towards the state. Lone parents were increasingly portrayed as problematic – in the words of Peter Lilley, Conservative Secretary of State for Social Security, part of the 'something for nothing society' (Lilley, 1992).

> We back parents' rights. But with rights go duties. All parents have a duty to support their children. Yet only one in three absent fathers pays a penny towards the maintenance of his children. That must and will change ... We will insist that absent parents contribute to the upkeep of their children. They will have the overwhelming support of parents throughout the country. (Lilley, 1992 – Extract from speech to 109th Conservative party Conference, as Secretary of State for Social Security)

THE FISCAL WELFARE STATE – THE TAXATION SYSTEM

Within the taxation system we can also see policy acting to support particular types of family through financial support. The system of income tax in Britain has long treated married couples as a single unit, and within that unit women have been seen as economically dependent on men until very recently (Fox Harding, 1996). Married men were thus eligible for a tax allowance – to reflect the additional costs a married man has – which women were unable to claim. A low rate of personal allowance for married women was introduced during the First World War – when women were drawn into the labour market and there was recognition of married women's financial needs whilst men were away from home. This was reduced in the inter-war years, and then brought up to equal the single person's allowance when women were once again drawn into paid work in the Second World War (Fox Harding, 1996).

However, in the 1990s the taxation system was changed, with the introduction of the married couple's allowance, which allowed married women to claim some or all of their partner's tax allowance if he was not in paid employment or if his earnings were so low that he could not claim the allowance himself (Glennerster, 1995; Fox Harding, 1996). From 1993 married couples have been able to choose how they divide this married couple's allowance and the allowance can now only be offset against the lower tax rate (Glennerster, 1995). However, an unmarried couple cannot claim such an allowance: taxation policy benefits those who are legally 'a family'. From 1976 onwards unmarried mothers or fathers have been able to claim an additional personal allowance, equal to the married allowance, to reflect increased costs of raising a child. However, again, unmarried couples are not allowed to benefit from this – lone parents who cohabit have been ineligible to claim this additional allowance since 1988 (Fox Harding, 1996).

DOMESTIC VIOLENCE

State intervention in the private world of the family was for many years reluctant to deal with domestic violence. In the early eighteenth century a judge ruled that a man was allowed to beat his wife with a stick no larger in diameter than his thumb (Gittins, 1993), and this acceptance of a man's right to chastise his wife continued well into this century. It was not until the early 1970s and the development of the women's refuge movement that violence between adult partners inside the family was viewed more seriously (Glennerster, 1995). Family policy, in failing to offer help to the victims of domestic violence and in failing to see such violence as a problem, had implicitly accepted that violence will at times occur within an 'ordinary' family (Rose, 1986). It took a long time for such violence to be problematised.

Domestic violence has been defined in a variety of ways:

> violence within, or as a result of, an intimate relationship between adults. It can comprise physical, mental, emotional/psychological, financial or sexual abuse and assault, often in combination. Threats of violence as well as actual violence are included. Women are abused by a range of violent perpetrators including husbands, boyfriends, partners and ex-partners, fathers, sons and other close relatives or friends. (Malos and Hague, 1993, p. 1)

Domestic violence occurs across all social classes and cultures, although some research has suggested that domestic violence is more likely to occur in stressful situations and particularly in deprived households (Segal, 1990). However, figures on domestic violence are extremely difficult to collect, and it may be that middle-class women are more able to escape domestic violence without seeking help from the refuge movement or police and thus are less often counted in both statistics and surveys (Segal, 1990; Pringle, 1995).

Estimates of the prevalence of domestic violence are problematic, because of the under-reporting of violence and because many studies are based on limited definitions of what constitutes violence. Domestic violence accounts for more than a quarter of all violent crime reported to the police, even though most cases of domestic violence are not reported to the police (Hague *et al.*, 1996). Over 90 per cent of domestic violence is against women (Malos and Hague, 1993), and studies have estimated that between 5 and 10 per cent of all marriages are violent (Segal, 1990). It is only in the last few years that rape within marriage has been seen as an offence, after the Law Commission recommended in 1990 that husbands should no longer be exempt from prosecution for rape, and after the 1991 decision in the House of Lords that it was unacceptable to presume that, within marriage, a wife gives her general consent to sexual intercourse (Hague *et al.*, 1996). According to a national survey carried out in 1991, women are seven times more likely to be raped by their husband than by a stranger (Muncie *et al.*, 1995). However, it remains to be seen how many men will be prosecuted for rape within marriage.

The major source of help for women in violent situations, the women's refuge movement, is largely co-ordinated by the Women's Aid Federations. A number of refuges are not affiliated to these federations – many of these being refuges which have developed in recent years to meet the needs of black and minority ethnic women (Malos and Hague, 1993). In particular, criticisms of the largely white women's aid movement have argued for a recognition of the different issues for black and minority ethnic women – for example, that it may be difficult to go to the police for help when black people often do not experience the police force as protective of their rights (Mama, 1989; Cashmore and McLaughlin, 1991; Kirkwood, 1993).

The refuge movement continues to be largely self-organised and under-funded, with some financial help from local authorities but always with fewer spaces in the refuges themselves than are needed by women fleeing violence, or than are recognised as necessary by policy makers (Malos and Hague, 1993).

Legal protection from domestic violence has two elements: civil legislation, which should protect women who have suffered violence from further violence, and the extent to which the police are willing to take action within the criminal justice system. Before the 1970s, women suffering domestic violence could only get protection through an injunction or protection order from the civil courts if this was part of divorce proceedings (Glennerster, 1995; Hague *et al.*, 1996). The Domestic Violence and Matrimonial Proceedings Act 1976 allowed both married and unmarried women to apply to the county court for civil protection orders, without this being part of divorce action. These could be either non-molestation or personal protection orders, to deter further acts of violence by the abuser, or exclusion or 'ouster' orders which required the violent partner to leave the home. Whilst the Domestic Proceedings and Magistrates Court Act 1978 gave similar powers to grant protection orders to magistrates, it applied only to married women and required more evidence of physical violence (Malos and Hague, 1993; Fox Harding, 1996).

Provisions under the 1996 Family Law Act relating to non-molestation orders replaced the earlier Acts. Much of the new law relating to domestic violence came from the Homes Affairs Select Committee Report, in 1993. In particular, the new Act extended the powers of both courts and police – to arrest and to remand in custody – and should reduce the need for women to seek action in the civil courts.

The police are an important agency in protection against domestic violence. However the police have often been criticised by the women's movement for failing to take such violence seriously, and for failing to intervene in cases of domestic violence (Pringle, 1995). In more recent years, the police response to violence within the home has improved, after a Home Office Circular in 1986 and a later one, in 1990, which encouraged the police to tackle domestic violence more seriously (Pringle, 1995; Hague *et al.*, 1996). The 1990 circular encouraged police forces to be proactive in preventing domestic violence and to set up specialist domestic violence units to support women and children in this situation. Since the 1990s there has been more emphasis on the need for collaboration between different agencies involved in responses to domestic violence – including housing departments, the police, women's refuges and the social services (Hague *et al.*, 1996).

CHILD PROTECTION

Child protection is an important aspect of family policy, with legislation to protect children from neglect or cruelty going back to the turn of the century. During recent decades there has developed increasing concern over the failure of policy to achieve such protection. In the 1970s and early 1980s a series of scandals involving the death of children brought the issue of physical abuse to the attention of the public. In the late 1980s the cases in the public eye more often concerned child sexual abuse, and the debate began to shift from outcry at parental neglect and the failure of social workers towards a concern at the invasion and over-policing of the private family (Glennerster, 1995).

This debate is covered in the chapter on personal social services. What is important to highlight here, however, is the extent to which the understanding of the state's right to intervene in family life to protect children shifted during this period, and the way this in turn reflects the model of the family which is at the heart of policy.

Many of the well-known cases of children who have died as a result of physical abuse have come from poor areas and working-class rather than middle-class families who were already under the surveillance of the social services. The blame has mostly been seen as lying with both adults, the mother as well as the father or other male in the household (Pringle, 1995). The rise in cases of child sexual abuse during the latter half of the 1980s, however, was not restricted to working-class homes, nor to those already under the gaze of the social services (although those who were, were more readily detected). One of the most significant aspects of the Cleveland affair in the 1980s, where during a period of a few months over 120 children were diagnosed as having been sexually abused, was that middle-class families were also under scrutiny (Campbell, 1988). However, the outcome of Cleveland is also interesting, for whilst publicly it appeared that public outrage at the removal of children from their home was justified, only one fifth of the children were later determined to have been wrongly diagnosed (Campbell, 1988).

During the same period there was an increase in the visibility of 'survivors' – adult women and some men who were beginning to talk to others about their experience of being sexually abused as children within the family. This was a clear challenge to the notion that the private family is a safe haven, and always represents the best option for the raising of children. Estimates of the true incidence of childhood sexual abuse can only be approximate, as many survivors either do not remember their abuse or choose not to talk about it. However, with research suggesting that anywhere up to a fifth or a third of adults have experienced sexual abuse as a child (Russell, 1986, 1995; Kelly, 1991) it is clearly significant. Not all abusers are within the family, though it would appear that the majority are (Segal, 1990; Russell, 1995). Not all abusers are men, although again the overwhelming majority are (Pringle, 1995), and not all of those abused are female – figures suggest that up to 10 per cent of those abused may be boys (Segal, 1990).

Social service and official responses to childhood abuse within the family setting – physical, sexual and emotional – have changed over time. Immediately after the Second World War the objective was to keep families together whilst turning 'dysfunctional families' into healthy ones. During the 1960s there was a belief that sexual abuse was relatively rare (Segal, 1990), and the focus of social services was the needs of deprived families and neglected children. In the 1970s there was a move to keep children away from abusive families, and encourage children to form bonds with other carers (Segal, 1990; Fox Harding, 1996). During the 1980s social work practice focused on removing children at risk or placing such children on 'at risk' registers, which allowed monitoring of further incidents. However, the conclusions of various reports after the death of a child have largely been that social services and individual social workers have failed in their duty to protect. What such cases have highlighted is that families do not always represent safety for those within their private world, and that constructing policies and delivering services which are neither overly intrusive nor unable to properly protect children is very difficult indeed.

FAMILY LAW

One aspect of state intervention in family life is legislation around particular circumstances in which families might find themselves. Some of this legislation has been covered already in this chapter, but there are also laws to determine what happens in marriage and divorce, children's rights, the needs and the care of children, the procreation of children (in the law on abortion and also on human embryology), and legislation relating to sexuality. Such legislation not only affects those in families but also contributes to our understandings of what is the norm in wider society and helps to standardise or legitimise what 'the family' represents (Land, 1995).

However, whilst this legislation exists to deal with the situation when families form or when they break down, there was for a long time, and today there is still, relatively little which governs what goes on inside families. For example, whilst the division of resources on the breakdown of a marriage is governed by the legal system, the division of resources inside the family which remains together is not subject to specific legislation. Parents who deny their children food would be open to the charge of neglect, but most of the time inequalities in resource allocation within families are a private affair (Payne, 1991; Millar and Glendinning, 1993).

Exhibit 16.3

Family Law – Examples of major legislation

Marriage and divorce
Family Law Act, 1996: major changes in divorce law, changes in relation to domestic violence.

Reproduction
Abortion Law (Amendment) Act, 1967: Abortion legal up to 28 weeks of term where woman gains approval of two doctors. Linked with risk to woman's physical and mental health.

Human Fertilisation and Embryology Act, 1990: Restricted use of embryos in infertility treatment; also reduced legal limit of abortion to 24 weeks.

Children
Children Act, 1989: Shift in emphasis from parental rights to parental responsibilities and best welfare of the child.

Child Support Act, 1991: Requires absent parents to contribute to financial cost of child's upkeep.

Family law is an extremely powerful indicator of the ways in which family life and the roles of individuals both inside and outside families have changed over time.

EXPLAINING FAMILY POLICY

What we have seen is that family policy not only appears to cover a range of policies but also appears to have a range of effects, both intentional and unintentional. How can we explain the direction of family policy? One way of assessing this question is to explore the ways in which different theoretical perspectives have addressed this question. Analysing the family and the family's role in welfare has appealed to some theorists more than others. In particular, feminists have focused on the family and women's position within the family to explain women's subordination on a wider scale.

Functionalist theory, as in the work of Talcott Parsons (1964), views the modern nuclear family as an inevitable part of society's development and, in particular, a function of modern industrial capitalism. The modern state has taken over some of the former welfare functions of families – in particular education – leaving

Exhibit 16.4

Who does what in the home? Division of household tasks by married and cohabiting couples			
	Always/usually the woman (per cent)	Equal/ together (per cent)	Always/usually the man (per cent)
Washing and ironing	79	18	2
Deciding what to have for dinner	59	35	4
Looking after sick family members	48	45	–
Shopping	41	52	5
Small repairs around house	5	18	74

Source: *Social Trends*, 1996.

Note: Again, note how the selection of statistics reinforces ideas about the 'natural' family. Here, we are presented with figures on the division of labour in the home for married and cohabiting couples only, whilst other families – for example, lesbian or gay couples with children, or extended families – are excluded. This could appear to be a statistical convenience – after all, the majority of couples with children *are* heterosexual – however, there would be a different understanding of 'family' if the researchers simply took into account all households where there are children and adults.

One of the ways we can detect assumptions about families, then, is by carefully considering the assumptions which underpin the statistics on 'the family' which are produced routinely by the government and others.

families as specialist institutions providing mutual support. Within the nuclear family, however, men and women are seen as having different roles, with a naturally determined sexual division of labour (Segal, 1990).

Feminist theory covers a wide range of ideas. For many, both familial ideology and families as a reality are seen as oppressive to women. Radical feminists, for example, see families as patriarchal, with men having power over women's sexuality and reproductive nature. However, black feminists have been critical of the feminist view of the family as oppressive, highlighting the ways in which families – within a discriminatory and racist society – may be a source of support for women in the face of other forms of oppression (Bryan *et al.*, 1986; Williams, 1989).

Feminists criticise family policy as serving to maintain women's subordinate position (Segal, 1990). The family which is supported is the traditional nuclear family with an economically dependent wife – as in Beveridge's 1942 plan (Wilson, 1977). Others have argued that one of the tasks of social policy is to coerce people into patriarchal households, in which they might learn the importance of deference to patriarchal authority, both within the family itself and in wider society (Gittins, 1993). Black feminists have argued that social policy is 'ethnocentric': for example, in assumptions that Asian families are extended families, and the best providers of welfare for dependants. Similarly, the censure of lone mothers is problematic, given the higher proportion of black women who are lone mothers. The point they would make is that many of these women are single parents only in the conventional policy definition, as these women are involved with the fathers of their children, who take on family responsibilities (Watt and Cook, 1992).

New Right theory attacks what is seen as the 'dependency culture' created by the welfare state. Family policy has too often taken away the right of the individual to make decisions regarding the welfare of their family. Individuals should provide for their family – usually envisaged as economic provision through employment, savings and insurance against need – together with provision for dependants by family welfare, primarily through the domestic labour of women (Glennerster, 1995). One of the writers often associated with New Right thinking in the 1980s, Ferdinand Mount, views the family as the last site of resistance against the intrusive state, arguing that the private world of the family should be free from state intervention (Mount, 1982). However, others would support the role of the state in creating disincentives for particular kinds of action – as in the Child Support Act, for example. Thus the role of the state is viewed by some on the Right as the defender of the traditional family against attacks from feminists and others.

These are some very brief examples of the ways in which different writers might view both 'the family' and family policy. The annotated reading list at the end of the chapter offers advice on more reading in this area.

CONCLUSION

Family policy is, as we have seen, a broad subject which can potentially include policies across a spectrum of arena and interests within the welfare system. We have pointed to a range of policies that affect families and the way they live their lives – through inclusion or exclusion, through the creation of an ideal type against which family life is measured or through policing the family, on behalf of the members themselves, as in child protection or intervention in other intra-familial violence, or on behalf of society more widely, as when children are forced to attend school.

However, we should also be aware that in adopting this very broad view, we are not necessarily identifying what might be taken as family policy by the political parties of the time. If a government was to create a Ministry of the Family, with special responsibility for family policy, there is no doubt that some of what we have discussed would be included within its brief – child protection, family breakdown, divorce, marriage laws, and perhaps the economic support of the family, whilst other aspects may be left on the margins or ignored altogether. Would a government acknowledge, for example, that the direct impact of its immigration policies may be to prevent some families from staying together and supporting each other, whether financially or emotionally? It will always be necessary and valuable to question both implicit and explicit assumptions and effects of 'family policy', and the implications of policy for a diverse range of family types, whilst keeping in mind the broad identification of what might be taken as 'family policy'.

REFERENCES

Austerberry, H. and Watson, S. (1986) *Housing and Homelessness: A feminist perspective*, London: Routledge and Kegan Paul.

Beveridge, Sir W. (1942) 'Social Insurance and Allied Services', Cmnd 6404, London: HMSO.

Bryan, B., Dadzie, S. and Scafe, S. (1986) *The Heart of the Race*, London: Virago.

Campbell, B. (1988) *Unofficial Secrets*, London: Virago.

Cashmore, E. and McLaughlin, E. (1991) *Out of Order: Policing Black People*, London: Routledge.

Conway, J. (ed.) (1988) *Prescription for Poor Health: The crisis for homeless families*, London: London Food Commission.

Cook, S. and Watt, S. (1992) 'Racism, Women and Poverty', in Glendinning, C. and Millar, J. (eds), *Women and Poverty in Britain in the 1990s*, Hemel Hempstead: Harvester Wheatsheaf.

Deacon, A. (1995) 'Spending More to Achieve Less? Social Security Since 1945', in Gladstone, D. (ed.), *British Social Welfare: Past, present and future*, London: UCL Press.

Elashtain, J. (1981) *Public Man, Private Woman*, Oxford: Martin Robertson.

Firestone, S. (1972) *The Dialectic of Sex: The case for feminist revolution*, London: Paladin.

Fox Harding, L. (1996) *Family, State and Social Policy*, London: Macmillan.

Gittins, D. (1993) *The Family in Question*, Basingstoke: Macmillan.

Hague, G., Malos, E. and Dear, W. (1996) *Multi-agency work and domestic violence: a national study of inter-agency initiatives*, Bristol: Policy Press/Joseph Rowntree Trust.

Hill, M. (1993) *Understanding Social Policy*, 4th edition, Hemel Hempstead: Harvester Wheatsheaf.

Kelly, L., Regan, L. and Burton, S. (1991) *An Exploratory Study of the Prevalence of Sexual Abuse in a Sample of 16–21 Year Olds*, University of North London: Child Abuse Studies Unit.

Kirkwood, C. (1993) *Leaving Abusive Partners: from the scars of survival to the wisdom for change*, London: Sage.

Land, H. (1995) 'Families and the Law', in Muncie, J., Wetherell, M., Dallos, R. and Cochrane, A. (eds), *Understanding the Family*, Milton Keynes: Open University Press.

Lasch, C. (1977) *Haven in a Heartless World: The family besieged*, New York: Basic Books.

Lilley, P. (1992) *Speech to Conservative Party Conference 1992*.

Malos, E. and Hague, G. (1993) *Domestic Violence and Housing: Local Authorities' Responses to Women Escaping Violent Homes*, Bristol: Women's Aid Federation/Bristol University.

Malpass, P. and Murie, A. (1994) *Housing Policy and Practice*, 4th edition, London: Macmillan.

Mama, A. (1989) *The Hidden Struggle – Statutory and Voluntary Sector Responses to Violence Against Black Women in the Home*, London: Race and Housing Research Unit/Runnymede Trust.

Midwinter, E. (1994) *The Development of Social Welfare in Britain*, Buckingham: Open University Press.

Millar, J. and Glendinning, C. (1993) *Women and Poverty in Britain: The 1990s*, Hemel Hempstead: Harvester Wheatsheaf.

Mount, F. (1982) *The Subversive Family: an alternative history of love and marriage*, London: Cape.

Muncie, J., Wetherell, M., Dallos, R. and Cochrane, A. (1995) *Understanding the Family*, London: Sage.

Murdock, G. (1968) 'The Universality of the Family', in Bell, N. and Voge, E. (eds), *A Modern Introduction to the Family*, New York: Free Press.

Murie, A. (1995) 'Housing: On the edge of the welfare state', in Gladstone, D. (ed.), *British Social Welfare: Past, present and future*, London: UCL Press.

Oakley, A. (1974) *The Sociology of Housework*, Oxford: Martin Roberts.

Parsons, T. (1959) 'The Social Structure of the Family', in Anshem, R. (ed.), *The Family, its Function and Destiny*, New York: Harper and Row.

Parsons, T. (1964) *The Social System*, London: Routledge & Kegan Paul.

Pascall, G. (1986) *Social Policy: A feminist analysis*, London: Tavistock.

Pascall, G. (1997) *Social Policy: A new feminist analysis, London: Routledge.*

Payne, S. (1991) *Women, Health and Poverty*, Hemel Hempstead: Harvester Wheatsheaf.

Pringle (1995) *Men, Masculinities and Social Welfare*, London: UCL Press.

Rose, H. (1986) 'Women and Restructuring the Welfare State', in Oyen, E. (ed.), *Comparing Welfare States and their Futures*, London: Gower.

Russell, D. (1986) *The Secret Trauma: Incest in the lives of girls and women*, New York: Basic Books.

Russell, D. (1995) *Women, Madness and Medicine*, Polity Press: Cambridge.

Segal, L. (1990) Slow Motion: *Changing Masculinities, Changing Men*, London: Virago.

Van Every, J. (1991) 'Who is 'The Family'? The Assumptions of British Social Policy', *Critical Social Policy*, 11: 62–75.

Watson, S. (1986) *Accommodating Inequality: Gender and Housing*, Sydney: Allen & Unwin.

Watson, S. (1987) 'Ideas of the family in the development of housing form', in M. Loney et al (eds), *The State or the Market*, London: Sage.

Weeks, J. (1991) *Against Nature: Essays on History Sexuality and Identity*, London: Rivers Oram Press.

Williams, F. (1989) *Social Policy: A Critical Introduction*, Polity Press: Cambridge.

Wilson, E. (1977) *Women and the Welfare State*, London: Tavistock.

Woods, R. (1996) 'Women and Housing Policy', in Hallett, C. (ed.), *Women and Social Policy: An Introduction*, London: Prentice Hall/Harvester Wheatsheaf.

Young, P. (1995) *Mastering Social Welfare*, Basingstoke: Macmillan.

ANNOTATED READINGS

The textbook by Muncie *et al.* (1995) *Understanding the Family* (Sage) offers a good introduction to issues in family policy and some of the important areas in analysing both family policy and how families behave. The chapter on 'Family Law' by Hilary Land is a particularly good discussion of the ways in which the legal system affects families. The second edition of Gittins (1993) *The Family in Question* (Macmillan) is also a good introductory text with useful sections on other family forms and changes in family life over time. Fox Harding's 1996 text, *Family, State and Social Policy*, is a very detailed discussion of family policy in Britain.

Housing and social security as they affect families are both well discussed in Gillian Pascall's new edition of the book, *Women and Social Policy*. For more on the subject area of domestic violence the work of Dobash and Dobash (1992) *Women, Violence and Social Change*, together with Pringle's (1995) *Men, Masculinities and Social Welfare* (London, UCL Press), are good.

Bea Campbell's book about the Cleveland affair, *Unofficial Secrets* (Virago), is a thoughtful and well written discussion of the issues it raises. Fiona Williams' (1989) book, *Social Policy: A critical introduction* (Polity Press), is a valuable discussion of feminist theories of welfare, including feminist perspectives on family policy. For other theoretical perspectives chapters 1 and 2 in the Muncie book referred to above are also good introductory material.

17 Explanations of criminal justice policy, process and practice: A theoretical approach

by Tony Colombo

OBJECTIVES

- To consider the role of the criminal justice system within British social policy.
- To compare different 'models' of delivering criminal justice policy.
- To debate the question of 'inequality before the law' in terms of both race and gender.

INTRODUCTION

It is probably fair to say that Britain has become a nation for which crime is an obsession. 'True Crime' and crime fiction paperbacks, magazines and newspaper articles can be found on the shelves of every High Street bookshop and news-agents. Almost all television dramas are crime related, with series focusing on virtually every conceivable aspect of the criminal process, including: brilliant detectives, police surgeons, crown prosecutors, criminal psychologists and defence lawyers. The popular image of the criminal justice process generally personified by such media exposure is one in which the values of both truth and justice are shown to predominate.

Since the late 1980s, however, revelations concerning numerous 'miscarriages of justice' have increasingly made the public aware that such a view is, to some extent, nothing more than a popular myth. More generally, public fear and anxiety about becoming a victim of crime, along with a decline in confidence in the ability of our system of criminal justice to identify offenders and not lock up the innocent, has led to claims that 'English criminal justice is in crisis without precedent' (Rose, 1996, p. ix).

Before being able to make such a claim, however, it would surely be prudent to try and gain a clearer understanding of the primary purpose of our criminal justice process. In other words, what are the key values, issues and debates influencing, shaping and promoting the policies, processes and practices which are responsible for driving forward our system of criminal justice? For example, is the criminal process simply driven by an unwavering desire to catch, try and punish criminals or is this commonsense notion too simplistic?

In an effort to provide some answers to these questions, an attempt will be made in this chapter to examine the function/purpose of the criminal justice system from a series of key theoretical perspectives originally derived from the work of Packer (1969) and King (1981). Each perspective – due process, crime control, welfare and rehabilitation, and power (dominance) – will be presented as an 'ideal type' and should be interpreted as a window through which it is possible to gain a particular (though partial) insight into what drives both criminal justice policy and its processes.

DUE PROCESS MODEL

During the last two decades a string of miscarriages of justice including the 'Confait Affair', the 'Guildford Four', Judith Ward, the 'Cardiff Three' and most dramatically of all the 'Birmingham Six' have led to the Royal Commissioning of two reports into the operational nature of criminal justice procedures, namely the Philips Commission, reporting in 1981, and the Runciman Commission which reported in 1993. The goal of the system according to the Philips Commission was to develop a 'fair, open, workable and efficient' system, achieved through developing a fundamental balance between the rights of the suspect and the powers of the police. By 1993 the criminal justice system of England and Wales, once heralded as the finest and fairest in the world, was perceived by many as in desperate need of urgent repair.

In its raw form the due process perspective prioritises concern for the civil rights of the individual, emphasising the need for a criminal process which is fair and equitable. Generally, supporters of this approach lack confidence in the ability of pre-trial fact-finding measures, such as interrogation and identification parades, believing that within the course of the criminal justice process there are many factors that may contribute towards the mistaken apprehension and conviction of a suspect. Indeed, due process advocates would not have to look too hard in order to find evidence to substantiate their concerns, citing, in addition to the above miscarriages, recent revelations concerning the West Midlands Serious Crime Squad whose unlawful practices led to the wrongful conviction and eventual release in 1993 of 14 people.

In order to safeguard against the potential for such errors, due process insists upon the establishment and strict adherence to a series of formal rules and adjudicative adversarial processes. Packer (1969) has likened these rules to an obstacle course by stating that each successive stage in the criminal justice system should be designed to present 'formidable impediments' to carrying the accused any further along the process.

The present framework of rules governing both the treatment of the suspect and the operation of police powers are now enshrined in two major pieces of legislation that were enacted following the Philips Commission, namely the Police and

Criminal Evidence Act (PACE 1984) and the Prosecution of Offences Act 1985. Along with their associated Codes of Practice, the underlying intention of these statutes was to try to create a balance between the power of the state and the rights of the accused. *Inter alia* (among other things), PACE 1984 places limits on the length of time a suspect can be held for questioning, requires the police to notify the suspect of their right to legal advice and sets out the conditions for the admissibility of evidence, such as, the recording of interviews and notifying the accused of his/her right to remain silent. Meanwhile, the Prosecution of Offences Act 1985 made provision for the establishment of a new stage within the criminal justice process known as the Crown Prosecution Service (CPS). All papers relating to a suspect's charge are now to be passed on to the CPS for an independent assessment of its merits, i.e. each case is examined in order to determine whether or not the police have, in accordance with the rules of PACE 1984, obtained sufficient evidence against the accused in order to form a 'realistic prospect of conviction'.

Some due process advocates have argued that this framework of rules does not go far enough and cite several post-PACE miscarriages such as the 'Cardiff Three' to support their case. Alternatively, they suggest that rather than tinker around the edges a more fundamental overhaul of our legal system is required. In particular, it is claimed that as Britain lacks a written constitution like France or North America, there are no entrenched rights and principles governing the operation of the criminal justice system. Instead, we must rely only on parliamentary legislation and common law rights created by judges which can easily be redefined or repealed altogether.

An important safeguard afforded to suspects within the criminal process, which is also central to the due process model, is the presumption of innocence. Essentially, there are two aspects to such a presumption: First, the principle stipulates that it is the duty of the state to prove that the defendant has broken the criminal law. Thus, the police cannot simply go out and arrest on the basis of a hunch and then demand that the suspect prove their innocence, and, secondly, the standard of proof required in order to establish guilt is higher on a criminal charge, where the case against the accused must be proven 'beyond reasonable doubt', than for a civil charge, where it is only necessary to prove guilt on 'a balance of probabilities'.

The requirement of such a high standard of proof in criminal cases not only helps guard against wrongful convictions but more fundamentally symbolises the acknowledgement of an important due process philosophy officially remarked upon as long ago as 1823 by Holroyd, J. in the Hobson case, namely: 'it is a maxim of English law that ten guilty men should escape rather than one innocent man should suffer'. The question that remains unresolved, however, is precisely how high should this evidential threshold be? If the criminal courts employed the lower standard of proof as applied in civil cases, i.e. by determining each case on a balance of probabilities, then obviously many more factually guilty suspects could be successfully prosecuted. For due process supporters, however, the unacceptable corollary is that it would also be easier for many more factually innocent people to slip through the net and be convicted. Alternatively, the demand of due process for a suspect's presumption of innocence, which could only be challenged through strictly proving their guilt beyond any doubt at all, would certainly protect the innocent but suffer from the diverse corollary of rarely achieving a successful prosecution. With regard to this point, it is interesting to note that Holroyd, J. did not suggest that it was better that 100 or indeed 1000 guilty men should be set free in order to protect against a single innocent conviction.

Regarding the 'burden of proof' aspect of the presumption of innocence principle, it has been claimed that a 'golden thread' runs throughout the criminal law, which embodies the due process approach that it is for the prosecution to bear the burden of proving the guilt of the accused (Sankey LC in *Woolmington* v *DPP* 1935). Fundamental to this principle is the classic due process position enshrined in the Judges Rules in 1912 and now the PACE 1984 Code of Practice relating to the suspect's right to remain silent, i.e. the right to avoid self-incrimination by saying nothing, either to the police or the courts and from which no adverse inferences about the accused's level of guilt may be drawn as a consequence.

In practice, however, the evidence suggests that this right has been undermined in a whole variety of instances, juries and magistrates can and probably do draw adverse comment from silence (Sanders and Young, 1994). Furthermore, the former Conservative government under John Major, in an effort to develop tougher law and order policies, introduced a clause into the Criminal Justice and Public Order Bill (cl 27-31) aimed at abolishing the right of silence altogether. Their attempt failed as many politicians, particularly in the House of Lords, felt that any attempt to remove such a right may possibly have a fundamental impact on everyone's right to be presumed innocent until proven guilty.

The due process model also believes that the best way to uphold moral standards and to encourage law-abiding behaviour is to lead by example. Thus, due process advocates insist that the legal system should never benefit from its own illegalities, such as through the use of unlawfully obtained evidence. This level of concern for the abuse of power could, however, lead to inefficiencies within the system. For example, if the police obtained evidence showing beyond any doubt that a suspect had committed a murder and it was also discovered that the evidence had been obtained illegally, i.e. not in accordance with the established rules for obtaining confessions, etc., then due process thinking would, nevertheless, insist that the suspect walks free because of this procedural irregularity. Their justification for such an action would be based on the premise that to accept such procedural irregularities would encourage future abuses of power to take place, which in the long term would be far more damaging to society than releasing one murderer.

In summary, the primary concern of the due process model is to inject justice into the criminal process through the establishment of policies and procedures which fairly and equitably balance the rights of the accused against the power of the state. In England this approach is most likely to be found among the attitudes of lawyers, particularly those involved in defence work, and the goals of key organisations such as Liberty and the National Council for Civil Liberties who continue to highlight the need for a more liberal approach towards our system of criminal justice.

CRIME CONTROL MODEL

In direct contrast to the due process model, a pure crime control perspective views the repression of all criminal conduct, regardless of the consequences to people's civil rights, as the most significant function to be performed by the criminal justice system. Without this degree of control, it is envisaged that disrespect for the criminal law would develop, resulting in the collapse of public order, creating fear and anxiety amongst law-abiding citizens.

In order to avoid such an infringement of our social freedom, a high rate of detection and conviction of suspects must be upheld and this can only be effectively achieved through minimising the opportunities for a case to be challenged. Thus, according to the crime control perspective, the criminal justice system should function much like a conveyor belt, where the police are given extensive powers and freedom to act on their own hunches and working assumptions in order to establish the facts necessary to differentiate the innocent from the guilty, leaving the remaining stages as the task of swiftly trying and sentencing the offender.

Earlier it was noted that under PACE 1984 a number of due process safeguards were introduced in an attempt to redress the 'balance' between the power of the state and the rights of the individual. However, a closer look at the way the criminal process actually operates in practice reveals the presence of a number of features highly characteristic of the crime control model. Focusing specifically on PACE 1984, the Philips Commission also advocated giving greater powers to the police so that they could be more effective at repressing crime. Thus, many of the operational rules that were once informally used by the police have now been legitimised. For example, before 1984 many suspects were induced to come to the police station without being charged on the basis that they were 'helping the police with their inquiries', PACE 1984 now formalises this practice by allowing for pre-charge detention. Hence, popular crime control lines such as 'the police are forced to break the law in order to get results' have in some cases been removed: 'police and court officials need not abuse the law in order to subvert the principles of justice; they need only use it' (McBarnet, 1983, p. 156).

Advocates of the crime control paradigm would also assert that the judicial 'conveyor-belt' process of dealing with offenders could be made significantly quicker and simpler if those accused of a crime could simply be persuaded to admit their offence at the outset and so enter a guilty plea, thus leap-frogging the trial phase altogether and moving directly on to sentencing.

Reading in the area of criminal law and policy for the first time, one might understandably be forgiven for thinking that the adoption of such an approach is more akin to a game of monopoly – move directly to jail – rather than a fair and equitable system of criminal justice. In reality, however, such an approach is a typical feature of the criminal process. In both England and America a large majority of defendants plead guilty and forgo their right to an adversarial trial (Baldwin and McConville, 1977). Thus, the alleged evidence against them is never heard, the reliability of witness statements are not cross-examined and the all-important 'beyond reasonable doubt' presumption is never tested.

Supporters of the crime control perspective, therefore, clearly envisage a criminal justice system which is primarily managed and controlled by the police and although these advocates would accept that 'a few' mistakes may possibly be made during the police's efforts to try and identify the probably guilty from the probably innocent, such mistakes should be tolerated as they are insignificant relative to the larger goal of repressing crime. Ideally of course, the aim would be to secure as many guilty pleas as possible before the trial stage, thus eliminating the possibility for any potential errors to be uncovered, which might be interpreted as weaknesses in the system and so consequently reduce respect for the law.

If the system did show signs of weakness, perhaps through revealing that guilty defendants were being released or, as discussed earlier, that too many innocent defendants were being convicted, then the introduction of some degree of due process safeguard into the system would be tolerated. However, only those rules which may make fact finding more reliable, such as forbidding illegal arrests or preventing coercive interrogation practices, would be acceptable. To suggest, as due process supporters do, that illegally obtained evidence should be deemed inadmissible or that a conviction relying on such evidence should be quashed is viewed by crime control advocates as ridiculous: why should perfectly credible evidence be ruled as inadmissible simply because the methods used to obtain it were improper? Indeed, if the due process lobby had things entirely their way, the detective 'Dirty Harry' (alias Clint Eastwood) would have to look for another job! Harry's approach to law enforcement personifies the crime control approach, the means used by both the good and the bad guys end up being identical and it is only the end result that actually tells them apart – in such cases, the crime control ideal would assert that the ends always justify the means.

WELFARE AND REHABILITATION MODEL

Dealing with the illiterate, drug addicts, alcoholics or the mentally disturbed through the criminal process is of dubious morality. According to the welfare model, people should not be seen as responsible for their actions, instead they should be viewed as the product or victim of circumstances beyond their control. This approach views notions of free will and moral responsibility as nothing more than an illusion and so rejects concepts of guilt and punishment as meaningless, arguing instead that crimes are simply occasions for social intervention.

According to this perspective, the aim of the criminal justice system should not be to deter or seek retribution but to rehabilitate the defendant back to a state of social and mental health through treatment, better housing, job security, etc. A process, which in turn, will transform them into law abiding citizens, hence, reducing their threat to society.

In many respects the criminal justice system is seen as functioning in a similar way to a hospital, the aim being to diagnose, treat and cure the defendant – an approach very similar to the medical model adopted for the physically sick. Within such a framework the court functions much like a GP in that it can either administer treatment itself or refer the defendant to an expert who could provide the appropriate help, for example offering drug rehabilitation while the offender is on probation. More generally, the primary goal of the criminal justice agencies would be to collect information about the defendant on issues such as their mental history, family, educational and general social circumstances from which a diagnosis about their anti-social behaviour can be made and appropriate treatment recommended.

Such a welfarist perspective was particularly prominent in Britain immediately following the Second World War. At this time, it was felt that the formula for controlling anti-social behaviour rests not with politicians but with those psycho-social professionals claiming to collectively understand the criminogenic nature of offending. Tied in with the establishment of the welfare state was the belief that it would now be possible to tackle the root causes of crime, namely: poverty, unemployment, poor housing, educational disadvantage and family dysfunctions. No longer was the criminal justice system to be exclusively dominated by penal measures; instead, policies orientated towards treating and rehabilitating the offender, particularly juveniles, would be encouraged.

The post-war era was one of optimism – after all, Britain had just managed to control the expansion of Germany's Third Reich so, in comparison, how difficult could it be to manage a small domestic crime problem – which, along with improvements in the level of social affluence during the decades to follow, kept alive the dominance of the rehabilitative model for some time. By the 1970s, however, the vision of a crime-free society began to fade, the 'decade of discontent' increasingly saw crime creep back on to the political agenda and along with other socio-political problems, such as urban decline and increased IRA militancy, the public began to consciously feel unsafe and insecure, and, in turn, demanded greater protection through the imposition of tougher policies on law and order.

Since the 1970s the social democratic welfarist model has continued to take a 'back-seat' within the criminal justice arena. Today, key policy initiatives tend to focus on measures designed to protect the public and promote a wellmanaged and cost-effective system. Policies aimed at rehabilitating the offender are still practised but frequently they are watered down, form uneasy compromises, provoke professional disagreements or are openly criticised.

Supporters of the rehabilitative ideal would claim that one of the main reasons why the paradigm has been so strongly criticised as 'soft' on offenders and failing to stem the rising tide of crime, is because the key principles of the welfarist approach to criminal justice have always been presented in a diluted, half hearted form. Even at its inception, policy makers stopped short of proposing any radical systematic reform of the criminal justice system, preferring instead to introduce a gradual process of change. Such advocates would also point out that it is nonsense to abandon the whole idea of trying to rehabilitate offenders simply because past attempts have not shown themselves to be as effective as originally hoped. Disciplines such as sociology, psychology and criminology are still at a relatively early stage in their development, thus as knowledge in areas such as the cognitive-behavioural sciences improves, so ultimately will our skills in assessment, prediction and treatment. Until this time, rather than turn our backs, expert resources should be made available, directed towards improving the offenders so they are more able to adapt and cope in society without resorting to crime.

Realistically, even if during the optimistic post-war period the political will was there, it is clearly beyond the resources of the state to provide the welfare facilities for thousands of defendants who become caught up within the criminal justice process. At best only a modified version of the paradigm could ever be achieved, targeting resources primarily at those defendants who are likely to benefit from such rehabilitative measures.

Such a targeting policy, however, inevitably generates its own problems for someone must ultimately decide: who are the 'worthy' cases? Determining such issues can on occasion generate conflicting assumptions and misunderstandings between agencies (Colombo, 1997). For example, efforts by the various professions within the criminal justice system to divert mentally ill offenders away from prosecution and into care by health and social services may be hampered by mental health practitioners who do not consider the patient/offender as appropriate for treatment or suitable for the in-patient care facilities available.

The criminal justice agencies most likely to subscribe to the welfarist ideal are social workers and probation officers. As the courts' rehabilitation experts, their task is to prepare statements on the defendants, known as pre-sentence reports (PSRs), which contain details about the nature and circumstance of the crime, and other general background information about the offender. Such reports appear to be taken seriously by the courts (Hines *et al.*, 1978) and, therefore, seem to indicate an attempt by the judiciary to find a sentence that will meet the defendant's needs. More recently, some attempt has been made to standardise the content of PSRs so as to generate a higher standard of consistency and accuracy (Walker and Padfield, 1997).

There exists some evidence to suggest, however, that the probation service itself is in a state of flux. During the early 1990s the profession received a spate of unpopular press with regard to the issue of providing cash and holidays to juvenile offenders. Regardless of the broader welfarist intentions of such approaches, they clearly conflicted with the perceived traditional role of the criminal justice system as an administrator of punishment and as a consequence, such actions succeeded in undermining still further popular beliefs about the underlying intentions of the rehabilitative ideal. Today, the probation service is under increasing pressure to redefine itself in terms of protecting the public (Home Office, 1990), the ideas associated with rehabilitating offenders still remain important in principle but at the present time their significance and impact on shaping policy initiatives appears less influential in practice.

On concluding, it would appear that the rehabilitative approach only occasionally finds expression within the criminal justice process. The original notion of welfarism has simply been imposed upon a traditionally punitive criminal justice structure, no fundamental changes to the system have been made, hence, conflicts and tensions remain so that even in those worthy cases where some form of help in the form of treatment is needed, there still linger many features of the overall criminal justice policy process which are cautious in their approach, thus remaining more in line with the objectives of punishment and crime control rather than with those of rehabilitation.

POWER (DOMINANCE) MODEL

Each of the aforementioned models is based on a consensus idea of society, that is, they start from the assumption that society functions as an integrated structure whose members agree on the rules and values which are to be uniformly respected and upheld. Thus, within this structure the criminal law simply represents the embodiment of all that the members of a society find most unacceptable or intolerable. More recently, however, several alternative ideas have emerged about the origin and nature of criminal law and criminal justice which collectively redefine how the primary functions of the criminal justice system should be interpreted.

These theorists, who reached broadly similar conclusions, were particularly prominent during the period 1960–75 and are collectively referred to in textbooks under a number of labels including: 'new criminology', 'conflict criminology' and 'radical criminology'. Essentially, a synopsis of their ideas would contend that rather than acting as a consensus, society is made up of a series of conflicting and competing groups and that the only way the wealthy and powerful can protect themselves from being usurped, and so defend the status quo, is to ensure that the criminal law reflects primarily their own perceptions of what is both socially and morally acceptable. Within this analysis, conflicts are resolved and behaviour controlled though the most powerful groups using the law in order to enforce its views.

Overall, the 'new criminologists' argue that neither individuals nor their behaviour are inherently criminal, instead they claim that, within the context of everyday social reality, crime should be seen as merely an artificially constructed phenomena. However, while traditional conflict criminologists (such as Taylor *et al.*, 1973) adopt a purely Marxist approach towards the basis of crime, claiming that the only behaviour to be criminalised is that which threatens the structure and dominance of capitalist society, many more recent conflict theorists have moved on and instead promote the view that state power is just one element leading to social conflict – others could include cultural differences and prejudice.

Thus, within this broader context, the criminal justice system may be defined as a weapon used by society's ruling groups in order to legitimise and preserve, not only economic/capitalist power, via the maintenance of class differences, but also various forms of socio-political domination, such as patriarchal and racial inequalities, through repressing the types of behaviour it believes should be defined as unacceptable and illegal.

Consequently, in order for such a power (dominance) perspective of the criminal justice system to be upheld, we would expect to find, inter alia, judges to be drawn from and so representative of only a small elitist section of society, more rigorous enforcement of only those crimes that threaten the status quo and differential treatment within the criminal process of men compared to women and 'whites' in comparison to other ethnic minorities. It is to a brief consideration of these issues that we will now turn.

The nature of the judiciary

With regard to senior judges, the evidence shows that they are predominantly male, white, fairly old (average age 61) and invariably drawn from a social and educational elite. It has been calculated that in 1994 of the 1,778 judges eligible to work in the Crown Court only 122 (6.9 per cent) were women. Furthermore, it has been observed that there were no black or Asian High Court judges and that there were only four circuit judges (Crown Court judges) from minority ethnic groups (Padfield, 1995). Regarding magistrates (JPs) the situation is very similar, for, although they are no longer predominantly male, the research still suggests that JPs tend to be overwhelmingly white, middle aged, middle class and 'middle minded' (Parker *et al.*, 1989).

A number of researchers and commentators would, however, assert that the climate is changing fast. The common claim that judges are elderly may be partly dispelled by the emerging evidence which shows that over half (56 per cent) are between the age of 40 and 45, while some QCs (senior barristers) would argue that individual talent and personality are now considered and not just a person's educational or parental background, a practice, it is claimed, which in time will be removed as a stepping stone (*Daily Mail*, 1993).

As a consequence of their background it has been argued that the independence or neutrality of the judiciary in cases of conflict can become highly strained. According to Chambliss and Seidman (1971), judges, mostly unconsciously, decide cases on the basis of their own personal values and then try and fit that decision into a specific legal rule. Their assertion that decisions are being made in the public interest simply means that the public interest element is being perceived from the point of view of their own class. A class which has been described as highly cloistered and detached from mainstream society (referring to the 'pop scene', a senior judge in the 1960s asked: 'who are these Beatles?') and whose main value system is orientated towards maintaining the established distribution of power (Griffith, 1991). Of course, such a generalisation ignores individual differences between judges where there are many instances when judicial decisions have not 'toed the party line' in favour of the ruling elite (Zander, 1989).

The nature of criminal behaviour

The legitimisation of certain ideas within society may also be highlighted by the types of actions or behaviours which are criminalised. Stabbing someone to death with a knife would be legally defined as murder and clearly taking and keeping property belonging to another would be labelled under the criminal law as theft. But how easily might one define over-charging for goods and services, misuse of the employer's telephone, photocopier or other facilities and a company's reckless negligence for the health and safety of employees or customers which results in someone's death? These latter examples typically receive very little media coverage and generally are not topics that lay people think of during the course of defining crime.

Criminologists generally refer to these types of activity as either white-collar or corporate crime. The former was not generally afforded much consideration in

Britain until the circumstances surrounding the Guinness Affair came to light in 1986 which eventually resulted in the prosecution of Geoffrey Collier for the, as then, new offence of insider dealing. Meanwhile, corporate crime still remains relatively obscure, few cases are ever tested or succeed in court, and the media, who contribute towards shaping our general perceptions of crime, have shown very little interest.

Both categories of crime appropriately represent the dominance of the ruling group. Typically, it is the powerful and wealthy who become involved in either white-collar or corporate crime, yet it is also these groups who, via political and economic power, ensure that what is defined as criminal activity and the extent to which this criminality is enforced are sufficiently controlled to suit their own interests. In order to redress this balance, conflict and critical theorists would argue that society requires tougher and more clearly defined criminal laws, more effective corporate controls and more severe sentences for such offenders.

Against this perspective it could be argued that in strict legal theory the law is actually only interested in the type of offence committed (the actus reus) and the level of mental intention associated with the act (mens rea), hence, the social class of the offender becomes an irrelevant factor for the purposes of deciding guilt or innocence. To support this fact we could highlight the successful prosecution and eventual conviction of both Geoffrey Collier and the chairman of Guinness, Ernest Saunders.

Furthermore, most white-collar offences tend to involve incidence of financial fraud such as embezzlement, insider dealing or deception. Offences of this type tend to involve fairly small amounts and are generally committed by people who are not publicly well known and rich. Such offences can, thus, be dealt with by the police and crown prosecution service in much the same way as any other crime. Even in the case of those white-collar offences where the sums involved are high and where corrupt investments or deals are made by a few very rich individuals, for example, the Guinness inside-dealing affair of 1986, the Blue Arrow rights issue fraud of 1987 or the Robert Maxwell's pension fund affair of 1992, there now exists a Serious Fraud Office (SFO) with the power to investigate such incidence. The SFO was set up under the Criminal Justice Act, 1987 and clearly gave the impression that it was now government policy to take such offences seriously.

Unfortunately, this optimistic approach towards the criminal justice system's management of white-collar crimes has, in practice, failed to produce encouraging results. Even minor fraud cases tend to be complex in nature which has made them expensive to investigate and prosecute. As a result, such cases tend to absorb police time and money normally used for dealing with other types of offence which have a more visible public and political profile. Thus, these crimes are generally considered as low priority and given a low profile by most police forces. Furthermore, serious fraud cases can become highly technical and lengthy, which has tended to stretch a juror's patience and comprehension of the case to their limits. A consequence which has resulted in a high number of acquittals, thus giving the impression that the SFO is ineffectual. Even when convictions are secured the sentences are often derisory relative to the severity of the offence, for example Ernest Saunders originally faced a five year sentence, however, this was later reduced to two and a half because he was reputed to be suffering from Alzheimer's disease (fortunately, the change in his sentence seems to have been just the tonic as he has made a miraculous recovery since!). Such examples, according to Levi (1993), can clearly be interpreted as a reluctance by judges to send their 'own kind' to prison even when they have let the side down.

Corporate crime is more difficult to define but may generally be explained as acts committed by employees of a corporation for the benefit of that corporation. An obvious, though hopefully rare example, would be the assertion made by Dowie (1977) against the Ford car manufacturers. In this instance it is claimed that the corporation showed blatant disregard for the health and safety of its customers by continuing to sell a particular model knowing that it was unsafe. The company had speeded up production in order to remain competitive in sales despite identifying a hazardous defect. It is alleged that the company had calculated that the amount they would have to pay in compensation in the event of an accident would be less than the loss in profits caused by the delay in production necessary in order to resolve the problem.

More generally, we could consider those pharmaceutical and industrial companies who disregard society and the environment for corporate gain through dumping toxic waste or emitting dangerous fumes into the atmosphere. Still others ignore or cost cut on safety standards for their employees which may result in death, injury or work-induced diseases, such as cancer or asbestosis.

In the light of such incidence it is quite distressing to think that for the vast majority of the population such corporate offences would not usually be listed amongst what would generally be perceived as important crimes. Equally worrying is the derisively low number of corporations who are ever successfully prosecuted and convicted for their criminal acts or omissions. Examples which have resulted in either acquittal for corporate manslaughter or the failure to even pursue a prosecution include: the Ford company of 1977 (mentioned above), the Bradford Football Stadium fire of 1986 and the Townsend Thoresen ferry disaster off Zeebrugge in 1987.

Thus, corporate crime is a real social problem which is no less morally reprehensible and damaging than most recognised crimes committed by individuals. Yet state authorities such as the criminal process as well as the mass media have succeeded in playing down the significance of such events, often passing them off as merely 'acts of God', or unfortunate accidents rather than testing claims that they represent serious criminal acts or omissions.

Discriminatory practices: race

Like the judiciary, police officers are not representative of the population. They tend to be drawn from the middle to higher ranks of society, to be more conservative in their outlook, white and male. Thus, as a result of the narrowly defined nature of this group, we should not be surprised to discover the existence of a specific pattern of values and beliefs which are not only homogeneous but continually reinforced via police training and general socialisation processes. Such a 'cop culture' (Reiner, 1985) has been shown to contain highly sexist and racist elements which have manifested themselves within both the rank and file of the police, via internal discriminatory working practices, as well as on the streets.

Following a review of several Home Office studies, Reiner (1985) concluded that the weight of police activity in terms of stop-and-search, and arrests generally falls more heavily on blacks and those from the lower working class. As a consequence of such biased actions, relations between the police, who represent the white ruling culture in our society, and black communities have become very strained. During the early 1980s saturation policing procedures were used in areas defined as having high crime rates. The locals viewed such practices, particularly the apparent targeting of black youths, as highly unjust. In retrospect the policy has been seen as one of the main factors 'triggering' the 1981 inner-city riots in Brixton (London), Liverpool and Bristol (Scarman, 1981) and the 1985 riots in Brixton and Broadwater Farm (London) (Gifford, 1986).

A further stage within the criminal justice system where there exists the possibility of racial discrimination is at the point of court sentencing. According to the 1991 census, ethnic minorities make up around 5.5 per cent of the total population in Britain, yet these groups represent about 16 per cent of the overall prison population. It would also appear that it is those defined as Afro-Caribbean who have the highest incarceration rates with males representing 10 per cent and females 29 per cent of their respective gender prison populations which is grossly in excess of the 1 per cent Afro-Caribbean presence in the general public. Furthermore, a recent study by Hood (1992) on a sample of 6,000 individuals sentenced at five different Crown Courts in the West Midlands, concluded that black males had a 17 per cent greater chance of imprisonment than whites and that such differences could, inter alia, be attributed to both direct and indirect discrimination by the courts.

It could of course be argued that blacks, perhaps because they generally occupy the lower socio-economic groups in our society, are more likely to become involved in criminal activity and so we should not be surprised that they are disproportionately represented in the criminal justice process (Graham and Bowling, 1995). Evidence to substantiate such a view is limited and so to take this point further would be highly presumptuous. What can be said with some degree of confidence, however, is that police stop-and-search and arrest patterns, as well as court sentencing practices are, at least partly, a product of race and class stereo-typing (Lea and Young, 1984; Hood, 1992). Perhaps more importantly, though, it should be recognised that the decisions made by various criminal justice agencies inevitably interact with each other. Thus, the cumulative effect of even the smallest amounts of discriminatory practice at key points in the process could have a fundamental impact on the way in which certain minority ethnic groups are managed and controlled by the criminal justice process (Reiner, 1993).

Discriminatory practices: gender

A further claim made by those who subscribe to the power (dominance) perspective is that the criminal justice system works towards legitimising and actively promoting the maintenance of a patriarchal society. In support of this claim it is generally believed that as most of the decision makers within the justice system are male (perhaps with the exception of the magistrates' court where the numbers are now about even), there is a tendency for them to adopt a more lenient approach towards women. This leniency is said to be based upon the chivalry hypothesis which asserts that most males are likely to respond to female offenders in much the same way as they would respond to their wives, daughters or mothers.

The evidence obtained from criminal statistics appears to substantiate this chivalry notion by demonstrating that women are more likely to be cautioned than prosecuted (Home Office, 1995), are less likely to receive a custodial sentence and even when imprisoned women are more likely to serve shorter sentences.

The important point to make here, however, is that these data are not sufficient in themselves to claim that women are treated more leniently than men, they merely show that both sexes are treated differently within the criminal justice process. The question of real significance is: why do these differences occur?

One suggestion, which may partially explain the differential treatment/processing of women, refers to the way in which they are perceived by the various agencies of the criminal process. Generally, the criminal justice system is viewed a little like a men's club and as a consequence women who enter the process are seen as 'out of place' or 'invisible' (Worrall, 1990). Explanations for women's behaviour are sought in terms of irrational behaviour or mental illness rather than as the product of such factors as boredom, greed or peer group pressure normally associated with male offending. It has also been shown that how respectable the female defendant appears to be is an important influential factor; thus, women are on trial not only for their criminal offence, but also because of their inappropriate feminine and gender role behaviour (Edwards, 1984).

It could, of course, be argued that women are not actually treated differently and that the degree of alleged leniency shown simply reflects the fact that they tend to commit the less serious types of crime. This is not unreasonable given that the statistics suggest that crime is overwhelmingly a male activity (Home Office, 1995). Furthermore, the evidence, substantiating the claim that the police afford preferential treatment to women simply because they are women, is weak and research findings with regard to the assertion that being female is a sufficient reason for differential treatment in respect of sentencing are at best controversial. For example, Farrington and Morris (1983) found that both sexes were dealt with in the same way and that sex was not related to sentencing severity independent of other factors, such as the nature of the offence. Moxon (1988), on the other hand, claims to have found conclusive evidence that women are dealt with more leniently than men, while Dominelli (1984) has claimed that women are generally dealt with more harshly.

Overall, however, it would appear that some women are treated in a discriminatory manner within the criminal justice process. Those who fit predominantly male stereotyped conceptions of 'respectable ladies' or 'nice girls' tend to be given generally more lenient, but most importantly for our purposes, different sentences. The evidence, however, is by no means conclusive on this point and significantly the experience of women, or for that matter blacks or the unemployed, should not be perceived in isolation. In a complex pluralistic society such as ours, each of these factors, and many more besides, continually interact with each other, for example, how might a black, wealthy mother fare under the present system of criminal justice. Furthermore, to assume that men are not the subject of sexual discrimination would be erroneous. Ultimately, in order to gain a more complete understanding of the nature of discriminatory practices within the criminal process it is essential that such issues are given the fullest consideration.

On reviewing this section, it is clear that many of the issues raised by the power (dominance) model are highly controversial and thought provoking. Some of the claims discussed above may be labelled by the reader as absurd or acknowledged with a sense of disbelief; however, whatever your views may be, there is no doubting the fact that this particular ideological approach has succeeded in developing our understanding of how institutions, such as the criminal justice system, help maintain and promote a social structure which is on occasion unjust, discriminatory and oppressive towards certain groups in our society.

CONCLUSION

From the discussion that has taken place in this chapter, it will be apparent that each of the four models offers a distinct ideological interpretation of how the operational nature of our criminal justice system should be understood. Three of the models – due process, crime control and welfarism – may be defined as 'participant approaches', in the sense that they reflect the values and perspectives of particular groups involved within the criminal process (King, 1981). For example, the police are most likely to favour a crime control approach, while defence lawyers would probably be more supportive of due process measures. Of course, such remarks are being made about 'ideal type' perspectives and so should not be taken to imply that all police officers or indeed that every last defence lawyer will support a particular paradigm to the total exclusion of all others. Nor should it be assumed that these perspectives are held exclusively by those who participate in the criminal justice process. On the contrary, these models provide the basis for public and professional debate on society's response to crime and criminals. The ideological context of each perspective addresses important questions about current social policy issues and so provides policy makers and those who take up causes with a clearly defined stance to be used when dealing with problems and issues raised during the course of the criminal process. From this multi-theoretical approach, some may well see issues, such as 'miscarriages of justice', as symptomatic of a harsh criminal justice system which is in crisis, while for others such issues are no more than an unfortunate consequence of a process ill equipped to effectively and efficiently repress crime.

The fourth perspective – power (dominance) – is in many respects very different from the other three approaches. Generally, this model tends to be much broader in its outlook, attempting to develop a more analytical and theoretical account of the way in which social institutions such as the criminal justice system shape and define the structural nature of our society. Unlike the other three models, this perspective does not start from the assumption that class, or indeed any other form of domination, is a laudable social objective, but instead highlights the fact that such problems may possibly be an operational characteristic of capitalist societies. Of course, as was the case with the participatory approaches, it would be nonsense to suggest that those individuals involved in criminal justice are all part of a huge conspiracy plot directed towards maintaining and perpetuating discriminatory practices, rather the process is far more indirect, unconscious and subtle. Ultimately, this important perspective contributes towards our understanding of both policy, process and practice within the criminal justice system through its ability to be able to look beyond the dull, routinised procedures that most of us take for granted and instead open up for debate questions and issues which are rarely, if ever, considered.

REFERENCES

Baldwin, J. and McConville, M. (1977) *Negotiated Justice*, London: Martin Robertson.

Chambliss, W. J. and Seidman, R. B. (1971) *Law, Order and Power*, Massachusetts: Addison-Wesley.

Colombo, A. (1997) *Understanding Mentally Disordered Offenders: A multi-agency perspective*, Aldershot: Ashgate.

Daily Mail 10 April 1993 (article by Anthony Doran).

Dominelli, L. (1984) 'Different Justice: Domestic labour, community service and female offenders', *Probation Journal*, 31: 100–103.

Dowie, M. (1977) 'Pinto Madness', *Mother Jones*, 2: 18.

Edwards, S. (1984) *Women on Trial*, Manchester: Manchester University Press.

Farrington, D. and Morris, A. (1983) 'Sex, Sentencing and Reconviction', *British Journal of Criminology*, 24(1): 63–73.

Gelsthorpe, L. (1996) 'Critical Decisions and Processes in the Criminal Courts', in McLaughlin, E. and Muncie, J. (ed.), *Controlling Crime*, London: Sage.

Gifford, Lord (1986) *The Broadwater Farm Inquiry*, London: Karia Press.

Graham, J. and Bowling, B. (1995) 'Young People and Crime', Research Findings No. 24, Home Office Research and Statistics Department, London: HMSO.

Griffith, J. A. G. (1991) *The Politics of the Judiciary*, 4th edition, London: Fortana.

Hines, J. *et al.* (1978) 'Recommendations, Social Information and Sentencing', *Howard Journal*, 17: 2.

Home Office (1990) 'Crime, Justice and Protecting the Public', Cmnd 965, London: HMSO.

Home Office (1995) *Criminal Statistics: England and Wales*, London: HMSO.

Hood, R. (1992) *Race and Sentencing*, Oxford: Clarendon.

King, M. (1981) *The Framework of Criminal Justice*, London: Croom Helm.

Lea, J. and Young, J. (1984) *What is to be Done about Law and Order?*, Harmondsworth: Penguin.

Levi, M. (1993) 'The Investigation, Prosecution and Trial of Serious Fraud', Royal Commission on Criminal Justice, Research Study No. 14, London: HMSO.

McBarnet, D. (1983) *Conviction*, London: Macmillan.

Moxon, D. (1988) 'Sentencing Practice in the Crown Court', Home Office Research Study No. 103, London: HMSO.

Packer, H. (1969) *The Limits of the Criminal Sanction*, Stanford: Stanford University Press.

Padfield, N. (1995) *Text and Materials on the Criminal Justice Process*, London: Butterworth.

Parker, H. *et. al.* (1989) *Unmasking the Magistrates*, Milton Keynes: Open University Press.

Reiner, R. (1985) *The Politics of the Police*, Brighton: Wheatsheaf.

Reiner, R. (1993) 'Race, Crime and Justice: Models of interpretation', in Gelsthorpe, L. and McWilliam, W. (eds), *Minority Ethnic Groups and the Criminal Justice System*, Cambridge: Cambridge University, Institute of Criminology.

Rose, D. (1996) *In the Name of the Law*, London: Jonathan Cape.

Sanders, A. and Young, R. (1994) *Criminal Justice*, London: Butterworth.

Scarman, Lord (1981) 'The Brixton Disorders 10–12 April, 1981 (Scarman Report)', Cmnd 8427, London: HMSO.

Taylor, I. *et. al.* (1973) *The New Criminology*, London: Routledge & Kegan Paul.

Walker, N. and Padfield, N. (1997) *Sentencing: Theory and Practice*, London: Butterworth.

Woolmington v *DPP* (1935) AC 462 at 481.

Worrall, A. (1990) *Offending Women: Female law breakers and the criminal justice system*, London: Routledge.

Zander, M. (1989) *A Matter of Justice: The legal system in ferment*, Oxford: Oxford University Press.

ANNOTATED READINGS

Perhaps the most useful text here, which provides an overview of the place of the justice system in the British polity is that by Griffith, *The Politics of the Judiciary*, whilst the role of the police force is most clearly examined in Reiner's *Politics of the Police*. A controversial viewpoint of prisons policy is provided in C. Murray (1997), *Does Prison Work?* London: IEA.

18 The international perspective

OBJECTIVES

- To consider the influence of the European Community in developing social policy legislation within member states and the effect on the development of social policy in Britain.

- To consider the potential for development of a particularly European social policy.

- To consider the usefulness of comparing social policies between countries.

- To describe the different roles of various European institutions in the making of social policy.

The aim of this chapter is to provide the reader with an overview of both the international context within which social policy in Britain is today made and to introduce the concept of 'comparative' social policy, that is how we can attempt to compare the social policies of different nations or indeed the role of international actors in social policy. The chapter will also identify those areas that are controversial or problematic in the study of social policy at an international or transnational level.

We will begin by trying to set the making of contemporary British social policy in its wider context and in particular we will focus on the emerging social policy focus being adopted by the European Union and with which Britain, whether we like it or not, is inextricably linked. The chapter will also introduce the notion of a developing 'European' social policy in areas such as employment legislation or equal treatment and will look at some possible future directions in European social policy, given the changing and dynamic nature of European politics at the end of the twentieth century.

BRITAIN IN EUROPE

Few of the readers of this text are likely ever to remember a time when Britain was not a member of the European Community or Union and to say that British social policies in the 1990s are inevitably influenced by the policies and activities in

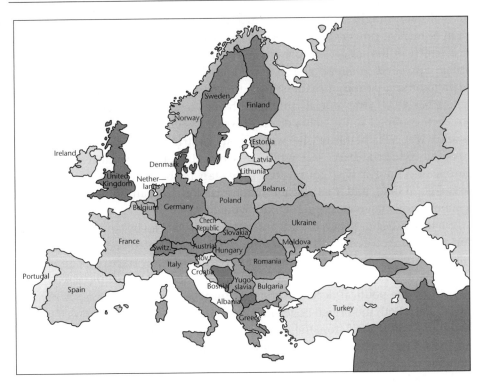

Fig. 18.1 Britain in the wider Europe

Brussels and Strasbourg may seem like stating the obvious. However, we must remind ourselves that British membership of this particular economic club can be dated back no further than 1973 and that the road to that membership was by no means smooth.

Britain emerged from the Second World War in a curiously paradoxical position. She had, after all, ended the war victorious and, politically at least, in a stronger position than her European allies and neighbours. Britain was, in 1945, still the largest imperial nation and as a victor who, singularly in Europe, had not seen the invasion of her homeland, could still lay claim to superpower status and a seat at the world's 'top-table'. Britain could also claim her 'special relationship' with the United States, one of a new type of economic and military superpower who now vowed not to return to her own years of economic isolation. Britain then seemed to have an 'ace in the hole' which guaranteed her status as a leading European nation. However, to paraphrase Prime Minister Macmillan, the winds of change were blowing across Britain.

The age of the imperial superpower had, almost without notice, passed by, the age of the new superpower was one which was built around both economic strength, some might say economic imperialism, and the possession and development of nuclear power. Britain's economic base was largely intact following the war which in the long term proved one reason for its later demise. For some Britain appeared to adopt, as it had done in 1919, a business as usual attitude wherein after a period of readjustment things would return to the normality of September 1939. One crucial difference here, however, was that this war had not been confined to the fields of north-western Europe but had indeed been a 'world' war which meant the widespread destruction of the European and Japanese industrial base. But whilst this meant that the countries of western Europe and the Far East got off to a slow start in the years after the war, they were rebuilding, and that meant modernisation. Britain soon then lost the economic advantage and began to fall behind.

Britain also began to lose the advantages she felt she had by continuing to maintain an Empire on every continent of the globe. As we noted above the age of the imperial superpower had come to an end; we can probably trace its beginnings to a time many years before 1945, but the decades of the 1950s and 1960s were to be marked by the political decolonisation of European empires all over Africa and the Far East. Both the British government and the prevailing international climate favoured a withdrawal from the Empire and the establishment of self-governance. For Britain the major step was to relinquish control of her Empire 'jewel' by the granting of independence to India and Pakistan in 1948 after many years of struggle led by Gandhi. The following three decades repeated this withdrawal of European rule across the world, often violently and with repercussions still felt today.

For Britain and her relations with Europe, however, the slow realisation of economic and imperial decline created a serious diplomatic dilemma. Winston Churchill had, in a speech given at Fulton, Missouri, described Britain as occupying a pivotal role within 'three circles of influence'. His argument was that Britain had crucial relationships with the United States, Europe and her Empire (which was of course transforming itself into a Commonwealth of nations of which Britain was naturally the titular head). Each of these circles was crucial to Britain's place in the world; the status of victor in the war allowed Britain the freedom to negotiate between the nuclear superpowers of the United States and Soviet Union but also to play a leading role in the reconstruction of Europe and the decolonisation of Empire. Similarly Britain felt that an equally special relationship existed between herself and her former Empire with whom trade relations would be damaged by closer economic ties with Europe. Maintaining a neutral balance between the three, for fear of damaging relations by favouring one over the other two, became central to Britain's foreign policy strategy through to the 1970s. Britain then, in the 1950s, did not want to pursue some vague European ideal at the expense of a wider international role.

But, although foreign policy proved vitally important, domestic considerations too were of crucial importance in steering Britain's relations with Europe. Britain, it seems, has always valued independence in policy making and whilst Britain's role in the world was changing, so too was the domestic situation. The 1945 General Election had returned for the first time a majority Labour government, and as we have seen elsewhere, the architects of the 'welfare state' who were not keen to have their socialist domestic policies derailed by the development of close relations with European neighbours. Such attitudes were shared, though perhaps for different reasons, by the Conservative governments of the 1950s and of course such arguments are resonant of more recent European debates surrounding the political direction taken by the EU and the development of a single currency.

We can see then that British relations with Europe at the end of the Second World War were, for a range of reasons, at their best tentative. At their worst they were positively hostile and suggested, somewhat arrogantly, that the new model of co-operation in Europe would be doomed to failure without British involvement and leadership. Overall Britain remained lukewarm to the idea of closer European economic co-operation or partnership and has apparently been trying, though maybe not too hard, to catch up ever since.

The nations of western Europe meanwhile went ahead with their discussions over closer economic co-operation and even floated ideas for closer co-operation on political and defence issues. Their discussions culminated in the signing of an agreement which established the European Coal and Steel Community in 1952 and later the European Economic Community in 1957. These two associations established the concept of closer economic (and political) co-operation between their signatories – initially Italy, West Germany, France, Belgium, the Netherlands and Luxembourg – although significantly the treaties themselves were cautious. Western Europe was itself unsure how far its nations would commit themselves to the economic support of their neighbours, and the treaties, therefore, represented a 'lowest common denominator' of what was politically feasible rather than the most desirable course of action. Thus social policy within the European Union has developed as a result of economic considerations (Hantrais, 1995).

Britain on seeing the success of European co-operation in the 1950s did attempt to set up a rival 'free trade area' (EFTA) which they hoped could deliver economic advantage without the implied commitment to closer political ties. But Britain had to concede that the EEC was likely to succeed with or without British membership and in 1961 submitted her own application for membership. This application together with a second application in 1967 were both vetoed by the De Gaulle government in France who feared British membership might represent a back door to increase American influence in European affairs. A third application in 1972, however, proved successful and Britain finally joined the EEC in 1973 along with Denmark and the Irish Republic.

British membership has, however, seemingly never been, or remained, assured. Even after the successful membership application by the Heath government both domestic political parties have remained divided over the issue of Europe. The Labour government which followed that of Heath promised, and delivered, a referendum over the issue of continued EEC membership and although that referendum produced a decisive public vote in favour of European membership the political parties have remained divided. (The Liberal and now Liberal Democrats are the only mainstream British political party to continually favour closer ties with Europe.)

Throughout the Thatcher years party political euro-scepticism has apparently been confirmed and reinforced. Initially Britain argued with her European partners over the size of her budget contribution which Whitehall and Westminster felt were out of proportion to the benefits Britain was receiving. Latterly and underlying most British political doubts has been the perceived threat of surrendering British sovereign power to Brussels 'eurocrats' and most persistently loss of control over British economic policy. British governments have remained cool over closer European ties from the signing of the Single European Act, the negotiations to amend the Treaty of Rome at Maastricht, entrance to and rapid departure from the Exchange Rate Mechanism (ERM) through to present day negotiations over the European Central Bank and Single Currency.

The British approach to such negotiations has been one of attempting to secure exceptions to or opt-outs from the provisions of European agreements and treaties. Through the 1980s and early 1990s first an exemption from the Social Charter and later an opt out from the Social Chapter of the Maastricht Treaty satisfied the demands of the Conservative euro-sceptics. But it also encouraged in the minds of Britain's European partners the feeling that Britain had never really joined the European club and that they might develop a 'two-speed' Europe – that the rest of Europe might move towards an ever closer union without British participation.

So deep did divisions over Europe appear to be within British politics that by the end of the 1980s the Conservative government had lost a Chancellor, Deputy Prime Minister and its longest serving twentieth century Prime Minister. In the summer of 1994 the new British PM, John Major, was forced to resign the leadership of his party in the face of continued conflict over Europe. But by 1997, with a change of government, Britain did sign up to both the Social Charter and Social Chapter which perhaps indicated a period of closer relations with Brussels, but the new Chancellor has remained reluctant to give any promise of when sterling might join the European Single Currency, continuing instead to rely on the vague suggestion that Britain would join when it was right for the economy to do so. Therefore the hot and cold relationship Britain has developed with its European partners since 1945 has continued as British governments continue their scepticism over conceding what they regard as sovereign political power. Yet at the same time they have had to recognise that closer economic and trade links make political progress an inevitability.

THE DEVELOPMENT OF SOCIAL POLICY IN THE EUROPEAN UNION

The debate surrounding the role of the European Union in the development of (common) social policies has, like British membership, a long and shaky history. The social dimension of Europe, which was not explicitly referred to in the founding Treaty of Rome, has developed as an adjunct to the economic concerns of the European project. The original European partners felt simply that social harmonisation would follow from their economic successes and although a social fund to help those areas of the economy in decline was established, it was to be on a small scale only (Hantrais, 1995).

Fig. 18.2 The European Union – 1997

The European partners stressed that the development of social interventions could only be justified where the laws and practices of member states were distorting competition and damaging the creation of an economic union, e.g. in the free movement of labour (Hantrais, 1995). Hantrais goes on to outline the chronological development of social policy as a concern of the European Community. The first stage was that laid down by the original Treaty of Rome which sought to promote closer co-operation between member states over social issues particularly those which related to the operation of the workplace. So emphasis was given to training or working conditions but there was, at this stage, no determination of what action should be taken, the Treaty simply emphasised closer co-operation. The European Social Fund (ESF) established under the Treaty was 'intended to make the employment and re-employment of workers easier and to encourage geographical and occupational mobility within the EEC' (Hantrais, 1995, p. 3).

The second stage in the development of European social policy as a legitimate sector of concern for the European Community came following its first enlargement. In 1974 the Council of Ministers resolved to create a 'social action programme' which would help to improve the quality of life alongside the pursuit of economic growth. The social action programme extended the social concerns of the Community into areas such as workers' rights, equality of treatment and health and safety at work. Still, however, the realm of social policy open for European consideration remained narrowly defined and poorly explored.

The 1980s witnessed the most significant development of social policy at the European level and is largely credited to the activities of the Commission President, Jacques Delors. Delors took up and expanded the notion of developing a social space (espace social) in Europe which stressed that social developments were necessary to Europe's future economic success. The EU could no longer guarantee continued economic expansion without addressing the social needs of the European population, beyond those simply associated with health and safety or equal treatment in the labour market. To this end the Commission established, or in places continued, a programme of research into what it saw as pressing social issues through a series of social policy 'Observatories', such as the European Observatory on old age, or alternatively by independent researchers.

The next stage in the development of a European social policy came with the development of the Community Charter of the Fundamental Social Rights of Workers or Social Charter. It marked a growing concern too with the issue of 'social dumping'. This was a concept which basically suggested that some EU member states might be able to gain unfair competitive advantage in the economic union by neglecting or taking a minimalist approach to their social responsibilities. The concern was initially one fuelled by a southern European expansion which incorporated Greece, Spain and Portugal into EU membership and one which continues today with present thoughts towards eastern expansion into the former communist bloc. The principal concern was that new members, with a relatively poorer standard of living, but therefore with lower labour costs, might be able to obtain an unfair competitive advantage and attract capital investment at the expense of other member states.

Although the concern was initially prompted by issues raised by the widening of Europe the most celebrated conflicts over social dumping have arisen because one member, Britain, refused to adopt the Charter. It appeared as though the British government of the day, under Margaret Thatcher, was itself seeking an unfair competitive advantage by refusing to accept what was regarded as a 'level playing field'. For the British government, though not always for British business, the issue was a more fundamental debate over the proper role of government in the regulation of economic relations. Britain felt that Europe was too ready to introduce new regulations over the economy and that instead Europe would do well to follow the British free market success of the 1980s. Over-regulation, it was particularly suggested in regard to the Social Charter, would create unemployment as it would impose unnecessary costs and burdens on the economy which would in the long term drive investment out of Europe altogether towards the so-called 'Tiger economies' of the Far East.

The issue raised too, however, more fundamental issues over the direction of Europe and questioned whether an ever-closer union, extending away from the economic and into the political and social arena, was either possible or desirable. Constitutionally Europe has appeared to lurch from one crisis to the next over referenda held on the Maastricht Treaty in both France and Denmark, over the widening of political powers for the European Parliament and of qualified majority voting in the Council and successively over the European Exchange Rate Mechanism and the single currency. Debate has periodically divided between those suggesting that Europe is in 'democratic deficit' and needs to develop wider and more generally recognisable duties and responsibilities for the elected Parliament and those suggesting that national governments remain the best guarantors of national interests and democratic legitimacy and resisting what is seen as further unnecessary cession of power to Brussels.

The wide-ranging debate which was launched with the advent of the Social Charter and the espace sociale continued at the end of the 1980s with the negotiations over the Maastricht Treaty and its 'social chapter'. Once again, as with the earlier Charter of workers' rights, Maastricht was adopted by 11 of the then 12 Union nations with Britain securing what it regarded as a vital 'opt out'. Maastricht introduced several important procedural changes to Europe alongside a widened social agenda in which a greater number of decisions could be taken on the basis of 'qualified majority voting'. 'The distinction between the areas subject to qualified majority voting and unanimous voting was important since it tended subsequently to dictate the social agenda, limiting it to topics where some degree of consensus already existed' (Hantrais, 1995, p. 12).

Exhibit 18.1

> ## Qualified majority voting
>
> Qualified majority voting is a system developed for progressing policy within the Council of Ministers of the Union which attempts to avoid the problem of attaining unanimity on all issues. Each member state has a vote with the following weightings:
>
> | | |
> |---|---:|
> | Germany, France, Italy and the United Kingdom | 10 votes |
> | Spain | 8 votes |
> | Belgium, Greece, Netherlands and Portugal | 5 votes |
> | Austria and Sweden | 4 votes |
> | Ireland, Denmark and Finland | 3 votes |
> | Luxembourg | 2 votes |
> | | 87 votes |
>
> In order for a proposal to be passed in the Council at least 62 votes must be cast in favour. By this method the Union hopes to ensure that the larger and more powerful members are able to neither press through legislation over the wishes of smaller states, nor to block the passage of legislation.

The most recent stage in the development of social policy at a European level is that embodied in the Green (1993) and White (1994) Papers on social policy. The Green Paper, a consultative document, sought the views of member states as to the agenda and direction of future Union social policy whereas the White Paper sought to lay down the direction of future social policies. Indeed, their publication marks a decisive shift in the development of European social policy, describing, as they do, the need for social rights for citizens, including those who are not in work and those resident within the Union who are not citizens of its member states. The emphasis now is of social cohesion hand-in-hand with economic success.

The Commission's White Paper on European Social Policy, published in July 1994, suggested that there would in future be a new mix between economic and social policies and that competitiveness and social progress could flourish together. Further it added that Europe needed, above all, an educated, adaptable and motivated workforce. The EU's role would be to provide a framework of economic growth, including the completion of the single market and the removal of protectionist barriers. Within this framework each member state would be able to target measures to address unemployment by vocational training or employment creation measures. The principal means by which the Union would develop its social policies would be the European Social Fund (ESF) which in the period from the White Paper to the end of the decade would have a budget of some 47,000 m ECU.

This new emphasis and new direction in European Social Policy has also been made within the context of further growth in membership for the Union. Since the collapse of the various communist regimes of Central and Eastern Europe those countries have made clear their desire to join in the economic success enjoyed by their western neighbours. The Commission has likewise made clear its readiness to welcome new members, but in doing so has laid down a range of guidelines for those governments. The guidelines have, in the main, stressed the importance of economic and fiscal stability as a pre-requisite to any future successful application. But alongside this the EU has underlined the development of sound social policies to underpin and support those economies. They have in particular stressed the need for support in time of transition, during which both unemployment and price inflation have risen rapidly. But the EU has also stressed the need for long-term social investment in the provision of social safety nets and securely founded pensions systems.

> The Commission adopted four main objectives for internal Community policies: establishing the conditions for lasting growth, basing growth on knowledge, undertaking the detailed modernisation of employment systems and promoting a safe society which is based on solidarity, takes the general interest into account and respects the environment. (Commission, 1997)

In July 1997 the Commission published its 'Agenda 2000' which sets out its proposed programme for the accession of new member states in Central and Eastern Europe. Accordingly negotiations for membership have begun with Hungary, Poland, Estonia, the Czech Republic and Slovenia to be followed by Cyprus, as the first stage of a proposed eastward enlargement. Further negotiations would later follow with other Central and Eastern European nations including Romania, Slovakia, Latvia, Lithuania and Bulgaria. The Commission's assumption in opening negotiations was that the first new members might be admitted after five years. In order to smooth the way into European Union membership the EU's structural fund has earmarked ECU 45 billion including ECU 7 billion in pre-accession aid, for the years 2000–6, in order to help achieve stable markets and economies. However, the economic crises felt by Eastern Europe but presaged by banking and economic crises in the Far East may delay any such negotiations. Much will depend on the strength of Europe's eastern economies in the decade since the transition began and the continued political goodwill of western European economies to continue to agree funds whilst attempting themselves to ride out any economic storm.

SOCIAL POLICY AND THE EUROPEAN UNION

In order to appreciate the role of the EU in making and developing social policy we need to have an understanding of both the structures within which social policy is made, how those structures differ from those of national policy-making structures and how they interact with national structures. Additionally we want to know whether and how European social policies develop their own identity distinct from those pursued by member states. In the European Union three institutions occupy central positions within the system of policy making; the Commission, the Council of Ministers and the European Parliament.

The European Commission itself lies at the heart of European policy making and comprises 20 Commissioners each appointed by the governments of member states for a period of five years. Each member may appoint one Commissioner with the exception of Germany, France, Italy, Spain and the United Kingdom who appoint two and although Commissioners are appointed by member states they act as representatives of the European Union rather than the member states. Indeed Commissioners are obliged to act impartially and to represent the interests of the Union as a whole rather than national interests. The Commission is headed by a President who is appointed by joint heads of government of the EU meeting in the Council of Ministers.

The central role of the Commission is to uphold the Treaties of the Union and to propose, develop and implement new European laws and policies. The Commission alone in Europe can propose new legislation, about which the other institutions may then express their 'opinion', and is responsible for monitoring the central aims of the EU, such as those developed in the form of the Common Agricultural Policy (CAP) or regional policy. The Commission is further responsible for the development of the external relations of the EU, such as those with the transitional economies of Eastern Europe, with the developing third world nations or in world trade negotiations held under the auspices of the General Agreement on Tariffs and Trade (GATT). The Commission's current occupation in policy terms is the continued development of the European Single Market which came into operation in 1993 and the future development of a European Single Currency.

The principal duty of the Commission is the proposal and development of new legislation, but the Commission does not have a free rein in this activity. Instead the Commission seeks to represent all opinion within the Union by discussing potential new initiatives with both the Council of Ministers and European Parliament. Additionally the Commission will consult those representative groups who have an interest in new legislation; so in social policy new directives on working conditions, for example, would be discussed with both employers and trades union representatives – the so-called social partners. In its day-to-day activities therefore the Commission depends heavily on the ability of the EU's three central institutions, and the other interest groups, to co-operate with one another.

The Commission carries out its duties with a staff of around 15,000, which may sound like a large bureaucracy but in reality is no larger than the number employed by an average-sized British municipal authority and yet serving some 370 million Europeans, organised through the Commission's 26 Directorates General. But in any of its activities the Commission also has a duty to respect the doctrine of subsidiarity, which holds that it is not appropriate for the Union to act where it would be more appropriate to carry out policy at national level. Thus

Exhibit 18.2

The Directorates General of the European Commission	
DGI	External Relations: Commercial Policy Relations with North America, the Far East, Australia and New Zealand
DGIA	External Relations: Europe and the New Independent States, Common Foreign and Security Policy and External Missions
DGIB	External Relations: Southern Mediterranean, TOP and Near East, Latin America, South and South-East Asia and North-South Co-operation
DGII	Economic and Financial Affairs
DGIII	Industry
DGIV	Competition
DGV	Employment, Industrial Relations and Social Affairs
DGVI	Agriculture
DGVII	Transport
DGVIII	Development
DGIX	Personnel and Administration
DGX	Information, Communication, Culture, Audiovisual
DGXI	Environment, Nuclear Safety and Civil Protection
DGXII	Science, Research and Development
DGXIII	Telecommunications, Information Market and Explanation of Research
DGXIV	Fisheries
DGXV	Internal Market and Financial Services
DGXVI	Regional Policies and Cohesion
DGXVII	Energy
DGXIX	Budgets
DGXXI	Customs and Indirect Taxation
DGXXII	Education, Training and Youth
DGXXIII	Enterprise Policy, Distributive Trades, Tourism and Co-operatives
DGXXIV	Consumer Policy and Consumer Health Protection

many European policies are expressed as Directives which lay down the aim or goal of a particular policy but leave member states to achieve those goals according to local tradition and circumstance. This too is the approach adopted in negotiations with potential new members who are told the economic and social conditions they need to achieve before they can accede to the Union but how those conditions are achieved are not prescribed.

The Council of the European Union, usually known as the Council of Ministers, acts within Europe as a guarantor of national interest. Its role is to set the political objectives of the Union and to co-ordinate and integrate their own national policies in accordance with those commonly defined objectives. The Council is presided over by each member state in turn who holds the presidency for a period of six months in rotation. Decisions within the Council of Ministers will be taken either by unanimous voting or Qualified Majority Voting (QMV – see exhibit 18.1) and since the adoption of the Maastricht Treaty the range of decisions taken by QMV has increased. The role of the Council is to consider any proposals brought forward by the Commission which it may choose to accept, to amend or to reject. The Commission, however, is limited in the range of legislation it may propose and the Council retains the right to propose new policy in the areas of Common Foreign and Security Policy (known as Pillar Two) and Justice and Home Affairs (known as Pillar Three).

The day-to-day operations of the Council of Ministers is carried out, not by national governments' ministers who have their own domestic agendas to pursue, but by the Committee of Permanent Representatives (COREPER). COREPER comprises senior diplomats from member nations' foreign ministry who meet on a weekly basis to prepare the ministerial meetings. The activities of both the Council and COREPER are supported by its permanent Secretariat. A more recent though crucial addition to the workings of the Council has been, since 1974, the European Council at which European Heads of Government meet, usually twice yearly. Like the Council of Ministers the leadership of the European Council is rotated on a six-monthly basis and at its summit meetings discussions take place which determine much of the future political direction for the Union.

The element of democratic legitimacy for Europe is provided by the European Parliament, although its operations appear very different from those adopted in national parliaments. Members of the European Parliament (MEPs) have been since 1979 directly elected and serve a period of five years. The Parliament meets for its monthly plenary sessions at the Parliament building in Strasbourg whilst its committee sessions are held in Brussels and the Parliamentary Secretariat is based in Luxembourg. The Parliament views its role as one which safeguards the interests of European citizens and which scrutinises the activities of the Commission and Council. This Parliament is notable, however, for its lack of legislative

Exhibit 18.3

The Presidency of the Council of Ministers

July–Dec. 1995	Spain	July–Dec. 1999	Finland
Jan.–June 1996	Italy	Jan.–June 2000	Portugal
July–Dec. 1996	Ireland	July–Dec. 2000	France
Jan.–June 1997	Netherlands	Jan.–June 2001	Sweden
July–Dec. 1997	Luxembourg	July–Dec. 2001	Belgium
Jan.–June 1998	United Kingdom	Jan.–June 2002	Spain
July–Dec. 1998	Austria	July–Dec. 2002	Denmark
Jan.–June 1999	Germany	Jan.–June 2003	Greece

authority; it has no power to propose or initiate new legislation nor any significant control over finances or money raising powers as we are more familiar with in Westminster. Instead the European Parliament has the right to be consulted in the preparation of new legislation and has the right to have its opinion heard which is supplemented by the right to pursue its concerns via 'Question Time' with Commissioners and the Council of Ministers. Although treaties adopted in recent years have sought to extend the role of the Parliament in making legislation (for instance at Maastricht) such changes have been slow to come and hard fought by European parliamentarians.

The Parliament does, however, hold significant powers in two areas. In both the appointment of a new Commission and the adoption of a new annual Budget the Parliament does have the power of amendment or even rejection. The Parliament also has power to pass a censure motion against the Commission and force its resignation as it did in early 1999, and the right to be consulted over the appointment of a new President of the Commission. Over the Budget the Parliament, through its Committee on Budgetary control, exercises scrutiny over spending and seeks to ensure that spending is in accord with the intention of the legislation. Additionally Parliament has an important function in the detection and prevention of fraud through its supervisory role. In particular areas of European policy the Parliament has developed and extended its role so that although the Council has the last word on most spending (particularly spending derived from the Common Agricultural Policy or international agreements) Parliament has the power to decide on spending, in close co-operation with the Council in areas such as education, social programmes, regional and environmental projects. Finally, and in exceptional circumstances, Parliament can vote to reject the Budget in its entirety.

The three institutions, and their functions, outlined above are core to the operation of the European Union, but there are others central to the operation of social policies. The Economic and Social Committee is made up of representatives of the so-called 'social partners', workers, employers and other interest groups, such as consumers and environmental interest groups. The Committee's task is to express its opinion on new Community legislation and to find 'common ground' between the different interested groups which it does through its nine sections. The European Investment Bank plays a central role in the development of regional policies and its role is to direct investment funds to what it refers to as the 'less favoured regions'. The EIB's role is therefore vital in the development of the European single market and a level economic playing field. Finally the European Court of Justice has the task of the interpretation and application of European treaties and has made important decisions in for example the harmonisation of income maintenance policies to ensure the equal treatment of men and women. The Court has been assisted in its task, since 1988, by the Court of First Instance which deals with disputes between individuals and companies and the

Community institutions and in enforcing competition rules. The Judges and advocates, appointed from member states must be qualified legal practitioners and must remain impartial throughout their six year appointment.

We have already seen that social policy in Europe has enjoyed a fitful existence often related to and deriving from the Union's economic role and measures to aid the implementation of the single market. But also, in recent decades Europe's notion of social policy has developed and changed to the effect that social and economic policy should develop hand in hand with one another. However that has not prevented the development of what we might conveniently term 'European Social Policy' in, for instance, training, care and support in old age or family policy.

The Commission has for instance put forward proposals for greater harmonisation in social security benefits across the Union which would possibly encourage an increase in the numbers of children born (Hantrais, 1994). Clearly the Commission is reflecting concern felt across Europe over the declining fertility and birth rate alongside the prospect of an increasingly elderly and possibly dependent population. But the Commission also seeks to avoid disadvantaging, and socially excluding, large families or those headed by lone parents.

The Commission also recognises that there may be issues for social policy raised by changing family structure. The trends of recent decades have been towards declining birth and marriage rates, but also towards later marriages and older first-time mothers. The period from the mid 1960s has also witnessed increases in the rates of cohabitation but also increases in the number of single households. Additionally employment rates have increased which has manifested itself in greater numbers of women entering the labour market and consequent demands for child care and for rights of equal pay and equal treatment. 'The picture which emerges . . . is that of an unstable family unit with fewer young children but more elderly relatives to support in a context where more women are likely to be employed outside the home in work which is increasingly insecure' (Hantrais, 1994). The Union has also become concerned over the apparent breakdown of traditional family structure in, for example, rural areas of Europe wherein young people migrate to urban locations in search of work. As a consequence of this process traditional patterns of caring, particularly of care for the elderly, break down and rural areas experience yet further economic and social decline (Walker, Alber and Guillemard, 1993).

However, whether such concerns amount to the development of an identifiable European social policy, distinct from that pursued by national governments, remains open to question. The development of a 'social Europe' might instead depend upon the development of common, or at least harmonised, economic, civil or political citizenship, but the development of a European social citizenship is by no means guaranteed (Leibfried, 1993). And, as Spicker clearly illustrates, there may be deep and impenetrable problems in trying to apply what amount to universal policy solutions to an entity as diverse as Europe (Spicker, 1993). The outcome is likely to be a social policy that is at the same time excessively generalised and delivered at the lowest common denominator rather than the highest.

The development of policies addressing the issues raised by third country nationals might usefully illustrate this point. Much of what is currently being developed as European immigration policy has been developed outside of the standards and notionally democratic channels of the Union. The negotiations of the Schengen group, which it was argued were creating a 'fortress Europe', have informed and indeed directed the development of Union policy itself. Proposals to develop a standardised police and security structure, to establish a European Police Agency, harmonisation of visa policies and procedures and harmonisation of security measures and checks on persons at external EU borders have derived from the negotiations of Schengen. That is they have developed outside the view of the European Parliament, but have since been adopted as Union policy following the Dublin summit in 1992 (Commission, 1990; Cruz, 1990).

SOCIAL POLICY IN THE WIDER WORLD

Although Europe occupies an increasingly important place in British politics and social policy since the adoption of both the Social Charter and the Social Chapter of the Maastricht Treaty by Blair's government in 1997, that is not the whole story. As the operation of the global economy becomes ever more complex and decisions taken by global capital are increasingly ignorant of national boundaries, nation states, it appears, become less effective. So, too, the social policies adopted by any particular government are often merely reactions to decisions taken in anonymous corporate boardrooms. The government in Whitehall finds itself, ever more so, pursuing social policies in response to company decisions or changes in markets in America or the Far East.

Social problems are now becoming international in their nature. Many of course have always been international and have demanded a co-operative international response; we might here point to policies to distribute aid to developing nations or the more long-term education and development programmes. Other issues, such as environmental pollution or global warming, are not within the realm of a single nation and therefore demand a supranational response. But increasingly decisions that may affect unemployment levels in one or a group of countries are taken out of the hands of governments and demand an international response. In this instance we must be aware of the increasing importance of international and global actors and agencies in the policy process. Organisations such as the United Nations or the Commonwealth have for many years adopted a social perspective, but we must look too to other actors such as the World Bank or

International Monetary Fund and their efforts to regulate world economics as an aspect of social policy (Deacon, Hulse and Stubbs, 1997).

The changing international dimension afforded to social policy is not only reflected in the social activities of international organisations as explored by Deacon, but also in new agendas adopted by governments. The British government announced in 1997 the establishment of a research programme emphasising the development of social capital for marginalised social groups, and the addressing of issues of social exclusion for those groups on a global scale (DfID, 1997).

REFERENCES

Commission of the European Communities (1990) *Policies on Immigration and Social Integration of Migrants in the European Community: Experts' report drawn up on behalf of the Commission,* Brussels: Commission of the European Union.

Commission of the European Communities (1997) *European Social Policy Forum: A summary,* Luxembourg: Office for Official Publications of the European Communities.

Commission of the European Union (1993) *European Social Policy: Options for the Union,* Brussels: Commission of the European Union.

Cruz, A. (1990) *An insight into Schengen, Trevi and Other European Intergovernmental Bodies,* Brussels: Churches Committee for Migrants in Europe.

Deacon, B., Hulse, M. and Stubbs, P. (1997) *Global Social Policy: International organisations and the future of welfare,* London: Sage.

Department for International Development (1997) *Research Programme on Social Policy,* London: HMSO.

Hantrais, L. (1994) 'Family policy in Europe', in Page, R. and Baldock, J. *Social Policy Review 6,* Canterbury: Social Policy Association.

Hantrais, L. (1995) *Social Policy in the European Union,* London: Macmillan.

Hill, M. (1996) *Social Policy: A comparative analysis,* Hemel Hempstead: Prentice Hall/Harvester Wheatsheaf.

Leibfried, S. (1993) 'Towards a European welfare state?', in Jones, C. (ed.), *New Perspectives on the Welfare State in Europe,* London: Routledge.

Room, G. (ed.) (1991) *Towards a European Welfare State,* Bristol: SAUS.

Spicker, P. (1991) 'The principle of subsidiarity and the social policy of the European Community', *Journal of European Social Policy,* 1(1): 3–14.

Spicker, P. (1993) 'Can European social policy be universalist?', in Page, R. and Baldock, J. *Social Policy Review 5,* Canterbury, Social Policy Association.

Walker, A., Alber, J. & Guillemard, A. M. (1993) *Older People in Europe: Social and Economic Policies: The 1993 Report of the European Observatory,* Brussels: Commission of the European Communities.

ANNOTATED READINGS

Social policy in the European Union is often regarded as a somewhat new and recent development within the study of social policy. However, interesting, thought provoking and thorough analyses of the development and role of social policy in Europe may be found in: S. Leibfried and

P. Pierson (1995), *European Social Policy: Between Fragmentation and Integration*, Washington DC: Brookings Institute; L. Hantrais (1995), *Social Policy in the European Union*, London: Macmillan and most recently in M. Rhodes (1998), *European Social Policy*, London: Longman. A most interesting and useful text is that by Deacon and Hulse, *Global Social Policy*, which explores the wider environment of social policy making and the effect of globalisation on social policy making.

19 Conclusion

The election of the first Labour government in almost 20 years in 1997 places the study of British social policy at an interesting crossroads though as yet some of the directions are still unclear. The Blair government it seems, as the party that brought the welfare state into being, has the opportunity to revisit many of its first principles and to design a welfare state for the twenty-first century. Yet, with one eye glancing back at the years of New Right dominance in British politics, Blair and his Cabinet inherited a welfare state vastly different to that of the last time their party held the reins of power. We seem then to be at one and the same time witnessing a new revolution in British welfare and also the consolidation of a new British welfare consensus.

A NEW BEVERIDGE?

We use the term 'a new Beveridge' not so much in the sense that it became known in post-war Britain, as emblematic of a state-led, run and funded welfare system providing, in theoretical and rhetorical terms, cradle to grave provision, but as a return to welfare principles. Blair and the Labour Party in opposition made much of a return to principles of responsibility and social solidarity as the antidote to what they perceived as the selfish individualism of the 1980s. 'New' Labour has also sought to gain, electorally, the ground occupied by the voters of 'middle England' and to shed its image as the party of the working class. Instead Blair has adopted a 'one nation' approach to both politics and social policy.

The social principles Blair has frequently espoused owe much to the works of communitarian thinkers (Etzioni; Hutton) and stress in particular the idea of duties incumbent upon anyone seeking to claim 'rights' in modern society. Thus the duty to find and keep a job in return for a right to claim welfare benefits has formed the cornerstone of Labour's welfare to work programme and in many ways seeks to re-establish a link set at the heart of the Beveridge solution. The connection of Beveridge's welfare principles to the economic principles espoused by Keynes, in particular the maintenance of full-employment as a counterpoint to the provisions of a welfare state, has much resonance in the rhetoric of New Labour. But to update this principle a notion of mass or maximum employment has overtaken the outdated and discredited idea of full (male) employment. In future not only will everyone have the opportunity to work but will be expected to have paid employment as welfare to work extends to the young unemployed, long-term unemployed, lone parents and the disabled. Alongside the opportunity and duty to work, the government has introduced the National Minimum Wage the clear message of which is that no longer will benefits dependency be an option. The resurrection of the Poor Law principle of less eligibility hopes to make reliance on the welfare state as unattractive as possible.

But Blair's back to basics message is not confined to the welfare to work programme. Initiatives across a range of policy areas hope to instill values of community, responsibility and social solidarity. In education the continued emphasis of basic skills of literacy and numeracy is to be reinforced by a greater role for parents in the form of homework 'contracts' and the widespread establishment of after school and homework clubs, and summer schools. Parental duties are to be further reinforced by proposals to make parents take greater responsibility for the criminal activities of their children or the introduction of child curfews and community safety orders under the Crime and Disorder Act.

Individualism in health too is to be reinforced following the introduction of 'targets' for improved health statistics (first announced under the Health of the Nation Report) in the incidence and treatment of conditions such as heart disease and smoking related illness. Health education programmes too are to be strengthened by the issuing of 'advice' to the public on such matters as healthy eating and exercise, alongside an intensified role for primary health care services. Indeed behaviour in general is to be identified as a legitimate concern of government social policy by the newly established Social Exclusion Unit which among its early pronouncements has called for initiatives to reduce numbers of people sleeping rough and proposals to reduce the high rate of teenage pregnancy.

With an apparent Damascene flash of inspiration Downing Street proposes 'joined up solutions to joined up problems' which it views as, in part, caused by the poor relationships and lack of co-operation between government welfare agencies. The inability of different social services to talk to one another, the government cites as a key cause for individuals to slip through the social 'safety net'. This is a feeling again reflected in the 'New Deal for Communities' which aims to improve social and environmental conditions in inner-city areas by enlisting the views of the local community itself but also by bringing together relevant government departments both central and local.

Perhaps, however, the underlying principle upon which much of the above is founded is that of 'attachedness' or social inclusion. The rise of the 'under-class' debate in British social policy in the decade before Labour's election victory has struck a chord with senior politicians. In particular the work of Charles Murray has stressed the lack of attachment to more widely accepted social norms and values as vital to the identification of an underclass – values such as the work ethic and values of family and community support. These ideas have found resonance in the writing of Frank Field, the erstwhile Minister for Welfare Reform, and Will Hutton who outlines a scenario of a 30:30:40 society exhibiting an increasing level of detachment for large numbers of Britain's population. It is with such issues firmly in mind that New Labour insists that the job of a modern welfare state should be to 'provide a hand up not a hand out'. In other words the task of welfare policy into the twenty-first century is to help people to help themselves – to create the economic climate for job creation and prosperity – wherein people are both able and duty bound to work.

A NEW WELFARE CONSENSUS?

How much the welfare programme of 'New' Labour owes to such a rediscovery of long-forgotten social-democratic principles is, however, not easy to uncover. Much of the rhetoric of New Labour echoes some of the themes and moral exhortations to good behaviour of Thatcherite Conservatives. We must then ask how far the altered political, social and economic environment that Blair has inherited is the basis of a new consensus in welfare policy.

Although Labour was quick to end the operation of the internal market in the National Health Service much of the reforms of the Thatcher and Major governments have remained untouched. And some of the proposals of earlier governments that they failed to introduce have been adopted by the new administration, for example the introduction of mechanisms of performance-related pay for school teachers. Labour has also been keen to steer itself away from anything that might be considered or characterised as 'Old' Labour and was elected on a promise to maintain for two years the public spending targets set by the outgoing government. Similarly Labour has promised that future well-being is to be built upon economic success and that the job of government is to create the economic conditions for that success and looks set to continue efforts to create a low-interest, high-productivity, low-cost economy. Labour it appears has managed to rid itself of some of its own economic and welfare sacred cows only to adopt a new economic orthodoxy.

It is unclear, however, how far this includes the adoption of similar political, social and welfare orthodoxies. The government has, for instance, created a climate for considerable political and constitutional change that signal both closer ties to a more powerful European Union and looser political ties at home. The creation of a devolved Scottish Parliament and Welsh Assembly and re-establishment of political power at Stormont in Northern Ireland promise to change radically the future development of social policy in Britain. So, too, the changes heralded by the Maastricht Treaty and reinforced by the Amsterdam Treaty which came into force in May 1999 will change the development of social policy on the European stage. A wider constituency in European social policy affairs, alongside an enhanced role for the European Parliament which maintains a strong interest in matters of social policy, exclusion and citizenship, suggest radical changes in this arena too. However, the interregnum caused by the collective resignation of the European Commission, leaves matters unresolved. It seems then that the creation of a new welfare consensus is, at this stage, only a partial one.

FUTURE DIRECTIONS

We would suggest that the tendencies outlined above are set to continue at least into the short-term future. Government's role in the provision and funding of welfare has, over the past quarter century, declined considerably and will continue to do so. A much enhanced role for the individual in welfare provision in the era of the stakeholder is, at least for the moment, the direction British policy is taking. The welfare state, as it developed in the years following the end of the Second World War, is no more (it probably never was). The role of government continues to develop as regulator and monitor of social policy – a regulator both of the vast range of welfare providers within the different quasi-markets that have formed but also of the behaviour of individuals as citizens and welfare recipients. A discussion of how well government is able to respond to such a vast and widespread regulatory task and an assessment of an emerging welfare consensus must, however, be the role of future texts.

Glossary of terms

Acts of Settlement: Name given to a number of Acts of Parliament passed from the sixteenth century that defined who was eligible for parish relief. In order to try to keep Poor Law costs down the parish was only responsible for paupers who were born within a parish or who had some other connection, for example through marriage.

Actus reus: The type of offence committed.

Adversarial: Description of the British legal system in which participants are pitted against one another either as plaintiff and respondent in civil law or prosecution and defendant in criminal law.

Beveridge: Sir William Beveridge, a civil servant/academic responsible for the publication of the Social Insurance and Allied Services Report of 1942 – the Beveridge Report – often considered the blueprint for much of the development of the post-war British welfare state.

Classical liberalism: Descriptive of a political doctrine usually associated with the nineteenth century and with early formulations of social policy. An interventionist role for the state may be justified where other social structures (markets) are seen to be failing and wherein state activity is minimal or residual.

Communitarianism: Range of ideas expressing the desire to re-establish or rediscover 'civil society', in which collective welfare is expressed through the agency of the active community and active citizen rather than that of a centralised state machinery.

Comprehensive schools: Schools offering education without attempting to differentiate between abilities of pupils along arbitrary academic or technical lines. Developed as the preferred method of state schooling during the 1960s and 1970s.

Consensus/welfare consensus: Term applied to the post-war political settlement characterised by the similarities exhibited in the economic policies of successive Labour (Gaitskell) and Conservative (Butler) Chancellors of the Exchequer. In particular the consensus was said to be built upon the acceptance of the role of the state in the pursuit of welfare and greater equality together with the pursuit of full employment as an economic principle.

Consumerism: Neo-liberal doctrine which stresses the role of the individual as consumer of welfare services within a market or quasi-market oriented welfare state. It regards consumers as having sovereignty within markets which individuals lack in any state-dominated system of welfare provision.

Contributory benefits: Range of cash benefits to which entitlement would be determined on the basis of the amount of contributions to and length of membership of the National Insurance system first introduced in 1911.

Corporate (or white collar) crime: Description of technically criminal actions not generally regarded as crimes, e.g. taking home pens or stationery from the office.

Crime control: Model of criminal justice policy that is concerned with attempts to suppress crime and criminal activity, often without regard to the consequences for civil rights.

Crown Prosecution Service (CPS): Government agency given responsibility for deciding whether to instigate, and pursue, criminal proceedings through the courts.

Democratic deficit: Term describing the lack or weakness of traditional democratic forms of control and scrutiny of the Executive arm of European policy making.

Deserving poor: Term applied to paupers thought to be more genuine and therefore deserving of parish relief. This might include those people who find themselves in poverty by virtue of illness, disability or old age.

Due process: Model of criminal justice policy that is concerned with the pursuit of justice within the criminal legal system.

Employment Training/Restart: Associated programme of retraining and reskilling for older workers following redundancy.

Enabling Authority: Term describing the developing role of local authorities, particularly in the Personal Social Services. The role of Social Service Departments would in future be to co-ordinate and monitor the quality of social services provision within its locale rather than acting as a provider of such services. The Enabling Authority was to be key in the development of an internal market in social services following the passage of the NHS and Community Care Act 1990.

Enlightenment: This term describes the historical period at the end of the middle ages during which rational and scientific methods of thought and investigation were developed.

Equal opportunities policies: A range of policies designed to narrow gender or other inequality within society, either by equalising outcomes of policy initiatives or equalising the environment within which policy operates.

Ethnocentrism: Term describing attitudes and the development of policies that explicitly or implicitly discriminate against minority ethnic groups.

European Community/European Union (EC/EU): The economic association developed among European countries following the Second World War which aims to create a single market on the continent of Europe and to guarantee economic progress.

European Free Trade Association: Alternative form of economic association to the EU designed around bilateral agreement between member states rather than common agreements across all member states.

Exchange Rate Mechanism: Monetary system established within the EU designed to tie the rate of currency exchange of its member nations more closely and to minimise rapid and wild currency fluctuation.

Fabianism: A range of political ideas associated with the rise of the Labour Party in Britain which promotes an active and redistributive role for the state. Often described as the 'Parliamentary road'.

Five giants: The most pressing social problems – Want, Ignorance, Disease, Idleness and Squalor – as defined by the Beveridge Report.

Forces of production: Marx's term to describe economic resources available within a society.

Full employment: Unwritten government goal throughout much of the post-war era which sought to maintain consistently low levels of (male manufacturing) unemployment.

Grant Maintained Status: Also known as 'opted out' schools, such schools are managed independently of their local authority and financed directly by the Education Department.

Health promotion: Describes a set of policies designed to induce personal and individual responsibility for health issues. Usually involves a programme of health education to promote healthier lifestyles, for example by discouraging health-damaging behaviour such as smoking, heavy drinking, poor diet or by promoting particular health issues such as more careful sexual behaviour.

Historical Materialism: Marx's theory of social development in which he suggested that all human societies were governed, in their development, by immutable historical laws.

Inter alia: Literally meaning 'amongst other things'.

Internal market: A system of internal organisation within the NHS introduced by the 1990 NHS and Community Care Act, which attempted to draw a distinction between the purchase and provision of health services. Market mechanisms were put in place in which NHS Trusts would compete with one another to earn contracts for treatment from Health Authorities or directly from (Fundholding) General Practitioners on behalf of their patients. The operation of the internal market was ended by the Labour Government in 1997, although it has attempted to maintain the distinction between the payment for and provision of health services.

Invisible Hand: Term coined by economist Adam Smith to describe the 'natural' operation of the free market and its tendency to self-regulation.

Laissez-faire: Economic and political principle which argues for freedom of action for individuals, especially in commerce and economics, and is, therefore, against extensive government activity or intervention.

Less eligibility: Principle of the Poor Law that suggested that the relief given to the poor should be at a level below that of the lowest paid of labourers to ensure that the poor would choose work rather than relief.

Life expectancy: The average period a person, of a given age, may expect to live.

Local management of schools: A system of management in schools in which much decision making is devolved to head teachers and boards of governors rather than LEAs.

Means-test: Test of income or wealth which determines entitlements to welfare benefits. Not all benefits, however, are subject to a means-test.

Mens rea: Intention to commit a criminal act.

Mode of production: Marx's term describing the organisation within a society of resources (forces of production) – capital, labour, land and raw materials.

Monetarism: Economic theory which emphasises the control of the money supply as a method of managing the economy and in particular of controlling inflation.

Morbidity: Measure of the rate of disease or illness in a society within a given period.

Mortality: Measure of the rate of death in a society within a given period.

National assistance: A system of welfare (mostly cash) benefits to which entitlement is most usually determined by the administration of a means-test. This system has operated under various guises over the past 50 years, developed as Supplementary Benefits and latterly Income Support.

National Curriculum: A standardised curriculum approved by the Department for Education which stresses the development of literacy and numeracy and allows for comparisons of achievement between schools.

National Insurance: A system of welfare (cash) benefits to which entitlement is determined by a National Insurance Contributions record.

National Minimum Wage (NMW): Introduced from April 1999, the NMW is to be a key element of Labour's Welfare to Work strategy by, they hope, making low paid employment more attractive.

Negative equity: A term coined after the slump in the private housing market in the early 1990s. Describes a situation wherein the market value of a property is less than the outstanding mortgage liability.

Non-contributory benefits: Range of cash benefits to which entitlement is determined by criteria other than National Insurance contributions.

People's Budget: Lloyd-George's redistributive Budget of 1909 which imposed higher levels of taxation on the rich in order to finance spending on social policies, including pensions and contributions to the National Insurance fund.

Polytechnic: A type of higher education institution developed in the 1960s offering degree-level study but specialising in the teaching of technical and vocational subjects. Polytechnics ceased to exist in Britain in 1991 as they were granted full university status.

Poor Law: A system of pauper relief developed in Britain between the sixteenth and nineteenth centuries. In its earlier form the parish was charged with responsibility for the poor living within its boundaries who would be helped with either outdoor relief – money or food and goods – which allowed the poor to carry on living and working within the parish. Alternatively the parish could provide indoor relief through workhouses, which would put the poor to work in return for assistance. The New Poor Law, which operated from 1834, did away with most outdoor relief and depended much more on the provision of help within the workhouse. The workhouse was intended to act as a deterrent and to encourage the poor to find work rather than rely on the help granted by the local Board of Guardians of the Poor who administered the new system.

Power (dominance) and new criminology: Model of criminal justice that sees crime as a 'social construct' such that neither individuals nor their behaviour should be regarded as inherently criminal.

Pre-fabrication: Method of rapid housing construction in which house components were constructed in factories and assembled on site.

Pre-Sentence Reports (PSRs): Documents prepared for a criminal trial which provide the court with background information about the accused person.

Primary Health Care: Health services provided often as the first point of treatment. Examples include General Practice, dentistry, health visiting services and locally based health clinics. Primary care has been identified as the cornerstone of 'New Labour' health policy, which intends to focus on the development of locality planning of health services.

Qualified majority voting: Description of some policy decisions taken in the European Council of Ministers for which unanimity is not required.

Queen's Counsel (QC): Senior barristers who usually work in the higher levels of the court system – High Court, Court of Appeal, House of Lords.

Reserve army of labour: Groups of workers maintained in capitalist societies who are available to work when the economic system enters one of its periodic boom cycles.

Serious Fraud Office: State-sponsored organisation responsible for the investigation of commercial malpractice such as insider trading.

Skills shortage/skills mismatch: two terms used to describe shortfalls in education and training policy. Skills shortage is a term particularly related to school leavers, who lack education in the skills relevant to and required by industry and the economy generally. Skills mismatch is a term referring to the type of skills possessed by workers and their inapplicability to the needs of the economy. An example would be where there have been redundancies in traditional industries, say engineering, and a rise in new technologies, computing and telecommunications, and the skills of the traditional industry are not readily transferred to the new.

Social Chapter: Annex to the Maastricht Treaty which lays down proposals to widen the concept of European social policy, initially without British participation.

Social Charter: More correctly called the Community Charter of the Fundamental Rights of Workers, this represents a key stage in the widening of the concept of European social policy beyond simply the rights attributed to those in employment.

Standard Attainment Tests: A system of assessing school children at ages 7, 11 and 14 which is used to both measure a child's progress and upon which School League Tables are based.

Subsidiarity: Doctrine of policy making in the European Union which holds that policy decisions should be taken at the lowest appropriate level and that national governments should take precedence over the European Commission.

Tenure: Set of legal rights to occupy property whether as rented, leased or owner-occupied property.

Tiger economies: Term describing in particular Far Eastern countries which went through a period of rapid economic growth in the 1970s and 1980s until able to challenge seriously the economic dominance of Western economies.

Transition economies: The states of Central and Eastern Europe (CEE) in the period following the collapse of communist state rule and the development of market economies and liberal democratic political systems.

Tripartism: A term denoting the 'three-way' organisation and management of compulsory and secondary education in Britain after the Second World War. Secondary schooling was split between the Grammar, Modern and Technical school, entry for which would be determined by assessment – the eleven-plus examination. Management in the education system was divided between the Ministry for Education, Local Education Authorities and teachers in schools.

Undeserving or indolent poor: Term applied to paupers thought to be less genuine and therefore not deserving of parish relief. This might include those simply unemployed and regarded as indolent or lazy, beggars and 'tramps' who moved about the country in search of work.

Underclass: A term describing a stratum of the poor within a population which is said to be living outside and detached from established social norms and is both reliant upon and encouraged by a generous welfare benefits system.

Utilitarianism: Philosophy expounded by (particularly) Bentham which argued that all human decisions were a choice between pleasure and pain and that rational individuals would usually satisfy (short-term) pleasure. In turn, Bentham argued that the correct role for the (welfare) state was to maximise human pleasure.

Welfare and rehabilitation: Model of criminal justice that seeks to rehabilitate the 'criminal' back into wider society.

Welfare to Work: Programme of employment assistance, more widely available than earlier targeted schemes, which employs a system of subsidy for employers who create permanent jobs for the unemployed. Initially targeted at the younger unemployed, it was later extended to include the long-term unemployed, single parents and the disabled.

Winter of discontent: Period of industrial unrest, particularly in the public sector, between the autumn of 1978 and spring of 1979, which marked the end of the Labour government's policy of wages control in order to control the economy.

Youth Opportunities Programme/Youth Training Scheme: Associated government initiatives aimed at tackling high levels of youth unemployment by establishing programmes of training and work experience.

Index